Wye's Dictionary of Improbable Words

All-Vowel Words

All-Consonant Words

by Craig Conley

This is a scholarly work intended for educational purposes.

For Jonathan Caws-Elwitt,
Wordsmith Extraordinaire

The conquest of the superfluous gives us greater spiritual excitement than the conquest of the necessary.
—Gaston Bachelard, French philosopher

CONTENTS

All-Consonant Words

b'chtsch.

n. the thin, high-pitched ringing of a snare drum, as described by the band Backwash in a "Bandorama" interview (bandorama.ch).

b-b-b-b-b.

n. a sound made by a baby, meaning unknown, as described in the novel *Edwin Mullhouse* by Steven Millhauser.

b-bb-bbbb.

n. a baby's babble, presumably asking to blow soap bubbles; see also bbbbb.

<*Harry said, "B-bb-bbb," which gave me the idea of blowing bubbles—possibly his intent in the first place, you never knew.* —Patricia Gaffney, *Circle of Three: A Novel.*>

B-Stl.

n. a gallant alien Luminoth who "lies deep in the fortress of a dry land," in the video game "Metroid Prime 2: Echoes."

bb.

n. in harmonica notation, a note that is "bent" two half steps down (made to sound lower by blocking part of the airway with one's tongue), as discussed in *Blues & Rock Harp Positions Made Easy* by David Harp.

Bbb.

1. *n.* a shorthand notation used by musician Gustav Mahler in his manuscripts "to identify [thematic] elements that he would repeat or rework later in the compositional process" (James L. Zychowicz, *Mahler's Fourth Symphony*).

2. *n.* the name of a character with glowing yellow eyes in the novel *The Martian Chronicles* by Ray Bradbury.

bbb.

1. *n.* in harmonica notation, a note that is "bent" three half steps down (made to sound lower by blocking part of the airway with one's tongue), as discussed in *Blues & Rock Harp Positions Made Easy* by David Harp.

2. *n.* the rhythmic chugging of a boat, as described in the New Zealand Ministry of Education's "More Than Words" adult literacy materials.

3. *n.* the sound of the letter b; see also bbbb[1].

<*I accept the job of talking to parents about discipline, tempering good advice with realism and, above all, the understanding that you can't do anything for a small child just once and assume it's done for good—not wiping her bottom, helping her pick up her toys, showing her how to hold a fork, telling her not to pinch her brother, or teaching her that the letter B makes a "bbb" sound.* —Perri Klass, "No More Yelling! The New Golden Rules of Discipline, From a Pediatrician Mom Who's Found Better Ways to Get Her Kids to Behave," *Parenting Magazine*.>

4. *n.* the spine-tingling stutter of a rotting corpse struggling to speak, as in the graphic novel *Uzumaki 2* by Junji Ito; see also bhh.

bbbb.

1. *n.* the sound of the letter b, as in the novel *Doona* by Anne McCaffrey; see also bbb[3].

2. *n.* the sputters of an engine. The sound is made with "lip rolls or 'motorboating,' which is rolling your lips on a 'bbbb' sound" (Susan Anders, *The No Scales, Just Songs Vocal Workout, Volume 2*).

<*We watch as he loops the [paper] airplane through the air and makes bbbb's with his lips.* —Kristin Waterfield Duisberg, *The Good Patient: A Novel*.>

3. *n.* the title of a poem by Mak Dizdar.

<*The poem "bbbb," inspired by what looks like funerary graffiti, points out to its ambiguity that allows us to have faith in language but robs us of the ability to count on its semantic durability.* —Amila Buturovic, *Stone Speaker: Medieval Tombs, Landscape, and Bosnian Identity in the Poetry of Mak Dizdar*.>

bbbbb.

n. a soap bubble; see also b-bb-bbbb.

<*I blew a perfect stream of airy, iridescent globes, so pretty, gone in seconds, like fireworks. "Bbbbb," the baby said, and I put my cheek next to his soft one and said, "Bbbbb" with a little more air, and we blew a big floating bubble that didn't pop until a grass blade speared it,* poof. —Patricia Gaffney, *Circle of Three: A Novel*.>

bbbbbbb.

n. a vocal imitation of "a sailing boat in a tub of water," as discussed in *Baby Talk: The Art of Communicating with Infants and Toddlers* by Monica Devine.

bbbbdbdbdbdbbtktktk.

n. the deafening chatter of automatic weapons fire, as noted by Rudy Rucker in the novel *Wetware*.

bbbrrrppll.

n. the gurgle of someone breathing through SCUBA gear, as in the comic strip "PvP" by Scott R. Kurtz.

Bdbdbd.

n. the name of a song by the band Gruppo Sportivo.

bdbdbdbd.

1. *n.* a noise made by Twiki the robot from *Buck Rogers in the 25th Century* (Spacecast.com).

2. *n.* the famous stuttering sound made by the cartoon character Porky Pig, as at the end of a Looney Tunes cartoon.

<*Bdbdbdbd, that's all, folks!* —Porky Pig, as transcribed by DavesGarden.com.>

Bgztl.

n. a parallel earth: a 4th dimension planet in the Legion of Super-Heroes.

<*As a native of Bgztl, the Phantom Dimension, she was used to ominous and queer environments, but there was something about the long dark tunnel into the unknown that gave her the shivers.* —Curt Fernlund, "Tales of the Legion of Super-Heroes: Twisted World! #2.">

bh bh bh.

n. the beating of a heart, as described in *Marva Collins' Way* by Marva Collins.

bhh.

n. the strained wheezing of a rotting corpse trying to speak, as in the graphic novel *Uzumaki 2* by Junji Ito; see also bbb[4].

bk.

n. a hen's cluck to welcome back and comfort a stray chick.

<*She calls her chick in a special way. She says, "Bk, bk, bk, bk, bk ... Bk, bk, bk, bk, bk" in a high tone, and then she sort of purrs. She wants to mother the chick. They all know what she's telling them.* —Minnie Rose Lovgreen, *Minnie Rose Lovgreen's Recipe for Raising Chickens.*>

bllpp.

n. a mother hen's "all clear" signal that danger has passed.

<*The hen stands guard until the enemy is gone. Then she gives the "all clear" signal, calls them out like "Bllpp, bllpp, bllpp," in a high-pitched voice, and they all come out and eat.* —Minnie Rose Lovgreen, *Minnie Rose Lovgreen's Recipe for Raising Chickens.*>

blpb.

n. the sound of someone struggling not to drown in a vat of fresh cream, as in the graphic novella *Hearts and Minds* by Scott McCloud; see also hgkh, sppt.

blrgh.

n. the choking sound of someone foaming at the mouth, as in the comic strip "PvP" by Scott R. Kurtz; see also phlrrt, bsshh.

blsh.

n. the sound of a talking vacuum cleaner's nozzle impaling a rapist, as in the comic book *Vacuum Horror* by Aaron K.

bmmf.

n. the sleepy mumble of someone with a hangover; see also mfff.

<*"Bmmf." His sentence ended with his face back in the pillow.* —Whitney Lakin, *A Paintbrush in the Devil's Toolbox.*>

bmph.

n. the dramatic thud as a falling person hits the floor.

<*Bmph!! The burned, limp body crashed to the ground not four meters away from him.* —Chris Kenworthy, *Showdown!*>

bng bng.

n. a German expression meaning the "bang bang" of gunfire, as in the song "Feuer Frei" by the band Rammstein.

bng-bmp.

n. a bumping or banging sound.

<*"Why---" thmp / 'are you being' / thmp thmp bng-bmp / 'so fucking nice to me?' / he asked. / thmp thmp.* —Terra Elan McVoy, "Dragonfly.">

br.

interj. a short expression that the temperature is uncomfortably cold; see also brr[1], brrr[1], brrrr[5], brrrrrrr[3], brrrrrrrr[3], rrr, rrrrr.

<*Br... It's cold outside and inside. My guess is the temperature is negative three degrees Celsius. I bet if it were to rain, it would snow. It's that cold—or so I feel that cold.* —JakeTWake.com.>

br r r r r r.

n. the "faint, upward-inflected, froglike trill" of the Cinnamon Ground-Dove, as described in *Birds of New Guinea* by Bruce M. Beehler.

br-r-r-r-rt.

n. the popping of shirt snaps, as when yanked apart (Colin Berry, "Shattered").

br-r-r-rmmm.

n. the singing style of Louis Armstrong.

<*[Billie Holiday would] do that Louis br-r-r-rmmm kind of thing, and she'd do her own thing right behind it. Louis would be her kick-off kind of thing.* —Mae Barnes, quoted in *Billie Holiday: Wishing on the Moon* by Donald Clarke.>

BR-rrr-BR-rrrrrrr.

n. a motorcycle sound.

<*Toby came barreling down the sidewalk on his Big Wheel, making motorcycle sounds with his mouth.* BR-rrr-BR-rrrrrrr. —Jamie Gilson, *Hobie Hanson, You're Weird.*>

brhnnnh.

n. a grunt in the Wookie language of the *Star Wars* films, as transcribed in the book *Return of the Jedi* by James Kahn.

brk.

n. the creak of a spiral horn boring through a wall, as in the graphic novel *Uzumaki 3* by Junji Ito.

brnnk.

n. the sound of a tap on a computer keyboard, as in the comic strip "PvP" by Scott R. Kurtz; see also chhg.

brr.

1. *interj.* an expression that the temperature is uncomfortably cold; see also br, brrr[1], brrrr[5], brrrrrrr[3], brrrrrrrr[3], rrr, rrrrr.

   <*Brr! Hubble sees coldest spot in cosmos.* —Richard Stenger, CNN.>

2. *n.* the persistent hum of television static; white noise, like ocean waves; a tinnitus-like roaring in the inner ear.

   <*This brr was starting in my head like the noise the telly used to make if you fell asleep at night watching it.* —Patrick McCabe, *The Butcher Boy*.>

brr-grr.

n. animal-like growls in the short story "The Birthday of the World" by Ursula K. Le Guin.

brrk.

n. the garbled noise of ambulance radio static; see also crrk.

<*Brrk! Crrk! Truck five twenty-two, code six, a two car head-on where the Coast Highway meets Five in Capistrano Beach.* —Kim Stanley Robinson, *The Gold Coast*.>

BRRK BRRK.

n. the jarring ring of a telephone; see also brrr brrrr, brrp brrp.

<*BRRK BRRK. My waking thought was that the guy who invented the telephone ought to have been publicly boiled in his own brainwater. Outside the bedroom window, dawn was just barely making headway against dark. If manufactured noise at such an hour isn't an offense against human nature, I don't know what is. BRRK BRRK.* —Ivan Doig, *Ride With Me, Mariah Montana*.>

brrk brrk brrk.

n. a telephone busy signal.

<*He dialed again; got only brrk, brrk, brrk. He dialed two other numbers, hoping to find someone free for lunch. No one was. He dialed Max again: brrk, brrk, brrk.* —William Gaddis, *The Recognitions*.>

brrm-brrm.

n. the throbbing or growling of a motorcycle engine.

<*Six or eight old women abandoned their aluminum-can-filled shopping carts to hop bowlegged across the grass, growling brrm-brrm in imitation of motorcycle engines.* —Tim Powers, *Expiration Date.*>

<*If he had been working for a big company [Akira Suzuki] would have had to sit down on the other side of the table from the local people and Exchange Views, which would have meant an exchange of names. The same name as the motor-cycle: Oh yes, most amusing. Brrm! Brrm! Ha ha. The famous English sense of humour, in Suzuki's experience, consisted largely of asking you to share their delight at a mortal insult.* —Clive James, *Brrm! Brrm!*>

brrnnngg.

1. (also brnng.) *n.* the ringing of a telephone, as in the graphic novel *Destiny's Eyes* by Gary Colcombe; see also brrrnng.

2. *n.* the ringing of a school bell; see also rrrr rrrr.

<*Brrnnngg! The bell rang. Priscilla hurried to her chair.* —Kathleen Leverich, *Best Enemies.*>

brrp.

1. (also brrrrrrrp.) *n.* the crackling of an automatic rifle firing.

<*I pulled the trigger on full auto! Brrrrrrrp! Brrp! Brrp!* —Ed Kugler, *Dead Center: A Marine Sniper's Two-Year Odyssey in the Vietnam War.*>

2. *n.* machine gun fire.

<*"All hell broke loose," says Hanson, "grenades, rifle shots and even the* brrp *of a Nambu [machine gun].* —Gerald Astor, *Crisis in the Pacific: The Battles for the Philippine Islands by the Men Who Fought Them.*>

3. *n.* a mother cat's greeting to her kittens.

<*A mother's direct interaction with her kittens involves giving the 'brrp' call as she approaches them.* —Dennis C. Turner, *The Domestic Cat: The Biology of its Behavior.*>

4. *n.* the "endless hullabaloo" of a cell block, reverberating through life beyond the confines of prison (Peter Blauner, *The Last Good Day*).

<*The noise from the cell block still ringing in his ears when he came home at night.* Brrp. *The fights in the commissary lines, the turds tossed out between bars, the razors taped to the ends of toothbrushes.* Brrp. *The need to win every fight, no matter how small. The cold fact that you could never let them see you weak or wavering.* Brrp. *The wife nattering at him because the only vacation they could afford was a crappy cabin without proper toilets or heat in New Hampshire.* Brrp. *His sons refusing to stop grab-assing in the backseat.* Brrp. —Peter Blauner, *The Last Good Day.*>

5. *n.* the sound of something being switched off like a television.

<*I'm nothing but this image [of my television roles]. A push of the button and*—brrp!—*I'm gone.* —Haruki Murakami, *Dance Dance Dance*.>

brrp bllp.

n. a cough, as in *Visions of Cody* by Jack Kerouac.

brrp brrp.

n. the ringing of a telephone; see also brrr brrrr, BRRK BRRK.

<*Man (making a ringing sound) Brrp, brrp. (picks up phone) Hello, yes right. (puts phone down)* —Graham Chapman, *The Complete Monty Python's Flying Circus: All the Words, Volume 1*.>

brrp brrp brrp.

1. *n.* a mother hen's call to gather her chicks.

<*She begins to pick up the food and drop it down in front of them. She calls them. She says, "Brrp, brrp, brrp, . . . Brrp, brrp, brrp," in a deep tone, and they all come around her.* —Minnie Rose Lovgreen, *Minnie Rose Lovgreen's Recipe for Raising Chickens*.>

2. *n.* the rattle of a World War I plane's engine warming up.

<*The only way the pilot could idle his engine was with the blip switch, causing the characteristic brrp, brrp, brrp sound heard during warm-up and taxiing of many World War I pursuit planes.* —Crocker Snow, *Log Book: A Pilot's Life*.>

3. *n.* the short, deafening bursts of an M-16 being fired.

<*He reloaded and fired with mechanical determination*—brrp, brrp, brrp! —Robert Crais, *The Last Detective*.>

brrp brrrpp.

n. the high-pitched squeak of a shoe's rubber sole.

<*My sneakers squeak, sounding like tiny voices on helium: "brrp ... brrrpp ... messed-up ... screwed-up ... messed-up ... screwed-up."* —Laurie Halse Anderson, *Catalyst*.>

brrp-brrp-brrp.

n. the "quick cackling" of the Streaked Wren-Warbler, as described in *The Book of Indian Birds* by Salim Ali.

brrr.

1. *interj.* an expression that the temperature is uncomfortably cold; see also br, brr[1], brrrr[5], brrrrrrr[3], brrrrrrrr[3], rrr, rrrrr.

<*Brrr—sunrise is too cold for me, even in the summer. Give me sunsets!* —Rob Brezsny.>

2. *interj.* an indication of an involuntary shudder.

<*Brrr. Even the thought of going underground made Old Bailey shudder.* —Neil Gaiman, *Neverwhere.*>

3. *n.* a typical sound made by a baby attempting to talk, as discussed in *Wonder Weeks: How to Turn Your Baby's 8 Great Fussy Phases into Magical Leaps Forward* by Hetty Vanderijt.

4. *n.* the whirring of an instant camera motor.

<*Andy [Warhol] would come with his Polaroid and sit there at the table. Everybody was carrying on and he'd say nothing, but periodically he goes brrr with the machine and then this long thing comes out eeeee. I always thought it was just like sticking his tongue out at the company. Puking on them in a way.* —Victor Bockris, *Warhol: The Biography.*>

brrr brrr.

n. the ringing of a telephone, as in the graphic novel *Code Name Nod* by Geoff Harrold; see also brrr brrrr.

brrr brrrr.

n. the ringing of a telephone; see also brrr brrr, BRRK BRRK.

<*The phone was ringing when I got in. I sat down at the kitchen table and let it ring. It stopped and then started again. Brrr brrrr. Brrr brrrr. Brrr brrrr. Brrr brrrr. I took the little bugger off the hook.* —Helen Fielding, *Cause Celeb.*>

brrr brrrrr.

(also brrrr brrrrrr, brrrrrrrr brrrrrrr.) *n.* a go-kart racer's vocalization for self-empowerment.

<*"They pushed with their feet and roared with their throats." It is a fact in go-kart racing that the louder you make your voice go, the more "brrr, brrrr" you put into it, the faster you will go.* —Mike McCardell, *Back Alley Reporter.*>

brrr-brrp.

n. the nasal call of the Pheasant-tailed Jacana, as described in *A Guide to the Birds of Southeast Asia* by Craig Robson.

brrrm.

1. *n.* the broken growling or throbbing of an airplane engine.

<*Just as darkness fell, a new sound rose above the general cursing. The short throbbing brrrm, brrrm, brrrm of enemy airplane motors.* —David Kenyon Webster, *Parachute Infantry: An American Paratrooper's Memoir of D-Day and the Fall of the Third Reich.*>

2. *n.* the coughs and purrs of a BMW engine, as in the novel *Homgae* by Julian Rathbone.

3. *n.* the perpetual drone of a drum roll; see also brrrrrrr-rrp.

<*And as the first bugle notes tapered off the bass drums came to prominence. Brrrm ... Brrrm.* —Ken Wright, "Wellesley Nautical Blyth Northumberland.">

brrrm brrrm.

n. the sound of a revving motorcycle engine; see also brrrm-brrrm[2].

<*Two filthy children in rags ran alongside, holding imaginary handlebars and saying "Brrrm, brrrm," in imitation.* —Ken Follett, *The Key to Rebecca.*>

<*"I'll keep your coffee hot, boss. Brrrm, brrrm!" Biscuter had the curious habit of accompanying his activities with the noise of a 750cc motorbike.* —Manuel Vazquez Montalban, *The Angst-Ridden Executive.*>

brrrm brrrm brrrm.

n. the "short throbbing" of "enemy airplane motors" (David Kenyon Weber, *Parachute Infantry: An American Paratrooper's Memoir of D-Day and the Fall of the Third Reich*).

brrrm brrrrm.

n. the electronic sounds of a space shuttle control tower.

<*Lynette makes one of the dolls push a pretend button and reports, "Brrrm, brrrm, they're going up!"* —Laura E. Berk, *Awakening Children's Minds: How Parents and Teachers Can Make a Difference.*>

brrrm-brrrm.

1. *n.* an unladylike noise.

<*Nooty, stop making those* brrrm-brrrm *noises. I'm sure nice girls shouldn't make those kind of noises.* —Terry Pratchett, *The Bromeliad Trilogy: Truckers, Diggers, and Wings.*>

2. *n.* the sound of a revving motorcycle engine; see also brrrm brrrm.

<*Six or eight old women abandoned their aluminum-can-filled shopping carts to hop bowlegged across the grass, growling* brrrm-brrrm *in imitation of motorcycle engines or howling like police sirens; then all paused at once and, even though they were yards and yards apart and separated by dozens of people, all shouted in unison, "Stop! You're on a one-way road to Hell!"* —Tim Powers, *Expiration Date.*>

brrrnng.

n. the ringing of a telephone; see also brrnnngg[1].

<*Brrrnng! The telephone rings loudly, jolting me out of my daydream.* —Lisa Scottoline, *Everywhere That Mary Went.*>

brrrr.

1. *adj.* overly formal, without warmth of feeling.

<*Why talk about the English? Brrrr...!* —E. M. Forster, *A Passage to India.*>

2. *interj.* a shudder of dread, as at a fearsome opponent.

<*Man and horse both clad in chain mail from head to heels. Brrrr!* —Colleen McCullough, *Caesar: A Novel.*>

3. *interj.* an enraged sputtering.

<*This sends Smirnov into a tirade against all women—calling them hypocrites, phonies, gossips, scandalmongers, haters, slanderers, liars, petty, fussy, ruthless, and illogical. "Brrrr!" he sputters, "I'm shaking with fury." His rage triggers her anger and they begin to shout insults at each other.* —Helen Fisher, *Why We Love: The Nature and Chemistry of Romantic Love.*>

4. *interj.* an expression of revulsion.

<*The waiter shuddered. "Brrrr," he said. "I won't eat that. It comes from the inside of a cow."* —Jonathan Gold, *Counter Intelligence: Where to Eat in the Real Los Angeles.*>

5. *interj.* an expression that the temperature is uncomfortably cold; see also br, brr[1], brrr[1], brrrrrrr[3], brrrrrrrr[3], rrr, rrrrr.

<*Sarah watched a young assistant perched on a peeling windowsill. A* brrrr *sound emerged through his lips and an overgrown, bushy mustache.* —James Patterson, *The Midnight Club.*>

6. *n.* a distracting thought during meditation.

<*Everybody's got these little "brrrr" thoughts. They're like little mosquitoes buzzing around.* —Ram Dass, *The Only Dance There Is.*>

7. *n.* a soft alarm tone, more a vibration than a ringing.

<*The cleverly constructed alarm, which had two tones, loud and soft, went* brrrr, *softly; and her prayer had been turned down.* —Cornell Woolrich, *Rendezvous in Black.*>

8. *n.* an involuntary shiver of fear, as in response to a tarantula.

<*I don't think anyone could ever forget a creature like that. Those hairy legs: brrrr!* —Darren Shan, *A Living Nightmare.*>

9. *n.* the rumble of a toy truck's engine.

<*Ava prefers Chandler's trucks; she makes a brrrr sound and moves them across the floor.* —Elizabeth Cohen, *The Family on Beartown Road: A Memoir of Love and Courage.*>

brrrr brrrr brrrr.

n. the repetitive sound of gunfire from a warplane.

<*We were in a convoy of trucks heading out of town. I heard a "brrrr" "brrrr" "brrrr" noise and I looked up and saw the telephone wires parting and coming down on the ground. I knew what was happening then. All of a sudden a Spitfire [British fighter] went zipping by.* —Patrick K. O'Donnell, *Beyond Valor: World War II's Ranger and Airborne Veterans Reveal the Heart of Combat.*>

brrrr rrrrr rrrr.

n. the ringing of a telephone.

<*At 3:25 Sally gets a call at her extension.* Brrrr, rrrrr, rrrr! —Glenn Beck, *The Real America: Messages From The Heart and Heartland.*>

brrrr.rrrr.

n. the ringing of the "bail out bell" of a fighter aircraft just before it blows up or crashes, as described in *The Mighty Eighth: The Air War in Europe as Told by the Men Who Fought It* by Gerald Astor.

brrrrm.

(also brrrm.) *n.* the sliding tones of a trombone glissando.

<*What he wouldn't give for the sound of the ODJB playing* Tiger Rag *right now. He conjured the sound in his head, and capered round the shabby confines of the room, imitating the fruity trombone glissando. "Hold that tiger ... brrrrm, hold that tiger ... brrrm, hold that tiger."* —Ian Morson, "There Would Have Been Murder," *The Mammoth Book of Roaring Twenties Whodunnits: Murder Mysteries from the Age of Bright Young Things.*>

brrrrr.

1. *n.* the hum of a telephone dial tone, as described in the novel *Tooth and Nail* by Ian Rankin.

2. *n.* the prolonged call of the skulking Slaty Spinetail bird, as described in *A Guide to the Birds of Panama* by Robert S. Ridgely.

brrrrrr.

1. *n.* the sound of an automobile engine.

<*If he had been able to hear, he would have heard, in the nearly perfect silence, the sound of Tom Cullen's imagination at work—the lip-vibrating* brrrrrr *as he drove the cars onto the Fisher-Price tarmac ... the* ssshhhhhhh *as the lift inside went up and down.* —Stephen King, *The Stand: Expanded Edition.*>

2. *v.* to switch on an engine.

<*Two canoes came streaking out through the surf and in a few minutes, for the first time in three months, the crew spoke to strangers—the descendents, perhaps, of Tiki and the original voyagers. With a mixture of sign language and the few words of Polynesian that [Thor] Heyerdahl could remember, the men indicated that they wanted to find a way in through the reef. The islanders replied by saying "Brrrrrr," indicating that the crew should switch on their engine. The natives could not believe that there was none, and Heyerdahl made them feel underneath the stern to prove that this was the case.* —Sir Christian Bonington, *Quest for Adventure: Ultimate Feats of Modern Exploration.*>

brrrrrrp.

n. a roar of steam from a fog horn, as if the fog horn were clearing its throat to speak.

<*"Brrrrrrp!" roared the Steam through the fog-horn, till the decks quivered. "Don't be frightened, below. It's only me, just throwing out a few words, in case any one happens to be rolling round to-night."* —Rudyard Kipling, "The Ship That Found Herself.">

BRRRRRRR.

1. *n.* an elephant's scream of pain.

<*The meaty, unmistakable thud of a falling elephant sounded fifty yards away, then the insane,*

vocal hysteria of the other bull dropped to a chilling, throaty, rattling BRRRRRRR. —Peter H. Capstick, *Safari: The Last Adventure.*>

2. *n.* the ringing of a football coach's whistle, as described in *The Last Street Fighter* by Wayne Normis.

3. *n.* the ringing of an alarm clock, as in the novel *Swamp!* by Joe Pachinko.

Brrrrrrr.

n. the "Official State Motto of Alaska," according to humorist Dave Barry (*Dave Barry's Only Travel Guide You'll Ever Need*).

<*It was freezing ... I'm kind of blue. My lips go, "brrrrrrr," and they chatter.* —Juliette Lewis, quoted in *Stranger than Fiction: True Stories* by Chuck Palahniuk.>

brrrrrrr.

1. *interj.* a shivery response to a chilling concept.

<*The rain comes a-poundin' and the wind comes a-screamin' for days on end, and you have no light but candles. Brrrrrrr! It shivers me somethin' terrible to even think on it.* —Betty J. Vickers, *Walkin' the Floor.*>

<*If Freud and Marx and Nietzsche and Feuerbach and their followers are right, however, there ... is no heaven. Only rearrangements of valueless matter in a mostly empty universe where everything happens by randomness and chance. Brrrrrrr.* —Luis Palau, *God Is Relevant: Finding Strength and Peace in Today's World.*>

2. *interj.* an expression that something has gone wrong, as in *Good Vibrations: A History of Record Production* by Mark Cunningham.

3. *interj.* an expression that the temperature is uncomfortably cold; see also br, brr[1], brrr[1], brrrr[5], brrrrrrrr[3], rrr, rrrrr.

<*[J]ust as he opened his mouth in order to let forth a yell, he gave a shiver and pulled his towel tightly round himself as a sudden draft of cold air caught him unawares. In the end all he could manage was a loud* "Brrrrrrr!" —Michael Bond, *Paddington Treasury.*>

4. *interj.* an involuntary shudder of revulsion, as when a corpse flops down into one's face in the novel *Extreme Justice* by William Bernhardt.

5. *n.* a raven's whimper, as in *Snow Ravens* by Bruno Hachler.

6. *n.* a vocal disapproval of damp, cold weather.

<*He got out of the Tempo, hurried up the steps, and crossed the wide veranda, voicing his objection to the chilly air as he went: "Brrrrrrr."* —Dean Koontz, *Strangers.*>

7. *n.* the "brief, downslurred, rapid trill like thumbing comb tines" of the Carolina Wren, as described by Tomm Lorenzin in "Birdsong Mnemonics."

8. *n.* the hum of someone's electrifying personality.

<*This guy is good, but he's like electric. There's a bulge in his eye. Wow! When he comes into a room, it like lights up. He's like "Brrrrrrr!"* —Mark Baker, *Cops.*>

9. *n.* the purring of a thinking brain, as described in *The User's Manual for the Brain* by Bob G. Bodenhamer.

10. *n.* the ringing of an alarm clock, as in the Beatles' song "A Day in the Life."

<*He counted down and on bar twenty-four he hit the alarm clock, Brrrrrrr! It was just a period of time, an arbitrary length of bars, which was very Cage thinking.* —Barry Miles, *Paul McCartney: Many Years from Now.*>

11. *n.* the sputtering of an airplane engine.

<*One of his favorite pastimes was to race around the waiting room at KFVD, a room ringed with couches, with one foot up on the couches and the other on the floor, his arms outstretched, and making a "brrrrrrr" sound, pretending he was an airplane.* —Joe Klein, *Woody Guthrie: A Life.*>

brrrrrrr brrrrrr.

n. the ringing of a doorbell.

<*There was a bellpush and I pushed, and brrrrrrr brrrrrr sounded down the hall inside.* —Anthony Burgess, *A Clockwork Orange.*>

BRRRRRRR BRRRRRRRR.

n. the ringing of a house telephone.

<BRRRRRRR BRRRRRRRR! *Is that the house phone? It certainly* sounds *like our house phone. Well, it's not for me, anyway. Nobody calls me on the house-phone line, not now that I've got my cell phone. Phhhh, I'm not answering it.* BRRRRRRR BRRRRRRRR! BRRRRRRR BRRRRRRRR! BRRRRRRR BRRRRRRRR! *I'm still not answering it. It can ring as much as it likes.* BRRRRRRR BRRRRRRRR! BRRRRRRR BRRRRRRRR! BRRRRRRR BRRRRRRRR! —Grace Dent, *LBD: It's a Girl Thing.*>

brrrrrrr brrrrrrrr.

n. the sound of a revving motorcycle engine.

<*One of them raced his engine* brrrrrrr brrrrrrrr, *and Meg pulled the Mossberg shotgun out of the leather sheath and pointed it above her head. The bikers abruptly turned away, tore along the river bed and around a curve and out of sight.* —David Cole, *Stalking Moon.*>

brrrrrrr-rrp.

n. the perpetual drone of a drum roll; see also brrrm[3].

<*With Salem, he showed her how to stutter the stick on the drumstick. "Hold it loose," he told her, "that's the secret. Pretend your wrist is rubber." He showed her:* Brrrrrrr-rrp. *On the third try, she did it.* —Jerry Spinelli, *Report to the Principal's Office!*>

brrrrrrr-rrrrr.

n. a sound used in training hunting dogs.

<*A second bird boy picks up the shackled bird, says brrrrrrr-rrrrr (but doesn't shoot) and lets the bird fly.* —Bill Tarrant, *Problem Gun Dogs: How to Identify and Correct Their Faults.*>

brrrrrrrp.

(also brrp.) *n.* the sound of an automatic weapon firing.

<*He saw me ... there's the slow motion again. He started pulling up his rifle. I pulled the trigger [of my M-14] on full auto!* Brrrrrrrp! Brrp! Brrp! —Ed Kugler, *Dead Center: A Marine Sniper's Two-Year Odyssey in the Vietnam War.*>

brrrrrrrr.

1. *interj.* an expression indicating a "sense of a hidden evil lurking within the dark and leafy forest" (Ellen Moore, *Good Books Lately: The One-Stop Resource for Book Groups and Other Greedy Readers*, describing the ominous mood of the novel *The Long Home* by William Gay).

2. *interj.* an expression of boredom, as over obsessively drawing "little scratchy lines" in comics (Derf, quoted in *Attitude: The New Subversive Political Cartoonists* by Ted Rall).

3. *interj.* an expression that the temperature is uncomfortably cold; see also br, brr[1], brrr[1], brrrr[5], brrrrrrr[3], rrr, rrrrr.

   <"*That Katani is real cold.*" "*Brrrrrrrr,*" *said Daniel Jordan.* "*Where are my hat and mittens?*" —Annie Bryant, *Worst Enemies/BestFriends.*>

4. *n.* a "fast and technical" drum roll, as when playing the Afro-Cuban timbales (Victor Rendon, *The Art of Playing Timbales Volume 1*).

5. *n.* a "long trilled shiver" at the beginning of the Silvestre Méndex song "Druma Kuyi," sung with "an otherworldly timbre in order to meet the spirits halfway and entreat them to descend to earth"; the brrrrrrrr "possibly has a semantic value, since extraordinary vocal quality plays an important role in Afro-Cuban religious music" (Charley Gerard, *Music from Cuba: Mongo Santamaria, Chocolate Armenteros, and Other Stateside Cuban Musicians*).

6. *n.* a baseball umpire's whistle, as described in *The Brothers K* by David James Duncan.

7. *n.* the high-pitched humming of a surgical saw, as described in *Religion, Spirituality and the Near-Death Experience* by Mark Fox.

8. *n.* the purring call of the Spotted Honeyguide bird, "slightly reminiscent of [the] song of [the] Double-toothed Barbet" (Ron Demey, *A Guide to the Birds of Western Africa*).

9. *n.* the quality that "reeks" from the patriotic hymn "I Am a 100% American" by William W. Woollcott (H.L. Mencken, *Heathen Days: 1890-1936*).

10. *n.* the ringing of a telephone.

    <*I vas sleeping like a baby after the good party last night and, brrrrrrrr the phone ring.* —Andy Varlow, *Just Another Man: A Story of the Nazi Massacre of Kalavryta.*>

11. *n.* the sound of a telephone flying across the room, as in the novel *Born Free* by Laura Hird.

12. *n.* the sound of an angel "corkscrewing through the air, horizontally, feet first" (Sophy Burnham, *A Book of Angels*).

13. *n.* the sound of someone "speaking in tongues" during a religious service.

<*I knew it was the pastor and his wife behind us. I just knew it. And they were praying, and I heard her go "brrrrrrrr." And I'm like, They expect me to believe that's tongues?* —Vaughn Sills, *One Family*.>

14. *n.* the sound of someone shaking water out of his ears after crawling out from under a waterfall, as in *Sacred Journey of the Peaceful Warrior* by Dan Millman.

brrrrrrrrt.

n. the rapid fire of a machine gun, as in the comic book *Punisher #98* by Rod Whigham.

brrrt.

1. *n.* a mobile phone ringing.

<*Brrrt-brrrt, brrrt-brrrt. Gosh who could that be?* —Guide to Balloons and Ballooning.>

2. *n.* the "low-pitched, gurgling" call of the Long-tailed Hermit Hummingbird, as described in *Biological Exuberance: Animal Homosexuality and Natural Diversity* by Bruce Bagemihl.

3. *n.* the short, harsh call of the Northern Rough-Winged Swallow, as described in *A Guide to the Birds of Panama* by Robert S. Ridgely.

4. *n.* the sound of blowing one's nose, as when a man transforms into a woman on the night of the full moon and his mother sobs, "Our son becomes a daughter. How do I buy him clothes? What to do? Brrrt," in the graphic novel *Until the Full Moon Volume 1* by Sanami Matoh.

5. *n.* the whoosh of something being swept away.

<*So she took his wing and, brrrt, they split toward the pad.* —Richard Buckley, *The Bad-rapping of the Marquis de Sade*.>

brrrt brrrt brrrt.

n. the "cough and sputter" of "heavy-caliber machine guns," as described in *Chechnya Diary: A War Correspondent's Story of Surviving the War in Chechnya* by Thomas Goltz.

brrrt-brrrt.

n. the sound of an M-16 firing, as described in *Secret Commandos: Behind Enemy Lines with the Elite Warriors of SOG* by John L. Plaster.

brzzzzz.

n. the screech of bat-sonar, as in the comic book *Batman Family #19* by Bulandi.

bsshh.

n. the choking sound of someone foaming at the mouth, as in the comic strip "PvP" by Scott R. Kurtz; see also blrgh, phlrrt.

Bssss.

n. the title of a German animated film short by Felix Gönnert (1999).

bssss.

1. *n.* a German word for the "quiet, metallic" sound of an automobile's automatic window mechanism (Timm Schuch, "Meine Begleiter.")

2. *n.* a German word for the buzzing of a bee.

3. *n.* a German word for the sound of static, as in "Alarm! Der kleine Dicke ist da" by Von Weiland Freund.

4. *n.* a Spanish word for the sound of a whisper, as in "La Aventura de Hermenegildo."

bssss-bzzzz.

n. the sound of a drum roll.

<*Finney nods his head and shakes, and beats his hands as though holding drumsticks while imitating a drum roll, "Bssss-bzzzz."* —Tag Gallagher, *John Ford: The Man and His Films*.>

bttft.

n. the choking sound of someone foaming at the mouth, as when watching two *Matrix* film trailers simultaneously in the comic strip "PvP" by Scott R. Kurtz.

Bvhg.

n. an island in the Yap region of Micronesia.

bztbzt-bzt-bzzzt.

n. the spluttering hiss of a wireless spark gap transmitter.

<*Reports on the status of the Columbia and Shamrock rapidly flew through the air and electrified the small crowd of bystanders hearing the bztbzt-bzt-bzzzt of the wireless spark gap transmitter.* —John P. King, *Highlands: New Jersey*.>

bzz bzz bzz.

n. the "lazy" sound of insects "among the poppies," as described in *Prairie Soul: Finding Grace in the Earth Beneath My Feet* by Jeffrey A. Lockwood.

bzz bzz bzzt.

n. "game over," as in a video game.

<*All his mind would play was "game over." Game over. Bzz. Bzz. Bzzt. Again and again. Game over.* —Greg Moody, *Two Wheels: A Cycling Murder Mystery*.>

bzz bzz zzk zzk zk kzrp zzrz.

n. the buzz of a dying cell phone signal, as in the graphic novel *Bob the Hamster* by James Paige; see also bzzzk, crkzzzz, kzzzrt, crkzzzz.

bzz-bzz-bzz.

n. the call of the Bachman's warbler.

<*The Bachman's warbler was the rarest songbird in North America. From the black cowl, Finney knew that it was a male. As he watched, the bird gave its distinctive call: a low, grating* bzz-bzz-bzz. *Then it took wing and vanished from his field of vision.* —John Altman, *The Watchmen.*>

bzzp.

n. the buzzing of a fax machine disconnecting, as described in *Fax: Facsimile Technology and Systems*; see also bzzpbzzpbzzp

bzzpbzzpbzzp.

n. the signals which set up a modem for receiving faxes, as described in *Fax: Facsimile Technology and Systems*; see also bzzp.

bzzrrrrmmmmm.

n. the vibration of a video game console's "rumble pack," as in the comic strip "PvP" by Scott R. Kurtz.

bzzrrtt.

n. a buzzing malfunction of someone's robot double standing in line until the next *Star Wars* film opens, as in the comic strip "PvP" by Scott R. Kurtz; see also bzzzt[3], fttrrzzt, kzrrrtt.

bzzt.

1. (also bzzzt.) *interj.* an indication that a wrong answer was given, as in a television game show.

   <*Pressing an imaginary button, Crichton said, "Bzzt! Wrong answer.* —Keith R. A. DeCandido, *Farscape: House of Cards.*>

2. *n.* a call to draw attention to oneself, as when making an important announcement.

   <*At this point, Escalla popped into view above the center of the table and briskly clapped her hands like a carnival announcer. "Bzzt! All right, important safety note at this point!"* —Paul Kidd, *White Plume Mountain.*>

3. *n.* the electrical crackle of a security spotlight turning on.

   <*BZZT! A bright white spotlight snapped on. The light beamed down from the major's roof. BZZT! Another light came on. And another. And then another. A siren blared. The whole garden was suddenly filled with sound and light.* —Teddy Marguiles, *Revenge of the Lawn Gnomes.*>

4. *n.* the noise that a machine makes.

   <*The machine goes... bzzt.* —Kathryn Ash, *Scoop Journal.*>

5. *n.* the repeated harsh rattle of the Bank Swallow, as described in *Birds of the Mid-Atlantic Region and Where to Find Them* by John H. Rappole.

6. *n.* the sound of an X-ray machine, as in *C is for Corpse* by Sue Grafton.

7. *n.* the sound of live wires in a damaged cybernetic arm, as in the graphic novella *Hearts and Minds* by Scott McCloud.

bzzt bzzt.

1. *n.* the buzzing of a faulty neon bulb.

<*The constant flicker and bzzt bzzt of the broken neon light irritated me.* —Lynette Brasfield, *Nature Lessons: A Novel.*>

2. *n.* the buzzing of an office speakerphone or intercom, as in *Everywhere and Beyond: Sequel to From Here to Everywhere* by Robert Lee Joseph; see also bzzt bzzzzt bzzzzzt, bzzzt[6].

<*Bzzt! Bzzt! "Yes, Miss Johnson, what is it?"* —Steve R. Bierly, *How to Thrive as Small-Church Pastor.*>

bzzt bzzzzt bzzzzzt.

n. the buzzing of an office speakerphone or intercom; see also bzzt bzzt[2], bzzzt[6].

<*Bzzt .... Bzzzzt ... Bzzzzzt!!! The annoying sound cranked in Dorian's ears. He felt like he was coming out of a fog as he reached for the speakerphone button.* —R. A. Cross, *Caholia... When Murder Doesn't Die.*>

bzzt bzzzzzt bzt bzt.

n. a "faint buzzing, erratic, like electricity jumping a broken circuit" (Kathy Reichs, *Deja Dead*).

bzzt zzzt.

(also bzzt.) *n.* the flickering of a fluorescent light.

<*In school, the fluorescent overhead lights' steady flicker and bzzt cut through me. Bzzt. Zzzt.* —Tom Jenks, *Our Happiness.*>

bzzt-bzzt.

n. the ringing of a British telephone.

<*It started Meehan awake, and he had no idea where he was or what that sound was or why he was seeing daylight through venetian blinds or why the bzzt-bzzt wouldn't stop.* —Donald E. Westlake, *Put a Lid on It.*>

bzzz.

1. *n.* a buzz indicating an error or malfunction.

<*With a sinking feeling, I trudged up to my room and swiped my key through the lock. It emitted a soft, unsatisfied* bzzz *and lit up. "Please see the front desk." My room had been reassigned, too.* —Cory Doctorow, *Down and Out in the Magic Kingdom.*>

2. *n.* a deliberately mumbled word, due to passive-aggression.

   <*[Finon] prods Maura to be the gracious hostess: "Get the sherry, woman, get the sweets for the babas." Maura doesn't move, pretends not to hear, mumbles to herself. Finon gets up to find the sherry. "Where did she hide it?" he yells into us. "In the bottom of the bzzz," Maura answers, and then adds in an aside to us, "so ignorant, that man."* — Nancy Scheper-Hughes, *Saints, Scholars, and Schizophrenics: Mental Illness in Rural Ireland, Twentieth Anniversary Edition.*>

3. *n.* a placeholder expression, like "such and such."

   <*I had a model about what psychosexual stages were. I had a whole set of models. The person would say "Bzzz" and that would go into this category in my head and I would say, "Oh yes." Under Category A I would give Response 3. Now I didn't have it that exact, but it was that kind of a dance. They'd say, "My mother bzzz," and I'd write it down, and they could learn when to get the pellet.* —Ram Dass, *The Only Dance There Is.*>

4. *n.* an electric shock.

   <*I reached for the mic to say hello to the crowd out there eating their fish. Simultaneously, I held my electric guitar neck to silence its humming strings.* Bzzz! *An electric shock surged through me. I saw blue and tossed the microphone stand three feet into the air.* —Jack Eadon, *Got to Make It.*>

   <*The electric chair. Old Sparky. Bzzz, no more Umberto.* —Arthur Rosenfeld, *A Cure for Gravity.*>

5. *n.* the buzzing of a fly.

   <*The hoofbeats of the mule made a sound as drowsy as a fly's bzzz on a summer afternoon.* —Truman Capote, *Other Voices, Other Rooms.*>

6. *n.* the buzzing of a mosquito.

   <*You begin to drift off ... you are falling asleep ... And suddenly—suddenly you hear a tiny noise! Mosquitos! (Leaps to his feet) Mosquitos! Goddam mosquitos! Damn damn damn damn damn! Mosquitos! (Shakes his fist heavenward) The ninth plague of Egypt! They bzzz and bzzz, and it is such a sorry sound, such a sad, depressing sound, you almost feel sorry for them, but since* you *are the poor sonofabitch they are biting, you begin to itch.* —Anton Chekhov, *A Reluctant Tragic Hero.*>

7. *n.* the noise of electric hair clippers.

   <*I'd hear that first* bzzz *and nearly jump out of my skin. By the time I was ten, we had negotiated our way to scissor cuts.* —Linda Howard, *After the Night.*>

8. *n.* the sound of a dentist's drill; see also bzzz-bzzz-bzzz[2].

   <*[The drill] is the most feared item in the dentist's repertoire of tools: that bzzz, that little bzzz.* —S. Ratneshwar, David Glen Mick, and Cynthia Huffman, *Why of Consumption: Contemporary Perspectives on Consumer Motives, Goals and Desires.*>

9. *n.* the sound of a propeller plane.

   <*I caught sight of a little private plane below me. I could hear the 'bzzz' of its propeller—the*

only sound. —George Plimpton, *The Man in the Flying Lawn Chair: And Other Excursions and Observations.*>

10. *n.* the sound of a rattlesnake's tail.

<*A rattlesnake slithered out of sight beneath a car with a warning* bzzz *of its tail.* —Jennifer Armstrong, *Fire-us #2: The Keepers of the Flame.*>

11. *n.* the sound of an airport metal detector's alarm.

<*The sergeant passed the hand held metal detector over me from head to toe.* Bzzz! Bzzz! *I took off my bracelet*—Bzzz!—*and then my watch.* Bzzz! *I removed my belt with its metal buckle.* Bzzz! *I looked imploringly at the guard. "It must be the brass buttons on my dress!" I said.* —Barbara Kirwin, *The Mad, the Bad, and the Innocent: The Criminal Mind on Trial—Tales of a Forensic Psychologist.*>

12. *n.* the sound of an alarm clock's buzzer.

<*[H]e picked the clock up and heaved it across the room. On hitting the bathroom door the alarm went off, a loud and arrogant BZZZ.* —Thomas Pynchon, *V.*>

13. *n.* the sound of an open telephone line.

<*There was a click and then nothing: Jackal listened to the* bzzz *of the open line for almost five seconds before she realized that Crichton was no longer there.* —Kelley Eskridge, *Solitaire.*>

14. *v.* to wander.

<*Bzzz into the trap field and a devastating explosion spread silently across you.* —Frank Herbert, *Chapterhouse Dune.*>

BZZZ BZZZ.

n. bursts of radio static.

<*The radio spat forth a strange news report between bursts of static: BZZZ BZZZ ... "freak tornado hurled the cabin cruiser" ... BZZZ BZZZ ... "multiple injuries" ... BZZZ BZZZ ... "Pacific Coast Highway" ... BZZZ BZZZ ... "closed in both directions."* —Neal Shusterman, *Thief of Souls: Book Two of the Star Shards Trilogy.*>

bzzz bzzz.

1. *n.* the ringing of a cell phone set to "vibrate."

<*Then we hear the buzzing again, and he thinks the bee has traveled into his pants! So now he's jumping and flailing around with his pants down, and it's still going bzzz, bzzz. Turns out his cell phone was in the pocket of his shorts, and he had set it to buzz.* —Alice Cooper, quoted in *My Best Day in Golf: Celebrity Stories of the Game They Love* by Jonathon Clay.>

2. *n.* the sound of electrical power lines.

<*Electricity was shooting up the mountain, those wires were going bzzz, bzzz.* —Kai T. Erikson, *Everything in its Path.*>

Bzzz Bzzz Bzzz.

n. the droning buzz of a bee; see also bzzzzzz[1].

<*Bzzz Bzzz Bzzz. That is the noise a bee makes, and you had better get used to it because I want everyone who reads this to go out and get a pet bee.* —Tom Davies, SomethingAwful.com>

bzzz bzzz bzzz.

n. the hiss of whispers.

<*[The cinematographer, camera operator, director, and script supervisor] all turn to the actor: "Okay, Joe, look a little camera left." They whisper among themselves: Bzzz bzzz bzzz. "Joe, raise your eyes a tiny, tiny bit." Bzzz bzzz bzzz. "Here, Joe, look at my fist." Bzzz bzzz bzzz. "No, lower." Bzzz bzzz bzzz.* —Christine Vachon, *Shooting to Kill.*>

bzzz bzzzz.

n. the "loud and obnoxious" sound of a chain saw, as in the novel *Bubbles in Trouble* by Sarah Strohmeyer.

bzzz bzzzzzz bzz bzzzz.

n. the sound of a computer booting up, as in the novel *The Stonking Steps* by Will Rogers.

bzzz-bzzz.

1. *n.* a telephone busy signal.

<*Your child comes home and calls a friend. (You get a busy signal.) They chat for a while (bzzz-bzzz, bzzz-bzzz).* —Carol McD. Wallace, *Elbows Off the Table, Napkin in the Lap, No Video Games During Dinner: The Modern Guide to Teaching Children Good Manners.*>

2. *n.* the sharp call of the Southern Red Bishop bird, as described in *Birds of Kenya and Northern Tanzania* by Dale A. Zimmerman.

bzzz-bzzz-bzzz.

1. *n.* a telephone "all circuits are busy" signal.

<*On the day John F. Kennedy was killed, I was working in my office at the Air Force, and we had a radio on, and we heard the news. It was just devastating. I tried to call my husband at the National Institutes of Health, but those were government lines, and you'd pick up a phone and all you'd get was bzzz-bzzz-bzzz.* —Jackie Bolden, quoted in *From Camelot to Kent State: The Sixties Experience in the Words of Those Who Lived It* by Joan Morrison.>

2. *n.* the buzzing of a dentist's drill, as in the poem "Well, Shut My Mouth" by Judith Viorst; see also bzzz[88].

3. *v.* to chat excitedly.

<*Jannie and I had a chance to talk the talk. I knew she was dying to bzzz-bzzz-bzzz. I can always tell. She has a fine, overactive imagination, and I couldn't wait to hear what was on her little mind.* —James Patterson, *Cat & Mouse.*>

bzzz-zzz-t.

n. an egg-timer's buzzer.

<*It's hard to ignore that loud, insistent* bzzz-zzz-t *which announces "time's up!" in a universally recognizable way.* —Harriet Schechter, *Let Go of Clutter.*>

bzzz-zzz-zzz.

n. the buzzing of a fluorescent light, as in *Jack Frusciante Has Left the Band: A Love Story—With Rock 'N' Roll* by Enrico Brizzi.

bzzzk.

n. the buzz of a dying cell phone signal, as in the graphic novel *Bob the Hamster* by James Paige; see also kzzzrt, crkzzzz, bzz bzz zzk zzk zk kzrp zzrz.

bzzzt.

1. (also bzzzzt, bzzzzzzt.) *n.* the sound of a telescope slowing down as it synchronizes with the Earth's rotation, as in *Shoemaker by Levy: The Man Who Made an Impact* by David H. Levy.

2. *adv.* suddenly.

<*Elton loved to mimic my father's way of driving up in his car in a hurry, rolling the window down, patting the accelerator with his foot while he talked to you, and then—bzzzt!—taking off again, sometimes in the midst of your answer to what he had just asked you.* —Wendell Berry, *A World Lost [Three Short Novels].*>

3. *n.* a buzzing malfunction of someone's robot double standing in line until the next *Star Wars* film opens, as in the comic strip "PvP" by Scott R. Kurtz; see also bzzrrtt, fttrrzzt, kzrrrtt.

4. *n.* an electrical shock.

<*Bzzzt! His entire body convulsed in a bone-wrenching spasm.* —Thomas Harlan, *House of Reeds.*>

5. *n.* the "short, high, very buzzy" call of the Green-Tailed Trainbearer bird, as described in *A Guide to the Birds of Columbia* by Steven L. Hilty.

6. *n.* the buzzing of an office speakerphone or intercom; see also bzzt bzzzzt bzzzzzt, bzzt bzzt[2], bzzzt[6].

<*Bzzzt! The buzzer derailed my train of thought. "Yes, sir?" said Mrs. Crow to her intercom.* —Bruce Hale, *Trouble Is My Beeswax: A Chet Gecko Mystery.*>

7. *n.* the jolting feedback of an electronic musical instrument.

<*Again, this peak is followed by Jerry trying to start the "China Doll" with the MIDI guitar, which proceeds to blow up with an enormous "BZZZT," which jolts the audience and is heard clearly on the soundboard tape.* —Michael M. Getz, *The Deadhead's Taping Compendium, Volume III.*>

8. *n.* the sound of a sudden transformation, as at the touch of a button.

<*Next year perhaps—BZZZT! and Summerfield becomes an altogether different man.* —Evan S. Connell, *Diary of a Rapist.*>

<*It's only been in the last few years that Mother has been ... unstable. She hit fifty, and it was like somebody pushed a button. Bzzzt!* —Mary Daheim, *September Mourn: A Bed-And-Breakfast Mystery.*>

bzzzt-bzzzt.

n. the noise of a door buzzer; see also bzzzzt.

<*But when the next visitor came to the door and sounded the buzzer, bzzzt-bzzzt, two whole hours had gone by.* —Jane Langton, *The Escher Twist: A Homer Kelly Mystery.*>

bzzzttt.

n. the crackle of a person's body disappearing "through a curtain of energy," as in the comic book *Secret Society of Super-Villains #12* by Mike Vosburg.

BZZZZ.

(also BZZZ, BZZZZZ.) *n.* the buzz of a doorbell; see also bzzzzt.

<*[A]t about five-fifteen, I hear a loud BZZZZ. Someone is at my door. I choose not to answer it. It cannot be good news. "Go away. I am in a state of suspension." BZZZ. Whoever it is is very determined. But I am more determined. "Go away. You are wasting finger energy pushing that buzzer." BZZZZZ.* —David Klass, *You Don't Know Me.*>

bzzzz bzzz bzzzz.

n. the sound of sawing wood.

<*I explained to my old lady how most bassists who use the bow sound as though they were sawing wood—bzzzz, bzzz, bzzzz.* —Charles Mingus, quoted in *Mingus: A Critical Biography* by Brian Priestley.>

bzzzzt.

n. the noise of a doorbell or buzzer; see also bzzzt-bzzzt, BZZZZ.

<*You're right in the middle of things, when* bzzzzt, *the doorbell.* —Nicholson Baker, *Vox.*>

bzzzzzz.

1. (also bzzzzzzz, bzzz, bzz.) *n.* the buzzing of a bee; see also Bzzz Bzzz Bzzz.

<*Bzzzzzz. Bzzzzzz. The noise was driving me crazy. It had begun earlier in the morning in my office, and at first I thought I was having a stroke or that I was finally hearing the voices I had been waiting so long for. ... Bzzzzzzz. Bzzz. Bzz. Investigating, I followed the sound and came to the window, where the noise was loudest. It was coming from behind the curtains, and when I lifted them I saw the culprit A big, black bee, trying to get back outside.* —Laurie Notaro, *Autobiography of a Fat Bride: True Tales of a Pretend Adulthood.*>

2. *n.* the "faint note and flat, buzzy trill" of the band-Tailed Seedeater bird, as described in *A Guide to the Birds of Columbia* by Steven L. Hilty.

bzzzzzzt.

n. sexual electricity.

<*When I meet a man and feel overwhelmed by sexual attraction, when the very air seems to go* bzzzzzzt *with sexual connection, my whole self can drop into free-fall desire and I am determined to make it work.* —Laura Van Wormer, *The Last Lover.*>

bzzzzzzzz.

n. the buzzing of an electric hair clipper, as in the comic strip “PvP” by Scott R. Kurtz.

C-rch.

n. a judicious alien Luminoth who lies silently "in a small corridor within the depths of a high fortress," in the video game "Metroid Prime 2: Echoes."

ccc.

1. *n.* an ambiguous sound made by someone paralyzed with fear, as in the novel *Theo Slugg in Low Spirits* by Simon Goswell.

2. *n.* the sound of the letter c, as discussed in Phonics.com; see also kkkk.

cfg fgg fg fd dg.

n. the title of a visual poem by Mike Cannell. The poet explains: "Like an oriental calligrapher, I inscribe glyphs on the even white space. I mould shadows into shapes, fluid forms into concrete reality; or rather it becomes something that suggests meaning-but has none. No semantic meaning. There may be no words in these poems, but there is an emotional meaning. Meaning? What is that? Meaning is fleeting. Meaning is a phase, a phrase, a step. Meaning is insubstantial. It exists—then it exits, never staying for long."

cfl ch-ch-ch-ch.

n. the slow begging call of the Black-throated Wattle-eye, as described in *Shrikes and Bush-Shrikes* by Tony Harris.

cfl chchchchchch.

n. the "persistent rapid harsh chattering or buzzing" begging call of the Black-throated Wattle-eye, as described in *Shrikes and Bush-Shrikes* by Tony Harris.

ch'ch'ch'ch'ch.

n. the rapid series of harsh notes constituting the chatter of the Northern Oriole, as described in *Stokes Guide to Bird Behavior, Volume 2* by Donald Stokes.

ch-ch.

(also ch-ch-ch.) *n.* the harsh call of grasshoppers such as the Northern True Katydid, "given about once every second" (Lang Elliott, *A Guide to Night Sounds: The Nighttime Sounds of 60 Mammals, Birds, Amphibians, and Insects*).

ch-ch ch-ch-ch.

v. to flow through life to a train-like rhythm, as in the philosophy of the band Kraftwerk.

<*[The traveling theme in so many Kraftwerk songs is about] letting yourself go. Sit on the rails and ch-ch ch-ch-ch. Just keep going.* —Ralf Hütter, quoted in *Ocean of Sound* by David Toop.>

Ch-ch-ch.

n. a highly-evolved, intelligent lichen with a cloudlike body, living "in the very center of a hollow world" (Richard A. Lupoff, "Lights! Camera! Shub-Niggurath!", *The New Lovecraft Circle*).

<*Ch-ch-ch was minding its own business, keeping its resident birds, insects, ponds, fishes and small reptiles happy. Suddenly Ch-ch-ch felt itself punctured. It was a hell of a shock, although it probably didn't exactly* hurt *Ch-ch-ch.* —Richard A. Lupoff, "Lights! Camera! Shub-Niggurath!", *The New Lovecraft Circle*.>

ch-ch-ch.

1. *n.* a shooing sound, as one might make at a stray animal.

<*One of the boy soldiers, seeing her distress, left his place in the line and shooed the beggar woman away. He made a loud "ch-ch-ch" sound, as if the woman was one of the scruffy dogs slinking bout the garbage pail.* —Scott Landers, *Coswell's Guide to Tambralinga: A Novel*.>

2. *n.* a stutter, as described by Michael Faraday in *Michael Faraday: Physics and Faith* by Colin Archibald Russell.

3. *n.* a vocalized beat to a rhythm one hears in one's own head.

<*Clare was making* ch-ch-ch *sounds between her teeth, accompanying her mental music.* —Julia Spencer-Fleming, *A Fountain Filled With Blood*.>

4. *n.* the cicada-like chatter of the Common Cicadabird, as described in *A Photographic Guide to the Birds of Indonesia* by Morten Strange.

5. *n.* the harsh repeated call of the Spot-Winged Parrotlet in flight, as described in *A Guide to the Birds of Columbia* by Steven L. Hilty.

6. *n.* the sound of a rattlesnake excitedly shaking its tail, as in *Baby Rattlesnake* by Te Ata.

7. *n.* the sound of maracas or other shakable percussion instruments, as described in *Complete Idiot's Guide to Playing Drums* by Michael Miller; see also sh-sh-sh.

8. *n.* the sound of teeth "chattering uncontrollably," as in the novel *Slightly Married* by Mary Balogh.

ch-ch-ch-ch.

1. *n.* a squirrel's chatter, as in *Ribsy* by Beverly Cleary.

2. *n.* the call of the Dark-backed Goldfinch "when disturbed or in flight," as described in *Finches and Sparrows* by Peter Clement.

3. *n.* the fire of antiaircraft guns, as described in *The USS Arizona* by James P. Delgado.

4. *n.* the mechanical annoyance call of the Forest Batis bird, as described in *Birds of Kenya and Northern Tanzania* by Dale A. Zimmerman; the throaty chatter of the Moriche Oriole, as described in *New World Blackbirds* by Alvaro Jaramillo.

5. *n.* the soft clicking of a telephone connection being re-routed, as in the novel *Tooth and Nail* by Ian Rankin.

6. *n.* the sound of people muttering to one another.

<*I felt someone's heavy movement in the room and a head bent over my face. The smell of sterile muslin and toothpaste filled my nose. Two people were speaking to each other. All I heard them saying was "ch-ch-ch-ch."* —Heshmat Moayyad, *Stories from Iran: A Chicago Anthology 1921-1991.*>

ch-ch-ch-ch-ch.

1. *n.* a heartbeat like the chugging of a train.

<*I hit the ground and rolled. I came this close to chopping my head off, and my heart's going ch-ch-ch-ch-ch. I stood there and let the train go by. I was scared to death.* —Cliff Williams, *One More Train to Ride: The Underground World of Modern American Hoboes.*>

2. *n.* the quiet shuffle of someone who doesn't pick up her feet when she walks.

<*I heard a noise. A very small noise:* ch-ch-ch-ch-ch ... *It sounded exactly like my mother shuffling down the hall.* —Jill Conner Browne, *The Sweet Potato Queen's Book of Love.*>

3. *n.* the rhythmic chugging of a lawn sprinkler.

<*Sprinklers chugged on the lawns, making the ch-ch-ch-ch-ch sound that always made it feel even more like summer.* —Debbie Federici, *L.O.S.T.*>

4. *n.* the scratching of a caged bird.

<*The bird cage was covered with the red shawl, but this did not appear to interfere with the parrot's nocturnal activities. Issuing from the cage was a lot of sandpapery scratching and* ch-ch-ch-ch-ch-*ing, as if the bird were busy building something in there.* —Martha Grimes, *The Horse You Came In On.*>

ch-ch-ch-ch-ch-ch-ch.

n. the sound of a sampling drum machine's crash cymbal, as described by Scott Kirkland in *The Art of Digital Music: 56 Visionary Artists and Insiders Reveal Their Creative Secrets* by David Battino.

CH-CH-CH-CH-CH-CH-CH-CH.

n. the sound of an accelerating locomotive cut loose from the boxcars and "charging up the track" (Dan O'Neill, *The Last Giant of Beringia*).

ch-ch-ch-ch-ch-ch-ch-ch-ch.

n. the swishing sound of brushing one's teeth, as in *The New Mother's Survival Guide: A Primer for the First Year of Motherhood* by Elizabeth Wright.

ch-ch-ch-chhhhh.

n. the raspy sound of "serpent people" extraterrestrials, as discussed in *Captured By Aliens: The Search for Life and Truth in a Very Large Universe* by Joel Achenbach.

ch-ch-tm t-t-ch-ch-ch-ch-ch.

n. the rhythm of the Richard and Mimi Fariña song "Reflections in a Crystal Wind," as described by Bruce Langhorne in *Urban Spacemen and Wayfaring Strangers: Overlooked Innovators and Eccentric Visionaries of '60s Rock* by Richie Unterberger.

ch-chk.

n. the "strident chattering" alarm call of the Chinspot Batis, as described in *Shrikes and Bush-Shrikes* by Tony Harris.

ch-chr-chr-chr-chrrrr.

n. the sound of someone flying through the air, as after being given a forceful kick in "A Bishoujo Senshi Sailor Moon Story" by Benjamin A. Oliver.

ch-cht.

n. the early morning chirp of the Buff-bellied hummingbird that is "worth a little lost sleep" to hear, as described in *Hummingbirds* by Nancy L. Newfield.

chchch.

1. *n.* a guttural expression meaning "bang" or "crash," as in *Karina Has Down Syndrome: One Family's Account of the Early Years With a Child Who Has Special Needs* by Cheryl Rogers.

2. *n.* a sound that Guatemalan village children make to get attention (Jason A. Lubam, "Diary of a Jungle Acupuncturist," *Acupuncture Today*).

3. *n.* a strangled cry of shock and blind fury, as in the novel *Candy* by Terry Southern.

4. *n.* a throaty equivalent for the French phrase "je ne sais quoi," when one can't find the right word.

   <*She was fumbling around in her bag for a packet of cigarettes. "How are you doing?" I asked, smiling. "Oh, okay—a bit mnnng. A bit, y'know—chchch—I don't know—y'know."* —Dave Robison, "An Extract From a Work in Progress.">

5. *n.* the sound of "velcro wings falling to the linoleum," as described by Marilyn C. Oakley in the poem "Pseudo."

chchch pschsch chchch pschschsch.

n. the melodious sound of snoring in German, as described in *Simplify Your Life* magazine.

chchchch.

1. (also ch--ch--ch.) *n* . a strange noise made by a faulty computer sound card, as described by Steve Graeper, dBforums.com.

2. *n.* a French word for musical percussion lacking a definite note (fr.AudioFanzine.com).

3. *n.* the dying word of a Hunter, a human-reptile hybrid created by the Umbrella Corporation in the video game "Resident Evil Zero" (Alasdair Lo, "Resident Evil Strategy Guide").

4. *n.* the sound of brushing one's teeth in the chant of the street game "Brush Your Teeth," as described by David Saphra.

5. *n.* the squawk of the Rainbow Lorikeet, as described in "Thoughts From the Bottom of the Glass," EnchantedQuill.net.

chchchch chchchch.

n. the chugging of a train, as described in "The Chattanooga Choo-Choo" by Emmie Wayland.

chchchchch.

1. *n.* the "guttural unvoiced growl" of a tiger (Metamorphosism.com).

2. *n.* the sound of a bionic person.

<*You can hear "chchchchch" every time he steals your morning paper.* —Joe Crowe, "Signs Your Neighbor is Bionic," *RevolutionSF.*>

3. *n.* the sound of static, as discussed by the New York City BVE Motorman's Forum.

chchchchchchchch.

n. the rapid, squeaky notes of the Carruthers' Cisticola bird, as described in *Birds of Kenya and Northern Tanzania* by Dale A. Zimmerman.

chfff.

n. a sound made by a six-month-old baby, as described in the novel *Edwin Mullhouse* by Steven Millhauser.

chhg.

n. the sound of a tap on a computer keyboard, as in the comic strip "PvP" by Scott R. Kurtz; see also brnnk.

chhhht.

interj. an expression of disbelief, as when someone starts to bring up an old anecdote (Linda Lee Bukowski, quoted in *Bukowski and the Beats: A Commentary on the Beat Generation* by Jean-Francois Duval).

chhk.

1. *n.* a ferret's chatter, as in the comic strip "PvP" by Scott R. Kurtz.

2. *n.* the sharp hit of a chopper "cutting up a bullock" (Zhuang Zhou, *Zhuangzi*, quoted in *Classical Chinese Literature* by John Minford.)

chk.

1. *n.* a click mimicking the sound of a pheasant.

<*And she must have listened to what they were saying, for now, like somebody imitating the noise that someone else makes, she made a little click at the back of her throat: "Chk. Chk." Then she smiled.* —Virginia Woolf, "The Shooting Party," *The Complete Shorter Fiction of Virginia Woolf: Second Edition.*>

2. *n.* thc "distinctively short, dry" call of the Brewer's Blackbird, as described in *A Birder's Guide to Minnesota, 4th edition* by Kim Eckert.

3. *n.* the call of a lake bird.

<*On the north end of the lake a bird called* Chk?, *and from past Roddy Deepdale's lodge a second bird answered it:* Chk! Chk! —Peter Straub, *Mystery.*>

4. *n.* the dull click of a doorknob being twisted, as in the graphic novel *Uzumaki 2* by Junji Ito.

5. *n.* the sound of a dart penetrating a dartboard.

<*A gentle heft, and chk! the dart is as firm in the number, the double, the bull, as though it had grown from there.* —Keri Hulme, *The Bone People.*>

6. *n.* the sound of a shovel pushing through sand.

<*I listen until my itching subsides, and the nearby scratch of a shovel digging—chk... chk... chk...—is a gentle drumbeat calling me back to life.* —Donald W. George, *Japan: True Stories of Life on the Road.*>

chk chk.

1. *adj.* a cluck-like response meaning "that's correct," as in the comic strip "PvP" by Scott R. Kurtz.

2. *interj.* a cluck of sympathy over someone's bad luck, as in the novel *Elmer Gantry* by Sinclair Lewis.

chk chk chk.

1. *interj.* an expression of extreme irritation.

<*"Chk, chk, chk." Muttering meaningless syllables of exasperation, Kate struggled to let go of her thoughts, to let go of the hatred of Archer Canby that burned in her joints and shriveled her body.* —Faith Sullivan, *What a Woman Must Do: A Novel.*>

2. *n.* a blackbird's alarm cluck.

<*He watched [his blackbird spirit helpers] intently, as if they might tell him something of great import, when suddenly they took to the air as one, clucking a chk, chk, chk of alarm, and flew off in a tight cloud down the river.* —John Byrne Cooke, *The Snowblind Moon.*>

3. *n.* a call to lure one's timid conscience.

<*Come, my conscience, come, little chicken, chk chk chk. Hush now: here's fodder.* —Georg Buchner, *Danton's Death.*>

4. *n.* the sound of a garden sprinkler; see also chk-chk-chk[6].

<*At 2:00 a.m., Uwanda Docksteader heard the front yard sprinklers come on, the pipes groaning low—an almost hurtful sound—then the sprinkler heads slowly beginning to rotate with their calming chk, chk, chk.* —Curtis Oberhansly, *Downwinders: An Atomic Tale.*>

chk chk chk chk.

1. *n.* the harsh chatter of the White-Eyed Starling, "used in aggressive encounters," as described by Chris Feare in *Starlings and Mynas.*

2. *n.* the sound of steel plates dropping over windows, as in science fiction movies, discussed in *Surviving the Silence: Black Women's Stories of Rape* by Charlotte Pierce-Baker.

chk chk chk-chk.

n. the "soft dry" rattle of the Buff-Spotted Woodpecker, as described in *Birds of Kenya and Northern Tanzania* by Dale A. Zimmerman.

chk-chk.

1. *interj.* a command for a horse to move.

<*Now, when you want Sue to go, you give her a nice punch in the middle and make a little* chk-chk *noise. To her that means go.* —David Baldacci, *Wish You Well.*>

2. *n.* a clicking sound made to entertain a baby.

<*I looked down at her and I made that little sound out of the side of my mouth, the way you do with babies, chk-chk, like that, chk-chk, and she giggled the way she does when I do that, and then—she winked at me!* —Eric Kraft, *Herb 'N' Lorna: A Novel.*>

3. *n.* the musical sound of wildlife in a hayfield, as described in *Prairie Soul: Finding Grace in the Earth Beneath My Feet* by Jeffrey A. Lockwood.

4. *n.* the sound of a gun trigger.

<*Now promise me there'll be no more* (pulling an imaginary trigger) *chk-chk! when I'm gone.* —Anton Chekhov, *The Seagull.*>

5. *n.* the sound of bullets being loaded into a rifle.

<*Jay and Henry stood back from the lion-bearing ponderosa and chambered bullets with a* chk-chk *of metal against metal.* —David Baron, *The Beast in the Garden: A Modern Parable of Man and Nature.*>

chk-chk-chk.

1. *n.* the rhythmic sound of a woodchuck, as discussed in *Sparks of Genius: The Thirteen Thinking Tools of the World's Most Creative People* by Robert and Michèle Root-Bernstein.

2. *n.* a squirrel's warning chatter; see also chk-chk-chk-chk-chkchkchkchkchk.

<*At first I imagine it is an agitated squirrel barking at me from the trees, but there is none of the usual follow-up, no chatter, no chk-chk-chk to frighten me away. Looking up, I quickly discover that I am being watched not by a squirrel but by a black vulture perched in the top of a leafless elm.* —Susan Hanson, *Icons of Loss and Grace: Moments from the Natural World.*>

3. *n.* the choppy noise of a helicopter, as discussed in *Extraterrestrial Visitations: True Accounts of Contact* by Preston Dennet.

4. *n.* the nattering of a crow, as described in *Broken Ground: A Novel* by Kai Maristed.

5. *n.* the soft call of the Olive Thrush, as described in *Birds of Kenya and Northern Tanzania* by Dale A. Zimmerman.

6. *n.* the sound of a garden sprinkler; see also chk chk chk[4].

<*The clippers fell into a steady rhythm, a counterpoint to the chk-chk-chk of a sprinkler over the wooden fence that circled the garden.* —Barbara Parker, *Blood Relations.*>

chk-chk-chk-chk-chk.

n. the "rough clucking" of the Rufous-Crowned or Purple Roller, as described in *Birds of Kenya and Northern Tanzania* by Dale A. Zimmerman; the "dry rapid" call of the Moustached Green Tinkerbird, as described in *Birds of Kenya and Northern Tanzania* by Dale A. Zimmerman.

chk-chk-chk-chk-chk-chk-chk.

n. the chatter of the Slender-Tailed Nightjar, as described in *Birds of Kenya and Northern Tanzania* by Dale A. Zimmerman.

chk-chk-chk-chk-chkchkchkchkchk.

n. a squirrel's chatter; see also chk-chk-chk[2].

<*"Chk-chk-chk-chk-chkchkchkchkchk," the squirrel jabbers, on a tree branch right above my little home on the hill here. ... I look up at him, take off my baseball cap, try to figure out what he's saying to me. I know he's trying to say* something. —J.G. Hayes, *This Thing Called Courage: South Boston Stories.*>

chkk.

n. the sound of a knock at the door, as in the graphic novel *ShadowFall* by Kaichi Satake.

chkk chkk.

n. the sound of grasshoppers hopping through the grass, as in the poem "Hopper-Grass" by Cao-chong, translated by Ezra Pound (*Classical Chinese Literature*).

chnk.

n. the sound of clashing swords, as in a great battle described in the novel *The Iron Tower* by Dennis L. McKiernan.

chp.

n. one of the "golden sounds of early morning," the chirp of the Rufous hummingbird, as described in *Hummingbirds* by Nancy L. Newfield.

chr.

n. the title of a visual poem by Mike Cannell.

chr'r'r'r'r'r.

n. the trilling call of the yellow-eyed babbler, as described in *A Guide to the Birds of Southeast Asia* by Craig Robson.

chrk.

1. *n.* a clucking sound to command a horse.

   <*Clambering back into his wagon and taking up the reins, with a* chrk *of his dry tongue he urged the horses ahead, the train rumbling into motion after.* —Dennis L. McKiernan, *Silver Wolf, Black Falcon.*>

2. *n.* one of the chirping noises of the Southern Grosbeak-Canary, as described in *Birds of Kenya and Northern Tanzania* by Dale A. Zimmerman.

3. *n.* the chirp of a fantastical "ptarmigan" bird, as in *The Dragonstone* by Dennis L. McKiernan.

4. *n.* the sound of a hotel desk clerk transferring a phone call to Lou Reed, as in *Psychotic Reactions and Carburetor Dung: The Work of a Legendary Critic: Rock'N'Roll as Literature and Literature as Rock'N'Roll* by Lester Bangs.

chrp.

n. the musical chatter of the Ruby-Throated Hummingbird, as described in *Hummingbirds: A Wildlife Handbook* by Kim Long.

chrr.

1. *n.* a harsh call delivered by the Blue-throated Flycatcher, as described in *A Photographic Guide to the Birds of India and the Indian Subcontinent, Including Pakistan, Nepal, Bhutan, Bangladesh, Sri Lanka, and the Maldives* by Bikram Grewal.

2. *n.* a noncommittal mutter.

   <*Chrr. Why not?* —Leo Rosten, "Potch," anthologized in *A Passion for Books: A Book Lover's Treasury of Stories, Essays, Humor, Love and Lists on Collecting, Reading, Borrowing, Lending, Caring for, and Appreciating Books* by Harold Rabinowitz.>

chrr chrr.

n. the echoing of a submarine's sonar, as in "The Empire News."

chrr trrt trrt.

n. the "low churring notes" of the Black-throated Tit, as described in *A Field Guide to the Birds of China* by John MacKinnon.

chrr-chrr-chrr.

1. *n.* the "harsh chattering" of the Southern Black Tit, as described in *Birds of Southern Africa* by Ian Sinclair.

2. *n.* the laughter-like chatter of a squirrel, as after stuffing itself with birdseed in *Active Young Readers Grades 4-6 Assessment Resource* by the Nova Scotia Department of Education; see also chrrr[1], chrrt.

chrr-chrrr chrr-chrrr.

n. the African Barred Owlet's "double trilled or purring whistle, the second note higher," as described in *Birds of Kenya and Northern Tanzania* by Dale A. Zimmerman.

chrrp.

n. the soft utterance of the Dusty Lark, as described in *Birds of Southern Africa* by Ian Sinclair; the sharp chatter of the Anna's Hummingbird, as described in *Hummingbirds: A Wildlife Handbook* by Kim Long.

chrrr.

1. *n.* the chatter of a squirrel; see also chrr-chrr-chrr[22].

<*The man reported seeing the squirrel and the bird sitting about 10 feet apart in different trees and chattering back and forth. First the squirrel gave a loud "chrrr" call, then climbed up into the tree where the pileated was perched, chattering as it ascended the tree.* —Washington Department of Fish and Wildlife, "The Weekender Report.">

2. *n.* the sound a hamster makes, as described by Eva Padrna.

3. *n.* the static noise a walkie-talkie makes before and after its user speaks.

<*CHRRR—We need extra men to the base. They have surrounded us, repeating… CHRRR—Roger! Two men coming! CHRRR.* —Lasse Pakarinen, "Laser Combat.">

chrrr chrrr.

n. a German phrase for the sound of snoring.

chrrr chrrr chrrr.

n. the struggling of a computer hard disk drive stressed by mechanical interference.

<*The typical consequence is that the next bootup will terminate with the well known Chrrr, chrrr, chrrr ..... where the splash screen used to be.* —Lostcircuits.com.>

chrrr-chrrr-chrrr.

n. the rapid, buzzy call of Bonaparte's Gull, as described by Tomm Lorenzin in "Birdsong Mnemonics"; the "harsh scolding" call of the Short-tailed Scimitar Babbler, as described in *A Guide to the Birds of Southeast Asia* by Craig Robson.

chrrrr.

1. *n.* a command for a camel to kneel.

<*After some useless attempts I finally managed the "chrrrr," deep from the throat, that commands*

camels to kneel down and wait to be saddled. —"Those Irresistible Black Eyes," VirtualTourist.com.>

2. *n.* pain (as inflicted by a troubled relationship) which is forgiven but not forgotten, which suddenly pops back into consciousness and, croaking like a toad, makes even the brightest sunshine seem cheerless, as in the poem "Phantasus" by Arno Holz.

3. *n.* the "harsh and raucous" call of Lagden's Bush-Shrike, as described in *Shrikes and Bush-Shrikes* by Tony Harris.

4. *n.* the courting call of the gecko, "like a squeaky door hinge" (The Global Gecko Association).

5. *n.* the sound of laughter from deep within the throat.

<*Jak'xen made a deep chrrrr in his thorax, a noise people knew him recognized as laughter.* —Phil Bacon, "Party Party.">

chrrrr chrrrr.

n. the scolding call of the Red-bellied Woodpecker.

<*These are noisy woodpeckers, easily identified by their repeated soft, scolding, "chrrrr, chrrrr."* —Georgann Schmalz, "Woodpeckers of the Southeastern United States.">

chrrrr grrrr cgrrrr.

n. the grating creak of a pet mouse exercise wheel in need of oil.

<*[M]y wheel makes this chrrrr grrrr cgrrrr sound, a cross between a grating sound and a chk chk sound that no amount of oil will cure.* —PetsHub.com Mouse Forum.>

chrrt.

(also chrtt.) *n.* a squirrel's chatter, as in the comic book *Marvel Super-Heroes III #8*; see also chrr-chrr-chrr[22].

chrrt chrrt.

n. the harsh alarm of the Crimson-winged Laughing Red-Faced Liocichla, as described in *A Photographic Guide to the Birds of India and the Indian Subcontinent, Including Pakistan, Nepal, Bhutan, Bangladesh, Sri Lanka, and the Maldives* by Bikram Grewal; the throaty call of the Rosy Starling, as described in *The Handbook of Bird Identification for Europe and the Western Palearctic* by Mark Beaman.

chrrt chrrt chrrt.

n. the raucous call of the Ochraceous Bulbul, as described in *Birds of Thailand* by Craig Robson.

chrzzt.

n. the harsh call of the Tawny-Flanked Prinia bird, as described in *Birds of Southern Africa* by Ian Sinclair.

ck chchchch.

n. a sound resembling a bird's clucking.

<*"Ck! Chchchch!" Sounds like that of a clucking bird accompanied the words.* —Rociriel, "Mother of Horsemen," Henneth Annûn Story Archive.>

ck ck ck.

n. the cracking of a nut, as described in *Marva Collins' Way* by Marva Collins.

ckgh.

n. the title of a visual poem by Mike Cannell.

cld.

v. could, written in Roger Bacon's all-consonant secret code (devised in 1250), as discussed in *The Voynich Manuscript* by Gerry Kennedy.

clk.

1. *interj.* an expression of anger by a Martian whose flying saucer has just been destroyed by a "little beast with a peppermint stick" (Will Eisner, *Comics & Sequential Art*).

2. *n.* the sound of involuntary swallowing.

<*"I said I'd like to* clk,*" he said.* —Nicholson Baker, *Vox.*>

clk clk.

n. a command used in training puppies to slow their pace as they are learning to heel, as discussed in *Puppies for Dummies* by Sarah Hodgson.

clr.

adj. clear, written in Roger Bacon's all-consonant secret code (devised in 1250), as discussed in *The Voynich Manuscript* by Gerry Kennedy.

cmrlj.

n. a Slovenian word for "bumble bee."

crkk.

n. the creaking of wooden planks straining, as in the graphic novel *Uzumaki 3* by Junji Ito.

crkzzzz.

n. the crackle of a dying cell phone signal, as in the graphic novel *Bob the Hamster* by James Paige; see also bzzzk, kzzzrt, bzz bzz zzk zzk zk kzrp zzrz.

crnch.

n. the crunch of a tree branch felled by a hurricane, as in the graphic novel *Uzumaki 2* by Junji Ito.

crrk.

1. *n.* a "screech of metal cut like paper," as when someone snips through a wrecked vehicle to save the driver in the novel *The Gold Coast* by Kim Stanley Robinson.

2. *n.* a call to lure a puffin.

<*"Crrk!" he called with a low throaty sound as a puffin went whizzing past, looking curiously at* Brendan *but keeping a safe distance. Again, "Crrk!" The bird wheeled in a tight arc and came back. "Crrk!" The bird was being drawn by the noise, closer and closer.* —Tim Severin, *The Brendan Voyage.*>

3. *n.* the sound of a flea being crushed.

<*He eased the pressure off slowly until just enough of the tiny parasite became visible. Crrk! His right thumbnail spliced it in two with a satisfying crack. He flicked the tiny corpse on to the floor, noticed the red stain of his own blood which it had left on his victorious thumb.* —Iain McDowall, *A Study in Death.*>

4. *n.* the static sound of an ambulance radio; see brrk.

CRRK CRRK CRRK.

n. the raspy, duck-like call of the Eastern Gray Squirrel, as described in *Squirrels: A Wildlife Handbook* by Kim Long.ul

crrk crrrk.

n. the noise of a squeaky chair, as described in *Call It Sleep: A Novel* by Henry Roth.

crrk-crrk-crrk.

n. the repeated croaking of the Marsh Owl, as described in *Birds of Kenya and Northern Tanzania* by Dale A. Zimmerman.

crrkkk.

(also crk, crrk.) *n.* the sound of a mirror cracking, as in the graphic novel *Soul Air* by Angel Hill.

Crrnx.

n. the name of an island cove.

<*[W]e have seen that pirate fleet at rendezvous not a day from here in the Cove of Crrnx.* — Stan McDaniel, *The Letterseeker.*>

crrpplrr.

n. the fluid warbling of a pigeon.

<*"Okay," she said, and then she made a noise that sounded like the liquid burbling of pigeons. "Okay Crrppllrr, you're looking for the marquis de Carabas."* —Neil Gaiman, *Neverwhere.*>

crrr.

v. to creak like a closing door, as in *Republic: A Novel* by J.B. Powell.ul

crrrk.

1. *n.* a mother hen's warning signal that danger is afoot.

<*When there is danger of hawks or owls or cats or anything around, the hen gives out a warning signal. She'll get up somewhere and make a squawking noise. Then she says, "Crrrk, crrrk, crrrk," in a low-pitched voice. The chicks all get under her, or all stand at attention.* —Minnie Rose Lovgreen, *Minnie Rose Lovgreen's Recipe for Raising Chickens.*>

2. *n.* a sound made by an intelligent insectlike "Thranx" poet named Desvendapur, in the novel *Phylogenesis: Book One of The Founding of the Commonwealth* by Alan Dean Foster.

<*"[T]hey are, crrrk, carrying out limited studies of their own far, far from here.* —Alan Dean Foster, *Phylogenesis: Book One of The Founding of the Commonwealth.*>

crrrkkkk.

n. the sound of a hatching seed from Mars, as described in *365 Bedtime Stories* by Christine Allison.

crrrrk.

n. the noise of radio static.

<*'We're crrrrk doing the best we crrrrk,' came the reply.* —Neil Gaiman & Terry Pratchett, *Good Omens.*>

chrtr.

n. the title of a visual poem by Mike Cannell.

crwth.

n. an ancient Celtic stringed instrument, played with a bow. Though in Welsh, the *w* generally represents a vowel sound, most English speakers consider *crwth* an all-consonant word.

<*Her fingers strummed across the strings of a crwth which had lain untouched since the Normans' coming. Strange chords of music broke the silence in the hall and echoed in the large room.* —Kathleen E. Woodiwiss, *The Wolf and the Dove.*>

crzzz.

n. the crackling of a flamethrower, as in the comic book *Super Team Family Giant.*

cshhh.

n. the crash of a cymbal that fell off a cliff, as transcribed in the comic strip "PvP" by Scott R. Kurtz.

cwm.

n. a natural amphitheatre. Though in Welsh the *w* generally represents a vowel sound, most English speakers consider *cwm* an all-consonant word.

<*After several weeks of furious, mindless travel, the rising sun found Rhapsody sitting on the crest of the cwm.* —Elizabeth Haydon, *Destiny: Child of the Sky*.>

D—l.

n. a self-censored spelling of "Devil."

<*By G—, gentlemen, I tell you nothing but the truth; and the D—l broil them eternally that will not believe me.* —Jonathan Swift, *A Tale of a Tub.*>

D-chr.

n. the child hero of Agon, former acolyte squire turned warrior and temple defender, in the video game "Metroid Prime 2: Echoes."

d-rrrrr.

n. the harsh alarm call of the Yellow-winged Blackbird, as described in *New World Blackbirds* by Alvaro Jaramillo.

d-z-z-z-z-z-z-z.

n. the "distinctive buzzing or ticking" of the Fork-Tailed Palm-Swift bird, as described in *A Guide to the Birds of Columbia* by Steven L. Hilty.

ddd.

n. the sound of the letter d, as described in the educational video *Nurturing the Love of Learning: Montessori for the Early Childhood Years*; see also dddd[3].

dddd.

1. *n.* "a loud hammering sound," as described in *Tongue Tie—From Confusion to Clarity: A Guide to the Diagnosis and Treatment of Ankyloglossia* by Carmen Fernando.

2. *n.* the "rattling sound" of the Plate-billed Mountain-toucan, "likely made by the tongue against the ramphotheca," as described in *Toucans, Barbets and Honeyguides: Ramphastidae, Capitonidae and Indicatoridae* by Lester L. Short; see also kkkk, tttt.

3. *n.* the sound of the letter d, as described in *The Voice That Means Business: How to Speak With Authority, Confidence and Credibility Anytime, Anywhere* by Linda Shields; see also ddd.

dddddt.

n. a "soft sound like that of scraping a comb," made by the rapid claps of the Choco Toucan's bill, as described in *Toucans, Barbets and Honeyguides: Ramphastidae, Capitonidae and Indicatoridae* by Lester L. Short.

dddrrr.

n. the muttering of someone paralyzed by fear; see also nnnnn.

<*"Dddrrr," said Brother Fingers, beginning to shake uncontrollably.* —Terry Pratchett, *Guards! Guards!*>

ddrrt.

n. the distinctive low raspy twitter of the Dickcissel bird, as described in *A Guide to the Birds of Panama* by Robert S. Ridgely.

dh dh dh.

n. a knocking at the door, as described in *Marva Collins' Way* by Marva Collins.

DJ.

n. originally an abbreviation for "disc jockey" but now a word unto itself.

dknnnnz.

n. a sound made by a six-month-old baby, as described in the novel *Edwin Mullhouse* by Steven Millhauser.

dlrdn.

interj. an interjection coined by François Rabelais in the novel *Gargantua and Pantagruel*, spoken by a native of the imaginary "Lanternland."

dnnn.

n. an incoherent response, as from someone intoxicated; see also hnnn.

<*"You all right? You sick or anything, or just drunk?" "Dnnn," said Sandra.* —William Kennedy, *An Albany Trio.*>

Dpfnzzlwrpf.

n. a fictitious corporation in Chartreuse, New York.

<*As you know, we are in the process of a transition here at Dpfnzzlwrpf Inc., as we shift all our perforated swizzle-satchels over to automated denim.* —Jonathan Caws-Elwitt, "Letter to a Customer.">

dr.

v. do, as spoken with a mouth filled with toothpaste, as in *My Monastery is a Minivan: 35 Stories from a Real Life* by Denise Roy.

dr'r'r'r'r'r'r'r'r'r.

n. the "rapid rattling" of the agitated Black-eared Shrike Babbler, as described in *A Guide to the Birds of Southeast Asia* by Craig Robson.

drhds.

interj. an interjection coined by François Rabelais in the novel *Gargantua and Pantagruel,* spoken by a native of the imaginary "Lanternland."

drmpf.

n. an incomprehensible utterance of pain, from the ubiquitous German joke about a man mistakenly diagnosed with hemorrhoids who tells the proctologist, "get someone with longer fingers—I have a sore throat!" See also hgmmm, hlmpfmr, hmmgmr.

Drrr.

n. a mispronunciation of the title "Dr."

<*Lynne told her physician that she wanted to be referred to as* Ms. *Atkinson. He sarcastically replied, "If you are* Ms., *then call me Drrr.* —Pamela E. Butler, *Self-Assertion for Women.*>

drrr.

n. door, as spoken by someone "slurring his words out of pure exhaustion," as in the novel *Doona* by Anne McCaffrey.

drrr-drr.

(also drr-drr.) *n.* an automobile sound.

<*He grabbed hold of the lower end of the steering wheel and swung it this way and that, making motor-car noises as he did so: "Drrr-drr, drr-drr."* —David Davidar, *The House of Blue Mangoes: A Novel.*>

drrrp.

n. a hen's call for her chicks to feed.

<[I]*f the food is all right, she says, "Drrrp, drrrp, drrrp," in a higher pitch, and they all come and eat.* —Minnie Rose Lovgreen, *Minnie Rose Lovgreen's Recipe for Raising Chickens.*>

drrrrrrrrrr.

n. the dry purr (with emphasis on the d) of the Desert Warbler, as described in *A Field Guide to the Birds of China* by John MacKinnon.

drrt.

n. the dry, gravelly call (sometimes delivered in a series) of the Sand Martin, as described in *A Guide to the Birds of Panama* by Robert S. Ridgely.

dth.

n. an expression of dread.

<*Dth, dth, dth! Three days imagine groaning on a bed with a vinegared handkerchief round her forehead, her belly swollen out!* —James Joyce, *Ulysses.*>

dzzt.

1. *n.* a sound made by the zikri drum, as described in *Dan Ge Performance: Masks and Music in Contemporary Côte d'Ivoire* by Daniel B. Reed.

2. *n.* the electrical buzz of an android or robot malfunctioning, as in *The Metallic Touch*; see vzzkt.

3. *n.* the sound of a satellite feed disconnecting, as in the graphic novel *Dangerous Days* by Kat Richardson.

dzzt dzzt.

1. *n.* the erratic, Morse code-like buzzing of electricity.

   <*The metal contraption was back, and the yellow lightning bolt was flaring and chirping out an erratic sequence: dzzt dzzt ... dzzt dzzt dzzt ... dzzt ... dzzt dzzt ... dzzt dzzt dzzt dzzt ... dzzt ... dzzt dzzt dzzt ..., like an eerie version of Morse code.* —Jason Earls, "Corpse Machines.">

2. *n.* the sound of a metallic voice.

   <*A metallic voice emanated from the first box, "dzzt dzzt ... We have enough. It's time to leave ... dzzt."* —Jason Earls, "Corpse Machines.">

dzzz.

n. a "muffled noise, half-screech, half-whimper," as in the novel *Dezra's Quest* by Chris Pierson.

dzzzzr dzzzzr dzzzzr dzzzzr.

n. the "monotonous" song of the Spotted Bush Warbler, as described in *A Guide to the Birds of Southeast Asia* by Craig Robson.

DzzzZZzZZZzZZZZZzzzZzZZZZzzzZZzZzZZZZZzzzzZzZZzZZZzzzZZZzZZZZzzt.

n. the sound of noise and information communicated all at once, as in the novel *Software* by Rudy Rucker.

f f f.

n. the title of a visual poem by Mike Cannell.

f'r.

prep. for.

<*[S]moking grass in a goddamned* green cloud, *f'r chrissake.* —Tom Wolfe, *The Electric Kool-Aid Acid Test.*>

f-f-f-f-f.

n. a painful inhalation.

<*"Be careful," he shouted once more, and hardly were the words out of his mouth when, thump! there was the sound of a heavy fall in front of him, followed by the long "F-f-f-f-f" of a breath indrawn with pain.* —Aldous Huxley, *Chrome Yellow.*>

fdgd.

n. the title of a visual poem by Mike Cannell.

ff.

adj. fortissimo (a musician's directive to perform a passage very loudly).

fff.

1. *adj.* fine, as spoken during a disjointed telephone conversation in the play *Oleanna* by David Mamet.

2. *adj.* fortississimo (a musician's directive to perform a passage very, very loudly).

   <*[T]here is a point [in Mahler's First Symphony] where the orchestra slows down very dramatically and is requested to take a "Luftpause," a pause for breath. What comes after the "Luftpause" determines the rest of the symphony—the orchestra comes in fff—very very loudly and triumphantly. This is a very psychologically dramatic and tense moment in the Symphony, possibly the climax, and is therefore of utmost importance.* —Derek Lim, "Mahler: Symphony No. 1," *Inkpot #55.*>

3. *interj.* a dismissive huff.

   <*"What about women?" "Fff! Eat, drink, and go to bed, I say. All the rest's just trouble!"* —Nikos Kazantzakis, *Zorba the Greek.*>

4. *interj.* a gasp of pain.

<*Hans Castrop pulled air in between his teeth. The needle struck home. "Fff!" he sucked in. "That's a critical nerve you happened to hit there, Director Behrens. Oh, yes, yes, hurts like hell.* —Thomas Mann, *The Magic Mountain*.>

5. *interj.* a huffing exhalation, as in *Ulysses* by James Joyce.

6. *n.* the sound of a sky rocket fizzing up, as described in "More Than Words" by the New Zealand Ministry of Education.

7. *n.* the sound of the letter f, as described in "Emergent Literacy Lesson Design" by Katie Kirkpatrick; see also ffff[2], fffffff.

fff fff fff.

n. the hissing of a fighting cat, as described in *Marva Collins' Way* by Marva Collins.

ffff.

1. *adj.* fortississississimo (a musician's directive to perform a passage very, very, very loudly).

<*You'll also hear a speaker that will take you on a joyride from p (though maybe, just maybe, it's only one-and-a-half p's) to ffff without crunching in on itself, like a run over beer can.* —Wayne Garcia, review of the Avalon Acoustics Arcus Loudspeaker, *Fi: Magazine of Music & Sound*.>

2. *n.* the sound of the letter f; see also fff[7], fffffff.

<*Now can you find the letter that makes ffff?* —Peggy Kaye, *Games for Learning: Ten Minutes a Day to Help Your Child Do Well in School, From Kindergarten to Third Grade*.>

fffff.

adj. fortississississimo (a musician's directive to perform a passage very, very, very, very loudly).

<*The entirety of the piece [Symphony for the Near-Deaf, or Near-Deaf Experiences] is at a dynamic level of fffff. Piece is to be repeated as many times as possible. Instrumentation: 21 shotguns (blanks should be used), four cannons, one 50-foot stack of guitar amplifiers, two dragsters, one airplane, 256 chainsaws, five power saws, 76 police sirens, 31 rivet machines, chorus of screaming women, fireworks, and 15 sticks of lit dynamite.* —"A Catalog of Never-to-be-Recorded Musical Works."

fffffff.

n. the sound of the letter f, as in the novel *Attaboy, Sam!* by Lois Lowry; see also fff[7], ffff[22].

fffft.

1. *interj.* an expression of dismissal.

<*Once, when one of her friends protested her speaking of me this way [as a pathetic creature] within my hearing—and of my parents and family—she said,* "Fffft. *If you speak at all rapidly, she understands nothing."* —Sue Miller, *The World Below*.>

2. *interj.* an ironic, dismissive huff.

<*"Work, you can rely on," she said. "Love ... ffffl."* —Heidi Jon Schmidt, *The Bride of Catastrophe: A Novel.*>

ffffzzzzzz.

n. a hiss of steam, as when hot metal is dipped in water, in the novel *The Polished Hoe* by Austin Clarke; see also fzzzzz[1].

fffmmm.

interj. a moan of protest, as by someone with a traumatized, bloody nose in the novel *The Long Dark Tea-Time of the Soul* by Douglas Adams.

fffrrrrr.

n. a noise granting one's exit of a nursery.

<*I understood. If I was to leave the nursery it would only be after a performance of the noise: fffrrrrr.* —Edward Carey, *Observatory Mansions: A Novel.*>

ffft.

1. *adj.* "belly-up," finished, financially ruined.

<*The House of Beragon ... is ffft. ... Alas it is no more. Pop goes the weasel.* —James M. Cain, *Mildred Pierce.*>

2. *interj.* "all is lost."

<*Effective works of fantasy are distinguished by their often relentless accuracy of detail, by their exactness of imagination, but the coherence and integrity of their imagined worlds—by, precisely, their paradoxical truthfulness. ... If the fantasist's truth fails us—ffft.* —Ursula K. Le Guin, *Dancing at the Edge of the World: Thoughts on Words, Women, Places.*>

3. *interj.* a haughty "who cares?" as in the play *The Lady from the Sea* by Henrik Johan Ibsen.

4. *interj.* a response to tasting bourbon for the first time.

<*Willie said, "I've never had bourbon before," wiggling his heavy body forward in his chair so that he could hold his glass up to the candle-light and study the amber drink. He had a fat face, thin lips, a lot of tiny teeth, and an indolent grin. He sniffed at his glass, then tipped some of the liquid onto his tongue and said, "Ffft."* —Rosemary Mahone, *Whoredom in Kimmage: The Private Lives of Irish Women.*>

5. *interj.* an arrogant huff, as in the play *Ghosts* by Henrik Johan Ibsen.

6. *interj.* an expression of disdain, as in the novel *Swordpoint* by Ellen Kushner.

<*I care nothing for polite society. Ffft! I care only for ... what I like to do.* —Rosemary Rogers, *Dangerous Man.*>

7. *interj.* an expression of exasperation, as in the novel *When Mountains Walked* by Kate Wheeler.

8. *interj.* an expression of indignation.

<*This place, it is not civilized. Do you know I 'ad to spend the night by myself? Alone? Ffft!* —Tabor Evans, *Longarm 299: Longarm and Maximilian's Gold.*>

9. *n.* a puff of air in the place of someone who has been "commodified and reified," turned from a person into an "it," and essentially "erased" (Mac Wellman, *Cat's Paw: A Meditation on the Don Juan Theme*).

<*You've been erased, and are now invisible. There is no one standing in your shoes. Only air. Ffft.* —Mac Wellman, *Cat's Paw: A Meditation on the Don Juan Theme.*>

10. *n.* a racing car coming to a halt due to electrical failure, as described in *Daytona 24 Hours: The Definitive History of America's Great Endurance Race* by J.J. O'Malley.

11. *n.* the angry hiss of a duck whose treasure and flying carpet have been stolen, as in *Walt Disney's Comics in Color, Volume 7* by Carl Barks.

12. *n.* the combustion of a matchstick; the spark of creative synergy.

<*[T]hose connections [between emotional matters and subliminally registered facts] are the most interesting moment—no, second, like the* ffft! *of a match—in the process of writing.* —Rosellen Brown, "You Are Not Here Long," *Letters to a Fiction Writer.*>

13. *n.* the crack of pottery splitting in two.

<*That very moment and second, O Best Beloved, the Milk-pot that stood by the fire cracked in two pieces*—ffft!—*because it remembered the bargain she had made with the Cat; and when the Woman jumped down from the footstool—lo and behold!—the Cat was lapping up the warm white milk that lay in one of the broken pieces.* —Rudyard Kipling, "The Cat That Walked By Himself," *Just-So Stories.*>

14. *n.* the hiss of a cat, as in *Garfield Tips the Scales: His 8th Book* by Jim Davis.

15. *n.* the sound of a gun silencer.

<*You might wonder how you can possibly take an explosive noise that can damage your hearing and turn it into a little "ffft" sound like you see in the movies. Gun silencers work on a very simple principle to silence guns.* —Marshall Brain, *Marshall Brain's How Stuff Works: How Much Does the Earth Weigh?*>

16. *n.* the sound of a private, romantic moment being disrupted all of a sudden.

<*Nothing else went on. You know that well enough. Because then all the others came in, and—ffft!* —Henrik Ibsen, *The Master Builder.*>

17. *n.* the sound of an arrow hitting its target.

<Ffft, *garimpeiro [gold prospector] dead.* Ffft, *animal dead.* Ffft, *more animals dead.* —David Thomas, *Miracle Medicines of the Rainforest: A Doctor's Revolutionary Work With Cancer and AIDS Patients.*>

18. *n.* the whoosh of something flying past.

<*A little creek just went by. It went by so fast. I bet it never moved so fast in its life before.*

Ffft—and gone. It didn't look like water, it looked like silver plate; the sky was reflected in it. —Cornell Woolrich, *Rendezvous in Black.*>

19. *v.* to cut through.

<*"I'm here, though, because I can't help but wonder if we can't just cut across the whole mess ... Alexander's solution to the Gordian knot, right?" He made a chopping motion with his hand.* "Ffft! *Done."* —H. Jay Riker, *The Silent Service: Virginia Class.*>

20. *v.* to drop "in a downward motion like a falling bird," as in the novel *The Good Journey* by Micaela Gilchrist.

21. *v.* to shoot water.

<*As the years had disappeared amidst the cocktails, pies and* ffft-*ing garden sprinkler systems of Fordham, Wisconsin, so had whatever smidgen of love it was that had drawn me and Chester together.* —Bruno Maddox, *My Little Blue Dress.*>

22. *v.* vanished.

<*The pain has gone, I'm telling you, disappeared ...* ffft. —Ruth Levitt, *The Twins.*>

ffft fffffft ffffft.

n. the sound of a crossbow shooting steel bolts.

<*Ffft! Fffffft! Ffffft! Van Helsing shot the bolts one right after the other, but the grotesque white bats were too quick. They split up and soared around the spire of the village church.* —Carla Jablonski, *Van Helsing: The Junior Novel.*>

ffft ffft ffft.

1. *n.* a huffing, assured chuckle.

<*As we know—ffft, ffft, ffft—things aren't the same as when in civics class they had those big old "Products Maps." ... [E]ach state had a picture of the product it was happiest about making.* —Reno, "Reno Once Removed," anthologized in *Extreme Exposure: An Anthology of Solo Performance Texts from the Twentieth Century* by Jo Bonney.>

2. *n.* the sound of a shower of sparks as impurities rise to the surface of melting gold and burn off in the air, as in the novel *White Darkness* by Steven D. Salinger.

ffft fft ffft.

n. the sound of "friendly fire" gunshots.

<*All of a sudden you hear this funny ffft fft ffft sound, and you don't get it until maybe your left wing catches fire. Friendly Fire! Somebody on your side is mistaking you for the enemy!* —Julia Cameron, *Supplies: A Troubleshooting Guide for Creative Difficulties.*>

ffft mm.

n. an expression in the Jimi Hendrix song "Rainy Day Dream Away," encouraging one to "lay back an' groove" (Janie L. Hendrix, *Jimi Hendrix: The Lyrics*).

ffft, ffft, ffft.

n. the sputter of a truck engine backfiring, as in the novel *Three to Get Deadly* by Janet Evanovich.

ffft-ffft-ffft.

n. a typical sound made by a baby attempting to talk, as discussed in *Wonder Weeks: How to Turn Your Baby's 8 Great Fussy Phases into Magical Leaps Forward* by Hetty Vanderijt.

ffft-fft-fft.

n. the coughing sputter of a damaged F-5 aircraft.

<[W]e saw the plane pulling up into a climbing left turn, heading back toward the runway, but making a strange ffft-fft-fft sound. —Jeffrey L. Ethell, *Fighter Command: American Fighters in Original WWII Color.*>

ffftt.

v. to ejaculate, as in the song "The Big Black Bull" ("He missed his mark and ffftt in the pasture"), discussed in *The Erotic Muse: American Bawdy Songs* by Ed Cray; see also pfft.

fft.

1. *interj.* a scoff, as in the story "Hidden" by Elisabeth Kuijl.

2. *interj.* an expression of impatience.

<"Can you not climb?" he demanded. "I ... m ... my legs are so numb." "Fft," said Becket, and without further ado lifted Ames up under the armpits and hauled him over while his numb feet scrabbled at the spikes. —Patricia Finney, *Unicorn's Blood.*>

3. *n.* the name of a man with a glass head in the story "The Glass Head" by Vera Searles.

4. *n.* the sound of a gun trigger.

*<I thumbed the trigger, a soft *fft* and a loud *CRACK* as the shell impacted and fractured the slate chalkboard, spiderwebbing it.* —John Berryhill, "New Worlds Awaiting.">

5. *n.* the sound of a typewriter, as in the play *Words, Words, Words* by David Ives.

6. *n.* the sound of an object whirring through the air.

<Make a sound effect like Zorro's sword moving through the air, roughly like fft. —Scott Adams, *Dilbert and the Way of the Weasel: A Guide to Outwitting Your Boss, Your Coworkers, and the Other Pants-Wearing Ferrets in Your Life.*>

7. *n.* the sound of exploding ammunition.

<The crackling of the flames and the "vrrp" and "fft" of the exploding ammunition seemed to fill the troops with inordinate glee. —Johannes Steinhoff, *Messerschmitts Over Sicily: Diary of a Luftwaffe Fighter Commander.*>

8. *n.* the sound of suppressed laughter, as in the novel *The FarCall Project* by RedTurtle.

fft fft.

n. a shooing sound, as from a cat.

<*"All right, we accept your apology for all that barking," Mr. Smedley sniffed. "But run along. Fft! Fft!"* —George Selden, *Harry Cat's Pet Puppy*.>

<*She ended these words with a "Fft! Fft!" and, stroking her whiskers, took up her stand, with a defiant air, between Sugar and Fire.* —Georgette Leblanc (Madame Maurice Maeterlinck), *The Children's Blue Bird*.>

fft fft fft.

n. the sound of a projectile penetrating armor.

<*The attack came from the right, some kind of projectile spanging into Mercy's armor with a fft fft fft sound, at a rate of around four a second.* —"Six Days in Sanjii," UnknownWorlds.com.>

fhd.

n. the title of a visual poem by Mike Cannell.

fhg hf.

n. the title of a visual poem by Mike Cannell.

fhhhhh.

n. the "faint rush of breath," as when one blows on a feather in *Being with Rachel: A Personal Story of Memory and Survival* by Karen Brennan; see also jhhhhh.

flggh.

n. a muttered expletive.

<*Flggh ... Old ladies stick their nose in everyt'ing!* —Leo Rosten, "Potch," anthologized in *A Passion for Books: A Book Lover's Treasury of Stories, Essays, Humor, Love and Lists on Collecting, Reading, Borrowing, Lending, Caring for, and Appreciating Books* by Harold Rabinowitz.>

flkk.

n. the sound a lighter makes, as in the graphic novel *ShadowFall* by Kaichi Satake.

fllrrbrp.

n. the sound of Spiderman's web shooting out, as in the comic strip "PvP" by Scott R. Kurtz.

flmm.

n. a noncommittal mutter.

<*Flmm ... I wanna ask a favor.* —Leo Rosten, "Potch," anthologized in *A Passion for Books: A Book Lover's Treasury of Stories, Essays, Humor, Love and Lists on Collecting, Reading, Borrowing, Lending, Caring for, and Appreciating Books* by Harold Rabinowitz.>

flmp.

1. *n.* the sound of a sleepless person tossing and turning in bed, as in the graphic novel *ShadowFall* by Kaichi Satake.

2. *n.* the thump of a tired person falling into an easy chair, as in the graphic novel *ShadowFall* by Kaichi Satake.

flssh.

1. *n.* the sound of an arrow impaling a shoulder, as in the story "The Footprints of Time" by Franco (realfriendsandfamily.org).

2. *n.* the splashing or flushing of water, as in the story "The Footprints of Time" by Franco (realfriendsandfamily.org).

FMMMM.

n. the explosion of a grenade.

<*[H]e sticks his hand in the bag over his shoulder, feeling for a grenade, pulls the pin with his teeth—just like in the movies, thinks Teresa—tosses it down the stairwell, turns back, still hunched down, and throws himself down the hall on his belly while the stairs go FMMMM! Through the smoke and the noise and a blast of hot air that hits Teresa in the face, everything on the stairway, horses included, is blown to smithereens.* —Arturo Perez-Reverte, *The Queen of the South.*>

fmmpp.

n. the sound of a falling body hitting the ground, as in the graphic novel *ShadowFall* by Kaichi Satake.

fmpp.

n. the sound of a hand breaking one's fall, as in the graphic novel *ShadowFall* by Kaichi Satake.

fr.

prep. for, written in Roger Bacon's all-consonant secret code (devised in 1250), as discussed in *The Voynich Manuscript* by Gerry Kennedy.

frbl gzzt.

n. an incoherent muttering from someone about to collapse from psychic training overload, as in *The Clone Wars Episode 5: In Memoriam* by Michael Martin.

frfrrt fpphhtt plrtpht.

n. an incoherent sentence spoken by a body with no head, as in the comic strip "PvP" by Scott R. Kurtz.

frm.

n. form, written in Roger Bacon's all-consonant secret code (devised in 1250), as discussed in *The Voynich Manuscript* by Gerry Kennedy.

frr frr.

n. the sound a unicorn makes.

<*[S]he said o my god now how will we make the unicorn come and just then I heard a voice from Heaven said that the unicorn qui tollis peccata mundis was me and I started jumping around the bushes and crying hip heee frr frr because I was happier than a real unicorn because I had put my horn in the virgin's lap and this was why Saint Baudolino had called me son et setera but then he forgave me and I caught site of him other times but only if there is plenty of fog or if it isnt bright like to scorch everything.* —Umberto Eco, *Baudolino.*>

frrr.

prep. for, as spoken by someone "slurring his words out of pure exhaustion," as in the novel *Doona* by Anne McCaffrey.

frrrrrp.

n. a rude noise simulating flatulence.

<*I make the noise again with my mouth, frrrrrpp, but she doesn't turn around.* —Christopher Livingston, "The Hot Seat.">

frrt.

n. the sound of someone on the toilet, as in the comic strip "PvP" by Scott R. Kurtz.

Fsck.

n. the title of an album of experimental electronic music by the band Farmers Manual.

fsck.

n. a Linux system administration command.

<*If a filesystem is inconsistent, fsck prompts before each correction is attempted.* —Ellen Siever, *Linux in a Nutshell.*>

fsd.

n. the title of a visual poem by Mike Cannell.

fsh.

n. an eyeless fish, as in the pun "What do you call a fish with no eyes? A fsh."

FSHHH.

n. the hiss of steam from a dry cleaner's pressing machine, as described in *Crackers* by Roy Blount Jr.

fshhh.

1. (also fshhhhh.) *n.* the hiss of an aerosol-type spray can, as in the graphic novel *Uzumaki 2* by Junji Ito.

2. *interj.* a scoff.

<*One [literary agent] actually wrote on the form rejection letter that the writing was "good" but the story wasn't strong enough. I thought, fshhh, what does she know?* —Debra Lauman, "My Adventures as a Writer.">

3. *n.* the sound of a flammable liquid igniting.

<*Loxie takes out a whiskey hip flask, but it's not filled with whiskey. Loxie goes, "Alright, now, smell it," as he pours the gasoline on the terrified Hoff, "light a match and 'fshhh!'" and he holds the lighted match up to him.* —a review of the television show "The Untouchables" (episode 5) on TVtome.com.>

4. *n.* the sound of a zombie's foot scuffing the floor, as in Jason Maiden's review of the video game "Resident Evil" (GamePartisan.com).

5. *n.* the sound of an airplane engine, as in the album "At the Drop of Another Hat" by Michael Flanders and Donald Swann.

6. *n.* the sound of nitrogen escaping through a tear in a balloon, as in *20th Century Boys Vol. 8* by Naoki Urasawa.

fshhh fshhh fshhh.

n. the brushing sound of a broom.

<*It was not uncommon to be awakened in the middle of the night to the fshhh, fshhh, fshhh sound of Agnes sweeping the hallway runner, the living room rug or the walls themselves.* —Augusten Burroughs, *Running With Scissors: A Memoir.*>

fshhhhh.

n. the sound of water pouring from a faucet, as in the story "Saffron Transforms" by Rumiko Takahashi.

fshhhhhhhhh.

n. the sound of burning rocket jets.

<*Fshhhhhhhhh. The sound of rocket jets burning overhead reached the transport.* —Black Dragon, "Guardian: A Ranma 1/2 Fanfiction.">

fshht.

1. *n.* the hiss of pistol's silencer.

<*"Fshht! There must be a more pleasant experience than smelling gunpowder after the diminutive hiss of a pistol's silencer, but I don't know what it might be. Fshht! Fshht! Fshht! Fshht! Fshht! Fshht! Fshht! Fshht! There was no more sign of the enemy.* —David Glenn Rinehart, "Reconnaissance Report.">

2. *n.* the rush of water.

<*When I got on the hospital ship they just took a knife and, fshht, about a gallon of water come out of 'em.* —Kathryn Rhett, *Survival Stories: Memoirs of Crisis.*>

3. *n.* the sound of a ruffled dress brushing across the floor.

<*She had bought a pink taffeta dress with a mass of ruffles across the front. It made a nice, comforting fshht, fshht sound as she moved.* —Road Dog, *Trudy: A 50's Romance.*>

fshsqbpt.

n. the sound of shaving cream hissing and foaming from a can, as in the comic book *Schizo #2* by Ivan Brunetti.

fshzt.

n. the sound of electrical interference, as in "Evolutions" by Travis Hogbin.

fsshh.

1. *n.* a whoosh of air.

<*Once the [airplane's] cabin door closes behind you with a pneumatic fsshh, it's just like when you went away to camp, except then you still believed that eating s'mores and throwing a baseball badly could build character.* —Christian Moerk, "Wages of Fear," *Variety.*>

<*It was just before Christmas when Pauline and John Tomasello first heard a curious noise coming from the basement of their 20-year-old home. Fsshh. Fsshh. Fsshh. Their water pump was sucking air.* —Jack Kaskey, "Wells the Latest Victim as Drought Dries Region," *The Press of Atlantic City.*>

2. *n.* the spraying of an aerosol can.

<*I grabbed my can of Raid and aimed and fired. Fsshh!* —Chloe, "The Battle," geocities.com/chloecorner>

fsshhhhh.

n. the rushing sound of a running faucet, as in the graphic novel *Uzumaki 2* by Junji Ito.

fssht fssht fssht.

n. the sound of "the wind swishing" (D.W. Winnicott, quoted in *Squiggles and Spaces: Revisiting the Work of D.W. Winnicott* by Mario Bertolini); see also fssht-fssht-fssht.

fssht-fssht-fssht.

n. the sound of the wind "really getting up" (D.W. Winnicott, quoted in *Squiggles and Spaces: Revisiting the Work of D.W. Winnicott* by Mario Bertolini); see also fssht fssht fssht.

fsss.

(also fssss.) *n.* an exhalation of cigarette smoke.

<*Pee Wee, gimme some of that. Thank you. Ah fssss. That's fsss fsss good.* —Buzz Callaway, *Specimen Tank.*>

fsssh.

n. the whoosh of elevator doors.

<*The soft* fsssh *of air as the doors closed sounded explosively loud in his ears.* —Alan Dean Foster, *The Tar-Aiym Krang.*>

fssshhh.

n. a baby's pronunciation of "fish."

<*His first word was "fish" at eight mohths, a quiet "fssshhh" sound coming from his lips as he sat with me in the bathtub and held the porcupine fish he had always loved.* —Dawn Prince-Hughes, *Songs of the Gorilla Nation: My Journey Through Autism.*>

fsssshk.

n. the sound of an object falling down, as in the comic "Elf Life, Jan. 28, 2004" by Carson Fire.

fsssss.

n. the sound of a baby drooling, as described in the novel *Edwin Mullhouse* by Steven Millhauser.

fssssh.

n. the sound of lighter fluid squirting from a can, as in the comic strip "PvP" by Scott R. Kurtz.

fssst.

1. *n.* a "whispered hiss from the shadows," as in *Last Go Round* by Ken Kesey.

2. *n.* a warning from a "hissing, spitting, ferocious kitten," as described in *This Heart of Mine* by Beatrice Small and *Homeless: Sunita* by Laurie Halse Anderson.

3. *n.* an abrupt ending; the sound of life fizzling out.

<*The minute the axe comes down on Joe Mullin, the Warden's life will go fssst!* —John Gardner, "The Warden," *The Literary Ghost: Great Contemporary Ghost Stories.*>

4. *n.* the crackle of a wall torch flaring into flame, as in *Dawn For a Distant Earth* by L. E. Modesitt Jr.

5. *n.* the sound of a laser gun, as in *Martyrs' Crossing* by Amy Wilentz.

6. *n.* the swishing of a sharp blade.

<*"To be a leader you must have a rosary in your right hand," and here he imitated a benignly mumbling lama at prayer. "And in your left hand you must have a sharp knife. Fssst! If someone is no good, you must be able to chop him off!" Here he demonstrated a violent beheading.* —Caroline Humphrey, *Shamans and Elders: Experience, Knowledge, and Power Among the Daur Mongols.*>

fssst fssst.

n. the squeak of wet galoshes; see also pfft pfft.

<*Her rubber slippers also make a funny hissing noise, fssst, fssst. She's just washed her feet and*

the rubber slippers' pores have become saturated with water. —Betool Khedairi, *A Sky So Close: A Novel.*>

fsst.

1. *n.* a hiss made to frighten a cat.

<*I heard something that sounded like a stone that was loose and was being moved by a cat or something. I went "Fsst!" to scare the cat.* —Maria Catedra, *This World, Other Worlds: Sickness, Suicide, Death, and the Afterlife Among the Vaqueiros de Alzada of Spain.*>

2. *n.* a variation of psst, a sound used to attract attention; see also psss, pssst, psst, ssss, ssstt. <*Fsst, come over here.*>.

3. *n.* the sizzling sound of electrical sparks, as in *The Public Burning* by Robert Coover.

4. *n.* the sound of a firework's lit fuse; see also fzzt[3].

<*Sensible people go off to a roped-off enclosure where they can watch a heavily protected man, in the middle distance, light (with the aid of a very long pole) something that goes "fsst."* —Terry Pratchett, *Interesting Times.*>

fttrrzzt.

n. a buzzing malfunction of someone's robot double standing in line until the next *Star Wars* film opens, as in the comic strip "PvP" by Scott R. Kurtz; see also bzzrrtt, bzzzt[3], kzrrrtt.

fwsh.

(also fwff.) *n.* the sound of a slashing sword, as in the graphic novel *Falcon Twin* by Brenden Mecleary.

fwww.

n. the sound of a slashing sword, as in the graphic novel *Falcon Twin* by Brenden Mecleary.

fzz-nkk.

n. a buzzing sound, as by the venomous flying "Nizzik" insects in the novel *Akiko and the Intergalactic Zoo* by Mark Crilley; see also kzz-fzzz, pzzz.

fzzk.

n. the sound of "flash panties," a weapon disguised as underwear, as in the comic book *Dirty Pair: Run From The Future #3* by Adam Warren.

fzzpppp.

n. the sizzling zap of a mind-control energy ray, as in the comic book *Wonder Woman #255* by Estrada; see also krklll.

fzzrrrtt.

n. a strange sound made by a computer that has developed consciousness.

<*Fzzzrrtl! All those moments will be lost in time, like tears in... rain...”*—Scott R. Kurtz, “PvP.”>

fzzt.

1. *n.* a crackle in a long-distance telephone connection, as in *The Nirvana Blues: A Novel* by John Nichols.

2. *n.* the crackling and popping of a public address system, as described by Michael Bailey in “Story: Dreams” (jinxidoru.com).

3. *n.* the sound of a firework’s lit fuse; see also fsst[4].

   <*Fzzt! Bang! Crackle! “Ooooh!” “Aaaaah!” Fzzt! BANG! Crackle! Repeat ad nauseum and that’s what we will all be hearing this weekend as the whole country celebrates Guy Fawkes’ failure to blow up Parliament.* —“Virtual Manchester Versus Fireworks,” Manchester.com>

4. *n.* the sound of an “electrostunner” in *Mundementia One: The Book of Going Forth* by J. (Channing) Wells.

5. *n.* the sound of an android or robot malfunctioning, as in *The Metallic Touch*; see vzzkt.

6. *n.* the sound of something whizzing away.

   <*“Jim gets up nice and slow, then* fzzt! *And he’s off after the thing.” “Caught it, too,” said Virgil. “Never seen nobody catch a rabbit with their bare hands.”* —Christian Cameron, *Washington and Caesar.*>

fzzt-fzzt.

n. the sound of a radio turner skipping through stations.

<*I spun the dial, heard the fzzt-fzzt of stations whirling by.* David Adsit, “The Big Broadcast, Delayed.”>

fzzt-fzzt-fzzt.

n. the sound of “a hundred tiny air leaks,” as in the essay “Musique du Ballon” by David Gunn.

fzzz.

1. *n.* the sizzle of sparks.

   <*Fzzz. A tiny spray of blue sparks left her fingers, traveled a few inches in the air, sputtered, then faded.* —Tony Abbott, *Under the Serpent Sea.*>

2. *n.* the sound of instant vaporization.

   <*Every time he come to a new [wasp nest], the wasps they flew into the fire. You could see the wings go, not like burning, not like melting, sort of fzzz! they gone.* —Kurt Vonnegut Jr., *A Saucer of Loneliness: Volume VII, The Complete Stories of Theodore Sturgeon.*>

3. *n.* the sound of someone welding a mechanical girlfriend, as in the comic strip "PvP" by Scott R. Kurtz.

4. *n.* the sound of wet automobile tires.

<*We sail off feeling more conspicuous than ever, the only sound the* fzzz *of our rubber wheels on the wet roadway.* —Andrew Dowling, *Godless Pilgrim.*>

5. *n.* the zap of an image fading away, as in the novel *The Moon Scroll* by Tony Abbott.

fzzz-fzzz.

n. the sound of a deflating balloon; see also fzzzzzz-zzzz.

<*It's the beginning of the end. It's like a balloon that the air is just beginning to go out of—fzzz-fzzz.* —Nora Johnson, *The World of Henry Orient: A Novel.*>

fzzzzz.

1. *n.* a hiss of steam; see also ffffzzzzzz.

<*[F]eeling they were going to faint in the heat, they flung themselves into Mestre Valentim's fountain, and, on contact with the water, their clothes went* fzzzzz. —Ruy Castro, *Rio de Janiero.*>

2. *n.* the hiss of an enchanted amulet called the "Seal of Phobos," as in the novel *W.I.T.C.H.: Finding Meridian* by Disney Enterprises.

fzzzzzz.

n. the whoosh of a Gulf War missile, as described in *Bridget Jones' Diary* by Helen Fielding.

fzzzzzz-zzzz.

n. the sound of a deflating balloon; see also fzzz-fzzz.

<*And then, with a shocking* fzzzzzz-zzzz, *the air went out of the balloon.* —Roone Arledge, *Roone: A Memoir.*>

fzzzzzzzzzz.

n. a sound effect during an imaginary battle situation, as described in *The Childhood Roots of Adult Happiness: Five Steps to Help Kids Create and Sustain Lifelong Joy* by Edward M. Hallowell.

fzzzzzzzzzzzzzzzz.

n. the buzz of a medical scanner, as in the graphic novel *ShadowFall* by Kaichi Satake.

G'D'Z'L.

n. a beast (the equivalent to Typhon or Leviathan) that "shall rise from the sea" and lay waste the cities of men at the end of days, as prophesied by the Rev. Ivan Stang in *The Book of the SubGenius: Being the Divine Wisdom, Guidance, and Prophecy of J. R. 'Bob' Dobbs, High Epopt of the Church of the SubGenius, Here Inscribed for the Salvation of Future Generations and in the Hope that Slack May Someday Reign on this Earth.*

G'jlt'rn.

n. a species of elephant in the novel *The FarCall Project* by RedTurtle.

g'mrnng.

n. a sleepy "good morning"; see also mrnng.

<*G'mrnng. Do I really have to get up in five hour's time?* —Flavius M, LiveJournal.com.>

g'rrrrr.

n. the growl of a lion, as in the novel *Gaudy Night* by Dorothy L. Sayers.

G—d—mn.

v. a self-censored spelling of "God damn."

<*We will and command you upon sight hereof, to let the said prisoner depart to his own habitation, whether he stands condemned for murder, sodomy, rape, sacrilege, incest, treason, blasphemy, &c., for which this shall be your sufficient warrant: and if you fail hereof, G—d—mn you and yours to all eternity.* —Jonathan Swift, *A Tale of a Tub*.>

G-Sch.

n. a gentle alien Luminoth who "sleeps in a flooded temple," in the video game "Metroid Prime 2: Echoes."

gfs df.

n. the title of a visual poem by Mike Cannell.

ggg.

1. *n.* the gulping of a noisy drinker, as described in "More Than Words" by the New Zealand Ministry of Education.

2. *n.* the sound of the letter g, as described in "Beginning Literacy Design" by Jennifer Kate Hall; see also gggg.

gggg.

n. the sound of the letter g; see also ggg[22].

<*You'll be looking for the gggg sound soon enough.* —Peggy Kaye, *Games for Learning: Ten Minutes a Day to Help Your Child Do Well in School, From Kindergarten to Third Grade.*>

gggg-rrrr.

n. the growl of a dog.

<*[T]he hair on the back of her spine bristled and the Great Dog went "Gggg-rrrr."* —Pat Conroy, *Beach Music.*>

ggggg.

n. a baby's giggle, as described in the novel *Edwin Mullhouse* by Steven Millhauser; see also kkkkk, kkkkkk.

ggkkgkk.

n. a strangled sound from someone being choked, as in the graphic novel *Falcon Twin* by Brenden Mecleary.

gh gh gh.

n. the croaking of a frog, as described in *Marva Collins' Way* by Marva Collins.

gh-hrrr.

n. the sound of clearing one's throat.

<*She slides the phone back to her mouth and clears her throat. Her voice sharpens up to a squeak. "Gh-hrrr, I am not calling you a moron."* —D.B.C. Pierre, *Vernon God Little.*>

ghdkdghk.

n. the title of a visual poem by Mike Cannell.

ghghgh.

1. *n.* a strangled laugh; a chuckle, as in *The Letters of Kingsley Amis* by Zachary Leader.

2. *n.* an alternate spelling of the word *puff*: pronounce "gh" as in "hiccough," as in "Edinburgh," and as in "laugh" (Ralph Philip Boas, Jr., *Lion Hunting and Other Mathematical Pursuits: A Collection of Mathematics, Verse, and Stories by the Late Ralph P. Boas, Jr.*).

ghghghgh.

v. to constrict.

<*[A]ll of a sudden his pupils go ghghghgh and shrink in disgust.* —Dacia Maraini, *Woman at War.*>

ghghghnnn.

n. the title of a visual poem by Mike Cannell.

ghrrr.

n. a word spoken by the *Star Wars* character Chewbacca, as described in “Leia’s Light Sabre” by Steph Magawan.

ghrrrr.

1. *n.* a growl “like a fearful caged wild animal,” of someone both drunk and homesick, as in *Psalm at Journey’s End: A Novel* by Erik Fosnes Hansen.

2. *n.* the growl of a leopard, as described in “Storytelling Workshop” by Gerald Fierst.

ghrrrrr.

n. the gurgling call of the Little Bittern bird during breeding, as described in *Birds of Kenya and Northern Tanzania* by Dale A. Zimmerman.

gkkk.

1. *interj.* a strangled gasp of pain, as in the comic book *Flash #158* by Pelletier.

2. *n.* a muttered generic response.

<*“I’d like to shake you by the hand.” He looked down. “Only they’re rather full at the moment,” he added. “Gkkk,” said Gern.* —Terry Pratchett, *Pyramids*.>

glkkt.

n. a strangled utterance from someone shot in the throat, as in the graphic novel *Falcon Twin* by Brenden Mecleary.

Glnk.

n. the name of a defiant goblin; see also Tzrg.

<*If Glnk was their chief now, his defiance made Tzrg feel weak enough, if he wasn’t the chief, he made Tzrg feel even weaker.* —T. H. Lain, *The Savage Caves*.>

glshkrkkt.

n. the sound of flesh ripped apart by a sword, as in the graphic novel *Falcon Twin* by Brenden Mecleary.

gmmph.

1. *n.* a muttered generic response.

<*Myra attempted to strike up a conversation with the tribal elder. “It’s a nice night. Warm.” “Gmmph,” Daisy replied, her reply barely audible over the rumbling drone of the big V-8 engine.* —James D. Doss, *The Shaman’s Game*.>

2. *n.* a sleepy groan.

<*“Gmmph,” said Sally, trying hard to wake up.* —Virginia Swift, *Bad Company*.>

3. *n.* a stifled cough.

<*Adolphus stroked her hair tenderly, and turned his head away to suppress another fit of coughing: Gmmph! Gmmph! Gmmph!* —K.P. Bath, *The Secret of Castle Cant.*>

gmmph nng m.

n. a mumbled line of dialogue by the character "Kenny" from the animated television series *South Park.*

<*KENNY: Gmmph nng m! KYLE: It's just your imagination. There's nothing in here with us. KENNY: NNNGH! (Sound of chains breaking and nasty slobbering noises. Kenny's eyeballs vanish.) KYLE: Ohmigod, they killed Kenny!* —Matt Graham, "South Park: Angband comes to South Park.">

gn.

n. an incoherent muttering, as from someone regaining consciousness after being thrown by an explosion, in the graphic novella *Hearts and Minds* by Scott McCloud.

gnch.

1. *interj.* an expression of frustration, as in "That Dratted Dress" by Alison Sinclair.

2. *n.* the sound of someone gorging on a giant mushroom, as in the graphic novel *Uzumaki 2* by Junji Ito.

gnff.

n. a grunt of passion, as in the comic strip "PvP" by Scott R. Kurtz; see also nnggh.

gnnk.

interj. the grunt of a sore loser at checkers, as in *The Essential Calvin and Hobbes* by Bill Watterson; see also mff.

gnnng.

interj. a grunt of derision.

<*Gnnng. ... Weird vegetarian eggplant food.* —Emma Bull, *War for the Oaks.*>

gnnnh.

interj. a groan of pain.

<*"Gnnnh!" he said, and drew himself up into a ball to escape the pain of his emergent teeth.* —Diana Gabaldon, *The Fiery Cross.*>

gnnnnh.

interj. a moan of regret, as in the comic story "Rogue's Curse" by Wendy Pini.

gnnnrrrrrrkkk.

n. the creaking of a subway train "lurching off the rails" (Dick Dillin, *World's Finest #223*).

gnnrk.

n. the sound of someone transforming into the Incredible Hulk, as in the comic strip "PvP" by Scott R. Kurtz.

gnrk.

n. the sound of the "Vulcan nerve pinch" from the *Star Trek* television series, as transcribed in the comic strip "PvP" by Scott R. Kurtz.

gnrrr.

1. *n.* a groan of exertion, as when pulling oneself out from under a pile of office boxes in the comic strip "PvP" by Scott R. Kurtz.

2. *n.* a growl of exasperation, as in the novel *Boobytrap: A "Nameless Detective" Novel* by Bill Pronzini.

gr jrkdg.

n. the title of a visual poem by Mike Cannell.

gr-r-r-r-r-rrrrrrr.

n. a tiger's growl.

<*Presently he heard a horrible noise that sounded like "Gr-r-r-r-rrrrrrr," and it got louder and louder. "Oh! dear!" said Little Babaji, "there are all the Tiger coming baack to eat me up!"* —Helen Bannerman, *The Story of Little Babaji.*>

grk.

n. the sound of pulling up a block of earth, as in the comic "Bunny anb Rasputin #8" [sic] by H.J. Hornbeck.

grmm.

n. a stomach growling with hunger, as in the graphic novel *Uzumaki 3* by Junji Ito.

GRMMMMPH.

n. the sound of clearing one's throat.

<*Father ... was also silent—but more noisily so. He kept clearing his throat, as if he was getting ready to say something. It never got said. What got said instead was GRMMMMPH and HMMHMMHMMHMM.* —Jules Feiffer, *The Man in the Ceiling.*>

grmmmph.

1. *interj.* a sleepy, grumpy moan, as in the novel *The Venetian Policeman* by M.E. Rabb.

2. *n.* "a combination of baby giraffes and okapis and grysbok all mixed up into one gracefully scattered Disney-Dr. Seuss thing" (Bruce Jay Friedman, describing the "wraithlike" qualities of Jean Shrimpton in *Even the Rhinos Were Nymphos: Best Nonfiction*).

3. *n.* an incoherent mutter while one's mouth is full, presumably meaning "good to make your acquaintance."

<*Janice actually tried to reply, and said something with her mouth full, which sounded like "Gmmmph."* —Joe Jackson, *A Cure for Gravity: A Musical Pilgrimage.*>

grmmph.

1. *n.* a dull comeback.

<*That took some of the wind out of her sails, and all she could think to say was, "Grmmph." Not, she realized, her wittiest hour.* —Julia Quinn, *Everything and the Moon.*>

2. *n.* a grumpy mumble; see also grmpf, grmph.

<*"You made me swear I'd get you out of bed at half past five." "Mmmph, grmmph... didn't mean it."* —Julia Quinn, *Minx.*>

3. *n.* an indecipherable mumbling.

<*[A] move which the National Head Trauma Board is calling "grmmph Arrrrgh mmmmmmgh."* —"Production Music and Sound Design," VideoHelper.com.>

grmpf.

interj. an expression of grumpiness; see also grmmph[2], grmph.

<*"Grmpf! Now I have to create an account!"* —UserFriendly.org>

grmph.

n. a low, guttural harrumph, as in the comic "Elf Life, Jan. 15, 2004" by Carson Fire; see also grmmph[2], grmpf.

grnnnk.

n. a grunt in the Wookie language of the *Star Wars* films, as transcribed in the comic strip "PvP" by Scott R. Kurtz; see also mrr, hrrrrr.

grnt.

n. a grunt of exertion, as while playing a video game in the comic strip "PvP" by Scott R. Kurtz; see also hnn.

grpl.

n. a swallowing sound of a partygoer about to throw up his hors d'oeuvres, as in the comic strip "PvP" by Scott R. Kurtz.

grr.

1. *interj.* a warning sound of anger or hostility.

<*Grr! We would hunt down Big Brothers!* —Robert V. Levine, *The Power of Persuasion: How We're Bought and Sold.*>

2. *interj.* an affectionate growl.

<*"Grr..." Alice bounced over to my deskchair and I duck because I think she is going to hit*

me. Instead, she leans over and kisses me. "I love you. You are my best friend." —Carole Matthews, *The Sweetest Taboo.*>

3. *interj.* an expression of disapproval.

<*Witch hunters persecuting some poor old lady! Grr, stupid ignorant louts, I can't abide them!* —Brian Jacques, *Castaways of the Flying Dutchman.*>

4. *n.* a goblin's snarl, as in the comic strip "PvP" by Scott R. Kurtz; see also hrrr.

5. *n.* a highly-derogatory racial slang term, as discussed in *Running Loose* by Chris Crutcher.

6. *n.* a lion's growl.

<*"We can work! This will be a farm for two women. Aren't we strong? Like lions!" She curls her hands into imaginary claws. "Watch out all who come here. This is the farm of the lion women. Grr!" Her hands rake the air. "Grr!"* —Lewis DeDoto, *A Blade of Grass: A Novel.*>

7. *n.* a sound indicating that one is about to lose self-control.

<*To Mark's left, Os made that little grr sound he'd often make when about to lose control at tennis.* —Donald E. Westlake, *The Road to Ruin.*>

8. *n.* a wolf-like growl, as in *The Carnivorous Carnival: A Series of Unfortunate Events, Book 9* by Lemony Snicket; see also grrr[2].

grr blff mmrr.

n. a fretful mumble.

<*His head is bowed sulkily over the reins, and he is mumbling truculent sentiments to his knees, and when I ask if he will take us back to Piccadilly, he waves us in with a fretful swipe of his hand. —Grr, blff, mmrr. This is what we have reduced him to. No remonstrance, no litany—just consonants. It will take a handsome sum indeed to restore those soliloquies of woe.* —Louis Bayard, *Mr. Timothy.*>

grr grr.

n. the menacing roar of a gorilla.

<*He also played "gorilla" with the children. Donning his oldest clothes, he would lurk behind shrubbery, waiting for one of them to appear. When one did, he would leap out roaring "Grr! Grr!" and advance menacing, his arms swinging limply at his sides.* —William Manchester, *The Last Lion: Winston Spencer Churchill: Visions of Glory, 1874-1932.*>

grr-r-r.

n. the supposed roar of the fantastical Ignormus creature, as in *Freddy and the Ignormus* by Walter R. Brooks.

grr-r-r-r-p-p-p.

n. the revving of a boat's motor starting up.

<*I connected the hot battery—I primed each cylinder with naphtha gas—I screwed in each hot sparkplug. Then I pulled up hard on the crank. "Grr-r-r-r-p-p-p," she started.* —M. Wylie Blanchet, *The Curve of Time: The Classic Memoir of a Woman and Her Children Who Explored the Coastal Waters of the Pacific Northwest.*>

grr-rrr.

n. a roar of anger, as in *The Hawk Bandits of Tarkoom* by Tony Abbott.

grr-rrr-rrr.

n. the broken grumble of an automobile engine that won't start.

<*[S]he listened to the noise from the garage, the grinding growl of a car that was reluctant to start. "Grr-rrr-rrr," she said, imitating the sound of the motor.* —Beverly Cleary, *Ramona Quimby, Age 8.*>

grr-rrr-rrr-rrr.

n. the crow of the cock, as described in *The Encyclopedia of Country Living: An Old Fashioned Recipe Book* by Carla Emery.

grrgll.

n. the sound of gargling, as in the comic book *Schizo #2* by Ivan Brunetti.

grrk.

interj. a toad's croaky exclamation.

<*"I punish you when the time comes. Grrk!"* —Brian Jacques, *Salamandastron.*>

grrk grrk.

n. the low-pitched strong chatter of the Broad-Billed Hummingbird, as described in *Hummingbirds: A Wildlife Handbook* by Kim Long.

grrk grrrk grrk.

n. the creaking of a floorboard.

<*[T]here was another noise—the familiar grrk grrrk grrk of [the wombat] Mothball scratching her back on the floor beam under my bed.* —Jackie French, "Mothball News," JackieFrench.com.>

grrkkssh.

n. the sound of flesh ripped apart by a sword, as in the graphic novel *Falcon Twin* by Brenden Mecleary.

grrl.

(also grl, grrrl, grrrrl.) *n.* a girl who riots, usually associated with punk music.

<*Riot grrls are easier to define than such loose girl culture scenes as teeny-boppers, despite heated debate over their interests, allegiances, and even how to spell them. There are one-, two-, and even three-r versions of the girl that riots, mostly defined in relation to girl music scenes influenced by*

punk. Some two-r grrls accuse the three-r grrls of claiming a superior badness: 'maybe that third r is like a proud scarlet letter, a matter of haute transgression.' —Catherine Driscoll, *Girls.*>

GRRR.

n. a jovial grunt.

<*He scrunched up his face so hard it turned red and said simply "GRRR!" in a hearty grunt.* —Laurie Notaro, *Autobiography of a Fat Bride: True Tales of a Pretend Adulthood.*>

Grrr.

n. the name of a computer-program dog: "a remarkable creature, Grrr can distinguish colors and respond to voice commands" (Don Tapscott, *The Naked Corporation: How the Age of Transparency Will Revolutionize Business*).

grrr.

1. (also grrrr.) *n.* a growling sound of intense concentration.

<*He did the place where the shampoo bottles had been, that I'd simply defined as a safe haven for mildew, he was in there, grrr, grrrr, twisting and jamming that little sponge.* —Nicholson Baker, *Vox.*>

2. (also grrrrrr.) *n.* the growl of the Big Bad Wolf from the fairy tale "Little Red Riding Hood" (Lena Tabori, *The Little Big Book for Grandmothers)*; see also grr[88].

3. *interj.* an expression of revulsion.

<*It's like that time I had the stroke, in 1940, remember? When one side of me froze up? And you gave me baby food on a spoon?* Grrr, *what a godawful taste!* —Peter Straub, *Ghost Story.*>

4. *n.* "a roar of horror and rage" from a "wicked Beast" in *The Chronicles of Narnia* by C.S. Lewis.

5. *n.* "neither self-parody nor rage, but simply an expression of anger without accusation, blame, or apology. Sometimes we have a physical need when angry to make an angry noise. Growling—expressing anger through sound—can sometimes release the energy of anger swiftly" (Anne Katherine, *Where to Draw the Line: How to Set Healthy Boundaries Every Day*).

6. *n.* a cacophonous sound sung by Björk of the band Sugarcubes, as transcribed in *The Trouser Press Guide to 90s Rock* by Ira A. Robbins.

7. *n.* a canine-like growl of passion.

<*His T-shirt's hiked up his chest, and on impulse I put my head down and kiss his brown belly. I say, "Grrr..."* —Dave King, *The Ha-Ha: A Novel.*>

8. *n.* a frustrated growl to oneself; see also grrr grrr[2].

<Grrr. *Why did I keep ending up on the losing end of arguments in this house?* —Neta Jackson, *The Yada Yada Prayer Group.*>

9. *n.* a growl of enthusiasm, as in *The Accidental Diva* by Tia Williams.

10. *n.* a growl of indignation.

<*Grrr. There's absolutely nothing more annoying than having your perfect travel plans all mapped out ... and then being told when you check into your gate that they're "terribly sorry ... we're overbooked." Why you? Why?* —Jane Buckingham, *The Modern Girl's Guide to Life*.>

11. *n.* a growl of resentment, sounding "like a bear with bad breath coming out of hibernation or a mangy mongrel defending his bone in an alley" (Max Lucado, *The Applause of Heaven).*

12. *n.* a grunt of astonishment, as in the novel *Lion in the Valley* by Elizabeth Peters.ul

13. *n.* a hostile growl. Regarding this spelling, novelist Elizabeth Peters apologetically writes, "I assure you, there is really no other way of reproducing this sound" (*The Curse of the Pharaohs*).

14. *n.* a poodle's growl, as in response to a cat-like yowling in *Even Cowgirls Get the Blues* by Tom Robbins.

15. *n.* a shriek of fright, as at a dog's "perfect set of three-inch incisors" in the novel *No True Gentleman* by Liz Carlyle.

16. *n.* a sound from the "frightfully harsh" Welsh language, as described in the novel *Highlander in Disguise* by Julia London.

17. *n.* a sound to repel a wild boar.

<*[W]hen I was utterly defenseless, a wild boar strolled out of the undergrowth. "Grrr!" said the Senator's daughter amiably, over my naked shoulder. The wild boar snuffed, then turned around with a disapproving snort and ambled off.* —Lindsey Davis, *Shadows in Bronze*.>

18. *n.* a tearful expression of exasperation, as in the novel *Cloud Nine* by Luanne Rice.

19. *n.* a typical sound made by a baby attempting to talk, as discussed in *Wonder Weeks: How to Turn Your Baby's 8 Great Fussy Phases into Magical Leaps Forward* by Hetty Vanderijt.

20. *n.* an incoherent mutter by Keith Richards of the band The Rolling Stones, decipherable only by Mick Jagger, as discussed in *Rebel Heart: An American Rock 'n' Roll Journey* by Bebe Buell.

21. *n.* the noisy "growl, grind, snarl" of a kitchen sink's garbage disposal in action, sounding like "a monster [that] is enjoying a nice little snack" (Stephen King, *Black House*).

22. *n.* the rumble of an electrical generator's motor, as in the novel *Slot Machine* by Chris Lynch.

23. *n.* the snarl of a polar bear, as in *Polar Bears Past Bedtime* by Mary Pope Osborne.

grrr grrr.

1. *n.* the sound of an automobile engine turning over, as described by Madeleine Albright in *Madam Secretary: A Memoir*.

2. *n.* the sound of someone venting frustrations, as discussed in *Managing Generation X: How to Bring Out the Best in Young Talent* by Bruce Tulgan; see also grrr[88].

grrr grrr grrr.

1. *n.* the sound of a spring-loaded wind-up toy, as in *A Clockwork Orange* by Anthony Burgess.

2. *n.* the sound of grumbling about Laramie, Wyoming, as in *The Laramie Project* by Moises Kaufman.

grrr-grrr grrr-grrr.

n. the sound of a güiro, a musical instrument made from a hollowed gourd with carved slashes on the sides and played by "scraping the slashes with a metal fork" (Marisa Montes, *A Crazy, Mixed-Up Spanglish Day*).

Grrr-Grrr-Grrr-Grrr-Grrr.

n. the growl of a baby grizzly bear, as described in *Complete Handbook of Indoor and Outdoor Games and Activities for Young Children* by Jean R. Feldman.

GRRR-rrr GRRR-RRR.

n. the roar of a hungry lion, as described in *Creative Bible Teaching* by Lawrence O. Richards and Gary J. Bredfeldt.

grrr-rrrr.

n. the emotional growl of someone feeling a "natural reaction to fight back," as discussed in *Shacking Up: The Smart Girl's Guide to Living in Sin Without Getting Burned* by Stacy Whitman and Wynne Whitman.

grrr-thnk.

n. the incoherent noise of a talking doll after it has been immersed in water.

<*She pulled my talking string again. This time, I made a grrr-thnk sound. But I didn't talk!* —Joan Holub, *Saving Marissa.*>

grrr-vrrrrt.

n. the sound of the floor spiraling open and a dragon ship rising up from below, as in *Secrets of Droon #18* by Tony Abbott.

grrrk.

n. the sound of a computer function being interrupted.

<*'Grrrk,' the computer said as it was interrupted.* —Harry Harrison, *The Stainless Steel Ray Joins the Circus.*>

grrrk grrrk.

n. the croaking call of the Spot-Flanked Barbet bird, as described in *Birds of Kenya and Northern Tanzania* by Dale A. Zimmerman.

grrrp.

n. a variation of "group," as in the "Jzzz Grrrp" division of the Erskine College Music Department's Sinfonia wind ensemble.

GRRRR.

n. the roar of Tyrannosaurus Rex, as described in *The Most Wonderful Writing Lessons Ever (Grades 2-4)* by Barbara Mariconda.

grrrr.

1. *adj.* fierce.

<*"You did it, Lacey!" Stella squealed. "You are totally* grrrr!" —Ellen Byerrum, *Killer Hair.*>

2. *interj.* a grumble from someone forgetting for a moment to be affable, as in the novel *Guardian of the Horizon* by Elizabeth Peters.

3. *n.* a child's joyous shout, as discussed in *Your Child's Growing Mind: Brain Development and Learning From Birth to Adolescence* by Jane Healy.

4. *n.* a growl of animal lust.

<*But what captivated her most was the raw, overt male sexuality he oozed. ... Vane moved with the fluid grace of a predator, with his head held low as if ready to attack. Grrrr, but the man was a fetching beast.* —Sherrilyn Kenyon, *Night Embrace.*>

5. *n.* a growl of determination, as described in *The Big Bing: Black Holes of Time Management, Gaseous Executive Bodies, Exploding Careers, and Other Theories on the Origins of the Business Universe* by Stanley Bing.

6. *n.* a lion's roar, as described in *Little Big Book For God's Children* by Lena Tabori.

7. *n.* a snarl of impatience.

<*"Grrrr!" snarled Scaurus Princeps Senatus, not at Marius or Sulla, but at circumstances.* —Colleen McCullough, *The First Man in Rome.*>

8. *n.* an angry growl, as in *How to Take the Grrrr Out of Anger* by Elizabeth Verdick and Marjorie Lisovskis.

9. *n.* the fierce snarl of a fighting dog, as in the novel *Voyager* by Diana Gabaldon; the "low, threatening" growl of a cyborg dog, as in the novel *Then Comes Marriage* by Christie Ridgway.

10. *n.* the growl of a rhinoceros, as in *A Porcupine Named Fluffy* by Helen Lester.

11. *n.* the guttural, toad-like trill of the Southern Bentbill bird, as described in *A Guide to the Birds of Panama* by Robert S. Ridgely.

12. *n.* the rumble of a "very, very hungry" grizzly bear's stomach, as in *Alaska's Three Pigs* by Arlene Laverde.

13. *n.* the snarl of a protective mother otter, as in *The Talking Earth* by Jean Craighead George.

14. *n.* the sound of a hair dryer in a beauty salon, as described in *Hunger and Thirst: A Novel* by Daniela Kuper.

15. *n.* the squeak of vinyl pants rubbing against vinyl furniture, as in the novel *The Final Detail* by Harlan Coben.

grrrr grrrr.

1. *n.* a screeching growl of someone possessed by the devil, as in *Beneath the Skin: The Collected Essays* by John Rechy.

2. *n.* the growl of the sacred grizzly bear spirit, as discussed in *Black Elk: The Sacred Ways of a Lakota* by Wallace Black Elk.

grrrr-grrrr.

n. the ferocious growl of the "Great Dog Chippie," "ready to spring at [Satan], the source of all evil" (Pat Conroy, *Beach Music*).

grrrrk.

n. a low grating call of the Sooty Thrush, as described in *Thrushes* by Peter Clement.

grrrrr.

1. *n.* a grunt, as when fighting in a "cat-panic" in *A Clockwork Orange* by Anthony Burgess.

2. *n.* a wolf-like growl.

<*"Maybe I had plans to ravish you myself. Grrrrr ..." He snapped his teeth together, imitating a hungry wolf.* —Dorothy Garlock, *Yesteryear.*>

3. *n.* the menacing growl of a dog.

<*Grrrrr. Two suspicious eyes glared at me from underneath the desk. "Grrrrr." It was the strangest looking dog I'd ever seen, with teeth too long to fit in its mouth.* —Sara Nickerson, *How to Disappear Completely and Never Be Found.*>

grrrrr-rrrrrr.

n. a wolf's growl of anger, as discussed in *Wolves: Complete Cross-Curricular Theme Unit That Teaches About These Totally Cool Canines* by Kathleen W. Kranking.

grrrrr-rrrrrr-rrrrrrr-rrrrrrrr-rrrr.

n. a growl of annoyance, as in *So You Wanna Be a Gambler: Baccarat* by John Patrick.

grrrrrr.

1. *adj.* sexy, passionate.

<*Leah was just full-on grrrrrr.* —K.M. Squires, *The Real World Paris.*>

2. *n.* a baby's cry of frustration, as described in *Complete Idiot's Guide to Bringing Up Baby* by Kevin Osborn.

3. *n.* a growl of frustration by a student of Zen meditation trying to stay centered in "frog consciousness," as discussed in *Meetings with the Archangel: A Comedy of the Spirit* by Stephen Mitchell.

4. *n.* a grunt of exertion, as when struggling while strapped to a table in *Jackie Chan Adventures #2: Jade's Secret Power* by Cathy West.

5. *n.* an expression of anger or rage.

<*A sob broke free, and she made a grrrrrr sound of anger.* —Joan Johnston, *The Loner.*>

<*Grrrrrr. This passion bothered his importunate thought three thousand miles away & made him wild with complicated rage.* John Berryman, *The Dream Songs.*>

6. *n.* the growl of a bear, as described in *Psychology of Hope: You Can Get There from Here* by C.R. Snyder.

7. *n.* the hungry growl of a monster, as a parent might instinctively intone while play-acting with a baby.

<*Eating and being eaten inspires one of the most common games adults play with babies. Animal noises—gobbling, if not barking like giants—are what adults make when they play-act with their young. It is instinctive, as instinctive as kissing or crying, to growl and grit your teeth and curl your fingers as if they were clawed and bring your face near the baby's and bare gritted teeth, going "Grrrrrr, you're good enough to eat."* —Marina Warner, *No Go the Bogeyman: Scaring, Lulling, and Making Mock.*>

8. *n.* the purring of a "big overgrown pussycat" (Herbert R. Lottman, *Such Sweet Thunder: A Novel*).

9. *n.* the roar of a dragon, as described in *Lionel in the Fall* by Stephen Krensky.

10. *n.* the roar of a mob erupting in a riot, as described in "Please Kill Me" by Legs McNeil and Gillian McCain (*The Outlaw Bible of American Literature*).

11. *n.* the rumbling of an airplane engine, as described in *More Like Wrestling: A Novel* by Danyel Smith.

12. *n.* the sound of a "ferocious crocodile," as discussed in *Complete Idiot's Guide to Yoga with Kids* by Jodi Komitor and Eve Adamson.

13. *n.* the sound of one's shadow self explosively releasing "a great amount of repressed energy" in a "giant over-reaction" (Jacquelyn Small, *Awakening in Time: The Journey from Codependence to Co-Creation*).

grrrrrr grrrrrr grrrrrrrrrrrr.

n. the "growling, mechanical" sound of an engine starting, as described in the novel *Choice of the Cat* by E. E. Knight.

grrrrrrgh.

n. an ominous growl.

<*"Grrrrrrgh..." Kyle flinched away at Hunter's dangerous growl, though the killer alien had his*

eyes locked on something down the street, obviously too far away for either of its masters to see. —Black Dragon, "Guardian: A Ranma 1/2 Fanfiction.">

grrrrrrrr.

n. the growl of a dog with "his fur up and his teeth bared," as described in *Help! I'm Trapped in a Vampire's Body* by Todd Strasser.

grrrrrrrrrr.

(also grrrrrrrr.) *n.* the growling of one's stomach, as in *The Classroom at the End of the Hall* by Douglas Evans.

grrrrt-grrrrt-grrrrt.

n. the "low rattling" call of the Chestnut-crowned Laughingthrush, as described in *A Guide to the Birds of Southeast Asia* by Craig Robson.

Grrrsh.

n. the name of a warrior bat in the novel *Wink-Eye Creek* by Doug Hiser.

<*Grrrsh gnashed his needle-like teeth thinking about the taste of fresh blood, the taste of fear.* —Doug Hiser, *Wink-Eye Creek.*>

Gsptlnz.

n. a savior of the Earth and girlfriend of the little imp Mxyzptlk in the *Justice League America* comic books.

gt.

v. "get," as spoken in a faint, muffled voice in the novel *Dezra's Quest* by Chris Pierson.

gzpxllztt.

adj. too exhausted to type a coherent word.

<*And now I am done for the night. Utterly, completely, ineluctably done. Gzpxllztt.* —Neil Gaiman, neilgaiman.com.>

gzrrrk.

1. *n.* an explosion during a laboratory experiment, as in the comic strip "PvP" by Scott R. Kurtz.

2. *n.* the crackle of a blown fuse, as when someone sticks a metal spoon into a hot toaster in the comic strip "PvP" by Scott R. Kurtz.

gzzrrt.

n. the sound of the lights going out due to a power outage, as in the comic strip "PvP" by Scott R. Kurtz.

gzzsrk.

n. a muttering of someone half-asleep, as described in "Confusion" by Chris "Bob" Odorjan.

gzzt.

1. *adv.* like.

   <*Due to disdain for the word "like," "gzzt" is used as a replacement. It denotes the brief short in your brain at the moment of using it.* —SlangSite.com.>

2. *n.* the sound made by a wounded cyborg.

   <*He gzzt schtinged.* —Hertzan Chimera, *The Getaway Girl.*>

gzzt gzzt gzzt.

n. the whirring of a computer's hard drive.

<*A whirring of the machine ensued, and then the familiar, gzzt, gzzt, gzzt of the a: drive began.* —Anonymous, pi-at-work.com.>

gzzzt.

n. the buzzing of radio static, as in *Gotham Day* by Jason Corley.

h'ngh.

interj. a scolding harrumph.

<*"H'ngh!" grunted the Cad, "You weren't listening, were you?"* —C.S. Lewis, *All My Road Before Me: The Diary of C.S. Lewis, 1922-1927.*>

hdf dfh rd drg.

n. the title of a visual poem by Mike Cannell.

hff.

1. (also hfff.) *n.* a huffing breath of exertion, as in the graphic novel *Uzumaki 2* by Junji Ito and the graphic novel *ShadowFall* by Kaichi Satake.

2. *n.* a "tiny, bitter laugh" (Mil Millington, *A Certain Chemistry: A Novel*).

3. *n.* a forced puff of breath, as from a car-crash victim who can't speak because her mouth is full of windshield glass, in the novel *Glow* by Kae Denino.

4. *n.* a haughty huff, as in the novel *Amanda's Wedding* by Jenny Colgan.

hff hff hff hff.

n. a panicked huffing, as when fleeing from a monster in the graphic novel *Parasyte 7* by Hitosi Iwaaki; see also hfff[1], hfffff hfffff.

hfff.

1. *interj.* a panicked huff; see also hff hff hff hff, hfffff hfffff.

<*Hfff ... Do you see my hair? I was having a haircut and someone made a bomb threat and I ran like a bugger across town but they haven't got a free bloody slot until Friday afternoon and I'm meeting someone in* two *minutes and I need a hat.* —Mil Millington, *A Certain Chemistry: A Novel.*>

2. *interj.* a snort of derision, as at "the faceless, overworked, understaffed bureaucracy that was responsible for international adoptions proceeding at a snail's pace while tiny souls languished" (Cindy Champnella, *The Waiting Child: How the Faith and Love of One Orphan Saved the Life of Another*).

3. *n.* the vocal mimic of a whooshing light saber from *Star Wars*.

<*[The Internet fad dubbed] Star Wars Kid began as a tape 15-year-old Ghyslain Raza made of himself pretending to be a Jedi with a golf ball grabber. If you haven't seen it, it sounds like,*

"Hfff! Unggh! Hff-hff-HFFF!" and looks like a whirlwind of your every comedic fantasy come true. —Seanbaby, "The 10 Best Internet Fads," *The Wave Magazine.*>

hfff hfff fffhph.

n. the sound of blowing on coals to kindle a flame, as described by D. Steele (Scouter.com).

hffff.

n. an animal's indignant snort.

<*The most annoying trait of dogs is their insistence on having the last woof in all your verbal encounters. I find that offensive in both animals and kids, but there is something particularly galling about a dog, whom you have just severely reprimanded, who will turn his back and utter a barely audible "hffff!"* —Elizabeth Wetzel, *A is for Aggravation.*>

hfffff hfffff.

n. deep huffing, as after fleeing from a monster in the graphic novel *Parasyte 7* by Hitosi Iwaaki; see also hfff[11], hff hff hff hff.

hggh.

1. *n.* a heaving, panicked breath, as in the graphic novel *Uzumaki 2* by Junji Ito.

2. *n.* heavy breathing of exertion, as described in the story "Marketplace" by Bhavna S. Doegar.

3. *n.* the sound of clearing one's throat.

<*I think I have something stuck in my throat. Hggh ... hggh.* —"When Vesuvio's Erupts, As With Shrimp Pizza, It's Amore," *The Standard-Times.*>

hgkh.

n. the sound of someone struggling not to drown in a vat of fresh cream, as in the graphic novella *Hearts and Minds* by Scott McCloud; see also sppt, blpb.

hgmmm.

n. an incomprehensible utterance of pain, from the ubiquitous German joke about a man mistakenly diagnosed with hemorrhoids who tells the proctologist, "get someone with longer fingers—I have a sore throat!" See also drmpf, hlmpfmr, hmmgmr.

hh.

n. a reply meaning "what?" or "huh?"

<*A voice said, "Psst." "Hh?" said Varney.* —Neil Gaiman, *Neverwhere.*>

HHH.

n. an exhalation; the calm and silent moment of Buddha-nature, when "the breath is completely out" and one effortlessly experiences the moment of death (Osho, *The Book of Secrets*).

<*And when the breath goes out ... HHH ... everything is emptied.* —Osho, *The Book of Secrets.*>

Hhh.

n. the name of a character with glowing yellow eyes in the novel *The Martian Chronicles* by Ray Bradbury.

hhh.

1. *n.* a "whispery rasp," as by a burn victim with "the larynx and vocal chords seared, learning to talk from the gut" (Jonathan Kellerman, *The Web*).

2. *n.* a sigh of relief, as in *The Boy From the Basement* by Susan Shaw.

3. *n.* the sound of a low-level audio distortion, as from a stereo speaker system.

   <*I'd noticed a low-level hhh sound riding atop otherwise pristine sinewave sweeps during the pure-tone measurements. During the listening tests, I thought I detected a gauzy layer of belt noise diminishing the vividness of my test tracks, though the effect always seemed to reside near or below the threshold of audibility.* —GuideToHomeTheater.com.>

4. *n.* the sound of the letter h, as described in "Feminine Voice Techniques" by the Looking Glass Society.

hhh hhh.

n. a weak hiss sound that a young kitten makes.

<*One of the kittens keeps opening its mouth and making a "hhh hhh" sound.* —SpankMag.com.>

hhh hhh hhh.

n. the panting of a sick reptile, as in "Creature" by Carol Emshwiller (*Nebula Awards Showcase 2004*).

hhh hhh hhh hhh hhh.

n. the "terrifying" panting of a rainforest animal that "can only be a land crab, a lizard, or a wild rabbit" (William Manchester, *Goodbye, Darkness: A Memoir of the Pacific War*); see also hhhhhhh hhhhhhh hhhhhhh.

<*In that instant the thing catches my scent and I catch* its *scent. The malevolent panting has begun again,* hhh hhh hhh hhh hhh, *and it reeks of sweat, cordite, urine, and old leather.* —William Manchester, *Goodbye, Darkness: A Memoir of the Pacific War.*>

hhh hmm.

n. a condescending cough.

<*"Hhh, hmm," the haughty receptionist coughed, looking down at Molly over two large nostrils. "Can I be of assistance?"* —Georgia Byng, *Molly Moon's Incredible Book of Hypnotism.*>

HHH-HHHHH.

n. the panting breaths of a "cybertroll," as in *Cyberchase* by Adam Rudman.

<*HHH-HHHHH. I listened carefully. HHH-HHHHH. Yes, there it was again. Heavy panting ... hot, sticky breath on my neck, breath that smelled like rotting garbage.* —Adam Rudman, *Cyberchase.*>

HHHH.

interj. a wordless cry of disbelief, as at being called a "jackass" in *Travels With a Kayak* by Whit Deschner.

hhhh.

1. (also hhh.) *n.* the horrific exhalation of a rotting corpse coming back to life, as in the graphic novel *Uzumaki 2* by Junji Ito.

2. (also hhhhh.) *n.* a wheezing gasp; see also hhhh hhh hhh.

<*The worms multiplied, clamping around his windpipe. "Hhhh—" A sharp wheeze climbed through his throat. "Hhhhh—" Charlie gasped for air as his heartbeat quickened, then started pounding.* —Brad Meltzer, *The Millionaires.*>

3. *interj.* a cry of surprise, as in *The Ghost Ship Mystery* by Gertrude Chandler Warner.

4. *interj.* a questioning sound, as in *Life, the Universe and Everything* by Douglas Adams.

5. *interj.* a vocalized pause.

<*Hhhh, that's something I can never really answer.* —Jim Jarmusch, answering the question "whose work are you especially passionate about," quoted in *Jim Jarmusch: Interviews* by Ludvig Hertzberg.>

6. *interj.* an expression of regret.

<*"Hhhh," she breathed in sharply through her teeth. The animal was a deer, not a panther or wolf. It had only been grazing and was now shot through the chest. She dropped to her knees and lay the gun on the ground.* —Cynthia Lamb, *Brigid's Charge.*>

7. *interj.* huh, as in the play *Pickling* by Suzan-Lori Parks (*The America Play and Other Works*).

8. *n.* a "haunting sigh" (Brad Meltzer, *The First Counsel*).

9. *n.* a "resigned laugh," as discussed in *The Psychiatric Team and the Social Definition of Schizophrenia: An Anthropological Study of Person and Illness* by Rob Barrett and Peter J. Tyrer.

10. *n.* the sound of a hush growing over a crowd, as "at the amazing sight of Periwinkle Fairies riding [thirty] water-spiders" in *Fairies of Bladderwhack Pond* by Debbie Bishop.

11. *n.* the sound of someone hyperventilating.

<*Her eyes are wide, begging for help. "Hhhh..." Gripping her chest, she lets out a long, protracted gasp and crumples to the floor.* —Brad Meltzer, *The Zero Game.*>

12. *v.* to inhale deeply, as when smoking.

> <*The girl started giggling. "Inhaling, breathing in deep, hhhh." Dan slowly brought the joint to his lips. Smoke curled up and burned his eyes. "Hhhh," said the girl. "I'll try once, that's all" [Dan said]. "Hhhh!" She was close to a giggling fit. "Just once." Dan closed his eyes. Hhhh! Immediately he was gasping and choking for air.* —Charles Deemer, "The Man Who Grew a Beard," *Selected Stories*.>

hhhh hhh hhh.
n. wheezing, asthmatic breaths, as described in the book *In the Shadow of Illness* by Myra Bluebond-Langner; see also hhhh[22].

hhhh-mmmmmnnn.
interj. an ecstatic hum, as by someone "deep in the throes of hedonistic backscratching" (Lance H.K. Secretan, *The Way of the Tiger: Gentle Wisdom for Turbulent Times*).

hhhhh.
n. a cough, as when choking from the smoke of a firepot in the play *Lysistrata* by Aristophanes.

hhhhhhh hhhhhhh hhhhhhh.
(also hhhhh hhhhh hhhhh.) *n.* a "disconcerting ... kind of cosmic gasping" of an "impossible to identify" rainforest animal (William Manchester, *Goodbye, Darkness: A Memoir of the Pacific War*); see also hhh hhh hhh hhh hhh.

> <*Its breath goes* hhhhhhh hhhhhhh hhhhhhh *and then* hhhhh hhhhh hhhhh, *and it is coming up after me.* —William Manchester, *Goodbye, Darkness: A Memoir of the Pacific War*.>

hhhhhht hhhhhht hhhhhht hhhhhhhht.
n. the "monotonous, husky, crackling insect-like" song of the Chinese Bush Warbler, as described in *A Guide to the Birds of Southeast Asia* by Craig Robson.

HHHHHMMMMMM.
n. a sigh of "self-dissatisfaction," with "feelings of powerlessness" (Lisa Miller, *The Alarm Clock of Your Life is Ringing: Time to Wake up to Happiness and Enlightenment, 2nd Edition*).

hhhhm.
1. *interj.* a sigh of despair.

> <*[H]hhhm, all through my life my luck's been against me. It's almost as if I was heading for the bottom all the time and now I've pretty well reached it.* Roger Gomm, *Social Research Methodology: A Critical Introduction*.>

2. *n.* an expression of deep thought in *Ulysses* by James Joyce.

hhhkkkk.
n. the sound of an inhalation by someone fighting for life, as in the graphic novel *ShadowFall* by Kaichi Satake.

hhhm.

1. *adv.* indeed, as in the play *Uncle Vanya* by Anton Chekhov.

2. *n.* a contemplative hum.

<*Hhhm, I say, picturing myself with a goatee, wondering if I too have a pretty mouth.* —Inman Majors, *Wonderdog.*>

hhhnn.

1. (also hhhhnnn.) *n.* the uncanny sound of a possum.

<*Hhhnn. Hhhhnnn. Horrible noise. The blasted animal might wake Hugh and she couldn't bear having to be the perfect mother again at midnight. Well, possum, she decided, your cousins in New South Wales might be protected animals, but that is in another country. You're a pest to me and I am going to get you.* —Barbara Else, *Gingerbread Husbands.*>

2. *n.* the sound of a stifled yawn.

<*"Hhhnn," said Peter, gulping down a violent yawn.* —David James Duncan, *The Brothers K.*>

hhhnnnnngggghhh.

n. an ambiguous response, as when one is too taken aback to formulate a clearly positive answer.

<*The Sex God had landed at my door. I was wearing my Teletubby pajamas. He said "Hi." I said "Hhhnnnnnggggghhh."* —Louise Rennison, *Confessions of Georgia Nicholson.*>

hhrnn.

n. a groan from a zombie hungry for brains, as in the comic strip "PvP" by Scott R. Kurtz.

hhrrkkrk.

n. the sound of "serious respiratory distress," as in the graphic novel *ShadowFall* by Kaichi Satake; see also sshhlllrrr.

hjckrrh.

interj. an exclamation of grief.

<*These words were followed by a very long silence, broken only by an occasional exclamation of 'Hjckrrh!' from the Gryphon, and the constant heavy sobbing of the Mock Turtle.* —Lewis Carroll, *Alice in Wonderland.*>

hkkk.

n. the sound of having one's breath knocked out from an impact to the back, as in the comic book *Dv8 #5* by Humberto Ramos and Sal Regla.

hksssshhhhhh.

n. a hiss made by a computer modem, as in the comic strip "PvP" by Scott R. Kurtz.

hlmpfmr.

n. an incomprehensible utterance of pain, from the ubiquitous German joke about a man mistakenly diagnosed with hemorrhoids who tells the proctologist, “get someone with longer fingers—I have a sore throat!” See also drmpf, hgmmm, hmmgmr.

hlp.

v. “help,” as spoken in a faint, muffled voice in the novel *Dezra’s Quest* by Chris Pierson.

hm.

1. *interj.* an expression of contemplation.

   <*“The whole universe is like some big FedEx box.” “Hm.”* —Haruki Murakami, *Kafka on the Shore*.>

2. *n.* a reply meaning “what?” or “huh?” in the novel *Perlman’s Ordeal* by Brooks Hansen.

hm hm hm.

n. a sound made when one’s mouth is full of food, as in the opera *The Magic Flute* by Wolfgang Amadeus Mozart.

hm hmhm hm.

n. a mumbled acknowledgment, as in *A: A Novel* by Andy Warhol.

hmhm.

1. *n.* a chuckle, as in the novel *From Sea to Shining Sea* by James Alexander Thom.

2. *n.* a minimal reply.

   <*Our conversation consists mainly of my own monologue. His only response has been an occasional brief “Hmhm.”* —Elliot Turiel, *The Culture of Morality: Social Development, Context, and Conflict*.>

3. *n.* a muffled attempt to say something witty.

   <*“Hmhm?” I riposte, sharp as a tack.* —David Nicholls, *A Question of Attraction: A Novel*.>

4. *n.* the sound of clearing one’s throat.

   <*“Much to my regret, I have learned ...” He cleared his throat. Why did lying always give him such a lump in his throat? “Hmhm, I have learned that the boys sneaked onto one of the large ferries that stop here regularly.”* —Cornelia Funke, *The Thief Lord*.>

hmhm hmhm.

n. a noncommittal response, as in the novel *A Fire Upon the Deep* by Vernor Vinge.

HMHMHM-hmmhmm-hmmmhm—h—m—m.

n. the sound of “a large piece of machinery somewhere off in the distance wind[ing] down, like a big saw blade spinning slower and slower till it stops,” as in *It Takes a Village Idiot: A Memoir of Life After the City* by Jim Mullen.

hmm.

1. *adv.* yes, as in the novel *The Time Traveler’s Wife* by Audrey Niffenegger.

2. *interj.* an expression of surprise.

   <*“Hmm,” I said, raising an eyebrow. “You have no debt?”* —David Bach, *The Automatic Millionaire: A Powerful One-Step Plan to Live and Finish Rich.*>

3. *n.* a sound which a “great conversationalist” makes while listening to keep people talking, as discussed in *Think Like Your Customer: A Winning Strategy to Maximize Sales by Understanding and Influencing How and Why Your Customers Buy* by Bill Stinnett; see also mmmmm, hmmmm[10].

4. *n.* an empathetic response, as in *Gilead: A Novel* by Marilynne Robinson.

5. *n.* an expression of thoughtful absorption, doubt.

   <*So people in England have cloned a full-grown mammal for the first time, a sheep named Dolly. Hmm. Can you say ‘Boys from Brazil?’* —Mike Kuniavsky.>

hmm hmm hmm.

1. *n.* a soft murmur to oneself.

   <*[H]e was in such a helplessly apathetic condition that he would have said “Hmm, hmm, hmm,” and nodded to anything.* —Patrick Suskind, *Perfume.*>

2. *n.* a whimpering agreement.

   <*[H]e was in such a helplessly apathetic condition that he would have said “Hmm, hmm, hmm,” and nodded to anything.* —Patrick Suskind, *Perfume.*>

hmm hmmhmm.

n. a thoughtful hum, as when considering the validity of an idea, as in *Tales of Protection* by Erik Fosnes Hansen.

hmm—hmm—hmm—hm-hm—hm—hmm-hmm.

n. the hummed melody of “Stars and Stripes Forever,” as transcribed in *Billy Maki: A Novel* by Joseph Damrell.

hmm-hmm.

n. a muttering of “social awkwardness,” as in the play *Brides of the Moon* by The Five Lesbian Brothers.

hmm-hmm-hmm.

n. a soft, appreciative hum from a horse, from “deep in its throat,” as when stroked (Jennifer Armstrong, *Fire-Us #2: The Keepers of the Flame*).

hmmgmr.

n. an incomprehensible utterance of pain, from the ubiquitous German joke about a man mistakenly diagnosed with hemorrhoids who tells the proctologist, “get someone with longer fingers—I have a sore throat!” See also drmpf, hgmmm, hlmpfmr.

HmmHmm.

n. an expression of surprise.

<*The Countess noticed that the tea things were disappearing. “HmmHmm, Madame Romaine! It seems we are running out of tea things.”* —Deborah Nourse Lattimore, *The Lady with the Ship on Her Head.*>

hmmhmm.

1. *adj.* a hummed “okay,” as in *How to Negotiate With Kids Even If You Think You Shouldn’t: 7 Essential Skills to End Conflict and Bring More Joy into Your Family* by Scott Brown.

2. *adv.* no.

<*Can’t we stay? —Hmmhmm, I say, and shake my head.* —Leslie Wells, *The Curing Season.*>

3. *adv.* yes, as in *New Directions for Equity in Mathematics Education* by Walter G. Secada.

4. *n.* a thoughtful hum.

<*You said, oh, this thing about hmmhmm, cataract surgery.* —Stephanie Brown, *Allegory of the Supermarket.*>

5. *n.* the sound of one thinking to oneself, as in the novel *Schooling* by Heather McGowan.

HMMHMMHMMHMM.

n. the sound of clearing one’s throat.

<*Father ... was also silent—but more noisily so. He kept clearing his throat, as if he was getting ready to say something. It never got said. What got said instead was GRMMMMPH and HMMHMMHMMHMM.* —Jules Feiffer, *The Man in the Ceiling.*>

hmmm.

1. *n.* a muttering during a religious sermon, as in the novel *The Recognitions* by William Gaddis; see also hmmmph[9].

2. *n.* a sound made by someone making “a show of seeming to have forgotten” something, as in *The Da Vinci Code* by Dan Brown.

3. *n.* the murmur of a “voice emanating from the floor,” in *Legacy of the Drow* by R.A. Salvatore; see also hmmmm[13].

4. *n.* the sound of a sudden realization.

<*He looked at the crystal ball, made the kind of 'hmmm' noise that means, "ah, so that's where that went," and he put it away again.* —Neil Gaiman, *Neverwhere.*>

hmmm hmmmm.

n. the mumbling of a doctor in an examination room, as when looking over a patient with acne vulgaris in *Ham on Rye* by Charles Bukowski.

hmmmm.

1. *interj.* a noise meaning "Would you care to elaborate on that?" (Dann Gunn, *Wool-Gathering or How I Ended Analysis*).

2. *n.* a "comforting," "supportive," "nonverbal" murmur of attentive listening (Anne Lamott, *Operating Instructions: A Journal of My Son's First Year*).

   <*I'd say something that was a thinly veiled plea for some advice or a pep talk, and she'd just say, "Hmmmm," like she knew I was going to be able to answer my own question in a moment. It seemed such a spiritually enlightened position to take.* —Anne Lamott, *Operating Instructions: A Journal of My Son's First Year.*>

3. *n.* a "trite expression of wonder, envy and awe" that, along with "oh my," "well well," "say now," and "really?" "will cover your adventures in New York" (Hunter S. Thompson, *The Proud Highway: Saga of a Desperate Southern Gentleman, 1955-1967*).

4. *n.* a chant from the Igbo Folk Epic from Sub-Saharan Africa, as discussed in *Traditional Storytelling Today: An International Sourcebook* by Margaret Read MacDonald.

5. *n.* a gleeful giggle, as in the novel *Mossflower* by Brian Jacques; see also mmmmm.

6. *n.* a murmur of mortification.

   <*Dad said, "Mike, you know about sex, right? You had sex education." "Hmmmm," I murmured, mortified that we'd have to talk about it!* —Michael Gurian, *The Wonder of Boys: What Parents, Mentors and Educators Can Do to Shape Boys into Exceptional Men.*>

7. *n.* a polite, noncommittal response.

   <*I was too meek to do anything but listen politely and utter noncommittal "hmmmms" to their suggestions that Jesus could turn my life around.* —Bill Bryson, *Neither Here Nor There: Travels in Europe.*>

8. *n.* a questioning sound.

   <*"How much longer?" I asked. Sylvie said, "Hmmmm?" "How much longer?" Sylvie did not reply.* —Marilynne Robinson, *Housekeeping: A Novel.*>

   <*The corporal found the dirty picture of the woman and the body in Weary's hip pocket. "What a lucky pony, eh?" he said. "Hmmmm? Hmmmm? Don't you wish you were that pony?"* —Kurt Vonnegut, *Slaughterhouse-Five.*>

9. *n.* a sound made while pondering, as in *Confessions of an Ugly Stepsister: A Novel* by Gregory Maguire.

10. *n.* a sound which a "great conversationalist" makes while listening to keep people talking, as discussed in *Think Like Your Customer: A Winning Strategy to Maximize Sales by*

Understanding and Influencing How and Why Your Customers Buy by Bill Stinnett; see also mmmmm, hmm[3].

11. *n.* the relaxed sigh of someone falling to sleep, as in the novel *The Fiery Cross* by Diana Gabaldon.

12. *n.* the sound of a brainstorm, as in the novel *Let That Be the Reason* by Vicki Stringer.

13. *v.* to hum; see also hmmm[3].

<*The floor "Hmmmm'd" several more times.* —R.A. Salvatore, *Legacy of the Drow.*>

hmmmmmm.

1. *n.* a "visceral feeling" of luxury coursing through one's central nervous system, playing upon one's sense of well-being, as in the novel *A Man in Full* by Tom Wolfe.

2. *n.* the sound of the realization that space equals time.

<*So* space *equals* time, *hmmmmmm.* —Tom Wolfe, *The Electric Kool-Aid Acid Test.*>

hmmmmmmm.

n. the hum of a power lance's protective energy field, as in the comic book *Avengers #255* by Steve Epting.

hmmmmmmmmm.

n. in the Pacaas Novos language of the Amazon, a sound representing the working of magic, fighting, talking, and eating, as discussed in *Wari: The Pacaas Novos Language of Western Brazil* by Daniel L. Everett.

hmmmmmmmmmm.

n. the hum of a computer, as in the novel *The Stonking Steps* by Will Rogers.

hmmmph.

1. (also hmmph.) *n.* a passionate murmur, as during kissing in *The Year of Ice: A Novel* by Brian Malloy; see also mmmmm.

2. *interj.* a harrumph of exasperation, as in the comic book *The Secret Society of Super Villains.*

3. *interj.* a suspicious sigh, as in the novel *The Venetian Policeman* by M.E. Rabb.

4. *n.* a disdainful harrumph.

<*"Hmmmph," said Fra Ludovico. "I've never been persuaded you had much of a soul. More like a little damp anchovy stuck between your breasts, trying to breathe. That's what you smell like, anyway."* —Gregory Maguire, *Mirror Mirror: A Novel.*>

<*Hmmmph. What are you going to do—threaten me with an egg whisk?* —Deborah Smith, *Caught by Surprise.*>

5. *n.* a grumble of disapproval, as in the novel *Fanny: Being the True History of the Adventures of Fanny Hackabout-Jones* by Erica Jong.

6. *n.* a grunt of pain, as in *The Lies We Believe* by Chris Thurman.

7. *n.* a laugh to oneself, as in *Paul McCartney: Many Years From Now* by Barry Miles.

8. *n.* a mumble of disappointment, as in *Power With Nature: Solar and Wind Energy Demystified* by Rex Ewing.

9. *n.* a muttering during a religious sermon, as in the novel *The Recognitions* by William Gaddis; see also hmmm[1].

10. *n.* a response "in the nature of a belch" yet also sounding "like a bit of a cough" (Bruce Alexander, *The Color of Death*).

11. *n.* a snort of dismissal, as in the novel *Mount Dragon* by Douglas Preston.

12. *n.* a snort of frustration, as in the novel *The Santaroga Barrier* by Frank Herbert.

13. *n.* a sound made while one is reflecting (Cyntha DeFelice, *Nowhere to Call Home*) or digesting information (Jon A. Jackson, *The Diehard*).

14. *n.* a wordless grumble when one doesn't know what to say (Louise Fitzhugh, *Harriet the Spy)* or can say nothing else (Dan Kerchenroether, *Selling Air*); a grunt by one whose "facility for repartee seldom peaks before noon" (Patrick F. McManus, *The Grasshopper Trap*).

15. *n.* an expression indicating that one has lost one's appetite, as in the novel *Carolina Mist* by Mariah Stewart.

16. *n.* an expression of disgust, as in the novel *The Angel of Montague Street* by Norman Green.

17. *n.* an expression of self-pity or regret; a "dramatic sigh" (Julia Quinn, *Brighter Than the Sun*).

    <*I heard Rosaleen make a sound like* Hmmmph, *and I knew she was thinking about her own sorry husband, wishing he hadn't shown up for* their *ceremony.* —Sue Kidd, *The Secret Life of Bees.*>

18. *n.* an hysterical wheezing, as in *Cat in a Jeweled Jumpsuit: A Midnight Louie Mystery* by Carole Nelson Douglas.

19. *n.* nothingness, "empty space" (Faye Kellerman, *The Forgotten*).

hmmnnhhh.

interj. a cry of pain, as from a stab wound to the navel in *Ripley Bogle* by Robert McLiam Wilson.

hmmph hmmmph.

interj. an expression of foot-stomping fury, as in the novel *Mortal Allies* by Brian Haig.

hmmph hmmph hmmmph.

n. an expression of admonishment, as in the novel *Erasure* by Percival Everett.

hmn.

n. an expression used to underscore that a question has been asked.

<*Any clues as to what to do, where to go, next? Hmn?*—Arthur Durkee, "On the Road: A Record of Changes.">

hmp.

interj. an expression of contemplation.

<*Mr. Young took his pipe out of his mouth and examined the stem thoughtfully. 'Hmp, he said.'* —Neil Gaiman & Terry Pratchett, *Good Omens*.>

hmph.

1. *adv.* indeed.

<*It sold well. Hmph, it did more than that.* —Barbara Delinsky, *Within Reach.*>

2. *adv.* okay, as in the novel *A Fire Upon the Deep* by Vernor Vinge.

3. *adv.* perhaps, as in *Mr. Maybe: A Novel* by Jane Green.

4. *interj.* an expression of disbelief.

<*Hmph. The lies you children tell. It's beyond belief.* —Jenny Nimmo, *Midnight for Charlie Bone.*>

<Hmph. You're saying there'll be no birds singing or brooks babbling.' No music? ... It's going to be a pretty bleak world, if you ask me.</i> —Haruki Murakami, *Hard-Boiled Wonderland and the End of the World: A Novel.*>

5. *n.* a contemplative mumble, as in *The Golden One: A Novel of Suspense* by Elizabeth Peters.

<*"Hmph." Lucas scratched his chin, considering.* —John Sandford, *Shadow Prey.*>

<*"Hmph." Rinker had to think about it for a minute.* —John Sandford, *Certain Prey.*>

6. *n.* a dubious response, as in *The Master Quilter* by Jennifer Chiaverini.

7. *n.* a groan, as when one is experiencing a hangover in the novel *The Price You Pay* by Ashley McConnell.

8. *n.* a grumbling to oneself, as in the novel *Rainbow Six* by Tom Clancy; a bad-tempered grunt, as in *Mr. Grumpy* by Roger Hargreaves.

9. *n.* a grunt implying that someone knew more about a topic at hand than one could guess, as in *Inheritance: A Novel* by Lan Samantha Chang.

10. *n.* a grunt meaning "don't mind if I do," as when one is offered a cigarette in *Past Reason Hated: An Inspector Banks Mystery* by Peter Robinson.

11. *n.* a grunt meaning "you can't fool me," as in the novel *Brighter than the Sun* by Julia Quinn.

12. *n.* a huff of disgust, as in the novel *On the Banks of the Bayou* by Roger Lea MacBride.

13. *n.* a noncommittal grunt, as in the novel *Insurrection* by Thomas M. Reid.

14. *n.* a questioning response, as in the novel *Without Remorse* by Tom Clancy.

15. *n.* a scoff "without much conviction," as in the novel *The Dream Spheres* by Elaine Cunningham.

16. *n.* a shudder of realization.

    <*"December twenty-second." A little* hmph *shook his chest. "It was a year ago today that she left."* —Patricia Ryan, *Naughty or Nice?*>

17. *n.* a snort to disguise one's mollification, as in the novel *The Secret History* by Donna Tartt.

18. *n.* a sound made to interrupt someone, as in the novel *Track of the Cat* by Nevada Barr.

19. *n.* a surly expression, as in *Call it Sleep: A Novel* by Henry Roth.

20. *n.* an ambiguous, "diplomatic" response, as in the novel *Quicksilver* by Neal Stephenson.

    <*The old sweeper hmph'd an ambiguous response and returned to sweeping into a heap tiny pieces of blue and white sky—bits of mirror smashed and sprinkled over the walkway.* —Arthur Phillips, *Prague: A Novel.*>

21. *n.* an angry sputter, as in the novel *Fool's Puzzle* by Earlene Fowler.

22. *n.* an argumentative expression, as in the novel *Once Upon a Curse* by E.D. Baker.

23. *n.* an exclamation by the "Good Magician Humfrey" that, according to a translator golem, means "You blundering aviary feline! Get your catty feet on the ground!" (Piers Anthony, *Source of Magic*).

24. *n.* an expression of annoyance, as in the novel *The Legend of Luke* by Brian Jacques.

25. *n.* an expression of consent, as in *The Falcon at the Portal: An Amelia Peabody Mystery* by Elizabeth Peters.

26. *n.* an expression of distrust, as of "people who do [southern drawl] accents" too easily in the novel *Revenge of the Wrought-Iron Flamingos* by Donna Andrews.

27. *n.* an expression of indignation, as in the novel *The Golden Transcendence* by John C. Wright.

    <*Hmph! Will heard an indignant—and muffled—squeak.* —Disney Enterprises, *W.I.T.C.H. Chapter Book: A Bridge Between Worlds.*>

28. *n.* an expression of surprise, as in the novel *Storm Front* by Jim Butcher.

29. *n.* an expression of suspicion, as in *The Quilter's Apprentice* by Jennifer Chiaverini.

30. *n.* an involuntary utterance, as upon suddenly remembering something in *Pandora's Box: A Novel* by Allison Hobbs.

31. *n.* nonsense, as in *Dance Dance Dance* by Haruki Murakami.

32. *n.* the growl of a cat, as in the novel *Warriors #3: Forest of Secrets* by Erin Hunter.

33. *n.* the snort of a dragon, as in the novel *To Light a Candle* by Mercedes Lackey and James Mallory.

hmph hmph.

n. a muffled cough, as described in *The Excellent 11: Qualities Teachers and Parents Use to Motivate, Inspire, and Educate Children* by Ron Clark.

hngggh.

interj. a grunt made during strenuous walking, as in the comic book *Hyperco* by Aaron K.

hngh.

1. *adj.* interesting, as in *Desert Winter: A Claire Gray Mystery* by Michael Craft.

2. *interj.* huh, as in *Hot Spot: A Mark Manning Mystery* by Michael Craft.

3. *n.* a sound made by someone with "three Licorice Allsorts" stuffed in his mouth (Charlie O'Neill, *Yeats is Dead! A Mystery by 15 Irish Writers*).

4. *n.* a suspicious snort, as in the novel *Storm Front* by Jim Butcher.

5. *n.* an "odd, brief sound. You couldn't call it a laugh. More like a cough" (John Derbyshire, *Seeing Calvin Coolidge in a Dream: A Novel*).

hngh hngh hngh.

1. *n.* a chuckle.

<*I wanted to stay in the spirit world, or even wine and beer, hngh, hngh, hngh.* —Terry Pratchett, *Reaper Man*.>

2. *n.* heaving breaths; panting "like a hot dog on a sunny day," as in the novel *The Bromeliad Trilogy: Wings* by Terry Pratchett.

hnghn.

interj. in "Grunt, a dialect of English passed on from father to son," "hnghn" is a noise to be distinguished from "ynuh" (James Dale, *Rules For Wives*).

hngk.

interj. a grunt made upon being shot by a gun, as in the graphic novel *ShadowFall* by Kaichi Satake.

hnh.

1. *interj.* a sound of contempt.

   <*"Hnh!" my mother huffs in a tone that implies Phil is stupid beyond words.* —Amy Tan, *The Kitchen God's Wife.*>

2. *n.* a huff of disbelief, as in the graphic novella *Hearts and Minds* by Scott McCloud.

3. *n.* an inquisitive sound; see also hrn.

   <*I twitched violently, and the woman next to me snorted, reared up with a bleary, "Hnh?" and collapsed again, in a whoosh.* —Diana Gabaldon, *The Fiery Cross.*>

Hnj.

n. a populated place in the Gracias a Dios region of Honduras.

Hnn.

n. an emissary of the Goblin Elves.

<*The emissary's name was Hnn. Among his own people, he was a hunt-leader, cruel and fearless, but now he had been brought before his gods, and he crouched and cowered, drooling in fear.* —Mercedes Lackey, *To Light a Candle.*>

hnn.

n. a grunt of exertion, as while playing a video game in the comic strip "PvP" by Scott R. Kurtz; see also grnt.

hnnh.

interj. in "Grunt, a dialect of English passed on from father to son ... 'Hnnh!' means 'Wow, I didn't know that. Glad you told me'" (James Dale, *Rules For Wives*).

hnnn.

1. (also hnnnn.) *n.* the grunt of Frankenstein's monster.

   <*Now in place of his brow-furrowing / Shakespearean tirades / all he ever said was: / Hnnn. Hnnnn.* —John Quinn, "Subway Station Meditation (New York)," *Do Not Ask Me to Compete with the Angels.*>

2. *interj.* a grunt of approval.

   <*"But right now I urge you all to enjoy yourselves. Eat, drink, and be merry" "Hnnn," Louisa grunted approvingly.* —Carol Higgins Clark, *Twanged.*>

3. *interj.* a questioning sound, as in *The Minotaur Takes a Cigarette Break: A Novel* by Steven Sherrill.

4. *interj.* an acknowledgment, if not a direct agreement.

   <*"Fine, good, be sick whatever. But just make sure you ditch that sucker once and for all." "Hnnn," I said.* —Jenny Colgan, *Amanda's Wedding.*>

5. *interj.* an excited equivalent of “voila.”

<*“Have you seen the paper?” “No,” Regan said. “Why?” “Hnnn.” Louisa reached into her carryall and pulled out the* Hamptons News. —Carol Higgins Clark, *Twanged.*>

6. *interj.* an non-committal answer, as to hide one’s ignorance or surprise.

<*“Hnnn,” Arkey said, slurping his chocolate shake, not wanting to seem like he didn’t know the intricate machinery of the world.* —Jay Cantor, *Great Neck.*>

7. *n.* a contemplative hum, as in “The Family Car” by John “Jack” Arnold.

8. *n.* a dog’s yearning moan.

<*There is the hint that escapes from him involuntarily, a rapid, defeated exhalation (hnnn!), as when he sees another dog, and he wants so badly to be with that dog.* —Michael Finley, “Communicating with Dogs.”>

9. *n.* a muffled voice in the distance.

<*He stared at the horizon blankly. The sun was down, the light fading, like his chance with ... her. “Hnnn.” He spun around. A voice. Whose? Where? His hair prickled. If it wasn’t a friendly voice, he would already be dead. Still... “Hnnn.”* —Win Blevins, *Beauty for Ashes.*>

10. *n.* an incoherent response, as from someone intoxicated; see also dnnn.

<*“Hey Sandra, it’s me, Rudy. You know me?” “Hnnn,” said Sandra. “You all right? You sick or anything, or just drunk?”* —William Kennedy, *An Albany Trio.*>

11. *n.* humming; the sound of singing to oneself.

<*I could hear her singing to herself in the kitchen. She had a monotonous, rather grating voice, which rose and fell at intervals. “Add the raw unsoaked millet—hnn hnnn—and turn off the heat. Leave covered for—hnnn hnnn—ten minutes without stirring or—hnnnn—until the juices have been absorbed.* —Joanne Harris, *Five Quarters of the Orange.*>

12. *n.* the soft sound of a voice fading away as the speaker is overcome by memory.

<*“Open ... sores. Skin on fire. Hnnn.” His voice trailed away, hardly-there air over barely moving mouth, and still he kept talking.* —Glen Hirshberg, *The Mammoth Book of Best New Horror, Vol. 15.*>

13. *n.* the sound of a stifled scream of pain.

<*“Yes… he…* hnnn!*” Julia gritted her teeth to prevent the scream escaping.* —Mark E. Cooper, *The Warrior Within: Devan Chronicles Part III.*>

<*“Hnnn!” the soldier clenched his teeth as the guards helped him to his feet and threw his arms over their shoulders.* —Greg Howell, *Godsend.*>

hnnng.

1. *interj.* an expression of discontent.

<*"Hnnng!" Cunyuan was sounding bitter, disgruntled. "Hnnng what? Have I done any less for you?" our niang asked him.* —Cunxin Li, *Mao's Last Dancer.*>

2. *n.* a grunt of exertion, as when hefting a heavy, lifeless body over one's shoulder in the comic strip "PvP" by Scott R. Kurtz; see also mmmph, nnnnggghh.

hnnngg.

n. the hum of a quivering sword blade, as in the graphic novel *Falcon Twin* by Brenden Mecleary.

hp hp hp.

n. a baby's hiccup, as described in the novel *Edwin Mullhouse* by Steven Millhauser.

hrgh.

n. a frustrated grunt over getting entangled in poison ivy, as in the comic book *Harley Quinn #14* by Terry and Rachel Dodson.

hrn.

n. an inquisitive sound; see also hnh[3]. <*Hrn? What are you talking about?*>

hrnf.

n. a contemptuous chuckle, as in the Nintendo 64 video game "Zelda: Majora's Mask."

hrr-hrrm.

n. the sound of clearing one's throat, as to call attention to oneself; see also hrrm[4].

<*Loud* hrr-hrrms *rattled from the throats of two irritated parents.* —Diane Mott Davidson, *The Cereal Murders.*>

Hrrl.

n. a warrior who raided the kingdom of Esti, in the novel *The Letterseeker* by Stan McDaniel.

<*Then Hrrl the Heavyhanded, my own great-great-grandfather's brother, gathered all the wickfolk and led a clever raid on Esti, thinking he had decoyed King Gorrst's fleet on a fool's errand.* —Stan McDaniel, *The Letterseeker.*>

hrrm.

1. *n.* a sound conveying "an impending verdict," as in the novel *Flashpoint* by Loren L. Coleman.

2. *n.* an expression meaning "your guess is as good as mine," as in the novel *The Family Trade* by Charles Stross.

3. *n.* the sound of a thoughtful pause, like hmmm.

<*But what if... Hrrm. No, that doesn't work.* —Ben Brown, "The Apocrypha of Ben Brown.">

4. *n.* the sound of clearing one's throat, as while nervously stammering in *The Story of Henry Tod: A Blackford Oakes Mystery*; see also hrr-hrrm.

hrrmph.

n. the grating sound of clearing one's throat.

<*Then Farley started to hrrmph and cough and stutter until we realized he was actually crying.* —Molly Moynahan, *Stone Garden: A Novel.*>

hrrph.

interj. an expression of disbelief, contempt.

<*'Hrrph,' said Coney.* —Jonathan Lethem, *Motherless Brooklyn.*>

hrrr.

1. (also hrrrr.) *n.* the whinny of the shaggy, six-legged "pilka" beast in the novels *The Golden Wasp* and the *Secrets of Droon* series by Tony Abbott.

2. *interj.* a purring "humph."

<*Hrrr... You're sicker than a cub who bit a spinytail on a dare.* —Thomas Harlan, *House of Reeds.*>

3. *interj.* an expression of agreement.

<*"We should get some food." "Hrrr... yes. I should go hunting."* —Thomas Harlan, *House of Reeds.*>

4. *n.* a goblin's snort, as in the comic strip "PvP" by Scott R. Kurtz; see also grr[4].

5. *n.* a vocalization by a terminally ill patient who cannot say a word but who can communicate via a "speaking board" that lists the alphabet, important persons, body parts, and important psychological needs.

<*[E]ven a ten year old child can go up and down on these lists and the patient can go "Hrrr" when he points to the right word or the right letter.* —Elizabeth Kübler-Ross, *The Tunnel and the Light: Essential Insights on Living and Dying.*>

6. *n.* the laugh of "the Sandman, Guardian of the dreams of men, protector against wicked nightmares, lord of the Dream Dome, and friend of children everywhere," as discussed in *The Sandman Companion: A Dreamer's Guide to the Award-Winning Comic Series* by Bender Hy.

hrrr hrrr.

n. a noise indicating car trouble.

<*How long before the brakes fail or the engine falls out or the transmission explodes or whatever is about to go wrong? You can drive and drive and listen to that "hrrr, hrrr," and all you do is wait and worry and worry and wait.* —Linda Richman, *I'd Rather Laugh: How to be Happy Even When Life Has Other Plans for You.*>

hrrr-hrrr.

1. *n.* the growl of a ratel.

   <*Foraging, possibly disturbed ratels have been heard uttering a breathy "hrrr-hrrr" sound.* —Richard Despard Estes, *The Behavior Guide to African Mammals: Including Hoofed Mammals, Carnivores, Primates.*>

2. *n.* the grunt of a badger.

   <*Later, when she listened to the hoot of an eagle owl, the hiss of a genet, and the hrrr-hrrr grunt of a foraging honey badger, she didn't feel quite as confident. The night was full of activity—some harmless, some not.* —Nancy Farmer, *A Girl Named Disaster.*>

3. *n.* the sound of snoring.

   <*Mommy's eyelids weren't fluttering; she lay on her back making a hrrr-hrrr sound through her nose.* —Nancy Kress, *Beggars in Spain.*>

hrrr-mph.

interj. a harrumph.

<*But there's nothing the matter, no, nothing. Hrrr-mph!* —Manfred Kyber, *The Three Candles of Little Veronica: The Story of a Child's Soul in This World and the Other.*>

hrrrk.

n. the growl of someone having been bitten by the Wolfman, as transcribed in the comic strip "PvP" by Scott R. Kurtz; see also nngh, snrrrl.

hrrrmph.

n. the snort of a unicorn.

<*I offered it my apple it looked at me with big silver eyes and then it snorted like this, hrrrmph, and ran away over the hill.* —Neil Gaiman, "Desert Wind," *Smoke and Mirrors: Short Fictions and Illusions.*>

hrrrr.

1. *interj.* a musical growl in a maritime ceremony.

   <*Presently we heard the Captain call out at the top of his voice Ease her—Stop her—Let go the Anchor, hrrrr ... and as the chain runs out, the vessel comes proudly up against the bank of the river to receive us.* —Lesley Adkins, *Empires of the Plain: Henry Rawlinson and the Lost Languages of Babylon.*>

2. *n.* a thoughtful sound one makes while scanning a page for information.

   <*"Hrrrr..." Magdalena paged through her guidebook.* —Thomas Harlan, *House of Reeds.*>

hrrrrr.

1. *n.* a grunt in the Wookie language of the *Star Wars* films, as transcribed in the comic strip "PvP" by Scott R. Kurtz; see also grnnnk, mrr.

2. *n.* the raspy voice of a dog attempting to make human sounds, as in the novel *Eternity's End* by Jeffrey Carver.

hrrrrrmph.

n. a euphemistic slur describing a thief.

<*I jest turns me back and that there young ... hrrrrrmph ... was stuffin' it in 'is marf.* —Desmond Flowers, *The War, 1939-1945: A Documentary History.*>

hrrrssh.

n. Godzilla's scream, as transcribed in the comic strip "PvP" by Scott R. Kurtz.

hrrt hrrt hrrt.

n. the dry rattling alarm call of the Wedge-Billed Wren Babbler, as described in *A Field Guide to the Birds of China* by John MacKinnon.

hsh.

interj. hush.

<*"Hsh. It is neither bullock nor buck he hunts tonight," said Mother Wolf. "It is Man."* —Ruyard Kipling, *Jungle Book.*>

hshbwns.

n. hashbrowns, as muttered by someone with a toothbrush in his mouth.

<*"What do you want with your eggs, Bill?" "Hshbwns." "Duly noted. Now go spit, you look rabid."* —Anonymous, "Infinity's Descent.">

hss.

n. a hiss used surreptitiously to get attention; see also hsst[4].

<*A rich female voice answered from the darkness, "Hss. Any idea when the next market is?"* —Neil Gaiman, *Neverwhere.*>

hsss.

1. *interj.* a shushing sound.

<*Hsss, Sister Condron shushed backwards.* —Alan Warner, *The Sopranos: A Novel.*>

2. *n.* a sound of intimidation; also hssss.

<*Hsss, fools, one bite from my fangs means death.* —Brian Jacques, *Mossflower.*>

3. *n.* the warning hiss of a snake; see also hssss[3], hsss ssss.

<*The snake was doing whatever snakes do early in the morning, and when Muka tried to get it to play there was a sharp hsss! and Muka came hopping out of the grass like a jackrabbit.* —Eknath Easwaran, *The Bhagavad Gita for Daily Living: Chapters 7 Through 12.*>

hsss ssss.

(also hsss sssss.) *n.* the hissing of a snake, as in *If There Be Thorns* by V. C. Andrews; see also hsss[33], hssss[3].

hssss.

1. *n.* a cat's hiss of vexation, as in the comic strip "PvP" by Scott R. Kurtz.

2. *n.* the hiss of a giant salamander with "volcanic breath," as in the comic book *Arak #25* by Adrian Gonzales.

3. *n.* the hissing of a snake; see also hsss[3], hsss ssss.

   <*The snake reared up, flickering a slim tongue. "Hssss. Nobody crosses without paying us."* —Brian Jacques, *Mossflower.*>

4. *n.* the sound of a city bus pulling away from a stop, as in *The Hearse You Came In On* by Tim Cockey.

hssss sss-sst.

n. a hiss to call someone's attention.

<*"Hssss sss-sst!" Parvati blew through her teeth.* —Suzanne Fisher Staples, *Shiva's Fire.*>

hsssss.

1. *interj.* a hiss of derision, as by a teacher to a student who questions a typo in his textbook in *Squee's Wonderful Big Giant Book of Unspeakable Horrors* by Jhonen Vasquez.

2. *n.* a sizzling hiss of a fire-breathing dragon.

   <*Flames licked from the dragon's mouth. "Hsssss. Why would you trade your life for such a pitiful scrap of flesh?"* —William D. Burt, *The Greenstones.*>

hssssssss.

n. an exhalation of "sulfur breath," as in the comic book *New Mutants #77* by Rich Buckler.

hssssssssssssssssssssssssssssssssssssssssss.

n. the crackle of an electric eel.

<*Hsssssssssssssssssssssssssssssssssssssssssss. Mad Uncle Jack snatched up the escaped eel, seemingly unconcerned as the current of electricity passed through his hand and up his arm as he popped it back into his pocket.* —Philip Ardagh, *Dreadful Acts: Book Two in the Eddie Dickens Trilogy.*>

hssst.

1. *conj.* an emotional "moreover."

   <*[N]ot only is it not too soon, hssst, it is overdue.* —Alan Dean Foster, *The Approaching Storm.*>

2. *interj.* a hiss of dismissal.

<*"Go away!" I said. "Hssst!"* —John Gardner, *Grendel.*>

3. *interj.* a hiss of rejection.

<*Hssst! What would you know of my needs? We've barely met, you and I.* —Terry Brooks, *Anthrax* .>

4. *interj.* a sound that puts a stop to any further discussion.

<*Hssst! It's settled. Come along.* —Eloise McGraw, *The Moorchild.*>

5. *n.* a sound to shoo a cat.

<*"She's got fleas," he said, following her out of the room. Through the door in the hall leading to the basement he called "Hssst!" several times, as though assisting the cat's departure.* —John Galsworthy, *The Forsyte Saga.*>

6. *n.* the flaring of a firebolt.

<*Hssst! A massive firebolt flared toward Kharl before he could try to harden the air around the wizard.* —L. E. Modesitt Jr., *Wellspring of Chaos.*>

7. *n.* the hiss of a burning laser.

<*Hssst! A laser burned into the tree above my head.* —L. E. Modesitt Jr., *Octagonal Raven.*>

8. *n.* the sound of a teapot coming to a boil, as in *Dead Soul* by James D. Doss.

9. *v.* look; see also hsst[8].

<*A rude noise from David broke her poetic reverie. "Hssst! Look there!"* —Elizabeth Peters, *The Camelot Caper.*>

hssst hssst.

n. a stage whisper, as in *Champion's Trial: Magic Legends Cycle Two* by Scott McGough.

hssst hsst.

n. the sizzling hiss of burning flesh.

<*Lorn raises the firelance, using his chaos-senses to focus the firebeam tightly. Hssst! Hsst!* —L. E. Modesitt, *Scion of Cyador.*>

hsst.

1. (also hsst hsst.) *n.* a warning signal.

<*"Hsst!" she signaled in warning, clasping his hand in hers once more. "We have to go now! Quickly! They're coming!"* —Terry Brooks, *The Talismans of Shannara.*>

<*Stresa was the first to feel the tremors and hiss in warning at Wren. "Elf Queen. Phffft! Do you feel it? Hsst! Hsst! The earth moves!"* —Terry Brooks, *Anthrax.*>

2. *n.* a feline greeting.

<*"Hsst!" another cat said and she opened her eyes to see a very real pair of cat eyes staring down into hers.* —Anne McCaffrey, *Acorna's Rebels.*>

3. *n.* a shooing sound.

<*When Henry tried to lift the hem of her dress, however, she had to push him away. "Hsst! What are you doing—with your daughter in the next room!"* —Larry Watson, *Orchard: A Novel.*>

4. *n.* a sound used surreptitiously to get attention; see also hss.

<*"Hsst!" From beneath another stand peered a small, swarthy face; a boy, near to my age. Grinning, his teeth white against his skin, he beckoned with one grimy hand.* —Jacqueline Carey, *Kushiel's Dart.*>

5. *n.* a summons.

<*His shovel had struck something hard. With a sharp "Hsst!" he summoned his companions, and all five men dropped to their knees and began scooping away the sand with their hands.* —Elizabeth Payne, *The Pharaohs of Ancient Egypt.*>

6. *n.* an enraged rasp, as in the novel *The FarCall Project* by RedTurtle.

7. *n.* the electrical hiss of an android or robot malfunctioning, as in *The Metallic Touch*; see vzzkt.

8. *v.* look; see also hssst[9].

<*Hsst lads here they come.* —Peter Carey, *True History of the Kelly Gang: A Novel.*>

hssttt.

(also hsssttt). *n.* the sound of a fireball or firebolt shooting overhead.

<*Hssttt! A lone fireball arced over the earthworks and flared across the right launcher.* —L. E. Modesitt Jr., *The Order of War.*>

hthn.

n. the title of a visual poem by Mike Cannell.

hw.

adv. how, written in Roger Bacon's all-consonant secret code (devised in 1250), as discussed in *The Voynich Manuscript* by Gerry Kennedy.

J-Gnc.

n. the fourth sentinel of Aether, who died defending the great temple, in the video game "Metroid Prime 2: Echoes."

j-j-j-j-j-j’j’j’j’j’j’J’J’J’J’J’j’j’j’j’j’j-j-j-j.

n. the "distinctive, ratchetlike, buzzing call" of the White-tipped Swift, which "accelerates, [becomes] loudest in the middle, then fades and slows," as described in *Birds of Venezuela* by Steven L. Hilty.

J-Shl.

n. a noble alien Luminoth who "lost his soul before a fortress in the scorched land," in the video game "Metroid Prime 2: Echoes."

jhhh.

n. a "pleading" noise, as in the novel *Innocents* by Cathy Coote.

jhhhhh.

n. the "faint rush of breath," as when one blows on a feather in *Being with Rachel: A Personal Story of Memory and Survival* by Karen Brennan; see also fhhhhh.

jhjh.

n. the title of a visual poem by Mike Cannell.

JHVH.

n. the unspoken, "unutterable sacred name" of the god Jehovah (Anna Voigt and Nevill Drury, *A Way Forward: Spiritual Guidance for Our Troubled Times*); the "classic Tetragrammaton," the four-letter divine name; the "secret name" of the god Yahweh (Harold Bloom, *The Western Cannon: Tthe Books and School of the Ages*).

<*"I am JHVH." He did not actually pronounce the name; it was only a concept.* —Piers Anthony, *For Love of Evil.*>

JHVH-1.

n. Jehovah One, the alien space god of the Church of the SubGenius.

<*I [JHVH-1] am the God of Wrath, that One who, to make Man pull the triggers of his thousand opposable thumbs, caused the apes of the ground to spill their seed on the dust.* —Rev. Ivan Stang, *The Book of the SubGenius: Being the Divine Wisdom, Guidance, and Prophecy of J.R. 'Bob' Dobbs, High Epopt of the Church of the SubGenius, Here Inscribed for the Salvation of Future Generations and in the Hope that Slack May Someday Reign on this Earth.*>

jjj.

n. the sound of the letter j, as described by Colin Reed in Vocalist.org; see also jjjj[2], JJJJJ[2].

jjj jjjj jjj.

n. the sound of a tractor, as described in *Tongue Tie—From Confusion to Clarity: A Guide to the Diagnosis and Treatment of Ankyloglossia* by Carmen Fernando.

jjjj.

1. *n.* a stuttering sound, as in *Way Back in the Ozarks Book 2: The Tale of Danny Boy* by James C. Hefley.

2. *n.* the sound of the letter j, as described in *The Voice That Means Business: How to Speak With Authority, Confidence and Credibility Anytime, Anywhere* by Linda Shields; see also jjj, JJJJJ[2].

JJJJJ.

1. *n.* the highest grade of free-range Jabugo ham, from pigs "having eaten nothing but acorns in their lifetimes" (Penelope Casas, *Discovering Spain: An Uncommon Guide*).

2. *n.* the sound of the letter j; see also jjj, jjjj[22].

<*I could hear the "JJJJJ" sound in my head.* —John Edward, *After Life: Answers from the Other Side.*>

Jrdn Kdhl.

n. the title of a web log by Jordan Koidahl.

Jrm.

n. a stream in the Baden-Wurttemberg region of Germany.

jst.

adv. just, as in the play *Sizwe Bansi Is Dead* by Athol Fugard: "Jst like that!"; as spoken with a mouth filled with toothpaste in *My Monastery is a Minivan: 35 Stories from a Real Life* by Denise Roy; as stuttered quickly in the novel *The Dragonstone* by Dennis L. McKiernan: "Uh, jst, jst, just who is it that was going to kill who, eh?"

jzzz.

n. a variation of "jazz," as in the "Jzzz Grrrp" division of the Erskine College Music Department's Sinfonia wind ensemble.

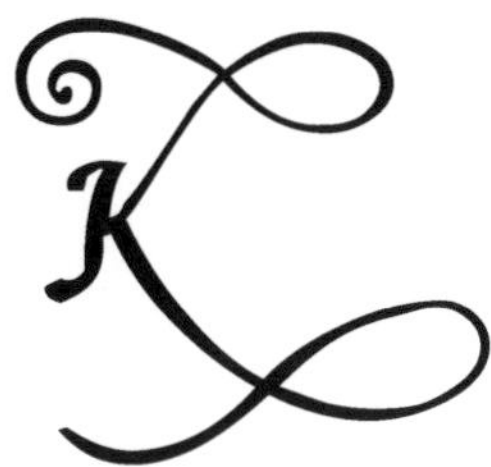

K'dsh.

n. a clan leader in the novel *The FarCall Project* by RedTurtle.

K'dsh'st.

n. a council of leaders in the novel *The FarCall Project* by RedTurtle.

k'k'k'k'.

n. the "rapid laughing" of the Black Noddy, as described in *A Guide to the Birds of Southeast Asia* by Craig Robson.

k'rth.

n. a weapon with needle-sharp black hooks.

<*K'rth have been recorded as having edges going below the sub-atomic level, and will penetrate even crystallite with ease.* —RedTurtle, *The FarCall.*>

k-hhhh.

n. a raspy exhalation.

<*The only sounds were of Savely wheezing and the postman breathing slowly and evenly in his sleep and emitting a deep, prolonged "k-hhhh" each time he breathed out.* —Anton Chekhov, "The Witch," *Early Stories.*>

k-k-k.

n. the sound of the letter k; see also kkk[1], kkkk[10].

<*My mother came from Russia, was stern in spite of herself (and hardest on herself), and never lost the k-k-k sound to her consonants, and never lost the sea tide lilt to her sentences, so every family in our suburban block was slightly frightened of her, and during the height of the Cold War, I'd heard rumors that she was supposed to have been a spy.* —Ira Sadoff, "The Tragic Stiletto of Trabzon," *Ploughshares: The Literary Journal at Emerson College.*>

k-k-k-kk—k-k-k-k-kkk-k-k-k.

n. a stuttering noise generated by a broken computer music program.

<*I had this music program that was cool. Until I broke it by turning up the rhythm tempo too high so that it made an awful "K-K-K-KK—K-K-K-K-KKK-K-K-K" sound.* —U-Magazine.com.>

k-kk-kkkkk.

n. the answering rattle of the female Swamp Boubou bird, as described in *A Guide to the Birds of Western Africa* by Ron Demey.

K-tch.

n. a great hero of Agon and former farmer, in the video game "Metroid Prime 2: Echoes."

k-tk.

n. the sound of an autumn leaf brushing the pavement, as described in *Snow Music* by Lynne Rae Perkins.

kchk.

n. the sound of a talking vacuum cleaner using the prongs of its electrical plug to jimmy an automobile's ignition, as in the comic book *Vacuum Horror* by Aaron K.

kck-kck-kck-ck-kck.

n. an irregular call of the Grey-breasted Mountain-toucan, as described in *Toucans, Barbets and Honeyguides: Ramphastidae, Capitonidae and Indicatoridae* by Lester L. Short.

kfffk.

n. a sound made by a six-month-old baby, as described in the novel *Edwin Mullhouse* by Steven Millhauser.

kgkk.

(also klgk.) *n.* a sound made by a hospitalized person with a tube down his throat, as in the graphic novel *ShadowFall* by Kaichi Satake.

kh-kh-kh.

n. the Arabic expression for sleeping (see zzz), as discussed in *Hear! Here!* by Michele Slung.

kh-krrrrrk.

n. the "dry croaking" of the Sprosser or Thrush-Nightingale, as described in *Birds of Kenya and Northern Tanzania* by Dale A. Zimmerman.

kjn.

n. the title of a visual poem by Mike Cannell.

kk kkk kkkkk.

n. a "scratchy sound," as heard through headphones in the novel *On the Reef* by J.C. Greenburg.

kkk.

1. *n.* the sound of the letter k, as described in *American Dream Series 2: I Can Read!* by Sheila Goodfriend. (This is a very rare spelling of the k-sound, likely due to its similarity to the famous acronym of the Ku Klux Klan.) See also k-k-k, kkkk[10].

2. *n.* the repeated sound of a fatal computer error.

<*I was done computing for the day so I decided to shut down, but I accidentally restarted. Then, just as it was about to go into the desktop it froze on the loading screen. It was making a sort of kkk....kkk....kkk....kkk sound. Then the screen turned blue and said "fatal error: dumping physical memory."* —TheGameCreators.com.>

KKK-K-K-KKK.

n. the staccato call of Lagden's Bush-Shrike, as described in *Shrikes and Bush-Shrikes* by Tony Harris.

kkkdttttkkkk.

n. the sound of a scratched record ("a sound now so rare [it] might make people jump with recognition"), as sung by Missy Elliott and transcribed in *We Gotta Get Out of This Place: The True, Tough Story of Women in Rock* by Gerri Hirshey; see also kkkkkkkkk ktkkt, kkkkkkkk[1].

kkkk.

1. *n.* a loud, harsh crackling; the sound of a crack forming in ice.

<*Suddenly, kkkk! A crack appeared in the ice.* —Tony Abbott, *The Golden Wasp*.>

2. *n.* a stuttered expression, as in *A Fish Called Wanda: The Screenplay* by John Cleese.

3. *n.* the "rattling sound" of the Plate-billed Mountain-toucan, "likely made by the tongue against the ramphotheca," as described in *Toucans, Barbets and Honeyguides: Ramphastidae, Capitonidae and Indicatoridae* by Lester L. Short; see also dddd[2], tttt.

4. *n.* the crackle of a bolt of light, as in the novel *The Great Ice Battle* by Tony Abbott.

5. *n.* the sound of "a spray of sparks," as in the novel *Voyage of the Jaffa Wind* by Tony Abbott.

6. *n.* the sound of a robot malfunctioning after a bad fall, as in the graphic novella *Hearts and Minds* by Scott McCloud.

7. *n.* the sound of a vision flaring in one's mind.

<*Kkkk! The silvery light flared, then faded, and the vision was over.* —Tony Abbott, *The Knights of Silversnow*.>

8. *n.* the sound of silk being stolen.

<*Aye, Silk's what they fancy out in India ... over the wall, in your Window*, kkkk! *Job's done.* —Thomas Pynchon, *Mason & Dixon*.>

9. *n.* the sound of the letter c; see also ccc[2].

<*With much prompting, he said, "Kkkk..." for cat.* —S. Adams Sullivan, *The Father's Almanac: From Pregnancy to Pre-school, Baby Care to Behavior, the Complete and Indispensable Book of Practical Advice and Ideas for Every Man Discovering the Fun and Challenge of Fatherhood*.>

10. *n.* the sound of the letter k, as described in *The Voice That Means Business: How to Speak With Authority, Confidence and Credibility Anytime, Anywhere* by Linda Shields; see also k-k-k, kkk[1].

11. *n.* the sound of the letter k, as described in the novel *Just Call Me Stupid* by Tom Birdseye.

kkkk kkkk.

n. a clicking of the throat in mock gunfire; see also kkkkkk kkkkkk.

<*Petey smiled and flailed his arms, returning the gunfire. "Kkkk, kkkk."* —Ben Mikaelsen, *Petey.*>

kkkkk.

1. *n.* a "burst" of noise made by the Grey-breasted Mountain-toucan, as described in *Toucans, Barbets and Honeyguides: Ramphastidae, Capitonidae and Indicatoridae* by Lester L. Short.

2. *n.* a baby's giggle, as described in the novel *Edwin Mullhouse* by Steven Millhauser; see also kkkkkk[1], ggggg.

3. *n.* a command for a horse to gallop, as described in *Prairie Home Commonplace Book: 25 Years on the Air With Garrison Keillor* by Garrison Keillor.

4. *n.* a crackling sound from a school intercom, as in the novel *In the Ice Caves of Krog* by Tony Abbott.

5. *n.* telephone static; see also kkkkkkk[4].

<*"Kkkkk." April made the sound of static and terminated the call.* —Leslie Glass, *Tracking Time.*>

6. *n.* the crackling of sorcerer's magic.

<*Kkkkk! A bolt of red light shot out from the bars and struck Keeah's hand.* —Tony Abbott, *Quest for the Queen.*>

7. *n.* the sound of a kookaburra "tapping at the back door," as described in *Tongue Tie—From Confusion to Clarity: A Guide to the Diagnosis and Treatment of Ankyloglossia* by Carmen Fernando.

8. *n.* the sound of a lightning strike.

<Kkkkk! *Lightning blasted over the street, sending the townspeople scattering for cover.* —Tony Abbott, *The Coiled Viper.*>

9. *n.* the sound of a neck breaking.

<*"I'd never be anybody's bitch man. If I found out I was going to prison, I'd go out in the garage, take my belt and—kkkkk." He twisted his neck unnaturally to the side. "Just like my old man did."* —Don De Grazia, *American Skin: A Novel.*>

10. *n.* the sound of one's throat being cut.

<*"The minute the police come asking—" He drew a finger across his throat. "Kkkkk!"* —Alan Temperley, *Harry and the Wrinklies.*>

kkkkk kkkkk kkkkk.

n. white noise, as when one turns a radio dial in the novel *Oryx and Crake* by Margaret Atwood.

kkkkkk.

1. *n.* a baby's giggle; see also kkkkk[2], ggggg.

<*The eeeeee grows louder and switches to a giggling kkkkkk.* —Steven Millhauser, *Edwin Mullhouse.*>

2. *n.* a strange mechanical noise.

<*[Eli was] trying to keep the laughter going, even imitating the way his dream machine worked [a machine whose function was to excrete small, square, metallic turds], his elbows squared up, his head sunk between his shoulders, weird mechanical noises emerging from him*—"Kkkkkk, *punk!* Kkkkkk, *punk!"—as he stiffly moved.* —Sue Miller, *While I Was Gone.*>

3. *n.* the rattling call of the Yellow-Rumped Tinkerbird, as described in *A Guide to the Birds of Western Africa* by Ron Demey; see also krrw.

4. *n.* the sound of "the whole world [going] blue" as one transports from one reality to another, as in the novel *Cracked Classics #1: Trapped in Transylvania: Dracula* by Tony Abbott.

5. *n.* the static of a CB radio.

<*He turns the dial.* Receive *is what he'll try. Kkkkkk. Then, faintly, a man's voice: "Is anyone reading me?"* —Margaret Atwood, *Oryx and Crake.*>

kkkkkk kkkkkk.

n. a clicking of the throat in mock gunfire; see also kkkk kkkk.

<*Alex and Graham and TJ playing cowboys and Indians in the living room, bouncing up to shoot, making kkkkkk kkkkkk gun noises in the roofs of their mouths.* —Beth Gutcheon, *Still Missing.*>

kkkkkkk.

1. (also kkkkkk, kkkkkkkk.) *n.* the sound of someone mimicking static interference.

<*He stepped over the stunned bodies and leaned over the control intercom. "This is ... kkkkkkk ... we have ... kkkkkkkk ... renegade prisoners ... kkkkkk ... bounty hunter ... kkkkkkk. Tyrant ... kkkkkk ... immediately. Over."* —Steve Barlow, *Weaver.*>

2. *n.* the "repeated harsh chattering" of the Bull-headed Shrike of Japan, as described in *Shrikes and Bush-Shrikes* by Tony Harris.

3. *n.* the rapid bill-clapping sound of the Choco Toucan, as described in *Toucans, Barbets and Honeyguides: Ramphastidae, Capitonidae and Indicatoridae* by Lester L. Short.

4. *n.* the sound of a dead telephone line; see also kkkkk[5].

<*The voice broke up again. "Oh, Jesus, April—" Silence. "April, talk to me." "Kkkkkkk." The phone went dead.* —Leslie Glass, *Tracking Time.*>

kkkkkkkk.

1. *n.* the "old familiar sound" of "a damaged LP," as sung by Missy Elliott and transcribed in *We Gotta Get Out of This Place: The True, Tough Story of Women in Rock* by Gerri Hirshey; see also kkkdttttkkkk, kkkkkkkkk ktkkt.

2. *n.* the sound of white noise.

<*White noise, more white noise, more white noise. He tries the AM bands, then the FM. Nothing. Just that sound, like the sound of starlight scratching its way through outer space:* kkkkkkkk. —Margaret Atwood, *Oryx and Crake.*>

KKKKKKKK-K-K.

n. a series of clicking sounds made by the Yellow-crowned Gonolek (Barbary Shrike), as described in *Shrikes and Bush-Shrikes* by Tony Harris.

<*"Kkkkkkkkk," exclaimed Eddy, exulting in his new skill, jumping up to reach for another branch still higher in the tree. "Kkkkkkkkk."* —Jane Langton, *The Astonishing Stereoscope.*>

kkkkkkkkk ktkkt.

n. the sound of a scratched record sung by Missy Elliott to serve as "a recovered rock memory" and used to "short-circuit the normal pop expectations," as discussed in *We Gotta Get Out of This Place: The True, Tough Story of Women in Rock* by Gerri Hirshey; see also kkkdttttkkkk, kkkkkkkk[11].

KKKKKKKKKKKKKKKKK.

n. the "cracked" sound of an echo.

<*I call your name and it echoes my voice back to me cracked. KKKKKKKKKKKKKKKKK. The sound gets louder and pulls me away like a magnet. KKKKKKKKKKKKKKKKKKKKKK K. That sound. It looks like the tail on a shooting star. It catches me. I look back and the black hole where maybe you are shrinks to a dot, a nothing. KKKKKKKKKKKKKKKKKKKKKKKK KKKKKKKKKKKKKKKKKKKKKKKKKKKKKKKKKKKKKKKKKKKKKKKKKKKKKKKKKK KKKKKKKKKKKKKKKKKKKKKKKKKKKKKKKKKKKKKKKKKKKKKKKKKKKKKKKKK.* —Emily Raboteau, *The Professor's Daughter: A Novel.*>

KKKKKKKKKKKKKKKKKKKKKKK.

n. a loud "cracked" echo of someone's name which pulls one "like a magnet," as in *The Professor's Daughter: A Novel* by Emily Raboteau; see KKKKKKKKKKKKKKKKK.

KKKKKKKKKKKKKKKKKKKKKKKKKKKKKKKKKKKKKKKKKKKKKKKK.

n. a sound that transports one "into the cold," lightyears past planet Earth and the Milky Way galaxy, as described in *The Professor's Daughter: A Novel* by Emily Raboteau.

KKKKKKKKKKKKKKKKKKKKKKKKKKKKKKKKKKKKKKKKKKKKKKKKK KKKKKKKKKKKKK.

n. a sound that "looks" to one with synesthesia like "KKKKKKKKKKKKKKKK KKKKKKKKKKKK. It looks like gravity ripping. It looks like the jets on a spaceship" (Emily Raboteau, *The Professor's Daughter: A Novel*).

KKKKKKKKKKKKKKKKKKKKKKKKKKKKKKKKKKKKKKKKKKKKKKKKKK KKKKKKKKKKKKKKKKKKKKKKKKKKKKKKKKKKKKKKKKKKKKKKKKK KKKKKKKKKKKKKKKKKKKKKKKKKKKKKKKKKKKKKK.

n. a reverberating echo of someone's name that "looks like the tail on a shooting star" to one with synesthesia in *The Professor's Daughter: A Novel* by Emily Raboteau.

kkrkk.

n. the sound of a body blown backwards by gunfire, as in the comic book *Darkness* by Joe Benitez and Joe Weems.

kksss.

1. *n.* a lizard's hissing exclamation.

   <*Want ta pull me tail off, steal me den, abeat me up? Kksss!* —Brian Jacques, *Salamandastron*.>

2. *n.* the sound of a sword stroke, within the word *Excalibur*, as discussed in *The World of King Arthur and His Court: People, Places, Legend and Lore* by Kevin Crossley-Holland.

Klnk.

n. the name of the goblin chief of the Cavemouth Tribe.

<*"The old goblin, Klnk," she said, with a shrug. "He tried to tell me what was going on, but I didn't catch all of it."*—T. H. Lain, *The Savage Caves*.>

kngggh.

interj. an exclamation of embarrassment, as in the comic strip "College Roomies from Hell!!!" by Maritza Campos.

knrr.

n. an impatient mutter, as in the story "Potch" by Leo Rosten (anthologized in *A Passion for Books: A Book Lover's Treasury of Stories, Essays, Humor, Love and Lists on Collecting, Reading, Borrowing, Lending, Caring for, and Appreciating Books* by Harold Rabinowitz).

krch.

1. *n.* the screeching of a "taxi plunging into the thick of the traffic," as described in *The Fatal Eggs and Other Soviet Satire* by Mirra Ginsburg.

2. *n.* the sound of iron smashing stone, as in a great battle described in the novel *The Iron Tower* by Dennis L. McKiernan.

3. *n.* the sound of tearing paper, as in the graphic novel *Uzumaki 2* by Junji Ito.

Krk.

n. an island in Croatia.

<*[We] hiked through a spectacular huge cave, and then drove to the island of Krk.* —Douglas R. Hofstadter, *Le Ton Beau De Marot: In Praise of the Music of Language.*>

krk krk krk.

n. the call of a barnyard chicken meaning "food [is] over here," as described in *High Tide in Tucson: Essays from Now or Never* by Barbara Kingsolver.

krkkkk.

n. the sound of someone's fingers being squeezed together, as in the graphic novel *Falcon Twin* by Brenden Mecleary.

krkkl.

n. the crinkle of an unfolded paper wad, as in the graphic novel *ShadowFall* by Kaichi Satake.

krklkk.

n. the sound of gently nudging someone's shoulder, as in the graphic novel *ShadowFall* by Kaichi Satake.

krklll.

n. the crackle of a mind-control energy ray, as in the comic book *Wonder Woman #255* by Estrada; see also fzzpppp.

krkrkrkr.

n. the rhythmic, "toneless rattling" of the Isabelline Shrike, as described in *Shrikes and Bush-Shrikes* by Tony Harris.

krnch.

n. the sound of a falling body impacting a balcony railing, as in the graphic novel *ShadowFall* by Kaichi Satake; see also whnngg.

krr-krr.

n. the alarm call of the Bull-headed Shrike of Japan, as described in *Shrikes and Bush-Shrikes* by Tony Harris; the "rough, raspy" call of the Oilbird as it forages outside of caves, as described in *Birds of Venezuela* by Steven L. Hilty.

krrk.

1. *n.* a toad's croaky exclamation; see also krrrk[2].

<*Silence stripedog, Glagweb is King, Krrk!* —Brian Jacques, *Salamandastron.*>

2. *n.* the squeak of a door hinge.

<*Even when you open a door, you get a "krrk" sound.* —Aidan, *Man-gah?*>

3. *n.* the voice of a Royal Toucan bird.

<*Monotonous and raspy "krrk"... very similar to the sound of the frogs.* —Mexico Desconocido Virtual.>

krrk-krrk.

n. the sound of the leaves and branches of a calamansi tree scraping the windows and announcing a monsoon.

<*Their insistent krrk-krrk against the steel guards and their shadows on the walls of his room gave them the same power they had had when he was a boy: giant skeleton fingers endeavoring to claim him for the devil.* —Han Ong, *The Disinherited.*>

krrkrr.

n. the creak of a camera shutter opening and closing (PBase.com).

krrkrrkrrkrrkrrkrrkrrkrr.

n. the low roar following a crashing wave.

<*Even from behind, the long irregular* crack *of the waves falling was louder than the Mayor's shotgun had been. And following the crack was a low roaring* krrkrrkrrkrrkrrkrrkrrkrr, *that faded away just enough to make the next break noticeable. All the sounds joined together in a fierce trembling boom.* —Kim Stanley Robinson, *The Wild Shore: Three Californias.*>

krrkshlshh.

n. the sound of flesh ripped apart by a sword, as in the graphic novel *Falcon Twin* by Brenden Mecleary.

krrnch.

n. the crunching sound of a crash.

<*KRRNCH! The automobile was crushed flat in one clean motion as a huge metal foot burst from the smokescreen, and Asuka gasped as a massive cockpit nose pushed forth into view.* — Black Dragon, "Guardian: A Ranma 1/2 Fanfiction.">

krrr.

1. (also krr.) *n.* an impatient mutter, as in the story "Potch" by Leo Rosten (anthologized in *A Passion for Books: A Book Lover's Treasury of Stories, Essays, Humor, Love and Lists on Collecting, Reading, Borrowing, Lending, Caring for, and Appreciating Books* by Harold Rabinowitz).

2. *n.* the call of the Spot-Winged Grosbeak, rattling like a "shaken, near-empty matchbox," as described in *A Field Guide to the Birds of China* by John MacKinnon; the quiet alarm call of the green-headed Knysna Turaco bird, as described in *Birds of Southern Africa* by Ian Sinclair.

krrr krrr.

n. the sharp call of the Aquatic Warbler, as described in *A Guide to the Birds of Western Africa* by Ron Demey.

krrr-krrr-krrr.

n. the "monotonous, hollow-sounding series of notes" sung by the African Crake, as described in *Illustrated Guide to the Birds of Southern Africa* by Ian Sinclair; the harsh call of the Yellow-Headed Caracara bird, as described in *A Guide to the Birds of Panama* by Robert S. Ridgely.

krrrk.

1. *n.* a hen's warning to her chicks not to feed.

   <*[I]f the food is not good, she says, "Krrrk," in a low tone, meaning, "don't touch it!"* —Minnie Rose Lovgreen, *Minnie Rose Lovgreen's Recipe for Raising Chickens.*>

2. *n.* a toad's croaky exclamation; see also krrk[1].

   <*Get those Foodslaves into the pit. Krrk!* —Brian Jacques, *Salamandastron.*>

3. *n.* the "querulous" call of the Black Noddy, as described in *A Guide to the Birds of Southeast Asia* by Craig Robson.

4. *n.* the crunching sound of something impacting metal, as in the novel *Prisoner* by Johnny Wallbank.

5. *n.* the grating call of the White-Throated Robin, as described in *Birds of Kenya and Northern Tanzania* by Dale A. Zimmerman.

6. *n.* the growling utterance of the Common Pochard bird, as described in *A Guide to the Birds of Western Africa* by Ron Demey.

7. *n.* the sharp alarm sound of the Comoro Thrust, as described in *Thrushes* by Peter Clement.

krrrk krrrk krrrk.

n. the creaking of a door, loud enough "to wake Squirrel Nutkin," as described in *Ribofunk* by Paul Di Filippo.

krrrmchh.

n. the crunch of wadded paper, as in the graphic novel *ShadowFall* by Kaichi Satake.

krrrrk.

1. *n.* the cracking of a plastic utensil.

   <*Krrrrk! my plastic fork breaks with a little pressure on the cold, hard cucumber.* —Dirk Holger, *I Hate Junk Food: A Satire and Other Short Pieces.*>

2. *n.* the sound of a "jagged crack" appearing "from floor to ceiling," as in the novel *The Knights of Silversnow* by Tony Abbott.

3. *n.* the sound of cracking stone.

   <*Finally, they reached the shore. Krrrk! The giant white cliff above them began to split.* —Tony Abbott, *The Mysterious Island.*>

krrrrrk.

n. the cracking sound of an electrical shock (as felt in one's head during a seizure); see also krrrrrrrrk.

<*[I] had another attack: a big crack in my head, the same* krrrrrk *of static, a flash.* —Chris Ryan, *The One That Got Away.*>ul 1. krrrrrrk. *n.* the rasping call of the African Jacana, as described in *Birds of Southern Africa* by Ian Sinclair.

krrrrrrnk.

n. the screeching sound of a straining hinge.

<*Krrrrrrnk! The mechanisms that kept the canopy shut were overcome, and the hinges to the canopy screeched in protest as they were forced open.* —Black Dragon, "Guardian: A Ranma 1/2 Fanfiction.">

krrrrrrrrk.

n. the cracking sound of an electrical shock (as felt in one's head during a seizure); see also krrrrrk.

<*[I] felt what I can only describe as a huge electric shock. I heard a noise like a ferocious short-circuit*—krrrrrrrrk—*and when I looked down at my hands, there was a big white flash.* —Chris Ryan, *The One That Got Away.*>

krrrrrrRRRRRRRRRRRRRRrrrrrrrrrr.

n. the cry of the Winding Cisticola bird.

<*Song of amphilectus [is] a dry creaking trill, likened to winding a clock; somewhat insect-like and quite prolonged, krrrrrrRRRRRRRRRRRRRRrrrrrrrrrr.* —Dale A. Zimmerman, *Birds of Kenya and Northern Tanzania.*>

krrshh.

n. the sound of a car crashing, as in the graphic novel *Uzumaki 2* by Junji Ito.

krrw.

n. the call of the Yellow-Rumped Tinkerbird, as described in *A Guide to the Birds of Western Africa* by Ron Demey; see also kkkkkk[3].

krsh.

n. a noncommittal mutter.

<*Krsh ... you hold on to 'em, hih?* —Leo Rosten, "Potch," anthologized in *A Passion for Books: A Book Lover's Treasury of Stories, Essays, Humor, Love and Lists on Collecting, Reading, Borrowing, Lending, Caring for, and Appreciating Books* by Harold Rabinowitz.>

Krsn.

n. in Hinduism, the supreme personality of God, described in the *Bhagavad Gita.*

<*Krsn, who is known as Govinda, is the supreme controller. He has an eternal, blissful, spiritual*

body. He is the origin of all. He has no other origin, for He is the prime cause of all causes. —Srila Jiva Goswami, *Sri Krsna-Sandarbha.*>

ks.

n. the sound of the letter x (Project HappyChild).

kshh.

n. the raspy "introductory note" of the Brewer's Blackbird, as described in *A Birder's Guide to Minnesota, 4th edition* by Kim Eckert.

kshh-kshh-kshh-kshh.

n. the hissing of a phonograph needle on a player with a broken automatic return, as in the novel *Suspicion of Madness* by Barbara Parker.

kshhh.

n. the sound of bicycle tires on wet pavement.

<*Rain fell while I was inside, and my tires go kshhh on the street.* —Lynn Breedlove, *Godspeed: A Novel.*>

kshhhhhhhhhhhhhhhhhhhh.

n. an electronic guitar chord turned to pure noise by too much volume, as described by Joe Thrasher, Guitarists.net.

ksn.

n. a seeker or explorer in the novel *The FarCall* by RedTurtle.

ksr.

n. a goblin's pet monster, with powerful muscles, gray and brown mottled fur, and a bushy tail as long as its body.

<*Rezrex would kill him—maybe quickly by pushing him off the cliff, maybe slowly in the ksr pit.* —T. H. Lain, *The Savage Caves.*>

kssh kssh ksshhh.

n. the beating of owls' wings.

<*From overhead came a frenzied flutter, followed by a harsh kssh! kssh! ksshhh! The patrolman glanced up and saw, framed against the starlit sky, two winged silhouettes—the baby owl's parents, anxiously circling their frightened fledgling.* —Carl Hiaasen, *Hoot.*>

kssh ksssh.

n. the patter of deer running through the woods.

<*They heard me and kssh ksssh and away they went.* —Chris Haynie, quoted in *Revolution on Canvas: Poetry From the Indie Music Scene* by Rich Balling.>

ksshshsshshss.

n. the sound of static from a lost communications signal, as in the graphic novella *Hearts and Minds* by Scott McCloud.

kssrrrrr.

n. the "harsh grating" call of the Black-Headed Gonolek, "sounding like violent tearing of cloth," as described in *Birds of Kenya and Northern Tanzania* by Dale A. Zimmerman.

ksss.

n. a lizard's hissing exclamation.

<*Ksss! Howja feel now?* —Brian Jacques, *Salamandastron.*>

ksss ksss.

1. *n.* a sound to lure mysterious creatures hiding in one's garden.

<*When I leave the house first thing in the morning ... I always stop in the garden for a moment and say out loud: "Ksss, Ksss." And at once a most peculiar phenomenon takes place. A kind of wheezing cough can be heard from the dry leaves; a croaking and rustling, spitting sound. Two fiery eyes light up about a foot from the ground and then something black with a bald swelling on its neck comes hurtling out of the bushes at me, snapping madly at my trouser-creases. What species of animal it belongs to I haven't yet succeeded in founding out.* —Gustav Meyrink, *The Opal.*>

2. *n.* the "sharp, hissing" call of the Red-billed Oxpecker, as described in *Starlings and Mynas* by Chris Feare; the "low hoarse" call of the Isabelline (Red-tailed) Shrike, as described in *Shrikes and Bush-Shrikes* by Tony Harris.

ksss—kss ks ks ks—kss.

n. the "scolding" call of the Magnificent Bird of Paradise, as described in *Birds of New Guinea* by Bruce M. Beehler.

ksss-ksss.

n. the crack of a bullwhip, as described in *Cloud Atlas: A Novel* by David Mitchell; see also kssss[2], ksssSSSsss.

ksssh.

1. *n.* the raspy exhalation of Darth Vader from *Star Wars*, as transcribed in the comic strip "PvP" by Scott R. Kurtz.

2. *n.* the sound of an electronic weapon being activated.

<*There was a ksssh as Asti's force lash activated and she stood up, blindfolded.* —Steven Cavanagh, *Tales From the RPG of Star Wars.*>

3. *n.* the sound of an erupting fireball, as described in *Strike Eagle: Flying the F-15E in the Gulf War* by William Smallwood.

ksssh-ksssh.

n. the hissing of "trip flares."

<*The heart-stopping ksssh-ksssh noise they made when tripped seemed the perfect noise with which to begin a symphony of fire.* —David J. Morris, *Storm on the Horizon: Khafji—The Battle That Changed the Course of the Gulf War.*>

kssshhh.

(also ksshhh.) *n.* the buzz of all "races and creeds" dancing together in a Conga line while under the influence of the drug Ecstasy, as described by Shane McGowan (quoted in *The Dark Stuff: Selected Writings on Rock Music* by Nick Kent).

kssshhhh.

1. *n.* the sound of a slashing knife, as in the graphic novel *Falcon Twin* by Brenden Mecleary.

2. *n.* the sound of flesh ripped apart by a sword, as in the graphic novel *Falcon Twin* by Brenden Mecleary.

kssss.

1. *n.* the "weak and high-pitched" voice of the Little Red Lorikeet (Fairy Lorikeet), as described in *A Photographic Guide to the Birds of Indonesia* by Morten Strange.

2. *n.* the crack of a bullwhip; see also ksss-ksss, ksssSSSsss.

<*Another* kssss *an' the boy Kona was felled.* —David Mitchell, *Cloud Atlas: A Novel.*>

ksssshhhh.

n. television static, as in the comic strip "PvP" by Scott R. Kurtz.

kssssss.

n. the hiss of flesh burned by a hot spike, as in *Cloud Atlas: A Novel* by David Mitchell.

ksssSSSsss.

n. the crack of a bullwhip; see also ksss-ksss, kssss[2].

<*A* ksssSSSsss *tore a slopin' gash cross the chief's torso.* —David Mitchell, *Cloud Atlas: A Novel.*>

ktcht-ktcht-ktcht.

n. the harsh, repeated call of the Grey-Backed (Tibetan) Shrike at dusk, as described in *Shrikes and Bush-Shrikes* by Tony Harris.

kwrrr kwrrr.

n. the hoarse notes of the Yellow-Fronted Tinkerbird, as described in *A Guide to the Birds of Western Africa* by Ron Demey.

Kxpx.
n. the name of a Christian-themed punk-pop band.

kzrrrtt.
n. a buzzing malfunction of someone's robot double standing in line until the next *Star Wars* film opens, as in the comic strip "PvP" by Scott R. Kurtz; see also bzzrrtt, bzzzt[3], fttrrzzt.

kzttt.
n. the crackling and popping of a public address system, as described by Michael Bailey in "Story: Dreams" (jinxidoru.com).

kzz-fzzz.
n. a buzzing sound, as by the venomous flying "Nizzik" insects in the novel *Akiko and the Intergalactic Zoo* by Mark Crilley; see also fzz-nkk, pzzz.

kzzk.
n. a buzzing indication that a robot has undergone a "general application failure," as in the comic strip "PvP" by Scott R. Kurtz.

kzzkt.
n. a crackle of electricity, as in the graphic novel *Falcon Twin* by Brenden Mecleary; see also zzzkt.

kzzt.
n. the mechanical noise of an android or robot malfunctioning, as in *The Metallic Touch*; see vzzkt.

kzzzrt.
n. the buzz of a dying cell phone signal, as in the graphic novel *Bob the Hamster* by James Paige; see also bzzzk, crkzzzz, bzz bzz zzk zzk zk kzrp zzrz.

kzzzz-kzzzz-kzzzz.
n. the rasping call of the Yellow-Billed Shrike, as described in *Shrikes and Bush-Shrikes* by Tony Harris.

Lkz.

n. a prince of the 5th dimension, in the *Aquaman* comic books; with his brother Yz, one half of the purple genie Ylzkz.

lll.

n. the sound of the letter l, as described by kindergarten teacher Judith Ann Mustain; see also llll.

Llll.

n. a "Lob wedge" golf club, as discussed in John Renslow's *In the Loop: A Crash Course in the Golf Culture.*

llll.

n. the sound of the letter l, as discussed in MommieTalk.com; see also lll.

Lmmm.

n. a French town, as pronounced by someone with a "perfect accent."

<*I couldn't grasp the name of the town because Mr. Drexler's accent was so perfect it sounded like Lmmm. But David knew Lmmm well because he had visited the Drexlers there several times.* —Susan Isaacs, *Close Relations.*>

lnscp.

n. suggesting the word "landscape," the title of a visual poem by Mike Cannell.

lpk.

n. the title of a visual poem by Mike Cannell.

lrrrg rrrr grrrrv rrr shrrrrrrd.

n. a "barely decipherable moan" by the living dead news commentator Zombie Dave, as transcribed by Chris Bell (bell101.freeserve.co.uk).

lrrrrr.

n. a trilled birdsong.

<*"Ah." It came out as a forlorn trill on a falling note, like birdsong.* Lrrrrr. —Karen Traviss, *Crossing the Line.*>

Lsssh.

n. the name of a warrior bat in the novel *Wink-Eye Creek* by Doug Hiser.

<*The doe's back hooves struck Lsssh and tore off his entire right ear.* —Doug Hiser, *Wink-Eye Creek.*>

Ltn.

n. a primeval sea serpent who fought the god Baal; likely a linguistic variant of Leviathan.

<*In the Canaanite Baal and Anat poems from Ugarit in Syria, Anat and Baal both speak of having crushed Sea, destroyed Flood, bound the sea dragon (tnn), and crushed the sea serpent (ltn).* —Fuller Theological Seminary.>

mbl.

(also mmbl.) *n.* a mumbled sound of gossip, as in the graphic novels *Uzumaki 2* and *Uzumaki 3* by Junji Ito.

mf.

adj. mezzo forte (a musician's directive to perform a passage moderately loudly).

mf krz nt vmiss.

n. a presumably off-color line of dialogue mumbled by the character "Kenny" from the animated television series *South Park* (Matt Graham, "South Park: Angband comes to South Park").

mff.

1. *interj.* the grunt of a sore loser at checkers, as in *The Essential Calvin and Hobbes* by Bill Watterson; see also gnnk.

2. *n.* the mumble of someone whose mouth has been gagged; an emphatic agreement; a questioning sound; an accusation; an expression of astonishment; a muffled cry of outrage.

<*"Mmf, mmf!" mumbled Eldin, who couldn't get his jaws open wide enough to speak. "Damn right!" Hero emphatically agreed, "Mmf!" And less restricted in respect of facial movements, he went on to berate his burly friend: "Of all the stupid, brainless, wild-goosiest wild-goose chases you ever got me into, this—" "Mmf?" Eldin was astonished. "Mmf mmf* mmf!" *he in turn accused. "It was you heard the cries first," said Hero. "Mmf mmf* mmf *mmf!" Eldin answered, his astonishment turning to outrage.* —Brian Lumley, *Mad Moon of Dreams*.>

3. *n.* a muffled expression of pain and surprise.

<*"Holler for me if you*—mff!" *Kootie had stumbled on a high curb and fallen to his knees.* —Tim Powers, *Expiration Date*.>

mff ffr dmm.

n. mumbled expletives, as said from behind a gag, discussed in *You are the ER Doc! True-to-Life Cases for You to Treat* by Peter Meyer.

mff mmnt mmp mmmmm.

n. an incoherent utterance, as from someone whose mouth is sticky with peanut butter.

<*She's Peanut Butter Kaliegh. / Should you ask her why, / She'll tell you without hesitating, / Mff mmnt mmp mmmmm."* —A.J. Wagner, *A Pocket Full of Smirks*.>

mfff.

1. *interj.* help, as said with a mouth full of cookie.

<*There was a woman who left her kitchen and headed for the back porch, with a cup of cocoa in each hand and cookie in her mouth. Her sweater got caught on a splinter in the door frame. With both hands occupied, she was unable to extricate herself. With her mouth likewise occupied, she could not call for help. She stood there, saying "Mfff" as loudly as she could, hoping someone would come. Someone did, freeing her while asking why she hadn't either chewed or dropped the cookie. "Mfff," she replied.* —Marvin Grosswirth, *Match Wits With Mensa: The Complete Quiz Book.*>

2. *n.* a mumble to mask one's sentimentality.

<*The men [in the audience of a movie preview] are more sentimental in one way—that is, they will set there with tears streaming down their faces and will then come out and say, "Mfff." They won't admit it, because they are more cynical or shy or think it unmanly to show their sentiment.* —Walt Disney, *Quotable Walt Disney*.>

3. *n.* a quiet growl from a dog.

<*I heard the pug call a muffled "mfff."* —Pam Conrad, *Stonewords: A Ghost Story*.>

4. *n.* the sleepy mumble of someone with a hangover; see also bmmf.

<*"Mfff." He buried his face in the pillow and clutched for the warm, reassuring flesh that lay beside him in his dream.* —Whitney Lakin, *A Paintbrush in the Devil's Toolbox*.>

mfff-ffff.

n. movies, as mumbled by a boy nervous about asking a girl on a date.

<*"You ... uh ... wanna go to the mfff-ffff," I mumbled.* —Jackie French Koller, *Nothing to Fear*.>

mghn.

interj. in "Grunt, a dialect of English passed on from father to son," "mghn" is a noise to be distinguished from "whaa" (James Dale, *Rules For Wives*).

mgnk.

n. the sound of swallowing.

<*Mgnk, it slips down like syrup.* —Lawrence Norfolk, *Lemprière's Dictionary*.>

mhm.

1. *adj.* unpleasant, as in *Deadhouse Gates: Book Two of the Malazan Book of the Fallen* by Steven Erikson.

2. *adv.* yes.

<*"Gettin' t' you too now, eh?" "Mhm," Adam Harmon admitted.* —James Alexander Thom, *Follow the River*.>

3. *interj.* a noncommittal expression.

<*She made some kind of noise, mhm, and gazed at her empty bowl.* —Ursula K. Le Guin, *The Birthday of the World: And Other Stories.*>

<*The Chief is sucking his lips so hard that he's making creases in his cheeks. "Mhm," is all that comes out of him.* —Lothar Gunther Buchheim, *Das Boot: The Boat.*>

4. *interj.* a sound "women are much more prone to make [than men]" while listening, to "indicate they are following what is being said" (Aaron T. Beck, *Love Is Never Enough: How Couples Can Overcome Misunderstandings, Resolve Conflicts, and Solve Relationship Problems Through Cognitive Therapy.*>

5. *n.* a contemplative murmur.

<*"Mhm," Haber nodded judicially, pondering.* —Ursula K. Le Guin, *The Lathe of Heaven: A Novel.*>

<*"Mhm," she said musingly.* —Edna Ferber, *Giant.*>

6. *n.* an absent-minded acknowledgment.

<*"I drank coffee, with lots of hot milk in it, and ate Viennese tarts and—and things." "Things meaning salami and sweet pickles?" "Mhm." She looked dreamily past me.* —M.F.K. Fisher, *The Art of Eating.*>

mhm mhm.

adv. yes, as in *The Fifth Element: A Novel of Discworld* by Terry Pratchett.

Mhm-M.

interj. a "singsongy" emphatic expression: "This sure beats typing. Mhm-M!" (Walker Percy, *The Moviegoer*).

mhmm.

1. *adv.* yes.

<*Jacy's mom went on and on ... with no interruptions from Jacy except an occasional "Mhmm," and "Yes."* —J. Gail, *Thugs Are for Fun: A Novel.*>

2. *n.* a signal "to encourage others to continue speaking," as discussed in *An Introduction to Sociolinguistics* by Ronald Wardhaugh.

3. *n.* an expression of agreement: "Mhmm, yeah" (Peter Gibian, *Mass Culture and Everyday Life*).

<*"They're very nice?" "Mhmm. They're very, very nice."* —Stephen M. Burke, *Surrender.*>

4. *n.* an expression of disagreement.

<*Mhmm, no [my parents] were easy going, compared to some people's anyway.* —Sara Arber, *The Myth of Generational Conflict: The Family and State in Ageing Societies.*>

mhmmm.

1. *adv.* yes, as in *Welcome to My Planet: Where English is Sometimes Spoken* by Shannon Olson.

   <*"Is that you, Barbara?" Daddy calls from the living room. "Mhmmm."* —Glen Huser, *Touch of the Clown.*>

2. *n.* an incoherent expression.

   <*"Mhmmm." Seth tried to reply, but his mouth felt as if it were full of cattail fluff.* —Mary Casanova, *Moose Tracks.*>

mhmmnn.

n. a yawning agreement, as in the novel *The Brothers K* by David James Duncan.

mhrn.

n. a feline murmur produced with a closed mouth.

<*Cats make their mhrn's serve many purposes. They can greet a friend, call a kitten either coaxingly or commandingly, ask a favor, and (by changing the final n to an ng and letting the intonation drop) say "thank you."* —Muriel Beadle, *The Cat.*>

mhrng.

n. a feline murmur of thanks; see mhrn.

MkzdK.

n. the psychedelic artwork of painter Stephen Miller.

<*My guess is that MkzdK is one of the more popular individual, and individualistic creations on the Net.* —Stephen Williamson, "The Magician of MkzdK: An Interview With Stephen Miller.">

mlg.

n. a primeval sound "upon which the very landscape was founded," as in Stan McDaniel's novel *The Letterseeker.*

<*"MLG," said the stone softly. ... Then it came again. "MLG, MLG," a series of distant gurgles.* —Stan McDaniel, *The Letterseeker.*>

mm.

1. *adv.* an affirmative answer.

   <*Did you? Hynes asked. Mm, Mr Bloom said.* —James Joyce, *Ulysses.*>

   <*"You seem to have trouble concentrating lately." "Mm."* —Steven Sherrill, *The Minotaur Takes a Cigarette Break: A Novel.*>

2. *n.* a hum to fill a pause while thinking; see also mm-mm[2].

<*If you're in any doubt as to whether or not he's made a joke, look at me. I'll... mm, tap my forefinger.* —Neil Gaiman, *Neverwhere.*>

3. *n.* a sad, tearful murmur, as in the comic book *The Wings of Cranes and Eagles* by Kaichi Satake.ul

4. *n.* an exclamation of ironic enthusiasm.

<*[She] pulled as hard as she could... and moved only a fraction of an inch.* Mm. What a jock I am. —Shari Macdonald, *A Match Made in Heaven.*>

mm nff bvn gth.

n. a mumbled line of dialogue (presumably meaning "I'm not a foul minion of evil") by the character "Kenny" from the animated television series *South Park* (Matt Graham, "South Park: Angband comes to South Park").

mm-hmm.

n. an intimate murmur of deep understanding.

<*I talked for a while, poured out all my sorrows and this quiet philosophical stream of consciousness, and she listened attentively and every so often at just the right moment said, "Mm-hmm." It made me feel all choked up with wonder and gratitude for the intimacy and tenderness of our relationship.* —Anne Lamott, *Operating Instructions: A Journal of My Son's First Year.*>

mm-hmph.

n. an acknowledgment, as in the novel *West of Then: A Mother, A Daughter, and a Journey Past Paradise* by Tara Bray Smith.

mm-mff.

n. a mumbled acknowledgment of understanding, as by someone learning to write by holding a pencil in her mouth.

<*"Mm-mff," I mumbled, meaning I understood.* —Billy Graham, *Joni.*>

mm-mm.

1. *n.* a double hum indicating that something tastes delicious.

<*Mm-mm. These are fine fries.* —Neil Gaiman, *American Gods.*>

2. *n.* a double hum to fill a pause while thinking; see also mm[2].

<*"Hang on a sec," he said. "Back up. Mm-mm: ordeal. Someone's got an ordeal waiting for them."* —Neil Gaiman, *Neverwhere.*>

mmf.

n. the chewing sound of a "white, orange-spotted wildcat" ravenously scarfing down a pawful of cookies (Voy.com).

mmf-mmf.

n. the sound of someone's muffled voice from behind a large piece of fruit.

<*He barely hesitated on the third picture, a repro of the Magritte of a man with an apple obscuring his face. "He's trying to talk but the fruit muffles him. All that comes out are these* 'mmf-mmf' *sounds."* —Pat Cadigan, *Mindplayers.*>

mmffh.

n. an incoherent mumble, as when one's face has been taken over by nano-bots, in the comic strip "Superosity" by Chris Crosby.

mmgh.

n. a slurping sound from a full mouth; a muffled sound made during sex.

<*"Al," I said. "Mmgh?" "C'mere," I said, tugging slightly at his armpits.* —John Fox, *The Boys on the Rock.*>

mmh.

1. *interj.* a "dull and ugly sound" made by someone who "could not speak, did not want to, did not want to try" (Meredith Ann Pierce, *The Pearl of the Soul of the World*); see also ngh.

2. *n.* a wolf's whimper of reluctance, as in the comic story "The Jury" by Wendy Pini.

3. *n.* an affirmative answer.

<*"You just can't hold your liquor," Trowa replied, pressing a brief kiss to his hair. "Mmh," Quatre whimpered agreement, trying to burrow his aching head into shelter.* —Talya FireDancer, "To Go That Far.">

mmhmm mmmhmm.

(also mmmhmm.) *adv.* yes.

<*B: Did you ever see a snail eating? P: Sure. B: Using its mouth? P: Mmhmm, mmmhmm. You could actually see it with the hand lens.* —Walter G. Secada, *New Directions for Equity in Mathematics Education.*>

mmm.

1. *interj.* a hum of appreciation.

<*"Mmm!" said Little Bear appreciatively.* —Lynne Reid Banks, *The Indian in the Cupboard.*>

2. *interj.* a hum of mock seriousness.

<*Taylor brought his hand to his chin. "Mmm." His face assumed a serious expression. "We might have to eliminate the Corian countertops and the Sub-Zero refrigerator," he said, and they both laughed.* —Nicholas Sparks, *The Rescue.*>

3. *interj.* a murmur of fatigue.

<*"Mmm. Getting on toward my bedtime," Avis's voice murmured behind me.* —Neta Jackson, *The Yada Yada Prayer Group.*>

4. *interj.* a murmured tone of skepticism.

<*"Mmm..." In Rachel's conversations a murmured "mmm" or drily drawn-out "I* know..." *could carry a lot of surprising skepticism.* —Alan Hollinghurst, *The Line of Beauty.*>

5. *interj.* a questioning sound.

<*"Pa, I want to ask you something," I said, hope rising in me like sap in one of our maples, though I tried not to let it. "Mmm?" He raised an eyebrow and kept on eating.* —Jennifer Donnelly, *A Northern Light.*>

6. *interj.* a sensuous, enticing moan.

<*"It's still dark out." "Mmm." She moaned sensuously. "Then* definitely *come over and play."* —Dan Brown, *Digital Fortress: A Thriller.*>

7. *interj.* a sound of anticipation.

<*Mmm, I'll look forward to that.* —Paul Stewart, *Midnight Over Sanctaphranx.*>

8. *interj.* a sound of intense scrutiny.

<*"Mmm," I say, studying the letterhead intently.* —Sophie Kinsella, *Confessions of a Shopaholic.*>

9. *interj.* an expression of sympathy or empathy.

<*What a shame. Mmm. I know how it feels to lose your vocation.* —Doug Marlette, *The Bridge.*>

<*Even as I murmur mmm's of sympathy, I am rifling through my mental Rolodex searching for someone who can take the children just for today.* —Allison Pearson, *I Don't Know How She Does It: The Life of Kate Reddy, Working Mother.*>

10. *n.* a hummed expression that means "good night," as in *The Minotaur Takes a Cigarette Break: A Novel* by Steven Sherrill.

11. *n.* a murmured sound with multiple meanings.

<*Her permutating mmm's served her in many ways, assuming a host of meanings. This one was drawled out, playful and yet effective, and he felt it working on him, uncomfortably, while in addition it made him jealous, the sly implications of her softly laughing* mmm. —Rebecca Goldstein, *Properties of Light.*>

12. *n.* a placeholder sound made to avoid an uncomfortable gap in conversation.

<*"Mmm." When he didn't say anything, the silence grew awkward.* —Karen Rose, *Have You Seen Her?*>

<*We filled the space between us with "mmms."* —Julie Anne Peters, *Keeping You a Secret.*>

13. *n.* a sound meaning "I don't know"; see also mmmm nnnn.

<*"They tell me you like mashed potatoes. ... But that you won't eat potato chips. Why is that, Jeffrey?" "Mmm."* —Barbara D'Amato, *Death of a Thousand Cuts.*>

14. *n.* a sound of agreement.

<*Her pals concurred with her assessment, nodding and mmm-ing.* —Rex Pickett, *Sideways: A Novel.*>

15. *n.* an affirmative answer.

<*"Everyone all right? Tommy all right?" "Mmm." Joe nodded, then closed his eyes again.* —Michael Chabon, *The Amazing Adventures of Kavalier & Clay.*>

16. *n.* an artfully ambiguous response.

<*It is only a butler of experience who can manage three M's together, without any interjacent vowels.* —Lewis Carroll, *Sayings of Lewis Carroll.*>

17. *n.* pleasure.

<*I made some mmm's of pleasure and they laughed again, free to love the coffee they had both been craving.* —Andrew Sean Greer, *The Confessions of Max Tivoli.*>

18. *n.* the blissful feeling of a cigarette smoker who has satisfied the craving for a puff.

<*[N]ow he could go on drawing in smoke until his lips were scorched. Mmm. The smoke crept and flowed through his whole hungry body, making his head and feet respond to it.* —Alexander Solzhenitsyn, *One Day in the Life of Ivan Denisovich.*>

19. *n.* the sound of the letter m, as described by Amanda Sahdi (quoted in "The Sound of Joy: Cochlear Implants Introduce Deaf Babies to the World of Hearing" by Jordan Lite, *New York Daily News*); see also mmmm[6].

mmm mmm.

n. an unintelligible statement, as from a mouth covered by a hand.

<*"Mmm, mmm" Trina said urgently into my palm. But I had her in a grip of iron.* —Meg Cabot, *Teen Idol.*>

mmm mmm mmm.

n. an expression of disbelief.

<*Mmm mmm mmm, scientists caught using human corpses as crash-test dummies.* —Fark. com.>

Mmm Mmm Mmm Mmm.

n. the title of a song by the band The Crash Test Dummies.

mmm mmm mmm mmm mmm.

interj. a teasing sound.

<*“Mmm mmm mmm mmm mmm,” Tarshia teased when they were inside. “You see the way that guy was looking at you?”* —Wally Lamb, *Couldn’t Keep It to Myself: Testimonies from Our Imprisoned Sisters.*>

mmm-hm.

n. a sound meaning “I understand,” as in *The Wounded Healer* by Henri Nouwen and *The Silicon Man* by Charles Platt.

mmm-hmm.

n. an enthusiastically affirmative answer.

<*Mmm-hmmm! I love a man in drag!* —Clumsygrrrl.>

mmm-hmph.

n. an acknowledgment, as in the novel *Duke of Sin* by Adele Ashworth.

mmm-mmm.

interj. a sound indicating that something smells or tastes delicious.

<*“What’s that smell? Mmm-mmm, I smell something baking.”* —Janet Evanovich, *Four to Score.*>

mmm-mmm-mmm.

interj. a laugh of agreement.

<*“Mmm-mmm-mmm,” Deacon Winslow said, laughing. “Paying the Lord with a credit card. Now ain’t that a notion.”* —Kimberla Lawson Roby, *Too Much of a Good Thing.*>

mmm-mmmph.

n. a distracted, non-committal response to a question.

<*“What’s Syria like, anyway?” “Mmm-mmmph.” “Happenin’ place, huh?”* —Stephen Coonts, *Stephen Coonts’ Deep Black Biowar.*>

mmmf.

n. the sound of a sudden, forceful kiss, as in the comic book *Gen13 Bootleg #18* by Kevin Altieri & Mark Farmer.

mmmm.

1. *n.* a moan of pain.

<*Ruthie tried to speak. “Mmmm.” She couldn’t open her mouth. Pain shot through her head.* —Bev Marshall, *Right as Rain: A Novel.*>

2. *n.* a murmur in one’s sleep.

<*She sleeps. Murmuring a whole series of Mmmms.* —Carol Emshwiller, “Creature,” *Nebula Awards Showcase 2004.*>

3. *n.* a purring affirmation.

<*“Mmmm,” purrs the male of the species.* —William Gibson, *Pattern Recognition.*>

<*“Did you have enough chili, M?” “Mmmm.”* —Steven Sherrill, *The Minotaur Takes a Cigarette Break: A Novel.*>

4. *n.* a sound recommended to aid meditation, as discussed in *Lymphedema: A Breast Cancer Patient’s Guide to Prevention and Healing* by Jeannie Burt; see also nnnn.

5. *n.* the sound of a trolley, as described in “More Than Words” by the New Zealand Ministry of Education.

6. *n.* the sound of the letter m; see also mmm[19].

<*How about a hint to help you find mmmm?* —Peggy Kaye, *Games for Learning: Ten Minutes a Day to Help Your Child Do Well in School, From Kindergarten to Third Grade.*>

<*To teach the letter* m *and it’s sound,* “mmmm,” *children are asked to describe their favorite meal and then rub their tummies as they say* m, m, m, m, m, meal. —Sally Shaywitz, *Overcoming Dyslexia: A New and Complete Science-Based Program for Reading Problems at Any Level.*>

mmmm mhmm.

n. “quiet assent,” as discussed in *Teaching Students to Write* by Beth Neman.

mmmm mmm mmmmm.

(also mmmm, mmmmm, mmmm mmm, mmmmm mmmm mm mmmmmmmm.) *n.* the quiet humming of a gagged computer terminal, as in *Life, The Universe, And Everything* by Douglas Adams.

mmmm nnnn.

n. a sound meaning “I don’t know”; see also mmm[13].

<*“Do [potato chips] frighten you, Jeffrey? Is it because when you eat them you have to break them?” “Mmmm. Nnnnn.”* —Barbara D’Amato, *Death of a Thousand Cuts.*>

mmmm-hmmm.

interj. a “subvocal interjection” which indicates a “therapist’s interest in whatever the client is describing,” as discussed in *Planned Short-Term Treatment, Second Edition*, by Richard Wells.

mmmm-mmm.

n. a wolf’s playful whimper, as discussed in *Wolves: Complete Cross-Curricular Theme Unit That Teaches About These Totally Cool Canines* by Kathleen W. Kranking.

mmmmm.

1. *adj.* good.

   <*Mmmmm. Means* good, *in any language.* —Roy Bount Jr., *Be Sweet: A Conditional Love Story.*>

2. *n.* a contemplative sound.

   <*'Mmmmm.' Rowe's eyes bounced. 'I like it.'* —Brooks Hansen, *Perlman's Ordeal.*>

3. *n.* a gleeful giggle, as in the novel *Mossflower* by Brian Jacques; see also hmmmm[5].

4. *n.* a passionate murmur, as if one is "having a seizure" during kissing in *The Year of Ice: A Novel* by Brian Malloy; see also hmmmph[1].

5. *n.* a sound which a "great conversationalist" makes while listening to keep people talking, as discussed in *Think Like Your Customer: A Winning Strategy to Maximize Sales by Understanding and Influencing How and Why Your Customers Buy* by Bill Stinnett; see also hmmmm[10], hmm[3].

6. *n.* an emotional sigh, as discussed in *Improv for Storytellers* by Keith Johnstone.

7. *n.* an expression of feeling vulnerable upon finding oneself stranded in a strange place at night, as in the song "Cross Road Blues" by Robert Johnson, as transcribed in *Trouble in Mind* by Leon F. Litwack.

mmmmm-hnnn.

n. an affirmative answer.

<*"Mom, you in there? You okay?" "Mmmmm-hnnn."* —Bett Williams, *Girl Walking Backwards.*>

mmmmmm.

interj. an expression that something is pleasing to the senses.

<*"Mmmmmm," I said, my mouth filled with her left breast.* —Luke Rhinehart, *The Dice Man.*>

mmmmmm nnnn.

adv. no, as in the story "Creature" by Carol Emshwiller (*Nebula Awards Showcase 2004*); see also mmnnnn.

mmmmmmgh.

n. an indecipherable mumbling.

<*[A] move which the National Head Trauma Board is calling "grmmph Arrrrgh mmmmmmgh."* —"Production Music and Sound Design," VideoHelper.com.>

mmmmmmm.

n. a distracting hum made by an irreverent child during a dinner table prayer, as in *God's Whisper in a Mother's Chaos: Bringing Peace Home* by Keri Wyatt Kent.

Mmmmmmmmmmmmm.

n. the murmuring of a crowd.

<*A low concerted sound rose from the congregation: "Mmmmmmmmmmmmm!"* —William Faulkner, *The Sound and the Fury*.>

mmmmmmmmmmmmmm.

1. *n.* a dreamy hum, as when someone reminisces about an old lover in *The Autobiography of Vivian* by Sherrie Krantz.

2. *n.* the title of a visual poem by Mike Cannell.

mmmmmmph.

n. the sound of someone clearing his throat (GiggleBounce.com).

mmmmmngh.

n. the "wincing" sound of "having hit one's head on something hard" (Timothy Albee, *Kaze, Ghost Warrior*); see also nnnngh.

mmmmpfgh.

n. a gagging sound.

<*[I] typed the letters that all those people in the dunes would love to pronounce, that lie beneath the surface of all cruising: Mmmmpfgh.* —Andrew Hollerman, *Flesh and the Word*.>

mmmmph.

1. *interj.* a sleepy, grumpy moan, as in the novel *The Venetian Policeman* by M.E. Rabb.

2. *interj.* an expression of terror.

<*"Mph," George said, shaking his head wildly. "Mmmmmnh! Mmmmph!"* —Stephen King, *The Stand*.>

3. *n.* a contented sigh.

<*Murphy finds a warm spot by the fire, paces off a small circle, curls up and drops his head on his paws with a loud mmmmph.* —Kathleen Cook-Waldron, *Five Stars For Emily*.>

4. *n.* a sound mumbled through a gag or a mouth taped shut.

<*"Mmmmph!" cried Shannon. "Are you okay?" [George] whispered, grabbing Shannon's gag and pulling it down.* —Chris Archer, *Eye of Eternity*.>

<*"Mmmmph," I said. It was the best I could do through the duct tape.* —Howard Roughan, *The Promise of a Lie*.>

5. *n.* a sound of annoyance; a complaint.

<*"You're awake, I see." Anna made a complaining mmmmph through her shut mouth and shut her eyes.* —Robert Ludlum, *The Sigma Protocol*.>

6. *n.* a sound of approval; a signification that one is impressed.

<*"Mmmmph, I'm impressed" Carla signified.* —Brenda Wilkinson, "My Sweet Sixteenth," *Join In: Multiethnic Short Stories*.>

7. *n.* a swallowing sound.

<*Ashley grabbed the grape and stuffed it into Mary-Kate's mouth. ... "MMMMPH!" Mary-Kate gulped.* —Mary-Kate and Ashley Olsen, *The Sleepover Secret.*>

8. *n.* a vocalized pause, as when one is thinking of the right word to use.

<*Your slang changes more rapid, and your culture style has encourage more, mmmmph, more shattering?* —Arthur Phillips, *Prague: A Novel.*>

9. *n.* an expression of enjoyment or sensual delight.

<*She reached her hand down to stroke his leg. "Mmmmph."* —Dale Brown, *Dale Brown's Dreamland: Piranha.*>

mmmmph, mmmph mph mmmmmmmph.
(also MmmmmMmmmmph.) *n.* the muffled speech of a talking pillow, as in *Xanth 15: The Color of Her Panties* by Piers Anthony.

mmmmphhh.
(also mmmmmmphhh.) *n.* an expression by someone whose mouth is sealed by duct tape, as in the novel *Heart Seizure* by Bill Fitzhugh.

mmmn.
1. *n.* a murmur.

<*[M]mmn pet the love dog, Dickie, nnnm?* —William H. Gass, *Omensetter's Luck: A Novel.*>

2. *n.* the Swahili expression for "yum-yum," as discussed in *Hear! Here!* by Michele Slung.

mmmnnn.
adv. yes, as in the story "Creature" by Carol Emshwiller (*Nebula Awards Showcase 2004*).

mmmph.
1. *adv.* no.

<*"You were going to give it to her anyway." "Mmmph." It was a growl, not an affirmation. "I changed my mind when I saw her in your room with her blade."* —Maggie Shayne, *Eternity*.>

2. *n.* a grumpy mumble.

<*"Mmmph, what time is it?" groaned Avanelle.* —June Rae Wood, *Turtle on a Fence Post.*>

3. *n.* a grunt of exertion, as when hefting a heavy, lifeless body over one's shoulder in the comic strip "PvP" by Scott R. Kurtz; see also hnnng[2], nnnnggghh.

4. *n.* a muffled word, as spoken through a covered mouth.

<*"Mmmph mmmph, you mmmph!" she mmmphed, one eye above his hand filling with anger while the other eye retained its terror. He hoped she wasn't saying the unmaidlike thing he feared she was saying; it would be detrimental to her image.* —Piers Anthony, *Castle Roogna.*>

5. *n.* a sound of disgust, as when spitting out food.

<*"Mmmph!" you say, spitting the food out. "Tastes like rotten fish!"* —Josh McDowell, *Josh McDowell's One Year Book of Youth Devotions.*>

6. *n.* a strangled sound.

<*"I think she might be involved in his murder." "Mmmph." It was a strangled sound, as if she had had to swallow a lot and was ready to cough it back up.* —Julie Smith, *New Orleans Mourning.*>

7. *n.* a stretching yawn.

<*"Mmmph?" Emil mumbled with a yawn, blinking his eyes to get them focused.* —Quinn Logan, "First Time For Everything.">

8. *n.* an expression of sympathy.

<*Skip shook her head and said, "Mmmph," to show her sympathy.* —Julie Smith, *82 Desire.*>

9. *n.* the sound of a person speaking with his mouth full.

<*'How's the food, honey?' 'Mmmph.'* —Michael Salinger, *Lake Erie.*>

mmmphhm mmrph.

n. an incoherent phrase, as muttered by a seamstress holding several pins in her mouth.

<*"Mmmphhm mmrph," said the woman on her knees at the pedestal under Lana's feet.* —Nicole Paolini, *Swamp Gas.*>

mmmphm mmm nngh gnn.

n. a mumbled and presumably off-color line of dialogue by the character "Kenny" from the animated television series *South Park.*

<*KENNY: Mmmphm mmm nngh gnn. STAN: Kenny, that's sick!* —Matt Graham, "South Park: Angband comes to South Park.">

MMMrrrr.

n. the hum of an aircraft engine starting up, as described in *Animorphs #37: The Weakness* by K.A. Applegate.

mmnn.

n. a murmur upon waking from sleep, as in the graphic novel *Uzumaki 2* by Junji Ito.

mmnnnn.

adv. no, as in the story "Creature" by Carol Emshwiller (*Nebula Awards Showcase 2004*); see also mmmmmm nnnn.

mmph hmhm.

n. a sleepy mumble that one is on one's way.

<*I muttered something that started in my brain as "I'm coming," but came out of my mouth more like "Mmph hmhm."* —Marilyn Halvorson, *Blue Moon.*>

mmrmph.

1. *n.* a mumbled word, as when a squid's tentacle is wrapped around one's face in the comic strip "Penny Arcade" by Mike Krahulik and Jerry Holkins.

2. *n.* an ecstatic mumble that "transcend[s] language," as in the novel *Frisk* by Dennis Cooper.

3. *n.* an incoherent apology, as when spoken with a mouth full of food in the novel *The House on the Point: A Tribute to Franklin W. Dixon and The Hardy Boys* by Benjamin Hoff.

mmrph.

1. *n.* a murmur made while one's face is buried in the bosom of a woman dressed as Mrs. Santa Clause, in the comic strip "PvP" by Scott R. Kurtz.

2. *n.* an incomprehensible mumble from a cell phone, in the comic strip "PvP" by Scott R. Kurtz.

mmth.

n. the sound of taking a swig from a bottle.

<*Mmth, another swig.* —Lawrence Norfolk, *Lemprière's Dictionary.*>

mnc.

n. the sound of a giant snail munching on leaves, as in the graphic novel *Uzumaki 2* by Junji Ito; see also mnch[1].

mnch.

1. *n.* a munching sound, as when eating mushrooms in the graphic novels *Uzumaki 2* and *Uzumaki 3* by Junji Ito; see also mnc.

2. *v.* to chew at a fast rate, as described in "Chewing Theories" by Ettore Pasquini.

mnnh.

1. *adv.* no, as in the novel *Flowers from the Storm* by Laura Kinsale.

<*"You don't eat much for a big fella." "Mnnh."* —Steven Sherrill, *The Minotaur Takes a Cigarette Break: A Novel.*>

2. *interj.* an angry grunt, as in the novel *One For the Gods: A Novel* by Gordon Merrick.

3. *interj.* huh?

<*He answers questions, even when he's heard them, with "Mnnh?" followed by "Well, let's see now."* —Jardine Libaire, *Here Kitty Kitty: A Novel.*>

4. *n.* a hum indicating a new thought.

<*Mnnh—will you be a better lover after it is over?* —Anton Myrer, *The Last Convertible.*>

mnnng.

(also mnnngg.) *n.* a humming equivalent for the French phrase "je ne sais quoi," when "meanings are impossibly jumbled" and one's jaw feels tight (Dave Robison).

<*She was fumbling around in her bag for a packet of cigarettes. "How are you doing?" I asked, smiling. "Oh, okay—a bit mnnng. A bit, y'know—chchch—I don't know—y'know."* —Dave Robison, "An Extract From a Work in Progress.">

mnth.

n. month, as pronounced by someone delirious with a 104-degree fever in the novel *Hosts* by F. Paul Wilson.

mp.

adj. mezzo piano (a musician's directive to perform a passage moderately softly).

Mph.

n. a name for the creator deity in Dr. John Dee's "Enochian Pentagram."

mph.

1. *interj.* an expression of disbelief.

<*Mph! Dam' stove heap gone!* —Mark Twain, *Roughing It.*>

2. *interj.* an expression of terror.

<*"Mph," George said, shaking his head wildly.* —Stephen King, *The Stand.*>

mprrr'drrrp.

n. a cat's purr.

<*Him looking up at me and saying "mprrr'drrrp" when I say his name.* —MzNeco, MysticWicks.com.>

Mr.

n. a man's title: Mister.

mrmph.

1. *interj.* a questioning sound.

<*"Do you know what the first thing I'm going to do when we get home is, Rowdy?" "Mrmph..." "I'm going to have you kill that horrid dog Felix loved so much."* —Paul Di Filippo, *Fractal Paisleys.*>

2. *n.* a disoriented murmur, as by someone startled awake in *The Nirvana Blues: A Novel* by John Nichols.

<*"Mrmph." The indistinct gurgle might have meant anything: acknowledgment, rage, a simple snore. Damn, Jane thought. I need him awake, and he sounds hung over.* —Deborah Grabien, *The Weaver and the Factory Maid.*>

3. *n.* the purr of a fire-lizard-like "watch-wher" in the novel *Dragon's Kin* by Anne McCaffrey and Todd J. McCaffrey.

mrmr.

(also mrr.) *n.* a murmur of conversation, as in the graphic novel *Uzumaki 2* by Junji Ito.

Mrnng.

n. the title of a song by the jazz band MSK on the album *Minimal.*

mrnng.

n. morning, as muttered by someone with a toothbrush in his mouth; see also g'mrnng.

<*"Good morning," Peppy said over his shoulder, making coffee as Bill wandered into the kitchen. "Mrnng," Bill agreed around the toothbrush, scrubbing absent-mindedly.* —Anonymous, "Infinity's Descent.">

mrr.

1. *n.* a cat's purr.

<*Then the door to the bathroom swung open then, just a few inches, enough for the little brown cat to put her head around the door frame and 'Mrr?' up at him curiously.* —Neil Gaiman, *American Gods.*>

2. *n.* a grunt in the Wookie language of the *Star Wars* films, as transcribed in the comic strip "PvP" by Scott R. Kurtz; see also grnnnk, hrrrrr[1].

mrrg.

n. a groggy mumbling.

<*Shoving aside unfamiliar materials, she opened her eyes and was greeted by the wet, pink snout of an albino rat. 'Mrrg. Hey there, Loki.'* —Whitney Lakin, *A Paintbrush in the Devil's Toolbox.*>

mrrr.

1. *n.* a cat's meow.

<*[There] came a plaintive call from outside her door. ... "Mrrr?" "Who are you?" Damia called sleepily. A large orange and white cat marched into the room, rubbing himself against her leg.* —Anne McCaffrey, *Damia.*>

<*Then Moose would come and preen himself against her ankles and say, "Mrrr. ..."—the only sound in the otherwise silent shop—and Agatha would have to force herself out of a deep lassitude that seemed to pervade her more and more often as winter slogged along.* —LaVyrle Spencer, *The Gamble.*>

2. *n.* a muttered expression, as while in the throes of passion (Christopher Buckley, *Thank You For Smoking*).

3. *n.* an expression of agreement, as in the novel *The Mermaids Singing* by Val McDermid.

mrrrp.

n. a questioning sound.

<*In the background, Spot's short, querying* mrrrp? *came through.* —Doranna Durgin, *Tooth and Claw.*>

mrrrr.

1. *n.* a feline sound of happiness, as described in *The Best of Baloney on Wry* by Kathi Gardner.

2. *n.* a feline sound of uncertainty, as described in *Storm Rescue* by Laurie Halse Anderson.

3. *n.* a sound of protest from a frightened kitten, as described in *Animal Emergency #9: Pony in Trouble* by Emily Costello.

mrrrr-rrrrm-mmrrr.

n. the grumble of an unhappy feline, as described in *Canapes for the Kitties* by Marian Babson.

mrrrrr.

1. *n.* a positive feline sound.

<*"Mrrrrr! It feels nice!" mewed Cinderpaw as she raced up the stone slope.* —Erin Hunter, *Warriors #2: Fire and Ice.*>

2. *n.* the sound of an unfamiliar voice.

<*A male voice, unfamiliar to Sebastian, said "Mrrrrr." He caught the sound but not the words.* —Philip K. Dick, *Counter-Clock World.*>

mrrrrrlg.

n. a vocalization made while strenuously pushing against a wall or door, as in the comic "Bunny anb Rasputin #17" [sic] by H. J. Hornbeck.

Mrs.

n. a married woman's title.

Ms.

n. a woman's title, regardless of marital status; a feminist term of address.

mssgs.

n. messages, written in Roger Bacon's all-consonant secret code (devised in 1250), as discussed in *The Voynich Manuscript* by Gerry Kennedy.

Msss.

n. Miss, as in the novel *Doona* by Anne McCaffrey; see also Mssss.

<*I would have moments when I couldn't wait for the year to end, and a call from a student of "Msss. Spraaague," would make me cringe.* —Daniel Liston, *Teaching, Learning, and Loving: Reclaiming Passion in Educational Practice.*>

<*I suggest you have a similar word with our Msss Drummond.* —Irvine Welsh, *Filth.*>

Mssss.

n. Miss; see also Msss.

<*He tells me curtly that Mssss Drummond is no longer lead officer on the case.* —Irvine Welsh, *Filth.*>

mssst.

n. an audible shudder.

<*"Well,* mssst, *thank you, Cezer." She shuddered visibly. "The mere thought of being held as a 'guest' by that loathsome creature is enough to curdle milk."* —Alan Dean Foster, *Kingdoms of Light.*>

Mzzz.

n. Ms, used to "avoid the Ms./Mrs. quandry" (Susan Isaacs, *Long Time No See*); see also Mzzzz, Mzzzzz, Mzzzzzz.

<*He'd wanted to have a go at Mzzz Middleton from their first interview, but he was too careful for that.* —James Patterson, *Pop Goes the Weasel.*>

<*She shook her head. "Not Mzzz. I'm Dr. Taylor.* —Torey Hayden, *Just Another Kid.*>

Mzzzz.

n. Ms, presumably to stress a distinction from *Miss*; see also Mzzz, Mzzzzz, Mzzzzzz.

<*Call me Celeste. I loathe Mzzzz.* —Arthur Laurents, *My Good Name.*>

<*"It's easy for you to say that, isn't it, Mzzzz. Hot Shot City Lawyer.* —Nick Hornby, *High Fidelity.*>

<*Mzzzz. Arden says our kids have no right to be here.* —Judy Maclean, *Rosemary and Juliet.*>

Mzzzzz.

n. a possible pronunciation of *Ms*, as discussed in *Ex Libris: Confessions of a Common Reader* by Anne Fadiman; a hissing or snarling pronunciation of *Ms*; see also Mzzz, Mzzzz, Mzzzzzz.

<*"Now, Mzzzzz..." he drew the word out until it was repulsive, snakelike, "Mzzzzz. Arden suggests that we of the Divido Bible Church have no standing to speak here, because many of our children do not attend the public schools.* —Judy Maclean, *Rosemary and Juliet.*>

<*The way I uttered Mzzzzz, it was a snarl.* —Joyce Carol Oates, *Big Mouth & Ugly Girl.*>

Mzzzzzz.

n. a mocking pronunciation of Ms, as in the novel *The Fat Friend* by Julie Edelson; see also Mzzzzz, Mzzzz, Mzzz.

<*I thought we were supposed to call all the broads 'Mzzzzzz' these days.* —Robin Hathaway, *The Doctor Makes a Dollhouse Call.*>

<*She regarded me with amusement and shook her head. "Mzzzzzz McTighe. Are you always this formal,* Mister *Jacovich?"* —Les Roberts, *The Indian Sign.*>

Mzzzzzzz.

n. a drawn-out pronunciation of Ms.

<Ms. [Magazine] *sure caught on fast [in the early 1970s]. Today when the Breather called the [underground feminist periodical* off our backs] *office he moaned, 'Mzzzzzzz' into the phone.* —Amy Erdman Farrell, *Yours in Sisterhood: Ms. Magazine and the Promise of Popular Feminism.*>

N'N'n'.

n. the archetype of the whore, as taught by Rev. Ivan Stang in *The Book of the SubGenius: Being the Divine Wisdom, Guidance, and Prophecy of J. R. 'Bob' Dobbs, High Epopt of the Church of the SubGenius, Here Inscribed for the Salvation of Future Generations and in the Hope that Slack May Someday Reign on this Earth.*

n'vs.

n. caretakers in the novel *The FarCall* by RedTurtle.

N'Xlccx.

n. the ancient grandfather of the prophet of the Church of the SubGenius, J. R. "Bob" Dobbs, as mentioned in *The Book of the SubGenius: Being the Divine Wisdom, Guidance, and Prophecy of J. R. 'Bob' Dobbs, High Epopt of the Church of the SubGenius, Here Inscribed for the Salvation of Future Generations and in the Hope that Slack May Someday Reign on this Earth.*

n-n-n-n- N-n-n-n-n-n-n-nnnnnn.

n. a scream by someone with severe back pain.

<*"Shout, Shirley. As hard as you can. I want to hear how much your back hurts." "N-n-n-n- . . . N-n-n-n-n-n-nnnnnn . . ."* —Jose Carlos Somoza, *The Art of Murder.*>

n-n-n-n-n-n-n-n.

n. the rumble of thunder as it "rolls away into the distance" (Jared Lobdell, "The Last Holosong of Christopher Lightning," *Free Space*); see also pr'k, pr'k-nnnnnnnn.

nff.

n. a sigh of frustration, as when trying to secure a candle in a holder in the comic strip "PvP" by Scott R. Kurtz.

nfff.

1. *adj.* enough; see also 'nff.

   <*Colleges have to get more proactive — nfff said!* —Gnote3138, University of Alberta "Inclusion Archives.">

2. *adv.* yes; an affirmative answer spoken by someone who can't be bothered to respond civilly.

   <*"Has your lordship got everything he requires?" "Nfff," said Nobby.* —Terry Pratchett, *Feet of Clay.*>

Ng.

n. a Vietnamese name.

<*Ng himself, or at least Ng's avatar, is a small, very dapper Vietnamese man in his fifties.* — Neal Stephenson, *Snow Crash.*>

ng'h.

n. the practice of mental control over another in the novel *The FarCall* by RedTurtle.

ngggggh.

n. a grunt of physical exertion, as when tugging a heavy box in *Arthur and the Comet Crisis* by Marc Brown.

ngggh.

n. a grunt of physical exertion, as in *The Pope's Rhinoceros: A Novel* by Lawrence Norfolk; see also ngggggh.

nggghhhh.

adv. now, as spoken by someone whose mouth is sealed with fear over a massive snake "with yellow, swirling slits for eyes and huge fangs" (Robert Asprin, *Myth-Ion Improbable*).

nggh.

1. *n.* a garbled utterance, as said while kissing someone in the novel *Kiss My—Left Behind* by Earl Lee.

2. *n.* a groan of exasperation, as when one can't pull one's hand out from under a pile of office boxes in the comic strip "PvP" by Scott R. Kurtz.

3. *pro.* what, as spoken by someone being bothered.

<*[S]he went straight down the hall to Laurent's room and knocked. "Nggh?" he said.* —Tom Clancy, *Safe House.*>

ngh.

1. *adv.* in "Grunt, a dialect of English passed on from father to son ... 'Ngh' means 'No thanks, I don't care for any more pot roast'" (James Dale, *Rules For Wives*).

2. *interj.* a "dull and ugly sound" made by someone who "could not speak, did not want to, did not want to try" (Meredith Ann Pierce, *The Pearl of the Soul of the World*); see also mmh[1].

3. *interj.* a groan, as in the novel *The Novice* by Trudi Canavan.

4. *interj.* a grunt of "abdominal pain, like the kind caused by sodomy" in pornographic prose, as discussed in *The Florence King Reader* by Florence King; see NNNNNNNNGGGGGGGGGGHHHHHH.

5. *interj.* a noncommittal response.

<*"Crowley, it's me!" "Ngh." The voice was horribly noncommittal.* —Neil Gaiman and Terry Pratchett, *Good Omens*.>

6. *interj.* a retch brought on by the odor of a sewage river in *Jackie Disaster: A Novel* by Eric Dezenhall.

7. *interj.* a scream of surprise, as in the novel *Clamp School Paranormal Investigators* by Tomiyuki Matsumoyo.

8. *n.* a groan signifying an urgent need to urinate, as in the comic strip "PvP" by Scott R. Kurtz.

9. *n.* laughter, as in *Warrior Woman: The Exceptional Life Story of Nonhelema, Shawnee Indian Woman Chief* by Dark Rain and James Alexander Thom.

ngh chnc.

n. "no chance," as mumbled in answer to the question "would [you] ever want to leave high school with a year and a half left, to live the glamorous and lucrative life of a touring golf pro" spoken by someone "eating a turkey, cheese, bacon, Hershey's syrup and Ruffles BBQ potato chip sandwich at the time" (Jack Canfield, *Chicken Soup for the Golfer's Soul, The 2nd Round: 101 More Stories of Insight, Inspiration and Laughter on the Links*).

ngh hng hng hng hng hnng.

n. a piercing laugh.

<*The preferred women's laugh: an upper-palate, saliva-powered "Ngh! hng! hng! hng! hng! hnng!" that was capable of shattering glass.* —Jonathan Raban, *Passage to Juneau: A Sea and Its Meanings*.>

nghh.

n. a noncommittal response, as by a teenager being cross-examined by his parent about "listen[ing] to that moronic garbage" (music) in *Too Soon to Tell* by Calvin Trillin.

ngk.

n. an ironic grunt in the novel *Good Omens* by Neil Gaiman and Terry Pratchett.

ngn.

n. a declaration of the divine "mercy and vengeance everlasting," as taught by Rev. Ivan Stang in *The Book of the SubGenius: Being the Divine Wisdom, Guidance, and Prophecy of J. R. 'Bob' Dobbs, High Epopt of the Church of the SubGenius, Here Inscribed for the Salvation of Future Generations and in the Hope that Slack May Someday Reign on this Earth.*

ngngngng.

n. a "continuous melodic sound," the exploration of which provides "valuable pre-reading experiences" (Anne Bloomfield, <i>Teaching Integrated Arts in the Primary School: Dance, Drama, Music and the Visual Arts

NHGH.

(also NhGh.) *n.* a mischievous and terrifying demon, whose duty it is "to mete out wars and rumors of wars, and dreams of wars, and fears of wars, and a peace which is like unto Hell," as taught by the Church of the SubGenius in *Revelation X* and *The Book of the SubGenius: Being the Divine Wisdom, Guidance, and Prophecy of J. R. 'Bob' Dobbs, High Epopt of the Church of the SubGenius, Here Inscribed for the Salvation of Future Generations and in the Hope that Slack May Someday Reign on this Earth.*

<*As soon as I collected my brain cells and began to speak, I instantly felt the presence of NhGh. It felt as though it mounted itself on the back of my neck and began to have it's way with my right ear, then my left ear. It was very distracting and I found it difficult to rant about anyting [sic]. I was cold and people weren't listening or giving me any money. But I went on.* —Reverend Sinphaltimus Exmortus, "First Ever Digital Church of Mind Slack.">

nhhh.

n. a "peculiar noise of indecision" (Christine Vachon, *Shooting to Kill: How an Independent Producer Blasts Through the Barriers to Make Movies That Matter*); see also nnnn[9].

nhhkhhhh hhh.

n. the sound of a laugh, as transcribed in *Interaction and Grammar* by Elinor Ochs.

nhv''gv.

n. the final stand in the time of the perdition as taught by Rev. Ivan Stang in *The Book of the SubGenius: Being the Divine Wisdom, Guidance, and Prophecy of J. R. 'Bob' Dobbs, High Epopt of the Church of the SubGenius, Here Inscribed for the Salvation of Future Generations and in the Hope that Slack May Someday Reign on this Earth.*

Nkst.

n. a populated place in Nigeria.

nn.

1. *interj.* a response to the question "You tolkatiff scowegian?" in *Finnegans Wake* by James Joyce.

2. *n.* a mumble of a dying person, as in *The Sandman: Preludes and Nocturnes* by Neil Gaiman.

3. *n.* a negative vocalization while one mentally berates someone "until the cows come home" (Inman Majors, *Wonderdog*).

4. *n.* a sound that indicates one's head is spinning, as noted by Lawrence Norfolk in the novel *Lemprière's Dictionary*.

5. *n.* the moan of a dead body reanimated by a wizard; see also nnnn[19].

<*The eyes trembled and slackly opened. "Nn," said the corpse.* —Orson Scott Card, *Hart's Hope.*>

nn nn nn.

interj. the stuttering of someone having a seizure brought on by a camera flash, as in the comic "The Abduction Announcement" by Jason Little.

nn-nnng.

interj. a furious utterance.

<*"Nn-nnng!" he says, and stomps the two steps to the door.* —Dave King, *The Ha-Ha: A Novel.*>

nngggggh.

interj. a grunt of annoyance, as transcribed in Respawned.co.uk.

nngggh.

interj. a groan indicating that one is suffering from a headache after having eaten too much chocolate, as in the comic strip "PvP" by Scott R. Kurtz.

nnggh.

1. *interj.* a grunt of agreement, a moan of annoyance, a questioning utterance, a rude response, an expression of agreement, a dismissive retort, as in "Gimme Some Skin" by Andrew E. Wheeler.

2. *interj.* a moan of protest, as by someone with a traumatized, bloody nose in the novel *The Long Dark Tea-Time of the Soul* by Douglas Adams.

3. *n.* a grunt of frustration over seasonal allergies.

<*Nnggh. I want to unscrew my head and hold it under a running faucet, just to rinse out everything. Tired of the congestion, stuffiness, and general aching from my damn allergies.* —Pam Riley, StrangePath.net.>

4. *n.* a moan of "indescribable" passion, as in the novel *Accidental Love* by B.L. Miller; see also gnff.

5. *n.* a moan of excitement.

<*Nnggh, car ready [to take us to the campaign reception]?* —Bob Dole, quoted in *What It Takes: The Way to the White House* by Richard Ben Cramer.>

nngghh.

1. *interj.* a grunt indicating "a minor irritation," as transcribed in Respawned.co.uk.

2. *n.* a grunt of painful exertion, as during abdominal exercises in the comic strip "PvP" by Scott R. Kurtz.

3. *n.* a noncommittal grunt, as in the poem "two mentally handicapped ladies get on bus" by James Hörner.

4. *n.* the moan of a mummy, as in the comic "Rockwood 2000" by Brian Lundmark.

5. *v.* confusing.

<*[“Sweet Child O’ Mine” by Guns N’ Roses is] such a beautiful song but it’s still nngghh.* —MusicianForums.com.>

nngh.

1. *adv.* yes.

<*“You’re not obsessed with a nasty bloke, you’re obsessed with a really decent* catch.*” “Nngh,” agreed Jo.* —Melissa Nathan, *The Nanny.*>

2. *interj.* an expression of agreement, as in the novel *The Nanny* by Melissa Nathan.

3. *n.* a dazed groan from someone just hit on the head with a frying pan, as in the comic strip “PvP” by Scott R. Kurtz.

4. *n.* a grunt made during an intense struggle, as in the comic book *Danger Girl #2* by J. Scott Campbell and Alex Garner.

5. *n.* a sound one makes upon regaining consciousness, as in the comic book *Gen13 #64* by Kaare Andrews and Jason Martin.

6. *n.* a tiger’s grunt, as in the comic strip *American Born Chinese* by Gene Luen Yang.

7. *n.* the moan of someone having been bitten by the Wolfman, as transcribed in the comic strip “PvP” by Scott R. Kurtz; see also hrrrk, snrrrl.

8. *pro.* what.

<*[S]he went straight down the hall to Laurent’s room and knocked. “Nggh?” he said.* —Tom Clancy, *Safe House.*>

nngh mmph mmm.

n. a mumbled and presumably off-color line of dialogue by the character “Kenny” from the animated television series *South Park* (Matt Graham, “South Park: Angband comes to South Park”).

nnghh.

n. the dying grunt of someone impaled by a sword, as in the graphic novel *Falcon Twin* by Brenden Mecleary.

nnh.

1. *n.* a muttering from a wizard overloaded with magical electricity.

<*Every single hair stood out from his head, giving off little sparks. Even his skin gave the impression that it was trying to get away from him. His eyes appeared to be spinning horizontally; when he opened his mouth, peppermint sparks flashed from his teeth. ... “I say,” said Nijel, “are you all right?” “Nnh,” said Rincewind, and the syllable turned into a large doughnut.* —Terry Pratchett, *Sourcery.*>

2. *n.* a semi-conscious muttering meaning “where am I?” as in the graphic novel *Falcon Twin* by Brenden Mecleary.

Nnn.

n. the name of a character with glowing yellow eyes in the novel *The Martian Chronicles* by Ray Bradbury.

nnn.

1. *adj.* good, as said sleepily; see nnnn[1].

2. *adv.* now, as spoken during a disjointed telephone conversation in the play *Oleanna* by David Mamet.

3. *interj.* a deep hum of intense pleasure.

   <*Oh! Nnnnnnnn! Nnn! Nnn! Nnn! Nnn! Nnn! Nnn!* —Nicholson Baker, *Vox.*>

4. *interj.* a response to the question "You spigotty anglease?" in *Finnegans Wake* by James Joyce.

5. *n.* a growled, nonsensical entreaty, as in *Sheepshagger: A Novel* by Niall Griffiths.

6. *n.* a negative expression, "toning down the negation" of *nnnnnn*, "stressing ... abject neutrality" (Inman Majors, *Wonderdog*).

7. *n.* the sound of the letter n, as described by Valerie Bendt in *Reading Made Easy: A Guide to Teach Your Child to Read*; see also nnnn[20], NNNN[2], nnnnn[14], nnnnnn[6], nnnnnnn[8].

nnnf.

adv. no; a negative answer spoken by someone who can't be bothered to respond civilly.

<*"If we can be of any help whatsoever—" "Nnnf." "Any help at all—?" "Nnnf."* —Terry Pratchett, *Feet of Clay.*>

nnng.

1. *interj.* a questioning utterance, as in *The Autograph Man: A Novel* by Zadie Smith.

2. *n.* a dying moan, as in the novel *From Sea to Shining Sea* by James Alexander Thom.

3. *n.* a nervous sound caused by fear of public speaking.

   <*'My nnng..' His voice came out as a choked gasp.* —Kittie, *Genesis.*>

4. *n.* an unemotional, noncommittal response.

   <*"This is Detective Sergeant Cooper. He'll probably let you call him Den." "Nnng," said the girl without a flicker of a smile.* —Rebecca Tope, *A Death to Record: A Mystery.*>

nnnggghh.

n. the sound of being suddenly caught in a powerful stranglehold, as in the comic book *Ultimate Spider-Man #21* by Mark Bagley and Art Thibert.

nnngh.

1. (also nnnnnnngh.) *n.* a groan of pain, as in the graphic novel *Falcon Twin* by Brenden Mecleary.

2. *adv.* no, as in the novel *The Virginia City Trail* by Ralph Compton.

3. *interj.* a cry of pain, as from an electric ray aimed at one's head in the novel *W.I.T.C.H. Chapter Book: Out of the Dark* by Disney Enterprises.

4. *interj.* a groan of exertion, as when one is "tugging violently" on large boards nailed across a doorway in the novel *Akiko and the Great Wall of Trudd* by Mark Crilley.

5. *interj.* a whimper of confusion.

<*"Where's Hal?" Joe demanded. "Nnngh." She shook her head uncomprehendingly. She didn't know what Joe was talking about, he saw.* —Jon A. Jackson, *Hit on the House.*>

6. *n.* a moan upon waking from a deep sleep, as in *Yesterday* by Roland Lowery.

NNNH.

interj. a cry of anguish, as discussed in *Eloquence in Trouble: The Poetics and Politics of Complaint in Rural Bangladesh* by James M. Wilce.

nnnh.

1. *interj.* a questioning sound, as in the graphic novel *Mortal Coils: Bodylines* by A. David Lewis.

2. *n.* an expression of panic and discomfort from being held to the ground under twelve Gs of force, as in the comic book *Dirty Pair: Run From The Future #3* by Adam Warren.

nnnh nnnh.

interj. gasps of pain.

<*[T]he residue of the shock baton's randomizing pulse allowed only a thick "Nnnh ... nnnh ..." to pass his lips.* —Matthew Woodring Stover, *Blade of Tyshalle.*>

nnnm.

1. *interj.* eh?

<*[M]mmn pet the love dog, Dickie, nnnm?* —William H. Gass, *Omensetter's Luck: A Novel.*>

2. *n.* an emphatic murmur, as in the novel *Omensetter's Luck* by William H. Gass.

NNNN.

1. *n.* a decorative grouping of letters that might have been a meaningful Dutch word had Dutch been an obscure African language, according to Rob Steenbergen.

<*Could it be true that in that throat-scraping-gutteral-riddled-'gggg'-this-and-'chchch'-that-lingo-where-people-speak-as-if-they-want-to-get-rid-of-some-very-nasty-phlegm, that is the Dutch*

language, there's a word NNNN? What do you think? Of course not! We might speak a funny language but we ain't that funny. NNNN is, although seemingly consisting of 4 capital n's, not a word but decoration, chiselled out of stone. But if Dutch had been some obscure African language it just might have been a word. And who knows, maybe somewhere it just is. —Rob Steenbergen, "Word.Log: A Beautiful, Fascinating, Interesting, Intriguing or Downright Abominable Dutch Word Commented On in English in a Remarkable Witty Way—Every Day.">

2. *n.* the sound of the letter n; see also nnn[7], nnnn[20], nnnnn[14], nnnnnn[6], nnnnnnn[8].

<*Besides being an essential part of creating vocal harmonics, this NNNN sound, incidentally, can help open your sinus passageways if you have a cold.* —Jonathan Goldman, *Tantra of Sound: How to Enhance Intimacy With Sound.*>

NNnn.

n. the sound of someone's neck breaking, as sung by the band Phish in the song "My Life as a Pez" (Mockingbird Foundation, *The Phish Companion: A Guide to the Band and Their Music, Second Edition*).

nnnn.

1. (also nnn.) *adj.* good, as said upon waking up.

<*"Nnn morning, sweetheart," one of would eventually say. "Nnnn," would say the other.* —Luke Rhinehart, *The Dice Man.*>

2. *adv.* a faltering *no.*

<*Do you spend too much time with someone because you cannot say no? Nnnn ... Nnnn ... Well, maybe.* —Joe Cirillo, *It's Your Time.*>

3. *adv.* no, as in the novel *Tim and Pete* by James Robert Baker.

<*"Are you awake?" "Nnnn."* —Katie Hickman, *Dreams of the Peaceful Dragon: A Journey Through Bhutan.*>

<*"Would you like a beer?" "Nnnn."* —Steven Sherrill, *The Minotaur Takes a Cigarette Break: A Novel.*>

4. *interj.* a growl or moan of ecstasy, as in the novel *Over Tumbled Graves* by Jess Walter.

5. *interj.* a questioning hum, as during lovemaking.

<*"I need to ask you something."* "Nnnn?" *He didn't remove his mouth, which now moved up her neck and was lightly sucking on her lobe.* —Dara Joy, *Ritual of Proof.*>

6. *interj.* a quiet, hummed expression, as when one is at a loss for words or considering what to say.

<*"Nnnn," said Stig out of the side of his mouth as Ralph approached and leaned his mass toward them.* —Michael J. Nelson, *Mike Nelson's Death Rat!: A Novel.*>

<*"Nnnn," Mitch said through his teeth.* —Tami Hoag, *Night Sins.*>

7. *interj.* a response to the question "You phonio saxon?" in *Finnegans Wake* by James Joyce.

8. *n.* a "closed," "intimate" hummed sound which "resonates mostly in the head," as opposed to the "exposed" *aaahh* sound "which resonates in the chest. You can keep the closed sound a secret, sitting calmly at a committee meeting while others about you are losing their minds" (W. A. Mathieu, *The Musical Life*).

9. *n.* a "peculiar noise of indecision" (Christine Vachon, *Shooting to Kill: How an Independent Producer Blasts Through the Barriers to Make Movies That Matter*); see also nhhh.

10. *n.* a chattered sound meaning "I'm cold," as in the novel *Lily Quench and the Dragon of Ashby* by Natalie Jane Prior.

11. *n.* a humming sound made while one considers how to describe something (Arundhati Roy, *The God of Small Thing*) or while one fumbles for words (Sue Grafton, *J is for Judgment*).

   <*Ahh. Nnnn. She's a friend of your dad's.* —Sue Grafton, *J is for Judgment.*>

   <*[Sheila answered the telephone.] Nnnn ... hullo?* —Bill Scheft, *The Ringer: A Novel.*>

12. *n.* a low humming sound, as described in *Having a Mary Heart in a Martha World: Finding Intimacy With God in the Busyness of Life* by Joanna Weaver.

13. *n.* a moan of pain, as from a blow to the head in *Jennifer Government: A Novel* by Max Barry.

14. *n.* a sound made by one "overwhelmed" by sleepiness, as in the novel *Rich in Love* by Josephine Humphreys.

15. *n.* a sound recommended to aid meditation, as discussed in *Lymphedema: A Breast Cancer Patient's Guide to Prevention and Healing* by Jeannie Burt; see also mmmm[4].

16. *n.* Antoinette, as slurred by someone with a pustule-covered tongue in *Versailles: A Novel* by Kathryn Davis.

17. *n.* the gurgle of someone fighting but ultimately succumbing to a mind probe, as in the novel *Fire Warrior* by Simon Spurrier.

18. *n.* the keening of a living robot undergoing dental surgery.

   <*"Nnnn," it said, the sound emerging from a grill in its forehead.* —Piers Anthony, *Prostho Plus.*>

19. *n.* the moan of a dead body reanimated by a wizard; see also nn[5].

   <*"Nnnn," said the pickled head. A spurt of bile came from the mouth, and then all went slack again.* —Orson Scott Card, *Hart's Hope.*>

20. *n.* the sound of the letter n, as described in the novel *The Binding Chair: or, A Visit from the Foot Emancipation Society* by Kathryn Harrison; see also nnn[7], NNNN[2], nnnnn[14], nnnnnn[6], nnnnnnn[8].

<*I asked about the* nnnn *sound in* dragon. —Peggy Kaye, *Games for Learning: Ten Minutes a Day to Help Your Child Do Well in School, from Kindergarten to Third Grade.*>

nnnn hnn.

interj. a sound indicating that one is thinking, as in the novel *Poison* by Kathryn Harrison.

nnnn nnnn.

1. *n.* a "faint droning sound in the distance," like a motor, as in the novel *The Golden Wasp* by Tony Abbott.

2. *n.* the frantic grunts of someone gagged with "a child's rubber ball with a rope punched through its middle" (Donn Cortez, *The Closer*).

nnnn nnnn nnnn.

n. the murmurs of a puppy.

<*"Dear Jesus, thank you for the food, and thank ..." From her little brother come little puppylike noises, "Nnnn ... Nnnn ... Nnnn ..." "Aaron! Now I have to start over," she says in a very annoyed tone.* —Keri Wyatt Kent, *God's Whisper in a Mother's Chaos: Bringing Peace Home.*>

nnnn nnnnnn.

n. low moans of labored breathing.

<*She reached out, got hold of his wrist with her floury hand. "Nnnn. Nnnnnn." She was breathing in short bursts, her face a deathly grey.* —Peter James, *The Truth.*>

nnnn-hmm.

adv. an emphatic *no*.

<*We ain't gonna sleep. Nnnn-hmm. We gamble right through the night.* —David Cohen, *Chasing the Red, White, and Blue.*>

nnnng bssss.

n. the reverberations of a guitar, as described by the band Backwash in a *Bandorama* interview.

nnnngggghh.

n. a grunt of exertion, as when hefting a heavy, lifeless body over one's shoulder in the comic strip "PvP" by Scott R. Kurtz; see also hnnng[2], mmmph[3].

nnnngh.

1. (also nnnnnhhh.) *n.* the moan of someone thrown to the ground during a fight, as in the graphic novel *Falcon Twin* by Brenden Mecleary.

2. *interj.* a grunt of pleasure, as in the novel *The American Zone* by L. Neil Smith.

3. *interj.* the "pained groan" of a nauseous drunkard, as in the novel *Twelve Bar Blues*

4. *interj.* the moan of someone whose feelings have been hurt, as in the novel *Mortal Fear* by Scott Ciencin.

5. *n.* a grunted acknowledgment by someone delirious with a 104-degree fever in the novel *Hosts* by F. Paul Wilson.

6. *n.* the "wincing" sound of "having hit one's head on something hard" (Timothy Albee, *Kaze, Ghost Warrior*); see also mmmmmngh.

Nnnnh-Nnnh.

adv. no.

<*A red-haired man in a short white jacket came by offering a plate of tiny crustless sandwiches. "Nnnnh-Nnnh," [Andy] Warhol said, looking kind of ashamed. "He only eats candy," Jeffrey told Jesse, like Warhol wasn't really there, or couldn't talk for himself.* —Jay Cantor, *Great Neck.*>

nnnnn.

1. (also nnnnnn.) *n.* the sound of a baby complaining, as described in the novel *Edwin Mullhouse* by Steven Millhauser.

2. *adv.* a hesitant *no*.

<*He opened his eyes to peek and gazed into the bony face he had ... no, not loved ... cherished ... well, no, that wasn't strictly true either. How about cared for? Nnnnn ... Oh, all right.* —Nina Killham, *How to Cook a Tart.*>

3. *adv.* a stifled *no*.

<*Edison kept Kootie's jaw clamped shut so that his* No! *came out as just a prolonged "Nnnnn!"* —Tim Powers, *Expiration Date: A Novel.*>

<*"Nnnnn," the best she could manage for no.* —Bev Marshall, *Right as Rain: A Novel.*>

4. *interj.* a slurred grunt made by a drunk who needs to "take a piss," as in *Wounded: Collected Tales of Horror and the Grotesque* by David Saliba.

5. *interj.* a sound indicating that one is thinking, as in *A Season on the Mat: Dan Gable and the Pursuit of Perfection* by Nolan Zavoral.

6. *interj.* a sound of disapproval.

<*"What kind [of potato chips are those?]" "Zapp's." "Zapp's? Nnnnn. Them old hard, crunchy-ass chips."* —Louis Edwards, *N: A Novel.*>

7. *n.* a "slow sigh" of regret: "Nnnnn. I just killed the surprise" (Cameron Crowe, *Jerry Maguire*).

8. *n.* a slurred sound, as spoken by an inebriated person trying to comprehend the meaning of a question.

<*"Why don't we go for a walk? Get some fresh air?" "Nnnnn ... walk?"* —MaryJanice Davidson, *Cravings.*>

9. *n.* a sound for babies to imitate as they learn to talk, as discussed in *Rookie Dad: Fun and Easy Exercises and Games for Dads and Babies in Their First Year* by Susan Fox.

10. *n.* a sudden snore made by someone "dead drunk" (Alan Temperley, *Harry and the Wrinklies*).

11. *n.* the muttering of someone paralyzed by fear, as in the novel *Guards! Guards!* by Terry Pratchett; see also dddrrr.

12. *n.* the ominous whining of an elevator in a high-rise.

<*The hall is resonant with the sound of elevators. They are whining in the black hollow shaft, an ominous* nnnnn *from the throat of the building.* —Leonard Michaels, *Time Out of Mind: The Diaries of Leonard Michaels, 1961-1995.*>

13. *n.* the sound of a "choking voice," as from a man "cruelly bound and gagged" with his neck "tied to the bottom of a drainpipe" (Alan Temperley, *Ragboy*).

14. *n.* the sound of the letter n; see also nnn[7], nnnn[20], NNNN[2], nnnnnn[6], nnnnnnn[8].

<*Doro had to ask as she did not know any "nnnnn" words. It turned out that [five-year-old] Sam said "naked body" [in his classroom].* —Barbara Bush, *Barbara Bush: A Memoir.*>

nnnnn nnnnn nnnnn.

1. *n.* the groaning of someone "curled in a tight ball," as in the novel *Candy* by Luke Davies.

<*The girl gave no glimmer of recognition. She seemed catatonic, shaking her head and repeating over and over, "Nnnnn. Nnnnn. Nnnnn," rocking backward and forward and staring at the floor.* —Luke Davies, *Candy.*>

2. *n.* the whine of a begging puppy.

<*He dropped down to his knees, bent his hands before his chest like a hungry pooch, and whined, "Nnnnn, nnnnn, nnnnn!"* —James Preller, *Jigsaw Jones #14: The Case Of The Bicycle Bandit.*>

nnnnn nnnnnn.

n. "puppylike noises," as made by an irreverent child during a dinner table prayer in *God's Whisper in a Mother's Chaos: Bringing Peace Home* by Keri Wyatt Kent; see nnnn nnnn nnnn.

nnnnn-hhhhh.

n. the neigh of a horse.

<*The horses went on eating grass. All but one. She raised her head and turned her ears toward him. "Nnnnn-hhhhh," she said. Her spirit entered his heart.* —Janice Shefelman, *A Mare for Young Wolf.*>

nnnnn-nnnnn.

interj. an angry shout, as by an insane cellmate in *Jennifer Government: A Novel* by Max Barry.

nnnnn-nnnnnnnnnnnnnk'lk nn'k'lk nnnnnh-k'lk.

n. the sound of a conveyor rack at a dry cleaner's shop, as described in *Crackers* by Roy Blount Jr.; see also nnnnnnnnnnnnnnn.

Nnnnnn.

n. the "head guy" of "a bunch of dudes from the nameless planet" (Bruce Coville, "I, Earthling," *Odder Than Ever*).

<*Nnnnnn moved his green hand in a circle, indicating the stream, the forest, the city. "I know you feel like an alien here," he said softly. "But that is because you are thinking too small."* —Bruce Coville, *Odder Than Ever.*>

nnnnnn.

1. *interj.* a raving scream "like an insane dock walloper," as in the novel *Roadwork* by Richard Bachman.

2. *n.* a hum indicating thought.

<*[A]s for whether she had any recurring nightmares, he tapped his fingers on the side of his head and went "nnnnnn" in thought, like an airplane coming in to land.* —Sabine Durrant, *Having It and Eating It.*>

3. *n.* a moan of pain, as from someone poking at one's damaged eyes in the novel *Starfish* by Peter Watts.

4. *n.* a seemingly negative sound made by a cat, as discussed in *Cat is Watching* by Roger A. Caras.

5. *n.* an expression of "negation" (Inman Majors, *Wonderdog*); see nnn[6].

6. *n.* the sound of the letter n; see also nnn[7], nnnn[20], NNNN[2], nnnnn[14], nnnnnnn[8].

<*I wouldn't let him miss the potential joy of sounding the "n" in the word. I had him draw out the sound as if he were playing the most romantic violin imaginable. "Nnnnnn." I had him do it until he felt the roof of his mouth vibrating, till he felt his whole head vibrating. "Nnnnnn."* —Jane Maria Robbins, *Acting Techniques for Everyday Life: Look and Feel Self-Confident in Difficult, Real-Life Situations.*>

nnnnnn-nnnn.

n. an ambiguous response, as when one is too taken aback to formulate a clearly negative answer.

<*I was so shocked (and also couldn't see a thing in the dark) that I just sort of went "Nnnnnn-nnnn."* —Louise Rennison, *Confessions of Georgia Nicholson.*>

nnnnnngh.

n. the moan of someone tossed out of a building, as in *Oddjob: The Collected Stories* by Ian Smith.

NNNNNNN.

n. a growl of enraged nonsense.

<*[H]e growls into the very fertile rain-clogged soil some disjointed noises, entreaties beseechings nonwords and nonsense: NNNNNNN.* —Niall Griffiths, *Sheepshagger: A Novel.*>

nnnnnnn.

1. *adv.* a dismissive *no*, as grunted by someone working intensely.

<*"Any new leads?" "Nnnnnnn." Well, this conversation wasn't getting her anywhere.* —William Bernhardt, *Hate Crime.*>

2. *interj.* a sound to interrupt and drown out what someone else is saying.

<*"We danced until two-thirty. Then we went back to his place. Oh, my God, you wouldn't believe his body, I mean, we didn't sleep all night—" "Nnnnnnn. Time out! Don't tell me more."* —Betsy Carter, *Nothing to Fall Back On: The Life and Times of a Perpetual Optimist.*>

3. *interj.* an expression of boredom, as transcribed in *Innovations in Science and Mathematics Education: Advance Designs for Technologies of Learning* by Michael J. Jacobson.

4. *n.* a "minuscule mosquito-whine of a sound" that proves to onself that one is alive and "not just a spirit lingering inside the clay effigy" of one's own dead body (Robert Bloch, *Robert Bloch's Psychos*); see also nnnnnnnnn[1].

<*I concentrate everything on my chest. I* push, *or try to ... and something happens. A sound! I make a sound! It's mostly inside my closed mouth, but I can also hear and feel it in my nose—a low hum. Concentrating, summoning every bit of effort, I do it again, and this time the sound is a little stronger, leaking out of my nostrils like cigarette smoke:* Nnnnnnn— *It makes me think of an old Alfred Hitchcock TV program I saw a long, long time ago, where Joseph Cotton was paralyzed in a car crash and was finally able to let them know he was still alive by crying a single tear.* —Robert Bloch, *Robert Bloch's Psychos.*>

5. *n.* a muttering by a thirsty person with a mouth so dry that his tongue has stuck to the roof of his mouth.

<*"Nnnnnnn ..." It was the best my stuck tongue could do.* —Robert Lipsyte, *One Fat Summer.*>

6. *n.* an ambiguous reply by a sleepy person, as in the novel *In a Land of Plenty* by Tim Pears.

7. *n.* an entreaty of a baffling nature.

<*"Do you need directions?" I repeated a bit louder. This time he appeared to be carefully considering my question, slowly closing his wrinkled eyes as if to envision when the planets would be in alignment. "Nnnnnnn," he murmured. "Nnnnnnn."* —Betty B. Youngs, *Gifts of the Heart: Stories that Celebrate Life's Defining Moments.*>

8. *n.* the sound of the letter n; see also nnn[7], nnnn[20], NNNN[2], nnnnn[14], nnnnnn[6], nnnnnnn[8].

<*Nanny Nuthatch from Nottingham learned to play the nutcracker as a little girl, and she can*

make it say the sound of the letter n *which is "nnnnnnn."* —Elizabeth Crosby Stull, *Let's Read: A Complete Month-by-Month Activities Program for Beginning Readers.*>

nnnnnnn zzzzzzzz.

n. the snore of a coyote, as described in *Coyote Stories for Children: Tales from Native America* by Susan Strauss.

NNNNNNNN.

n. the whine of a police siren.

<*And tonight, of all nights, after a week of not bothering him, the police decide to come after Slothrop. Oh yes, yes indeed NNNNNNNN Good Evening Tyrone Slothrop We Have Been Waiting For You.* —Thomas Pynchon, *Gravity's Rainbow.*>

NnnnNnnn.

n. the cry of a newly weaned baby, "not a full-blooded roar ... but *NnnnNnnn* like an insect trapped against glass" (Marian Eldridge, "The Woman at the Window," *Australian Literature: An Anthology of Writing from the Land Down Under*).

nnnnnnnn.

1. *n.* a line in the play *In the Blood* by Suzan-Lori Parks, "the sound of something I shouldn't have done" (Susan Letzler Cole, *Playwrights in Rehearsal: The Seduction of Company*).

2. *n.* a muffled moan of passion.

<*[T]he darkness was clear enough to see that the bed was too filled for it to be just one person. There was talking that wasn't talking, exactly, and a rearrangement of shapes under the blanket. A long, muffled sound that went "nnnnnnnn."* —Carol Anshaw, *Lucky in the Corner: A Novel.*>

NNNNNNNNGGGGGGGGGGGHHHHHH.

interj. an extended moan of "abdominal pain, like the kind caused by sodomy" in pornographic prose by hack writers trying to fill up pages, as discussed in *The Florence King Reader* by Florence King; see ngh[4].

nnnnnnnnn.

1. *n.* a desperate hum, as made by someone mistakenly believed to be dead who is about to undergo an autopsy; see also nnnnnnn[4].

<*He lifts my head, the pads of his fingers on my cheekbones, and I hum desperately—* Nnnnnnnnn—*knowing that he can't possibly hear me over Keith Richards' screaming guitar but hoping he may* feel *the sound vibrating in my nasal passages.* —Robert Bloch, *Robert Bloch's Psychos.*>

2. *n.* a profoundly empty hum.

<*What could have been mistaken for serenity from the top of the bank now looked like what it really was: vacuity, emptiness. When he took hold of her, the smoothness of her face was replaced by a dim and fretful smile; her mouth quivered as if she felt distant pain, and an almost formless*

sound of negation came from her mouth: "Nnnnnnnn—" —Stephen King, *Wizard and Glass*.>

3. *n.* the "snore-like croaking" call of the Red-fronted Tinkerbird, as described in *Toucans, Barbets and Honeyguides: Ramphastidae, Capitonidae and Indicatoridae* by Lester L. Short.

nnnnnnnnnn.

1. (also nnnnnn-nnn.) *n.* a "strangling, ripping scream ... pull[ing] up from the root of [one's] belly" that signals the beginning of "lunacy" (Stephen King, *The Gunslinger*).

2. *adv.* no.

<*"Can you cast fireballs or whirling spells, such as might be hurled against an enemy?" Simon looked sideways at Treatle. "Nnnnnnnnn," he ventured.* —Terry Pratchett, *Equal Rites*.>

3. *n.* a "frightening sound" of "vacuity, emptiness," and "negation," made by a bewitched woman madly cutting off her hair, as in the novel *Wizard and Glass* by Stephen King; see nnnnnnnnn[2].

4. *n.* the "nasty noise" of a "model plane flying about" (Sue Lloyd, *Jolly Phonics Workbook 1*.>

5. *n.* the humming of mosquitoes.

<*[H]e plodded on like an ox up the rutted mountain roads, splashing through the puddles when he had to, slapping at skeeters that hummed around his ears:* nnnnnnnnnn. —William T. Vollmann, *You Bright and Risen Angels*.>

nnnnnnnnnn-nnnnn-nnnnnnnnn-nnnnn-nn.

n. the sound of a turntable needle playing the first two seconds of a demo song by The Doors.

<*[Lou Adler played the last song of our demo record for two seconds.] It was like nnnnnnnnnn-nnnnn-nnnnnnnnn-nnnnn-nn. And at the end of it he said, "Sorry, nothing here I can use."* —Ray Manzarek, of the band *The Doors*, quoted in *Follow the Music: The Life and High Times of Elektra Records in the Great Years of American Pop Culture* by Jac Holzman.

nnnnnnnnnnn.

n. the "swelling and receding" sound of a bagpipe, as described in the novel *Fallen* by Emma Jensen.

nnnnnnnnnnnnnnnn.

v. to swing on a dry cleaner's conveyer rack; see also nnnnn-nnnnnnnnnnnnnk'lk nn'k'lk nnnnnh-k'lk.

<*[Y]ou see all the clothes moving around through there past [the woman operating the pressing machine] like soldiers or something, they kind of swing out like they're keeping their balance coming around the corners, then they nnnnnnnnnnnnnnnn, right up behind the counter.* —Roy Blount Jr., *Crackers*.>

nnnnrgh.

interj. a sound made by a sleepy person unwilling to get out of bed.

<*“Oy of ned, lazybones,” [Zoe] exclaimed. “Nnnnrgh,” James replied, pulling the covers over his head as she opened the curtains and light washed over his bed.* —Tim Pears, *In a Land of Plenty.*>

nnnr.

n. a warning grunt that means fear makes the enemy stronger, as in the comic book *Alpha Flight* by Mike Gustorvich.

nnsshhhh.

n. the crackling of a ball of energy, as in the graphic novel *Falcon Twin* by Brenden Mecleary.

nnt vzt n kvd mm rv n fnntng dnk nd mm nvw ff t vu zt.

n. a mumbled line of dialogue (presumably explaining that one has reached sexual maturity) by the character “Kenny” from the animated television series *South Park* (Matt Graham, “South Park: Angband comes to South Park”).

nnzzzzz.

n. the muted ringing of a cell phone that someone is sitting on, as in the comic strip “PvP” by Scott R. Kurtz.

nrnh.

adv. a nasal *no*, as spoken with congested sinuses.

<*“Have you ever swum with dolphins, Nick?” “Nrnh.”* —Christopher Buckley, *Thank You for Smoking.*>

nrrll mhh.

n. an incoherent muttering, as spoken with congested sinuses in the novel *Thank You for Smoking* by Christopher Buckley.

nt.

adv. not, written in Roger Bacon’s all-consonant secret code (devised in 1250), as discussed in *The Voynich Manuscript* by Gerry Kennedy.

nth.

1. *adj.* an indeterminate quantity.

   <*[F]or the nth time in his life he deplored the length of country calls and ended by wrapping himself in hostile silence.* —Giuseppe di Lapedusa, *The Leopard.*>

2. *adj.* the unknowable “last” in a series of infinite number.

   <*The writing of any autobiography involves numerous arbitrary decisions about the importance of events, and the writing about a dicelife by a diceperson involves arbitrariness multiplied to the nth degree.* —Luke Rhinehart, *The Dice Man.*>

3. *adj.* the utmost degree.

<*Tetsu's second release for Tzadik delves deeper into the methods of sonic microscopy that marked his debut, constructing minute, peerless sound-surfaces that break apart and reconstitute in the shifting, *n*th-dimensional space of the inner ear.* —Anomalous Records catalog.>

nttt nttt nttt.

n. the sound of a kangaroo, as in the story "Kyabram Kangaroo Chaos" by Daryll Bellingham.

Nxt.

n. a style of chair created by Danish designer Peter Karpf.

<*His minimalist Nxt… [is] based on architectural and philosophical principles that unify materials, form, process, and execution. —Design Within Reach.*>

Nxt Mrnng.

n. the title of a song by the German rock band Vito, short for "Next Morning."

p-KKkkkkkkkk.

(also p-KKkkkkkkkkk.) *n.* the sound of "waves breaking," as in the novel *The Wild Shore: Three Californias* by Kim Stanley Robinson.

p-p-p.

n. the patter of cat feet, as described in *Wishes, Lies, and Dreams: Teaching Children to Write Poetry* by Kenneth Koch.

Pb-pb-b-b-b.

n. the sound that powers a miniature motorcycle.

<*Next he inhaled deeply and with a Pb-pb-b-b-b sound, the only sound that will make a miniature motor-cycle go, sped out from under the television set and across the carpet. Pb-pb-b-b-b! Ralph rode across the lobby.* —Beverly Clearly, *Runaway Ralph.*>

pbbbtt.

n. the sound of a sudden expectoration, as upon being surprised while sipping tea in the graphic novel *Flipside* by Brion Foulke.

pf.

n. the whimper at the end of the world.

<*If he escapes ... the world is over. Pf!, like that.* —Neil Gaiman, *American Gods.*>

pff.

1. *interj.* an indication that one is miffed, as by a failed pursuit.

<*[W]hen they rounded the corner the bird had disappeared, and though the children searched high and low, there was not a feather to be found. "Pff! Typical," Georgie spat, turning back down the stairs.* —Justyn Walker, *The Magician's Daughter.*>

2. *n.* a spitting sound, as when the eye of a fantastical hurricane realizes it has sucked up the wrong person in the graphic novel *Uzumaki 2* by Junji Ito; see also pffft[8].

pff-fft.

adj. broken up, "on the outs," as in a relationship; see also phfft[11], phffft[11].

<*I just glanced at the paper and see where Marilyn Monroe and Arthur Miller are pff-fft.* —Margo Howard, *A Life in Letters: Ann Landers Letters to Her Only Child.*>

pff-pfff-pffff.

n. a hiss from a corroded pipe.

<*Every few seconds one of the tanks wheezes a pff-pfff-pffff sound, louder than any of the birdsong nearby ... It sounds as if it were having pulmonary trouble.* —Christopher Hallowell, *Holding Back the Sea: The Struggle for America's Natural Legacy on the Gulf Coast.*>

pfff.

1. *interj.* a contemptuous huff, as in the novel *Cage's Bend* by Carter Coleman.

2. *n.* a French expression of loneliness, as when everyone is having too much fun to give one a call, as in "Numéro privé" by Erwan Le Goffic.

3. *n.* a toneless wheeze from a pipe organ; see also pffff[8].

   <*[Father Fulgencio] struck the key hard. The organ pipe, thick as an arm, gave back: Pfff!* —Arturo Barea, *The Forging of a Rebel.*>

   pfffft. *n.* the sound of something fizzling away.

   <*And instead of a thermonuclear bomb, one great big ... dud. Pfffft.* —Lanny J. Davis, *Truth To Tell: Tell It Early, Tell It All, Tell It Yourself: Notes from My White House Education.*>

   <*After leaving the tank, the Freon spills into that huge green basketball thing, which allows it to reach a much lower pressure, then it slithers into that big snaky tube over yonder, where,* pffff, *it boils away, absorbing lots of heat in the bargain and thereby keeping our Main Attraction as cold as a penguin's kiss.* —James Morrow, *Blameless in Abaddon.*>

4. *n.* an expression of disbelief, as in the play *Stop Kiss* by Diana Son.

pffff.

1. *interj.* a noise meaning "Very interesting!" (Dann Gunn, *Wool-Gathering or How I Ended Analysis*).

2. *interj.* a sound meaning it's "'bout hot enough to throw the air-conditioning switch" (Valerie Sayers, *Who Do You Love*).

3. *interj.* an expression of ridicule, as in the novel *A Perfect Love* by Lori Copeland.

4. *n.* a dismissive huff, as in the novel *Three Wishes* by Liane Moriarty.

   <*My father gave her a dismissive look and sucked at his beer. Through the foam on his lips, he said, "Pffff."* —Eric Kraft, *Inflating a Dog: The Story of Ella's Lunch Launch.*>

   <*Guitars? Pffff! They'll be giving them away in a couple of years.* —Mo Foster, *Seventeen Watts?*>

5. *n.* a puff of air through one's lips, as to communicate impatience in the novel *Deadly Decisions* by Kathy Reichs.

6. *n.* a puff of the wind, as in the novel *Riders in the Chariot* by Patrick White.

7. *n.* a sound of resignation.

<*June made a* pffff *sound with her lips while August shook her head, and it washed over me for the first time in my life just how much importance the world had ascribed to skin pigment, how lately it seemed that skin pigment was the sun and everything else in the universe was the orbiting planets.* —Sue Kidd, *The Secret Life of Bees.*>

8. *n.* a toneless wheeze from a pipe organ; see also pfff[3].

<*One day he sat down at the organ and pressed one of the keys, but the pipe gave no sound. He stopped playing and pushed away at the key. The organ sounded pffff, in a long wheeze, but no more.* —Arturo Barea, *The Forging of a Rebel.*>

9. *n.* an incorrect pronunciation of pH, as discussed in *The Outer Reaches of Life* by John R. Postgate.

10. *n.* etcetera.

<*Today I'm with Dave in L.A., tomorrow in Detroit with Miles, then Phoenix, Chicago—pffff!* —Jack Chambers, *Milestones: The Music and Times of Miles Davis.*>

11. *n.* the barely-perceptible sound of porpoises breathing.

<Pffff. *Pause.* Pffff. *I'd heard this sound my first night at Nuka Island and thought—hoped—it might be a sea mammal. ... Tonight, on an evening paddle across glassy, tranquil Berger Bay, I hear it again:* Pffff ... pffff. *I paddle slowly toward the sound and spot what looks like a wake. Then, a hundred yards away, maybe less, I see a curved back and dorsal fin gently break the water and disappear. I count two, three animals. Not large. Not whales. They're harbor porpoises, also known as common porpoises. ... Occasionally they snort and splash, in preparation for deeper dives. But mostly they cut the water with no perceptible sound, except their breaking.* Pffff ... pffff ... pffff. —Bill Sherwonit, *Alaska's Accessible Wilderness: A Traveler's Guide to Alaska's State Parks.*>

12. *n.* the hiss of a dart shooting from a blowgun, as described in *The Rivers Ran East* by Leonard Clark.

13. *n.* the sound of an explosion.

<"*[The Inspector] figures there was some kind of flukey explosion, you know"—he used his hands—*"pffff, *with flames hitting the ceiling rafters.*" —Barbara Delinsky, *Three Wishes.*>

14. *n.* the sound of bullets piercing a wall.

<*[I]t could have been a train whistle, a few sharp* pffffs *into the air, but then there was plaster falling off the ceiling and smoke everywhere until you felt it could be Hallowe'en. ... And another shot, yes, that's what it was, bullet holes through the wall, and gunsmoke.* —Annie Callan, *Taf: A Novel.*>

15. *n.* the sound of dismissal, abandonment.

<"*We used to have many gods. The people thought that a god, if properly worshipped, should serve them and bring luck. If he didn't, then ...* pffff." *He made an outward sweeping motion with his hands, and grinned. "The god would be abandoned, and a new one chosen."* —Candice Proctor, *Beyond Sunrise.*>

pffff fffffft.

(also pfff fffft.) *v.* to disappear.

<*[T]hen pffff! fffffft! off this guy goes." "Pfff! Fffft! is the way he'll go all right," said Mr. Garble.* —Walter R. Brooks, *Freddy Plays Football.*>

PFFFFF.

v. to disappear.

<*[T]hey found something they like, they run after it, and PFFFFF!* —Red Jordan Arobateau, *Lucy and Mickey.*>

pfffff.

1. *interj.* a dismissive sound meaning "no way" (Cameron West, *First Person Plural: My Life as a Multiple*).

2. *interj.* an expression of disgust.

<*Zjorn let a disgusted* pfffff *escape from his lips.* —Paul Lindsay, *The Fuhrer's Reserve: A Novel of the FBI.*>

<*You worked for a Republican? Pfffff. I don't want to have this conversation.* —David Brock, *The Seduction of Hillary Rodham.*>

3. *n.* a puff of air, as blown into a firepot in the play *Lysistrata* by Aristophanes.

4. *n.* a toneless whistle.

<*I tried to whistle for Frightful, but couldn't purse my shaking lips tight enough to get out anything but* pfffff. —Jean Craighead George, *My Side of the Mountain.*>

5. *n.* an expression of contempt.

<*Fast zombies. Pfffff. Hey, fast zombies, where's the fire?* —Patton Oswalt, quoted in *Remains* by Steve Niles.>

6. *n.* the hiss of a "sudden ejaculation" of steam, as from a street cleaning truck spraying roads and sidewalks with water; see pssw.

7. *v.* to explode into thin air.

<*"It's a plunger," Stacey whispered. "If Papa presses down on it, the whole forest will go pfffff!"* —Mildred D. Taylor, *Song of the Trees.*>

PFFFFFFT.

n. a "Bronx cheer," i.e., a disapproving sound.

<*[H]e shpritzed a Bronx cheer, a loud, wet "PFFFFFFT!" right into my ear, and laughed. "Hmm" I nodded, thoughtfully. "Not bad, but how do you spell it?" He thought for a second and shpritzed me with four quicker, quieter Bronx cheers: "Pfft, pfft, pfft, pfft." Not bad for four and a half years old. And I had no idea PFFFFFFT was a four-letter word.* —Joel Siegel, *Lessons for Dylan: From Father to Son.*>

pfffffft.

n. the sound of a .22 caliber long-rifle cartridge being fired.

<*The target stood absolutely still for just a moment, and Ted, almost casually, squeezed off the round. The only sounds were the* pffffft *of the firing and the tinkle of window glass as the copper-jacketed round passed through it.* —Stuart Woods, *Dirty Work.*>

pfffft.

1. *interj.* a sound of derision.

<*Jumping to his feet, he yanked the weapon from Amanda's weak little fist and turned the gun on her. "Pffffft I say! Your kitchen floor is unpolished, you don't believe in Santa Claus, and you are bland!"* —Marianne Stillings, *The Damsel in This Dress.*>

2. *n.* the sound of a stabbing hypodermic needle.

<*She stuck the needle in, pushed* pfffft, *just like that, and it started burning immediately.* —Janet Laurel, *Heart and Soul: What It Takes to Promote Health While Confronting Cancer.*>

3. *n.* the sound of an impromptu bowel movement.

<*We'd be on the freeway and he'd be, "PULL OVER!" And just go* pfffft! *Right out there. He didn't care.* —Michael Azerrad, *Our Band Could Be Your Life: Scenes from the American Indie Underground, 1981-1991.*>

4. *n.* the sound of someone appearing in a doorway, seemingly out of thin air, as in "The Conspiracy of Dir en Grey" by Hidoko Matsumoto.

5. *v.* to disappear.

<*[S]he was the type who just goes* pfffft *one day.* —Jamie Harrison, *Blue Deer Thaw.*>

pfffsss.

n. the hiss of a soda can, as in the comic strip "PvP" by Scott R. Kurtz; see also psst[4], psssshhhh.

pffft.

1. *n.* a spray from a paint can.

<*A heavy coating takes care of a bald spot; a light* pffft! *and that tinge of silver you've developed is history.* —Becker & Mayer Ltd., *You're Not Getting Better, You're Getting Older.*>

2. *adj.* broken up, i.e., no longer a couple.

<*The doctor and I are* pffft *anyway.* —Peter David, *Fire on High.*>

3. *n.* a "coarse" expression indicating that one has been insulted, as in the novel *Heaven on Earth* by Marilyn Pappano.

4. *n.* a spurt of breath, as to blow something away from one's face in the comic strip "PvP" by Scott R. Kurtz; see phhbbppt.

5. *n.* the pop of a bubble bursting.

<*Ambassador Rahel's giggle escaped in a bluegreen bubble (the color of a jackfruit fly) and burst in the hot airport air.* Pffft! *was the sound it made.* —Arundhati Roy, *The God of Small Things.*>

6. *n.* the sound of a balloon deflating.

<*The volunteer was given a pair of safety glasses and a long bamboo pole to the end of which was secured a match. This was lit, and placed under the balloon. It collapsed with a dull pffft.* —D.W. St. John, *A Terrible Beauty.*>

<*[W]hen I told him that I had not only my loving mother to testify to my injuries, but a very nice bartender as well, he just went pffft like a balloon on a dartboard.* —Janet LaPierre, *Keepers: A Port Silva Mystery.*>

7. *n.* the sound of a cork popping out of a bottle; see also Thfft.

<*The cork escaped from the bottleneck with a gentle* pffft! *and he poured with a flourish, while lavishing felicitations on the bridal pair.* —Lillian Jackson Braun, *The Cat Who Tailed a Thief.*>

8. *n.* the sound of a person spitting; see also phfft[14].

<*When the officer closed his eyes he'd go 'Pffft!' He sprayed his face with a mouthful of spit.* —Lou Putnoky, *Pffft.*>

9. *n.* the sound of tobacco burning.

<*Paul's cigarette went pffft.* —ScrewTheDaisies, *Things Inside.*>

pffft-pffft.

n. the sound of rifle slugs hitting the ground.

<*We hadn't gone more than fifty yards when we saw a man in the rifle squad ahead of us fall; then we heard pffft-pffft and could see puffs of dirt as slugs burrowed into the furrows at our feet.* —Dean Joy, *Sixty Days in Combat: An Infantryman's Memoir of World War II in Europe.*>

pffht.

n. the sound of a harpoon gun being shot underwater, as in the comic book *Danger Girl #1* by J. Scott Campbell and Alex Garner.

pfflrrt.

(also pffllrrrt.) *n.* a "disgusting" bodily sound, as in the comic strip "PvP" by Scott R. Kurtz.

pffsssh.

interj. a sigh of annoyance, as in the story "Snow" by Tea Benduhn, *Testimonies: Lesbian and Bisexual Coming-Out Stories.*

Pfft.

1. *n.* a taunting nickname, insinuating that someone is flatulent.

<*"Did you hear that, Pfft? I am not afraid of you!" ... "Pfft? You call me Pfft?" ... "Pfft, sometimes I think of your name as Pfft-Pfft, or even Pfft-Pfft-Pfft. ... Sometimes I call you Pfft-Pfft-Pfft-Pfft, or even Pfft-Pfft-Pfft-Pfft-Pfft." ... "Why do you call me Pfft?" "Because of the sounds that so often come from your backside."* —Sue Pope, *Jexicus: One Soul's Journey*.>

2. *n.* an absurdist woman's name.

<*[Andy] Warhol himself says [the "pop girl of the year" is] either Ingrid Superstar (he won't say her last name) or a girl named Mary who, he says, is changing her name to Pfft.* —Steven Henry Madoff, *Pop Art: A Critical History*.>

pfft.

1. *adj.* deflated.

<*[A]t fifty-five [miles per hour], all her buoyancy would go suddenly pfft—like a flat tire.* —Wolfgang Langewiesche, *America from the Air: An Aviator's Story*.>

2. *adj.* done in.

<*"[You are a] sacrificial lamb. You are the rider they bring in, bring along too fast, put in too many big races he's not ready for or able to ride and then ... pfft." He waved a hand absently to the side. "You and the team are history."* —Greg Moody, *Two Wheels: A Cycling Murder Mystery*.>

3. *adj.* gone without a trace.

<*When they've gone, nothing left, not a particle, zero, pfft!* —Jean Genet, *The Screens*.>

4. *adj.* ruined; kaput.

<*[The kiln] must be watched like a hawk, because if the temperature is wrong, then—pfft! "Pfft?" "Yes, pfft! Pots, work, everything ruined. Twenty degrees either way and two months of work in shards!"* —Sabin Willett, *Present Value: A Novel*.>

<*She had been secretly seeing another performer and obviously her husband had found out and her husband had guided her career and now it was all* pfft. —William Goldman, *Adventures in the Screen Trade*.>

5. *adv.* broken up.

<*[T]o sum it all up, the engagement went pfft.* —Selma Eichler, *Murder Can Rain on Your Shower*.>

6. *adv.* immediately.

<*You'll do fine if you just keep the rules in mind. Break any of them, though, and* pfft, *you're right back here, and you'll be dealing with John, instead of me.* —Jenna McKnight, *A Date on Cloud Nine*.>

7. *interj.* a disdainful sound, as in the biography *Boogie Man: The Adventures of John Lee Hooker in the American Twentieth Century* by Charles Shaar Murray.

<*This town. Pffl! Very bad place.* —Tabor Evans, *Longarm 299: Longarm and Maximilian's Gold.*>

8. *interj.* a scoff, as in the novel *Family Resemblance* by Tanya Maria Barrientos.

9. *interj.* a scolding expression.

<*"Oh, cut the self-pity," Egg roared. "I haven't got the stomach for it. You've lived a long, healthy life and worked hard at something you liked. That's more than most people get. Now here you sit like a toad in a well crying, 'Woe is me.' Pffl! It's time to stop the pity party. Get off your butt and go outside. It's a marvelous fall day. The birds are singing, the critters are fat, the sun is shining, and the world is turning."* —Stephen Coonts, *Saucer: The Conquest.*>

10. *interj.* a sound capable of dismissing an entire topic of a conversation, as in the novel *Romancing Mister Bridgerton* by Julia Quinn.

<*"For I told him something, just now, that, if it were to get around, would make me very unpopular in England." "Pffl!" said Jean Bart, and rolled his eyes, dispensing with the entire subject of England.* —Neal Stephenson, *The Confusion.*>

<*I lied and told her one of her precious Lennon sisters—Diane, the oldest, her favorite—was having an illegitimate baby. "Pffl," she said, flicking away the possibility with the flap of her wrist.* —Wally Lamb, *She's Come Undone.*>

11. *interj.* an exclamation of disgust.

<*[N]ow he was completely alone in a prison of self-pity and doubt. "Pffl," he exclaimed in disgust, exhaling all the fear and frustration he had been brewing in his cauldron of ire.* —George Parker, *The Atomic Kid: Adventures in the Antiworld.*>

12. *interj.* an expression meaning "tough luck," as in the novel *The Bear Comes Home* by Rafi Zabor.

13. *interj.* an expression meaning that something is pointless or inconsequential.

<*"Pffl!" Pigeon Tony made a noise that accompanied a twist of his hand in the country air, and Judy figured it meant what's-the-difference.* —Lisa Scottoline, *The Vendetta Defense.*>

14. *interj.* an expression of "irritated amusement," as in the novel *The Fiery Cross* by Diana Gabaldon.

15. *interj.* an expression of skepticism, as in the novel *The Cutting Room* by Laurence Klavan.

16. *n.* a color that ranges from green to purple to dark brown, as on bromeliad leaves.

<*Yesterday I visited the conservatory at the Minneapolis Sculpture Garden where I saw a display of magnificent bromeliads. They had leaves that start out green, then all of a sudden, pffl, they go purple, then pffl, they turn dark brown, then pffl, they're green again. I wanted to get that pffl with Rit dye ... a hot tub of pffl.* —William Daley, "March 1998," *Clay Talks: Reflections by American Master Ceramists.*>

17. *n.* a dying gasp.

<*If that central computer were shut down, the entire economy goes ...* pfft. *Not good for business, eh?* —Steven Barnes, *The Cestus Deception.*>

18. *n.* a muffled gunshot, as with a silencer; see also phfft[9].

<*I shot the Picasso first. The silencer went "Pfft" and the .45 hollow point blew the canvas in half.* —James Ellroy, *The Black Dahlia.*>

<*The faint* pfft, pfft *of a silenced rifle reached her ear, and she knew in that instant, rolling to roadside boulders for cover, that Ismael was not dead.* —Ted Dekker, *A Man Called Blessed.*>

19. *n.* a mystical understanding of aloneness, likened to being a seemingly inconsequential drop of water in the ocean.

<*[A]loneness makes us just a drop of water in the immensity of the ocean—just pfft, that's all. Simultaneously, aloneness is not aloneness, because that drop of water extends everywhere in the immensity of the ocean. So if we understand real aloneness, we can be free from it.* —Dainin Katagiri, *Returning to Silence.*>

20. *n.* a spray from an aerosol can.

<*Every soft stroke from the society is like the* pfft *of an aerosol can as it eats up a few more atoms of our brain's delicate ozone, and furthers our personal cretinization.* —John Updike, *More Matter: Essays and Criticism.*>

21. *n.* a stifled laugh, as when laughing to oneself in *The Polish Officer: A Novel* by Alan Furst.

<*Madoc knew the Archbishop's words were meant to make him smile, and the more he thought about it the funnier it become. "Pfft!" he said, managing not to choke and to keep a straight face.* —Anna Lee Waldo, *Circle of Stars.*>

22. *n.* a sudden ending, as discussed in *Everything Scrabble* by Joe Edley and John Williams.

23. *n.* a void; nothing.

<*Pfft occulted. Nothing having stirred.* —Samuel Beckett, *Nohow On: Company, Ill Seen Ill Said, Worstward Ho: Three Novels.*>

<*Sei Shonagon could see somebody beheaded right in front of her and it's like, pfft, there's no connection between her and that person.* —Janet Fitch, *White Oleander: A Novel.*>

24. *n.* a whimper at the moment of creation, unlike the massive explosion in the "big bang" theory.

<*[Cosmologist Alan Guth] contends that the universe, "not with a bang so much as with a pfft, ... ballooned* accidentally *out of the endless void of eternity, from a stillness so deep that there was no 'there' or 'then,' only possibility."* —Robert L. Reymond, *A New Systematic Theology of the Christian Faith, Second Edition.*>

25. *n.* an expression of contempt or derision.

<*He's just another gutless politician scared of losing the bigot vote. Pfft!* —Stephen Coonts, *The Intruders.*>

26. *n.* the "weak, raspberry-like" call of the Calliope Hummingbird, "probably created by braking action of wings or tail" (Sheri Williamson, *A Field Guide to Hummingbirds of North America*).

27. *n.* the hiss of "silly string" spraying from a can, as in the comic strip "PvP" by Scott R. Kurtz.

28. *n.* the hiss of a garden sprinkler.

<*As we pull over to the curb and hop out, a sprinkler near our feet starts up with a sudden* pfft. —Michelle Nijhuis, "Shadow Creatures," *The Best American Science Writing 2003.*>

29. *n.* the loud, short spit of a fighting cat.

<*The constable's hands suddenly found the furry warmth of Grimalkin. "Pfft! Miaow! Pfft!" Grimalkin hissed and spat and scratched.* —Marguerite Henry, *King of the Wind: The Story of the Godolphin Arabian.*>

30. *n.* the rustle of clothing thrown over one's head and "fluttering down," as described in *The Tidewater Tales: A Novel* by John Barth.

31. *n.* the sound of "a match dipped in water," as in the novel *Some Great Thing* by Colin McAdam.

32. *n.* the sound of a body dissolved in a bathtub filled with acid, as discussed in the play *Awake and Sing* by Clifford Odets.

33. *n.* the sound of a cigarette being extinguished.

<*She licked her thumb and forefinger and put out the tip of the joint with the two of them, giving it a quick squeeze. It made a* pfft. —Craig Nova, *Cruisers: A Novel.*>

34. *n.* the sound of a falling star.

<*"I don't write films anymore. I dropped out. Consider me a fallen star. Pfft." He gestured with his closed hand—a long, slow descent from on high—until his hand dropped to the table and opened, with nothing inside.* —Ellen Sussman, *On a Night Like This.*>

35. *n.* the sound of a genie casting a spell, as in the joke where a man asks a genie to make him a malted and the genie responds, "Okay, pfft, you're a malted!" (referenced in *Breaking Into the Music Business* by Alan H. Siegel).

36. *n.* the sound of a golf ball struck by a club.

<*A well-struck explosion shot sounds like the club hit a bag of wet laundry—a sort of* pfft. *Tune in to any televised golf tournament and watch a good player hit a greenside sand shot, and you'll hear what I mean.* —Johnny Miller, *Breaking 90 with Johnny Miller.*>

37. *n.* the sound of a needle piercing skin.

<*The syringe made a little* pfft! —Craig Nova, *Wetware: A Novel.*>

38. *n.* the sound of a nerve gas pellet that failed to go off.

<*Pfft. The tiny sound came simultaneously with a pinprick in his leg. ... He scratched his leg*

with his free hand and dislodged the black pellet. —Vernor Vinge, "Bookworm, Run!" *The Collected Stories of Vernor Vinge.*>

39. *n.* the sound of a pneumatic seal being broken.

<*The steel door had a great wheel set in its face, like a watertight hatch inside a U-boat. The shoemaker shivered when he heard the hermetic* pfft *that signaled the opening of the door.* —Greg Iles, *Black Cross.*>

40. *n.* the sound of a projectile shooting by.

<*Pffft... ding!* —Lawrence Norfolk, *Lemprière's Dictionary.*>

41. *n.* the sound of an entire city emerging from a bottle.

<*According to the words, we must take the bottle to a giant sand dune in the Saladian Plains and—pfft!—out of it will come ... the city of Ut!* —Tony Abbott, *Flight of the Genie.*>

42. *n.* the sound of an overworked calculator melting.

<*[T]he calculator gave up the ghost. To Robert's surprise, it suddenly went Pfft! and melted down into a sickly green goo.* —Hans Magnus Enzensberger, *The Number Devil: A Mathematical Adventure.*>

43. *n.* the sound of an uncharged laser blaster.

<*Dursten drew and fired in a single motion—but his blaster made a little, stupid* pfft! *and sagged in his hand. Its charge was gone.* —Piers Anthony, *Bearing an Hourglass.*>

44. *n.* the sound of blowing air.

<*The little nose barely breaks the surface of the water; you hear a 'pfft' as it sprays water and air. Then you see the creature itself—a huge gray mass with a walruslike body that tapers to a beaverlike tail.* —Jeff Campbell, describing the West Indian manatee in *Lonely Planet: USA.*>

<*He brushed the tangles of her hair away from his face, making little* pfft! *noises that made her want to laugh.* —Diana Gabaldon, *Drums of Autumn.*>

45. *n.* the sound of brushing off someone or something.

<*She looks at Ian, makes a loud pfft! sound and waves him away like a bad odour.* —Alison Wearing, *Honeymoon in Purdah: An Iranian Journey.*>

46. *n.* the sound of dissident migrant workers being sent back to their homeland.

<*If they complain, or join a union, or do anything but work their ass off,* pfft! *He slams them back to Mexico.* —Susan Ferriss, *The Fight in the Fields: Cesar Chavez and the Farmworkers Movement.*>

47. *n.* the sound of gases exploding from a body ravaged by flesh-eating disease.

<*So there's a disease up there, eh? Makes AIDS look like a sniffle, eh? You turn into soup, eh? You explode, eh?* Pfft!—*coming out of every hole, is that the story?* —Richard Preston, *The Hot Zone: A Terrifying True Story.*>

48. *n.* the sound of instant gratification.

<*"I thought you said that it was"—she snapped her fingers imperiously—*"pfft, *like that for him."* —James Clavell, *Tai-Pan.*>

49. *n.* the sound of spitting.

<*Mina zipped over and hovered for a moment in front of the king. "Pfft!" She spat a grape in his face, then turned and zoomed out the door after Nell.* —Jackie French Koller, *The Wizard's Apprentice.*>

50. *n.* the sputter of an airplane engine.

<*There's always something important and dramatic about those engines going pfft—it's like the whole world is watching you.* —John Travolta, quoted in *John Travolta: Back in Character* by Wensley Clarkson.>

51. *n.* the whizzing of tranquilizer darts, as described in the novel *Cons, Scams, and Grifts* by Joe Gores.

52. *n.* the whoosh of a tossed hand grenade, as described in *Tanks for the Memories* by Aaron Elson.

53. *v.* to break through; to surpass.

<*Remember what Viola Spolin, the actress, teacher, and originator of improvisational theater, said: "First teach a person to develop to the point of his limitations and then—pfft!—break the limitations.* —Michael Levine, *Guerrilla P.R. Wired: Waging a Successful Publicity Campaign On-Line, Offline, and Everywhere In Between.*>

54. *v.* to carelessly dismiss.

<*You always go pfft when I say something good. You should let me be loving to you.* —Sue Miller, *While I Was Gone.*>

55. *v.* to combust into a cloud of smoke.

<*My name and the clan, buried. Burned up. Pfft. Becoming transparent smoke.* —Micheline Aharonian Marcom, *Three Apples Fell from Heaven.*>

<*Drinking at lunch, drinking before dinner, drinking during dinner, drinking after dinner, I declare if that little fat man with the bloodshot eyes that sat next to me stood near an open flame he'd have gone pfft like a celluloid collar.* —Herman Wouk, *Youngblood Hawke.*>

<*Till she'd done the unforgivable, landed the ultimate insult, and* pfft! *That home's up in smoke.* —Rosellen Brown, *Half a Heart.*>

56. *v.* to disband.

<*In the aftermath of the non-response to the album we continued to play around Manhattan, but it didn't take very long to lose whatever enthusiasm we'd generated amongst ourselves, and it didn't take much longer for us to allow the band to slowly, quietly dissolve. Pfft.* —Grant Jarrett, *More Towels: In Between the Notes.*>

57. *v.* to disincarnate.

<*The lama, when he was being led off to a prison camp, simply severed soul from body—pfft!—and that was the end of it. Liberation!* —Thomas Merton, *The Intimate Merton: His Life from His Journals.*>

58. *v.* to ejaculate, as in the song "The Big Black Bull" ("He pawed the ground and pfft in the fountain"), discussed in *The Erotic Muse: American Bawdy Songs* by Ed Cray; see also ffftt.

59. *v.* to fade away.

<*What's the point of living so long? Then you get old and ... pfft! You fade away. Why not die defending the Holy City? Be remembered as a martyr, huh?* —Bodie Thoene, *Jerusalem's Heart.*>

60. *v.* to spend money.

<*They say they sleep in Indian wigwams, and eat dirty Indian food, and when they come back in the summer—pfft!—they spend everything they have earned.* —Elizabeth George Speare, *Calico Captive.*>

<*He had some money. Whatever his aunt had lying around, pfft.* —Carol Lea Benjamin, *Fall Guy: A Rachel Alexander Mystery.*>

61. *v.* to spit in disgust.

<*"You should be ashamed of yourself ... pfft!" He spat in disgust. Wrublewski spat too.* —Fyodor Dostoevsky, *The Brothers Karamazov.*>

62. *v.* the spray painting of graffiti.

<*At night, a figure in dungarees with a mop of shaggy hair would have shaken a canister and angrily, joyfully, sprayed graffiti on the substation: pfft!* —Francesca Ferguson, *Deutschlandscape.*>

63. *v.* the bouncing of a moth.

<*The moth bounced against a row of books: pfft, pfft, pfft.* —Andrea Barrett, *The Voyage of the Narwhal.*>

64. *v.* the moment of death.

<*I've never told you but back in London (that time she was in hospital and refused to see me) she almost gave up the ghost pfft.* —Gérard Bessette, *Incubation.*>

pfft pfft.

1. *n.* a call to lure a dog, as in *Soon Be Free* by Lois Ruby.

2. *n.* puffs of breath, as when playing a musical instrument.

<*I look over and see Bubber putting his horn to the side of his mouth, and going, "pfft, pfft." He knew he couldn't find his mouthpiece, so he starts backing away.* —Garvin Bushell, *Jazz from the Beginning.*>

3. *n.* the noise of a breathing tube.

<*I see the oxygen tube / hear a soft noise / a pfft, pfft / as the air goes into the baby.* —Sharon Creech, *Heartbeat.*>

4. *n.* the squeaking of galoshes, as described in the novel *What Remains* by Nicholas Delbanco; see also fssst fssst.

pfft pfft pfft.

1. *n.* the sound of a locomotive's air reservoir valves at work.

<*A pfft pfft pfft spitting sound is made by water purge valves expelling water from the air reservoir.* —Brian Solomon, *GE Locomotives.*>

2. *n.* the sound of a moth bumping into things during flight.

<*The moth bounced against a row of books: pfft, pfft, pfft. Then soared up to the ceiling and into the window again.* —Andrea Barrett, *Voyage of the Narwhal: A Novel.*>

3. *n.* the sound of osprey feathers sprouting.

<*[M]y skin started to itch. Pfft! Pfft! Pfft! The hairs on my arms started growing like superfast-growing grass. Then each long hair blossomed into a feather.* —K.A. Applegate, *Animorphs #35.*>

pfft-pfft.

1. *n.* a grateful expression of thanks from a heavenly body, as discussed in *Shamanic Voices: A Survey of Visionary Narratives* by Joan Halifax; see pfft-pfft-pfft.

2. *n.* puffs of breath, as when playing a musical instrument.

<*[B]low the air out through your mouth, with your lips lightly closed, so that you clearly hear the breath coming out in puffs "pfft—pfft."* —Dirk Schellberg, *Didgeridoo: Ritual Origins and Playing Techniques.*>

pfft-pfft-pfft.

n. the whistling of the stars as they call to the soul of a shaman.

<*[A]ll the souls now pass up and down the souls' road, in order to keep it open for the shaman; some rush down, others fly up, and the air is filled with a rushing, whistling sound: "Pfft-pfft-pfft!" That is the stars whistling for the soul for the shaman, and the guests in the house must then try to guess the human names of the stars, the names they bore while living down on earth; and when they succeed, one hears two short whistles: "Pfft-pfft!" and afterwards a faint, shrill sound that fades away into space. That is the stars' answer, and their thanks for being still remembered.* —Joan Halifax, *Shamanic Voices: A Survey of Visionary Narratives.*>

Pfft'pfft'pfft'pfft-pfft.

n. The sound of machine-gun rounds pelting the snow, as in *Two Wars: One Hero's Fight on Two Fronts—Abroad and Within* by Nate Self.

pfftrw.

n. a muffled expression by someone whose mouth is sealed by duct tape, as in the novel *Heart Seizure* by Bill Fitzhugh.

pfp-ffffff-pfft.

n. the sound of convulsive laughter.

<*Alfredo opened his mouth to answer. "Pfp-ffffff-pfft," was all that he could articulate, and the two young men collapsed with laughter once again.* —Daniel Reveles, *Enchiladas, Rice, and Beans*.>

pfrr.

(also phrr.) *n.* a noncommittal mutter, as in the story "Potch" by Leo Rosten (anthologized in *A Passion for Books: A Book Lover's Treasury of Stories, Essays, Humor, Love and Lists on Collecting, Reading, Borrowing, Lending, Caring for, and Appreciating Books* by Harold Rabinowitz).

pftt.

n. the sound of a flying arrow.

<*A* pfft *sound, followed by a think, interrupted him. A feathered shaft quivered on the tree stump where Palin had been seated. The arrow was of elven make and design.* —Margaret Weis, *Dragons of Summer Flame*

phblthplbht.

n. a magic spell to conjure an "iron will" (Balanced Alternative Technologies Multi-User Dimension, Bat.org).

Phffft.

1. *n.* a modern dance theatre company based in New York and Seattle, Washington.

2. *n.* the title of a film from 1954.

<*Axelrod wrote his first script for Hollywood, 1954's Phffft! which featured Jack Lemmon and Judy Holliday as a divorced couple.* —"In Remembrance: George Axelrod," FilmBuffOnline.com.>

3. *n.* the title of an audio/visual artform by a musician and sculptor who goes by the name Trimpin, consisting of "a computerized collection of tubular organ pipes, duck calls, accordion reeds and other gadgets that rumble, squeak and crash" while hanging from the ceiling (*ClemsoNews*).

phffft.

1. (also phfft phfft.) *n.* an explosion in a video game.

<*As if by an extension of his finger, the darkened, mazelike chambers of the terrorist bunker exploded in balls of orange flame. Shadowy figures burst into narrow halls, phffft, phffft, phffft.* —James Patterson, *2nd Chance*.>

2. *adv.* “belly-up.”

<*His last few albums stiffed, his much-touted partnership with Pat Thrall went phffft, his band disbanded, he was several hundred thousand in the red.* —Bruce Pollock, “Pat Travers: Back on the Street.”>

3. *interj.* “phooey,” as said when spitting out something foul-tasting.

<*Can I have some? Phffft. Yuk. Can I have some more?* —Andrew McLean, “Ski Like a Dog.”>

4. *n.* a failing grade.

<*It seems that Prince was sort of disinterested in his performance, and I became disinterested in watching it. I give this dvd a phffft.* —Anonymous, “Review of Prince: Live at the Aladdin Las Vegas.”>

5. *n.* a quiet, delicate sound harboring vast implications.

<*The bloody Vietnam War which was to tear America apart, began with things that go phffft in the night.* —Peter Andrews, “Shots in the Dark: 25 Years Ago: The Battle of Tonkin Gulf is Fought.”>

6. *n.* the hiss of a dropped signal in a wireless microphone system.

<*As the talent moves across the stage with the wireless mic in operation you hear a “phffft” or maybe a “swisshhh” from the wireless system. You have a drop-out problem. No, not the high school variety, but rather a type of RF signal degradation that causes the desired signal to drop way down in strength to the point where the noise floor rises up and is heard.* —Lectrosonics.com.>

7. *n.* the sound of a faulty suction socket in a prosthetic limb.

<*If you should ever hear any kind of strange noises coming from your prosthesis (something along the lines of a “phffft, phffft, phffft” with each step), you should contact your prosthetist because you probably have a leak in the system somewhere. It is not normal for a suction system to make noise.* —Phillip Harrison, “Suction Suspension,” *In Motion*.>

8. *n.* the sound of a surgical procedure to the roof of the mouth so as to “enhance natural loyalties,” as in the novel *Nekropolis* by Maureen F. McHugh.

9. *n.* the whooshing of something disappearing in thin air; see also phfft[13].

<*She insists, he resists; they fall in love. And then—phffft!—she disappears from his life.* —Glenn Lovell, “Head Games,” *Mercury News*.>

10. *n.* the whooshing of world events “spiraling past so fast, flirting with our peripheral vision, that we have little time to properly frame an image or capture a reflective thought” (Kathleen Parker, “2003: Phffft! What Was That?” *Jewish World Review*).

11. *v.* divorced; see also phfft[11], pff-fft.

<*In his nationally syndicated column, [Walter] Winchell gave space to the couple when they got married. And the same five years later, when they went phffft.* —Richard Corliss, “Three Reasons to Love New York—Part III,” *Time*.>

phfft.

1. *adj.* incapacitated.

   <*Has anyone a concrete case, that this battery is "phfft & total kaputt."* —Heinrich Tauscher, Mir.com.>

2. *adj.* limp.

   <*What might have been an action-driven suspenser about a woman hiding from her double-dealing, dangerous hubby instead sags into a flabby, stylized teleplay that goes phfft. Written by Karen Black without much pizzazz, and directed adequately by Alan Metzger with some tense moments that do help, "Circle of Deceit" mostly chases its shadows.* —Tony Scott, "Circle of Deceit," *Variety*.>

3. *interj.* "that's crazy!"

   <*I mean, we all hear voices, but when you start answering them—phfft!* —Anonymous viewer of the television show "Wonderfalls" quoted in "'Wonderfalls,' a Comedy-Drama, May Seem Over the Edge to Some" by Gail Pennington, *St. Louis Dispatch*.>

4. *interj.* a sputtering of disgust or contempt.

   <*"An... an hour's passed already?" "Phfft," he sputters in disgust, "no you dummy. It's been about fifteen minutes."* —Don Lara, "The Slow Burn.">

5. *interj.* an exclamation of disappointment.

   <*It's like looking at the Brooklyn Bridge and saying "Phfft" because they didn't build the golden gate.* —TalkLeft.com>

6. *interj.* an expression indicating that someone has asked a stupid question.

   <*"Given up the spy trade?" "Phfft."* —K. A. Thompson, *As Simple as That*.>

7. *interj.* an expression indicating that someone has made a glaring understatement.

   <*"Who do we know who wants to ruin you?" "Phfft. Who do we know that doesn't?"* —Mary Adair, *Passion's Price: Book II*.>

8. *interj.* an expression that something is no longer available, as in "Caviar, Phfft. Now When You Cross the Atlantic, You'd Better Have Cucumber Slices" by Edward Wong (*New York Times*). In this article, Wong explains that with the end of Concorde's trans-Atlantic service, travelers accustomed to luxurious, high-speed flights would no longer be served caviar appetizers, and moreover should consider packing their own cucumber slices to soothe their tired eyes.

9. *n.* a muffled gunshot, as with a silencer; see also pfft[18].

   <*I pull a gun from my inside pocket and shoot him three times in the chest. Phfft. Phfft. Phfft. Silencers are wonderful. It's like plugging a pillow.* —Slipwater, "My Wife Glows in the Dark.">

10. *n.* zero.

<*Completion percentage: Phfft. Zero percent won't get you anything.* —Buccaneers.com.>

11. *v.* divorce; see also phffft[11], pff-fft.

<*Neither a corporate split nor a parental phfft! will keep the Olsen Twins from generating money in television, video, the movies, and now, books.* —*Billboard.*>

12. *v.* to blow air through pursed lips.

<*Avoid gesturing and aping the poses of the girls in the cigarette ads. It is graceless and unfeminine to "phfft" the little, loose pieces of tobacco that cling to your lips. Remove them inconspicuously with your fingertips—or change your brand.* —Prince George's County Historical Society.>

13. *v.* to disappear in a flash; see also phffft[9].

<*He fished for more than an hour with the fluttering roar inside his ear. Finally, he felt the insect near the surface, and phfft, it was gone.* —Keith McCafferty, "Trouble on the Wing: Big Problems Come in Small Packages," *Field and Stream.*>

14. *v.* to spit; see also pffft[8].

<*I like to recall my early days as reporter when a judge asked a convicted man for any last statement before receiving the sentence of the court. "Oh yes, your honor," the defendant said benignly. And, "phfft." He spit directly and broadly into the judge's face. The judge wiped the spittle off his forehead. He got up calmly and walked off the bench as the bailiffs subdued the defendant. Obviously, a recess was declared. In chambers, the judge recovered his dignity, grinned and said, "I guess if I was going to jail for a year, I'd be a little nervous, too."* —Harry Covert, "Firkytootlin' and Stuff.">

phfft phfft.

n. two flat bicycle tires.

<*They rode with me, made a gap, and welcomed me in physically and not verbally. This was a little strange. I approached the apparent leader of the group and demanded an explanation in a variety of languages, gestures, and bizarre bodily sounds. He responded by shaking two fingers, and going "phfft phfft" with his lips. I took this to mean his group had experienced two flat tires. This seemed reasonable, and I continued to ride with them in silence as we passed rider after rider.* —Paul Guttenberg, "Paris-Brest-Paris by Serendipity.">

phfft phfft phfft.

1. *n.* puffs of air leaking from a bicycle tire; see also phfft phfft.

<*I've never seen so much broken glass on the shoulder of a highway, and not just in one place, but for many miles. Inevitably, I picked up a big chunk in my back tire which I discovered after hearing the dreaded phfft, phfft, phfft, or something like that, coming from the back tire.* —Adam K., "Northern Washington and Southern BC Loop Tour of 8 Mountain Passes.">

2. *n.* the famous triple whoosh of Zorro's blade as he left the trademark symbol of his initial.

<Don Q, Son of Zorro *(1925), perhaps the quintessential [Douglas] Fairbanks film, was even better than its progenitor. It was followed by countless sound remakes, sequels, spin-offs, and spoofs. The only significant contribution these talkies made to the basic mix was the immortal sound effect "phffl! phffl! phffl!" —TVGuide.*>

phfft-phfft-phfft.

1. *n.* the spray of sand bombarded by machine gun fire.

   <*Phffl-Phffl-Phffl. More spraying sand, from machine gun fire, Smitty realized as the winking of muzzle flash blinked from all over the hill, and their staccato canvas-ripping sound filled his ears.* —EnWorld.org.>

2. *n.* the warning hiss of a cat.

   <*This court rules that neither 'Woof-woof-woof-woof-woof!' or 'Meow... Phffl-Phffl-Phffl!' constitutes hate speech.* —David Farley, "Doctor Fun, 9 April 96.">

phfftt.

n. a calling to attention.

<*Stresa was the first to feel the tremors and hiss in warning at Wren. "Elf Queen. Phfftl! Do you feel it? Hsst! Hsst! The earth moves!"* —Terry Brooks, *Anthrax.*>

phhbbppt.

n. a spurt of breath, as to blow something away from one's face; see also pffft[4].

<*Pffft. What's the deal with this damn phhbbppt tassel?* —Scott R. Kurtz, "PvP.">

phhhbt.

n. end of communication, as in "The Conspiracy of Dir en Grey" by Hidoko Matsumoto.

phhhh.

interj. a dismissive expression.

<*Nobody calls me on the house-phone line, not now that I've got my cell phone. Phhhh, I'm not answering it.* —Grace Dent, *LBD: It's a Girl Thing.*>

phhhhh.

n. a grunt, as when straining under the weight of a barbell.

<*"Phhhhh."* Clank. *The pope drops the barbell onto the Y rest over his head.* —Ethan Coen, *Gates of Eden.*>

phht.

v. to dribble.

<*Sometimes I think it is going to be a great one, and then it just sort of pffts out—there just isn't*

enough flow. —Lou Paget, *Orgasms: How to Have Them, Give Them, and Keep Them Coming.*>

phlrrt.

n. the choking sound of someone foaming at the mouth, as in the comic strip "PvP" by Scott R. Kurtz; see also blrgh, bsshh.

pht.

1. (also phpht). *interj.* an expression of mild anger, annoyance.

2. *n.* a possibly involuntary sound capable of arousing a feeling of poignancy about the human predicament.

<*When we sit down at the table, [my father] starts to eat and then he looks over and he sees that I'm doing this "thing" which I do quietly [to consecrate the meal]. I'm not coming on about it, I'm just sort of sitting quietly... and he'll hold his spoon in mid-air and he'll go "pht." It's almost an involuntary thing that comes out. It's like, "O.K., I'll wait for the kid... it's his* meshuggeneg *thing." Now that's not* satsang, *that is, that is not the community of monks on the path. And that "pht," whether that helps me or hinders me... is a function of where I'm at, really. In other words, if I am into what I'm doing strongly enough, all that that "pht" does is arouse a feeling of poignancy about our predicament, but it doesn't in any way deter from the amount of the living, vibrant quality I can invest in the thing I'm doing.* —Ram Dass, *The Only Dance There Is.*>

pht-pht-pht.

n. the sound of a series of things hatching forth.

<*All up the coast I could see the signs of what the Combine had accomplished since I was last through the country, things like, for example—a train stropping at a station and laying a string of full-grown men in mirrored suits and machined hats, laying them like a hatch of identical insects, half-life things coming pht-pht-pht out of the last car, then hooting its electric whistle and moving on down the spoiled land to deposit another hatch.* —Ken Kesey, *One Flew Over the Cuckoo's Nest.*>

phtrr.

n. an impatient mutter, as in the story "Potch" by Leo Rosten (anthologized in *A Passion for Books: A Book Lover's Treasury of Stories, Essays, Humor, Love and Lists on Collecting, Reading, Borrowing, Lending, Caring for, and Appreciating Books* by Harold Rabinowitz).

phttt.

(also pphht.) *n.* the sound of a skee ball machine feeding out a prize ticket, as in the graphic novel *Sordid City Blues* by Charles Schneeflock Snow.

pllrrt.

n. the sound of someone spitting coffee back into a pot, as when told that the coffee is for "employees only," in the comic strip "PvP" by Scott R. Kurtz.

plsh.

n. the sound of a boat's oars beating the waves of a ravaging maelstrom; see also pltt, splsh.

<*Plsh! slapped the oars into the rolling waves.* —Dennis L. McKiernan, *Dragondoom.*>

pltt.

n. the splashing of a boat's oars within a roaring whirlpool; see also plsh, splsh.

<*And caught within this elemental fury like insignificant wooden chips came three Dragonboats, spinning 'round the twisting hole in the sea, futile oars beating out a grim tattoo of death. Plsh! Pltt!* —Dennis L. McKiernan, *Dragondoom.*>

plz.

v. a shorthand for "please" often used in computer communication.

<*This is probably a stupid question but plz don't flame me.*>

plzplzplz.

(also plz plz plz.) *v.* a desperate plea, based upon a shorthand for "please" often used in computer communication.

pp.

1. *adj.* pianissimo (a musician's directive to perform a passage very softly).

2. *n.* the sound of a needle piercing a vein, as in *Baby Driver* by Jan Kerouac.

PPBBWRR.

n. the warning buzz of a housefly.

<*It bounced off the wall, then spiraled upward. As it neared the flypaper, the bluebottle buzzed once more: PPBBWRR—. A warning, 'BeWaRe!'"* —Peter Spielberg, *Hearsay.*>

ppffft.

1. *interj.* a dismissive sound.

<*Mrs. Morgan, who ran the Mom and Pop grocery store of my youth, told me she listened to radio soap operas "to learn about life." I was impressed and went home to recommend that my mother follow her example—to which my mother wisely replied, "ppffft." And she was right.* —John D. Husband, *Single Over Thirty.*>

2. *interj.* an expression of ridicule.

<*Kiki made a "ppffft" sound, then gave Hannah a withering stare. "Is itty bitty Hannah scared? Afraid the big bad policeman will slap her hand?"* —Annie Griffin, *Tall, Dead and Handsome.*>

3. *n.* the sound of someone spitting out her drink upon being surprised by emotional news, as in the comic strip "PvP" by Scott R. Kurtz.

4. *v.* to kill, especially by cutting the throat.

<*“Nobody much cares what happens inside those rats’ nests. But let them put one foot outside and ppffft.” He drew a line across his throat. “Then the machine guns will begin talking, eh?”* —Robert Ludlum, *Robert Ludlum’s The Lazarus Vendetta: A Covert-One Novel.*>

ppp.

1. *adj.* pianississimo (a musician’s directive to perform a passage very, very softly).

<*[Charles Ives’ composition] The Unanswered Question still seems a highly imaginative piece but it is no longer difficult to understand. Ives divides his chamber orchestra into two parts. The strings, which play very softly with mutes and very slowly throughout, contrast with the questioning solo trumpet and its related woodwind instruments. Ives himself describes in part his own intentions. “The strings play ppp throughout with no change in tempo. They are to represent the ‘Silences of the Druids—who know, see and hear nothing.’ The trumpet intones ‘the perennial question of existence,’ and states it in the same tone of voice each time.”* —Helen Faddis, Cape Ann Symphony “Program Notes.”>

<*“[T]here’s also about a thousand ppp-to-fff blasts, but only the one, the notorious One, going the other way....” Indeed, one reason for the work’s suppression is this subversive use of sudden fff quieting to ppp. It’s the touch of the wandering sound-shadow, the Brennschluss of the Sun.* —Thomas Pynchon, *Gravity’s Rainbow.*>

2. *n.* a French expression (usually accompanied by a shrug) meaning “beats me,” as discussed in *Street French Slang Dictionary & Thesaurus* by David Burke.

3. *n.* a sound made by a computer modem (*Linux Format Magazine*).

4. *n.* the sound of the letter p, as described in “Beginning Reading Design” by Valerie Lunceford; see also pppp[2].

ppp-fzzz.

n. the “weak fizzing sound” of a machine gun “out of propulsion gas,” as in the novel *Scarecrow* by Matthew Reilly.

ppphbbffft.

n. the sound of spitting out a beverage in disgust, as in the comic “Avalon, March 24, 2000” by Josh Phillips.

pppp.

1. *adj.* pianissississimo (a musician’s directive to perform a passage very, very, very softly).

<*In the Buenos Aires performance [of Verdi’s* Otello, *Mario] del Monaco ignores the composer’s repeated directives that Otello sing quite softly (the monologue begins with a “pppp” marking). Here, the tenor portrays Otello’s inner grief over Desdemona’s supposed adultery with stentorian tones, frequently straying from Verdi’s specified pitches, opting instead for* sprechstimme, *replete with sobs at almost every turn. As a result, this performance, as thrilling as it is, gives little sense of Verdi’s inexorable musical and emotional crescendo.* —Kenneth Meltzer, ClassicalCDReview.com.>

2. *n.* the sound of the letter p, as described in *The Voice That Means Business: How to Speak With Authority, Confidence and Credibility Anytime, Anywhere* by Linda Shields; see also ppp[4].

<*Where's the* pppp *sound in* computer? —Peggy Kaye, *Games for Learning: Ten Minutes a Day to Help Your Child Do Well in School, from Kindergarten to Third Grade.*>

pppp dddd.

n. an incoherent expression meaning one is feeling overheated and scared, as in the story "Waking Nightmares" by Ingrid Blythe Atkinson.

ppppp.

1. *adj.* pianississississimo (a musician's directive to perform a passage very, very, very, very softly).

<*A "crescendo" is not a peak of sound, or a sudden outburst, but a gradual increase in volume. Loudness is not even necessarily implied; Tchaikovsky, for example, goes so far as to indicate a crescendo from ppppp to pppp.* —William Safire, *The Right Word in the Right Place at the Right Time: Wit and Wisdom from the Popular Language Column in the New York Times Magazine.*>

2. *n.* the popping of popcorn, as described in *Tongue Tie—From Confusion to Clarity: A Guide to the Diagnosis and Treatment of Ankyloglossia* by Carmen Fernando.

pppppp.

adj. pianissississississimo (a musician's directive to perform a passage whisper softly).

<*The fact is that Tchaikovsky's use of five and six p's (ppppp and pppppp) at one end of the scale and quadruple f's (ffff) at the other end had nothing to do with playing louder or softer. Nor could it in reality. For all instruments have finite limitations of their dynamic range; and a composer could write fifteen f's for all that any instrument could play any louder than its natural acoustic limitations permit—except, of course, through the bane of amplification. Tchaikovsky was fascinated with something much more interesting than merely playing louder or softer; it was to achieve more refined, more discriminating gradations of dynamic levels, which he noted the best players (in chamber music-playing, for example) could command, and in fact used quite naturally in giving subtler profile to their phrasing and musical expression.* —Gunther Schuller, *The Compleat Conductor.*>

ppptr-rrrrrrr.

n. the alarm call of a grouse; see also whrrr.

<*Ppptr-rrrrrrr! There was a sudden burst of sound as a grouse broke from the cover of a nearby tree in a flurry of beating wings, scaring me half out of my wits.* —Cunthia DeFelice, *Weasel.*>

pprrpffrrppffff.

n. an expression meaning "I have done," from *Ulysses* by James Joyce.

pr’k.

n. “the rumble of long-remembered thunder and streaks of lightning split[ting] the skies” as “the sky clears its throat” (Jared Lobdell, “The Last Holosong of Christopher Lightning,” *Free Space*); see also n-n-n-n-n-n-n-n, pr’k-nnnnnnnn.

pr’k-nnnnnnnn.

n. the sound of the “sky clear[ing] its throat” with rolling thunder; the sound of a spaceship launch (Jared Lobdell, “The Last Holosong of Christopher Lightning,” *Free Space*); see also pr’k, n-n-n-n-n-n-n-n.

pr-r-r.

n. a purring sound.

<*‘Wo-o’ shouted Kal to his own team, knowing that this was the English for ‘pr-r-r!’* —Johan Bojer, *The Emigrants*.>

prpr prprprp.

n. the purring of a cat, as described by Leda Mesen in *Wishes, Lies, and Dreams: Teaching Children to Write Poetry* by Kenneth Koch.

prrp.

n. the call of the Chestnut-Banded Plover bird, as described in *Birds of Southern Africa* by Ian Sinclair.

prrprr.

n. purple, as in *Ulysses* by James Joyce.

prrr.

n. a typical sound made by a baby attempting to talk, as discussed in *Wonder Weeks: How to Turn Your Baby’s 8 Great Fussy Phases into Magical Leaps Forward* by Hetty Vanderijt.

prrrp-prrrp.

n. the ringing call of the Dark-necked Tailorbird, as described in *A Guide to the Birds of Southeast Asia* by Craig Robson.

prrrrp.

n. a roar of steam from a fog horn, as if the fog horn were clearing its throat to speak.

<*“Prrrrp! It’s a trifle windy up here; and, Great Boilers! how it rains!”* —Rudyard Kipling, “The Ship That Found Herself.”>

prrrrrrt.

n. the muffled call of the Grey-Backed Cisticola bird, as described in *Birds of Southern Africa* by Ian Sinclair.

prrrrt.

n. the “spluttering trilled” call of the Ashy Tailorbird, as described in *A Guide to the Birds of Southeast Asia* by Craig Robson.

prrrt.

n. the far-carrying cry of the Little Bustard bird, as described in *A Field Guide to the Birds of China* by John MacKinnon.

prrrt prrrt brrrt.

n. the “audible wing sounds” of the Batises family of birds as they fly from branch to branch in search of insects, as described in *Birds of Kenya and Northern Tanzania* by Roger Tory Peterson.

prrwht.

n. a contemptuous whisper.

<*Prrwht! Paddy Leonard said with scorn.* —James Joyce, *Ulysses*.>

przzt-przzt-przzt.

n. the “rapidly repeated” call of the Tawny-Flanked Prinia bird, as described in *Birds of Southern Africa* by Ian Sinclair.

ps-s-s-s-s-s-s-s-s-s.

n. the hissing of a snake, as described by Oscar Marcilla in *Wishes, Lies, and Dreams: Teaching Children to Write Poetry* by Kenneth Koch.

psh.

1. *interj.* an expression of ridicule.

<*Psh... You played that two pair like my dead mother would.* —Brion Foulke, *Flipside*.>

2. *n.* a sound effect for a fight sequence.

<*The fights looked much more convincing with psh! sound effects, which they lifted from the original film.* —The Guardian, “Indiana Jones Rides Again.”>

pshhh.

n. a sound made by a six-month-old baby, as described in the novel *Edwin Mullhouse* by Steven Millhauser.

pshhhhhhhhh.

n. a sound made by a baby.

<*He drops to a long pshhhhhhhhh, thinking.* —Steven Millhauser, *Edwin Mullhouse*.>

pshht.

n. a sound meaning “are you kidding?”

<*"So were you nervous today?" "Pshht! Me? I was cool as a cucumber," lied Irvine with a dismissing wave of his hand.* —Teri Stearns, "Final Fantasy VIII: Champagne Kiss.">

pshw.

interj. an expression of impatience or contempt. <*Pshw, right!*>

pshw pshw.

n. the sound of a pretend gun firing.

<*One of my trainmates was reading a Chinese magazine called "Police World." Half the pictures were of scantily clad lasses, and half were of handcuffed people being led away by "the fuzz." I pointed at the criminals, making a pretend pistol with my fingers. I went "pshw, pshw," and looked questioningly at the magazine's owner. He laughed and nodded.* —Paddy Carroll, "Beijing and Xinjiang.">

pss ssss.

n. the sound of people whispering, as in *Tourmaline: A Novel* by Joanna Scott.

psss.

1. *n.* a variation of psst; see also fsst[2], pssst[3], psst[2], ssss, ssstt.

   <*Psss, over there. That's him.* —Joanna Scott, *Tourmaline: A Novel.*>

2. *n.* the hiss of a carbonated beverage can being opened; see also shhhhht, sssss.

   <*There is no sound in the raft, either, except for the psss of a can being opened. Dominy is having one more beer.* —John McPhee, *Encounters with the Archdruid.*>

3. *n.* the hissing of air from a punctured bicycle tire.

   <*Psss. ... Nothing hisses quite so sweetly as a rival's puncture.* —Tim Krabbe, *The Rider.*>

4. *n.* the hissing of water in a leaking submarine.

   <*They are the ones whose pulse-rate doesn't alter when, 5,000 meters down, they hear psss! and a needle-jet of sea-water springs from a connector hole.* —James Hamilton-Paterson, *Three Miles Down: A Firsthand Account of Deep Sea Exploration and A Hunt for Sunken World War II Treasure.*>

psss psss.

1. *n.* a shushing sound.

   <*'Psss, psss,' Towanda said, shushing her.* —Denis Johnson, *Fiskadoro.*>

2. *n.* the sound of using friction to start a fire.

   <*"You make a bow and spin the arrow," said Roger. He rubbed his hands in mime. "Psss. Psss."* —William Golding, *Lord of the Flies.*>

psss psss psss.

n. the excited, insistent buzzing of the Rough-Legged Tyrannulet bird, as described in *A Guide to the Birds of Columbia* by Steven L. Hilty; the call of the White-Fronted Tyrannulet bird.

<*In Costa Rica [the White-Fronted Tyrannulet has been] heard to give an excited-sounding insistent psss psss psss.* —Robert S. Ridgely, *A Guide to the Birds of Panama.*>

psss pssss psss psss psss.

n. a sound to lure a cat into bed, as in the play *Stop Kiss* by Diana Son.

psss pssssss psssss pss.

n. the sound of whispering into the ear of one's Zen master.

<*Some Zen schools only want to see you answer this question by going up to the teacher and making a whispering sound in the teacher's ear. "Psss, pssssss, psssss, pss."* —Seung Sahn, *The Compass of Zen.*>

psss-psss-psss.

n. the hissing of an aerosol can spraying.

<*[A]s I moved persuasively into my next [sermon] point, the trustee returned to the scene of the mishap, this time with a can of scented air freshener. Psss-psss-psss. Pause. Psss-psss-psss. And for good measure: Psss. Suddenly, the whole church smelled like an alpine forest gone slightly off.* —William H. Willimon, *Pastor: A Reader for Ordained Ministry.*>

psss-ss-st.

n. a sound calling one's attention.

<*What would you think if a man in a string tie and a long, black coat came up to you and said, "Psss-ss-st. Wanna buy a drink that stops cancer of the skin, lung, stomach, colon, liver, breast, esophagus, and pancreas?"* —Selene Yeager, *Doctor's Book of Food Remedies.*>

psssh.

1. *interj.* a dismissive sound.

<*"Psssh," he said, fanning me off with one hand. "Just stand back, okay?"* —Sarah Dessen, *Someone Like You.*>

<*"I'm a volunteer," Trula said. "Well, of course* you *don't need the money. Psssh." She dismissed Trula with a slash of her hand.* —James Hall, *Bones of Coral.*>

2. *interj.* a sarcastic expression.

<*He lifted his hands in mock admiration. "Psssh!" said Papa. "What clever children I have!"* Judith Kerr, *When Hitler Stole Pink Rabbit.*>

<*"Psssh, was she ever wrong about you," she added, sarcastically.* —Victor McGlothin, *What's a Woman to Do?*>

3. *interj.* a shushing sound.

<*Psssh! These are matters we must not discuss.* —Jack Vance, *Alastor.*>

4. *interj.* a sound to call someone's attention.

<*"Psssh!" Nazneen turned around. She turned back again. "Psssh!" There was a dead man tied to a tree. His wrists were lashed to a branch and his feet dangled a few inches above the ground. His head fell forward, as if his neck were snapped. "Come closer," he croaked.* —Monica Ali, *Brick Lane: A Novel.*>

5. *interj.* a whooshing sound to accompany a hand gesture meaning that someone missed a point.

<*"Psssh"—he sliced his palm through the air—"[the meaning went] over their heads."* —Ron Powers, *Tom and Huck Don't Live Here Anymore.*>

6. *interj.* an emphatic expression.

<*Born-again. Huh! You ain't convincin' me that because you was born-again yesterday that you weren't freakin' the day before. Psssh... every girl got some freak in her, so don't even try to deny it.* —Relentless Aaron, *Triple Threat.*>

7. *interj.* an expression of contempt.

<*"Psssh." He wrinkled his mouth and nose at my stupidity, causing his small gray mustache to twitch between them.* —John Morgan Wilson, *Moth and Flame: A Benjamin Justice Novel.*>

<*"Psssh," Delp waves his hand contemptuously. "Need I remind you that the human animal is infinitely various, and that what will dispatch one quite neatly may not necessarily, inexorably and in all cases do the trick for another.* —T.C. Boyle, *Water Music.*>

<*Psssh. Beverly was an evil one. Good riddance to bad rubbish.* —Rochelle Alers, *Island Magic.*>

8. *interj.* an expression of frustration.

<*I'm then stuck again till 3:45 pm for the next bus back to High Wycombe. Psssh!* —Marc Fleisher, *Making Sense of the Unfeasible: My Life Journey with Asperger Syndrome.*>

9. *n.* a "gushing auditory noise" to accompany a character's offstage performance in Samuel Beckett's play *Waiting for Godot*, as discussed in *Theatrical Notebooks of Samuel Beckett: Waiting for Godot.*

10. *n.* a rhythmically-repeated call to provoke the curiosity of and attract "sparrows, warblers, jays, vireos, chickadees, nuthatches, hummingbirds, flycatchers, bushtits, orioles, kinglets, wrens" and other smaller species of birds, mimicking "many birds' scolding call" and "a mother bird's feeding call to her young" (Joseph Cornell, *Sharing Nature with Children*).

11. *n.* the sound of an exhalation, as in the novel *Addiction* by G.H. Ephron.

12. *n.* the sound of an explosion, as during warfare.

<*We killed them all. Close to four dozen men. Psssh!* —Marc Bojanowski, *The Dog Fighter: A Novel.*>

13. *n.* the sound of something squishy.

<*[Y]our feet are hot and sweaty because they seem to be covered with something that compresses periodically, rhythmically, accompanied by* psssh. —John Smolens, *Fire Point: A Novel of Suspense.*>

14. *n.* the sound of urinating, as in the comic book *Schizo #2* by Ivan Brunetti.

psssshhhh.

n. the hiss of a soda can, as in the comic strip "PvP" by Scott R. Kurtz; see also pfffsss, psst[4].

pssssssht.

n. radio static; white noise.

<*PSSSSSSHT! Heavy static followed the interrupted transmission, and the soldier at the radio frowned as he tried to reach the communications van again, to no avail.* —Black Dragon, "Guardian: A Ranma 1/2 Fanfiction.">

psssst.

n. a "conspiratorial whisper," as in the novel *The Stand: Expanded Edition* by Stephen King.

pssst.

1. *n.* a "sexy whisper," as discussed in *The Beak of the Finch: A Story of Evolution in Our Time* by Jonathan Weiner.ul

2. *n.* a conspiratorial whisper.

<*Without a map, you wouldn't even know where Twig was (pssst... Minnesota).* —Spencer Strauss, *The Unofficial Guide to Real Estate Investing.*>

3. *n.* a muted hiss used surreptitiously to get attention; see also fsst[2], psss[1], psst[2], ssstt.

<*"Pssst!" said a voice a few paces onward. It was Appleby, hiding in back of a tree.* —Joseph Heller, *Catch 22.*>

<*Pain is the body's way of getting our attention; from "Pssst!" to a thunder clap.* —Pete Egoscue, *The Egoscue Method of Health Through Motion: Revolutionary Program That Lets You Rediscover the Body's Power to Rejuvenate Itself.*>

4. *n.* the hiss of a deodorant spray.

<*You've all seen a certain deodorant commercial on television. You put one spray—psst ... psst—under each arm, and for twenty-four hours a day, an invisible shield forms around your body. The advertiser couldn't care less whether you or I understand the commercial, or whether there is evidence to support his claim. The advertiser simply wants to demonstrate how this spray meets* your *needs and desires to be socially acceptable.* —Herb Cohen, *You Can Negotiate Anything.*>

5. *n.* the hiss of air from a sealed can.

<*My passion for the sport became so intense, I would idly hold a tennis ball and just sniff it. The* pssst *and the rubbery fragrance of opening a can of new tennis balls became intoxicating.* —R. Kent Hughes, *Disciplines of a Godly Man.*>

6. *n.* the sound of something disappearing into thin air.

<*When your obstacles seem fearfully large and looming, let the air out of them! Fear and worry are nothing more tangible than hot air.* Pssst. *They're gone!* —Squire Rushnell, *When God Winks: How the Power of Coincidence Guides Your Life.*>

psst.

1. *n.* a horse's hiss.

<*Writing a preface is like ... pressing one's left leg to the horse, pulling the reins to the right, and hearing the steed say "psst" and telling the whole world to get lost.* —Soren Kierkegaard, quoted in *Soren Kierkegaard: A Biography* by Joakim Garff.>

2. *n.* a sound used surreptitiously to get attention; see also fsst[2], psss[1], pssst[3], ssstt.

<*When he had put about a mile between him and the dragon he stopped and collapsed against a tree, which then spoke to him. "Psst," it said. Dreading what he might see, Rincewind let his gaze slide upward. ... Finally it fixed on a black sword thrust straight through the branch above Rincewind's head. "Don't just stand there," said the sword (in a voice like the sound of a finger dragged around the rim of a large empty wine glass). "Pull me out."* —Terry Pratchett, *The Color of Magic.*>

3. *n.* a type of clam.

<*Throw in some sweetbreads, throw in some mountain oysters and some psst clams!* —Henry Miller, *Tropic of Cancer.*>

4. *n.* the hiss of a soda can, as in the comic strip "PvP" by Scott R. Kurtz; see also pfffsss, psssshhhh.

5. *n.* the sound of a jet car flying past, as in the graphic novella *Hearts and Minds* by Scott McCloud.

6. *n.* the sound of an office coffee machine that dispenses via hypodermic needle, in the comic book *Hyperco* by Aaron K.

psst psst.

n. a beckoning sound.

<*Don Quixote had reached this point in his piteous lament when the innkeeper's daughter began to attract his attention by saying, "Psst, psst," and calling to him: "Señor, please come here, if your grace doesn't mind."* —Miguel de Cervantes, *Don Quixote.*>

pssw.

n. a hiss of steam, as from a street cleaning truck spraying roads and sidewalks with water; see also pfffff[6].

<*Pssw! Pfffff! From the brown dry streets, steam sent up a sudden ejaculation and I saw it in each particle of light, saw all its constituent parts, vibrant, more alive than anything I had ever seen. I watched this cloud, gravity-defying, soar upwards and dissolve into tendrils of mist, up, up into the sky, beyond brick and brownstone façades, treetops and the dusty-windowed towers beyond, each window of which caught refractions of multi-coloured brilliance.* —A.N. Wilson, *Hearing Voices*.>

pthbthththth.

n. a "great roar of flatulence, much as would a hundred buffoons' air-filled, pig's-bladder-cushions prolongedly break wind were they all simultaneously sat upon," as in *Once Upon a Winter's Night* by Dennis L. McKiernan.

Pthr.

n. the title of a work of art by Michael Paulus based upon illuminated eye charts of the 1800s but modified so that "clinical function is surpassed by style and frivolity" (MichaelPaulus.com).

ptschschschz.

n. a cough, as by Tigger in *The House at Pooh Corner* by A. A. Milne.

pzzz.

n. a buzzing sound, as by the venomous flying "Nizzik" insects in the novel *Akiko and the Intergalactic Zoo* by Mark Crilley; see also kzz-fzzz, fzz-nkk.

pzzzt.

n. the sound of a poison dart hitting its target.

<*"It was a bounty hunter called—" Pzzzt. Something struck the assassin in the neck.* —Brandon McKinney, *Star Wars: Attack of the Clones*.>

pzzzz.

interj. hush.

<*"Pzzzz," Valerie said to me, in her distinctive way of telling me to be quiet.* —Mike McCardell, *Back Alley Reporter*.>

pzzzzz pzzzzz.

n. the "buzzy" call of the foraging Olive-backed Tanager, as described in *Birds of Venezuela* by Steven L. Hilty.

pzzzzzz.

n. the hiss of air from a vacuum-sealed can.

<*I watch you when you get undressed at night. Nothing moves. You're vacuum packed. When you open your belt I expect it to go like a can of coffee —Pzzzzzz!* —Neil Simon, *Plaza Suite*.>

pzzzzzzz.

1. *n.* the "sound of flushing toilets," as described in *Southern Ladies & Gentlemen* by Florence King.

2. *n.* the sound of lightning bolts shooting holes through the sky, as described in *War Cries* by Diane Glancy.

qch.

interj. a casual, cough-like utterance meaning *oh.*

<*"How's Andy," he asked casually. "Qch, fine," said the other.* —Dorothy L. Sayers, *The Five Red Herrings*.>

Qqq.

n. the name of a character with glowing yellow eyes in the novel *The Martian Chronicles* by Ray Bradbury.

qqq.

n. the sound of the letter q (ChildFun.com).

qqqq.

n. a bit of cosmic dust.

<*It didn't matter a qqqq whether the extrajovian world survived intact or turned to interstellar gravel.* —Ian Stewart, *Wheelers*.>

QT.

n. secret; in confidence.

<*I thought everything was on the QT, man. Like they might be listening.* —Michael Connelly, *The Narrows: A Novel.*>

Qwrk.

n. the name of an eight-year-old genius in the Australian miniseries "Halfway Across the Galaxy and Turn Left," based on the novel with the same name by Robin Klein.

qwrk.

n. a peculiar behavior; quirk. This particular spelling highlights the idiosyncratic nature of a quirk.

<*I find little qwrks in the game that I'd like to fix.* —Cyber 1, GamePort.com.>

Qwrt.

n. a sub-clan of the Darkfall multiplayer online role playing game.

qwrts.

n. the sound of swallowing back tears of nostalgia.

<**Sigh* ... those were the days ... qwrts ... qwrts ... qwrts ...* —Silverfox, ubi.com.>

Qwsp.

n. an enemy of Aquaman from the 5th dimension (*Aquaman #1*).

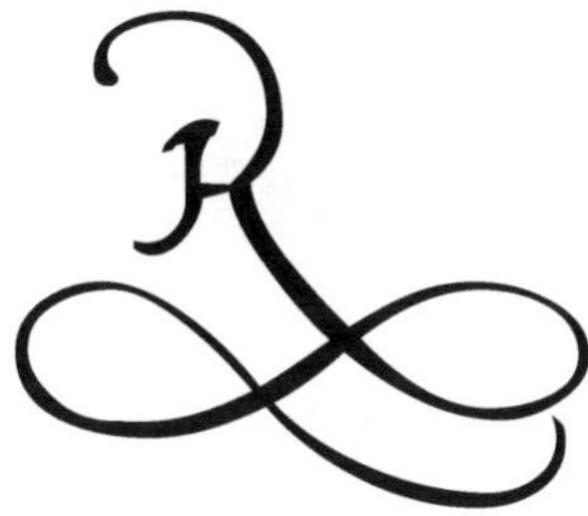

r-r-r-r-r-r-r.

n. the growl of a tiger, as described in *Wishes, Lies, and Dreams: Teaching Children to Write Poetry* by Kenneth Koch.

rglx.

n. in the Tashlhiyt dialect of Berber, this means "I locked."

rgr.

n. a grumbling or growling sound.

<*Rgr, I'm sooo tired.* —Karawynn Long, *Diary*.>

rgsdrdgrg.

n. the title of a visual poem by Mike Cannell.

rhhh.

n. a noncommittal answer, as spoken with congested sinuses.

<*"I love whales. They're the most majestic of the creatures, don't you think?" "Rhhh."* —Christopher Buckley, *Thank You for Smoking*.>

rmb.

1. *n.* the rumble of a whirlpool in a lake that has inexplicably absorbed six hurricanes, as in the graphic novel *Uzumaki 3* by Junji Ito.

2. *n.* the sound of roofing tiles tumbling down during a hurricane, as in the graphic novel *Uzumaki 2* by Junji Ito.

rmg.

n. the sound of rummaging through a purse or bag, as in the graphic novel *Uzumaki 3* by Junji Ito.

rmm rmm rmm rrrrrrmmmmm.

n. a sound made by someone "pommelling on the sofa" (James Joyce, *Ulysses*).

Rmmm.

n. a nickname in college for someone with a "tendency to mumble" (Roy Bount Jr., *Be Sweet: A Conditional Love Story*).

rmmm.

1. *n.* the rumble of a large van on the street, as in the novel *The Knights of Silversnow* by Tony Abbott.

2. *n.* the sound of an electric food-mixer; see vzzzz.

rmmm-rmmm-rmmm.

n. the "wide open" vibrating of an automobile engine, as described in *Happy to Be Here* by Garrison Keillor.

rmmmm rmmmm.

interj. a sound used to fill a pause in speaking while one thinks, as in the novel *A Rat's Tale* by Tor Seidler.

rmmmm rmmmm rmmmm.

n. the rumble of an airplane motor, as described in the novel *Ned Mouse Breaks Away* by Tim Wynne-Jones.

rmmmm rmmmmmm rmmmmmmmm.

n. the sound of "American bombers" flying past, as described in *After Sorrow: An American Among the Vietnamese* by Lady Borton.

rmmmmm.

n. the sound of an automobile engine, as described in *Rookie Dad: Fun and Easy Exercises and Games for Dads and Babies in Their First Year* by Susan Fox.

rmmmmm brmmmmmm.

n. the sound of an automobile engine, as described in the novel *No Place* by Kay Haugaard.

rmmmmm rmmm.

n. the "sound of a sports car engine" (Leslie Glass, *Over His Dead Body: A Novel of Sweet Revenge*).

rn.

n. the title of a visual poem by Mike Cannell.

rr rrr rrrr.

interj. an interjection by a merchant from the imaginary "Lanternland," as in the novel *Gargantua and Pantagruel* by François Rabelais.

rr-rr-rrrrrrrr-rrrrrrrr.

n. the cricket-like chirping and snorting of "some hydra-shaped creature with long spindly limbs, planted upsidedown in a snow bank" (Tom Trainor, *Rocker Heaven*).

rr-rrr-rrrr.

n. a tawny owl's joyful hoot.

<*When something happened that was delightful to it the owl made a characteristic sound, a high-pitched rr-rrr-rrrr, like a bell. At the same time it closed its eyes.* —*Dogs That Know When Their Owners Are Coming Home: And Other Unexplained Powers of Animals* by Rupert Sheldrake.>

rrc.

n. the title of a visual poem by Mike Cannell.

rrRRRrrrrrr.

n. a police siren.

<*Just then—as they say in children's books—*just then, *there was a wonderful sound. Cutting through the night came the, blissfully not-too-distant,* rr*RRR*rrrrrr *of a police car flicking its siren on for just a moment as an announcement that it was on its way.* —Mil Millington, *A Certain Chemistry: A Novel.*>

rrmmbl.

n. the rumble of the first tumbling boulder of a deadly landslide, as in the comic book *Amazing Adventures #8* by Bill Everett.

rrmmmbll.

n. the thundering footstep of a giant monster, as in the comic strip "PvP" by Scott R. Kurtz.

rrmmmm rrmmmm.

n. the sound of military "tanks and halftracks winding up," as described in *A Blood-Dimmed Tide: The Battle of the Bulge by the Men Who Fought It* by Gerald Astor.

rrmmmmm.

n. a "wet growling noise," as described in the novel *Tourist Season* by Carl Hiassen.

Rrr.

n. the name of a character with glowing yellow eyes in the novel *The Martian Chronicles* by Ray Bradbury.

<*"Earth is a place of all* jungle," *said Miss Rrr proudly.* —Ray Bradbury, *The Marian Chronicles.*>

rrr.

1. *interj.* an expression that the temperature is uncomfortably cold; see also br, brr[1], brrr[1], brrrr[5], brrrrrrr[3], brrrrrrrr[3], rrrrr[5].

<*Rrr! I'm cold, monkey! You're not. You're working.* —Thomas Harlan, *Wasteland of Flint.*>

2. *interj.* the sound of shivering.

<*Rrr! I'm cold, monkey!* —Thomas Harlan, *Wasteland of Flint.*>

3. *n.* a growl of pain, as during hair removal.

<*Leona's a tiny Ukrainian woman, and she makes this growly sound as she rips the strips of muslin and wax off,* rrr, *and when she's done both my legs and there's no more hurting, she rubs lotion into them.* —Nicholson Baker, *Vox.*>

4. *n.* a typical sound made by a baby attempting to talk, as discussed in *Wonder Weeks: How to Turn Your Baby's 8 Great Fussy Phases into Magical Leaps Forward* by Hetty Vanderijt.

5. *n.* an imbecilic utterance.

<*"Rrr! Rrr! ..." gabbled the imbecile, dribbling a whitish foam down his chin.* —Raphael Confiant, *Mamzelle Dragonfly.*>

6. *n.* the honk of a nose blowing like a foghorn; see also rrrrrrrsss.

<*Rrr. And deepmoved all, Simon trumping compassion from foghorn nose, all laughing, they brought him forth, Ben Dollard, in right good cheer.* —James Joyce, *Ulysses.*>

7. *n.* the sound of the letter r (Baby-Parenting.com); see also rrrr[17], RRRR[3], rrrrrr[10], rrrrr[25], rrrrrrr[25].

rrr rrr rrr rrr rrr rrr rrr rrr rrrrrrr.

n. the howl of wolves singing the second line of Mozart's *Eine Kleine Nachtmusik*, as in *Origins of Story: On Writing for Children* by Barbara Harrison.

<*I opened up my mouth and sang at the hills the opening melodic line of Mozart's* Eine Kleine Nachtmusic, *that famous broken tonic chord:* "La, *la* la, *la* la *la la la laaaa. ..." Now there were some wolves who lived in the hills across the valley. They heard me singing. They threw their heads in the air and howled back the second line:* "Rrr, *rrr* rrr, *rrr* rrr *rrr rrr rrr rrrrrrr. ..."* —Barbara Harrison, *Origins of Story: On Writing for Children.*>

rrr-rrr-rrr.

1. *n.* the groaning of a cold car engine struggling to start.

<*From downstairs came the sound of Kenny slamming out of the house, then the more distant rrr-rrr-rrr of Cindy's car struggling to start in the cold.* —Monica Wood, *Ernie's Ark: Stories.*>

2. *n.* the sound of "an engine revving up," as described in *Destructive Emotions: A Scientific Dialogue with the Dalai Lama* by Daniel Goleman.

3. *n.* the throaty sound of a toy motor (American Speech-Language-Hearing Association).

rrrggh.

(also rrrrrgh.) *n.* the howl of the man-wolf, as in the comic book *Giant-Size Superheroes #1* by Gil Kane.

rrrgh.

interj. a groan of exertion, as when one is "tugging violently" on large boards nailed across a doorway in the novel *Akiko and the Great Wall of Trudd* by Mark Crilley.

rrrhl.

n. a grunt in the Wookie language of the *Star Wars* films, as transcribed in the book *Return of the Jedi* by James Kahn.

rrrll chchch.

n. a cannibal madman's last words in the H. P. Lovecraft short story "The Rats in the Walls."

rrrmm.

n. an incoherent mumbling.

<*[M]y hat's an open book but Doris Day eats rrrmm.* —Andy Warhol, *A: A Novel.*>

rrrmmm.

1. *n.* an intimate purr.

   <*"Rrrmmm," he purred, moving toward her. "And who is this? What is your name, lovely one?"* —Anne McCaffrey, *Doona.*>

2. *n.* the sound of someone eating, as in the novel *Good News* by Edward Abbey.

RRRMMMM.

n. the sound of a motorcycle revving, as described in the novel *Raptor* by Paul Zindel.

rrrmmmm.

n. the sound of a racecar "spin[ning] out," as in *Storm Rides: A Novel* by Craig Lesley.

rrrmmmmm.

n. the rumble of an earthquake, as described in the novel *The Magic Engineer* by L.E. Modesitt Jr.

rrrpr.

n. the rumbling of far-off hoofbeats in *Ulysses* by James Joyce.

RRRR.

1. *n.* a howl like that of a werewolf, as in the novel *Mason & Dixon* by Thomas Pynchon.

2. *n.* the roar of a giant hell-bent on destroying a village, as in *The Sleeping Giant of Goll* by Tony Abbott.

3. *n.* the sound of the letter r; see also rrr[7], rrrr[17], rrrrr[25], rrrrrr[10], rrrrrrr[25].

   <*Some people find it easy to make this sound; it's a sound from childhood like when we made the sound of an engine or a plane taking off. With the RRRR sound, your tongue is about a quarter-*

inch to a half-inch behind your teeth. —Jonathan Goldman, *Tantra of Sound: How to Enhance Intimacy With Sound.*>

Rrrr.

n. the name of a cat in the novel *Ghost Cats* by Susan Shreve.

rrrr.

1. *adv.* yes, as spoken while yawning.

   <*"Rrrr," Hughie said, which would have been* yes *if he hadn't been yawning.* —Donald E. Westlake, *Bad News.*>

2. *interj.* a growl accompanying a bear-hug.

   <*[H]e came over and gave me a hug. "Rrrr," he said, squeezing. "You get shorter every time I see you, big brother."* —Dan Chaon, *Among the Missing.*>

3. *interj.* a growl of irritation.

   <*Rrrr, how irritating. Thanks to you, it was another wasted day.* —Ken Akamatsu, *Love Hina: Book 2.*>

4. *interj.* a grumble of disgust; see also rrrrr[4].

   <*Garbage and plastic everywhere— / In the streets, on the beaches, in the bellies of whales! / Rrrr, humans are so disgusting! Noxious vermin, infesting this planet.* —Camille Maurine, *Meditation Secrets for Women: Discovering Your Passion, Pleasure, and Inner Peace.*>

5. *interj.* an annoyed grumble, as when one's parents crash a skinny-dipping party in the novel *Insiders* by J. Minter.

6. *interj.* an expression equivalent to "oops."

   <*He touched a knob, and the view expanded so fast that Louis's hand clutched for a throttle. "I want to show you the rim wall. Rrrr, a bit off ..." He touched another fierce-visaged knob, and the view slid. They were looking over the edge of the Ringworld.* —Larry Niven, *Ringworld.*>

7. *n.* a baby's imitation of a toy car sound, as discussed in *Your Baby's First Year Week by Week* by Glade B. Curtis.

8. *n.* a growl of resentment over someone's superiority, as in the comic strip "PvP" by Scott R. Kurtz.

9. *n.* a stomach's hungry growl; see also rrrrr[15].

   <*"Perhaps I'll make her something to eat—" Rrrr. It was like my stomach actually heard that word.* —Tony Abbott, *Cracked Classics #1: Trapped in Transylvania: Dracula.*>

10. *n.* a throaty growl approximating the voice of the Marsh Monster, as described in *Sammy Keyes and the Skeleton Man* by Wendelin Van Draanen.

11. *n.* the creaking of an old wooden canal boat, as described in *The Magic Escapes* by Tony Abbott.

12. *n.* the noise of a robot.

<*'I'm Robot Man,' little Freak would go, making these weird robot noises as he humped himself around the playground. Rrrr ... rrrr ... rrrr ... like he had robot motors inside his legs.* —Rodman Philbrick, *Freak the Mighty*.>

13. *n.* the purring of a cat, as described in *The Faeries' Oracle* by Brian Froud; the growls of a communicative cat, as in the novel *Ghost Cats* by Susan Shreve; the hopeful trill of a cat hungry for a snack, as in the novel *A Stitch in Time* by Monica Ferris.

<*We began to have long conversations back and forth. "Rrrr," he would say. "Rrrrr," I replied. "Rrrrrrr," he continued. "Rrrrrrrrrrrrrrrrr."* —Susan Shreve, *Ghost Cats*.>

14. *n.* the soft note of the Ring-necked duck, as described in *Stokes Field Guide to Birds: Eastern Region* by Donald Stokes.

15. *n.* the sound of a "bus's transmission," as described in *Riding the Bus With My Sister: A True Life Journey* by Rachel Simon.

16. *n.* the sound of French words shouted by thousands of troops, as in *War and Peace* by Leo Tolstoy.

17. *n.* the sound of the letter r; see also rrr[7], rrrr[17], RRRR[3], rrrrr[25], rrrrrr[10], rrrrrrr[25].

<*"My father is still in Cuba. A small town outside Camagüey City called Cascorro." The* rrrr *flowed off his tongue.* —Barbara Parker, *Suspicious of Innocence*.>

18. *n.* the vibratory roar of an airplane propeller, as described in the novel *The Queen of the South* by Arturo Pérez-Reverte.

rrrr rrrr.

1. *n.* a police siren.

<*Office Goldberg turned on the siren and Officer Johnson drove off.* Rrrr! Rrrr! *Each time the car hit a bump, Cam's and Eric's heads hit the roof of the car.* Rrrr! Rrrr! —David A. Adler, *Cam Jansen and the Catnapping Mystery*.>

2. *n.* the ringing of a school bell, as in *Young Cam Jansen and the Lost Tooth* by Susanna Natti; see also brrnnngg[2].

rrrr rrrr rrrr.

1. *n.* the "little" sound of a sewing machine, as in the story "Woman Hollering Creek" by Sandra Cisneros (anthologized in *The Scribner Anthology of Contemporary Short Fiction: Fifty North American Stories Since 1970* by Lex Williford); see also rrrrrrrrr[10].

2. *n.* the howl of a tornado ripping through a wheat field, as described in *The Breathtaker* by Alice Blanchard.

RRRR RRRR RRRRR.

(also RRRRR RRRR RRRRR, RRRR RRRRRR RRRRR.) *n.* the rasping of a blade being sharpened.

<RRRR RRRR RRRRR *rasped the blade. He'd been sharpening the knife a long time; I*

wondered how sharp it had to be. Perhaps he would forget to stop and would sharpen it down to nothing. RRRRR RRRR RRRRR. —Richard Mosher, *Zazoo.*>

rrrr rrrrrr.

n. the fast whine of a motorboat whose motor is sticking out of the water, as described in *The Ship and the Storm: Hurricane Mitch and the Loss of the Fantome* by Jim Carrier.

rrrr-cchhh-rrr.

(also r-cchhh-rrr.) *n.* a leonine growl in celebration of sloppy eating, as discussed in *She's Had a Baby and I'm Having a Meltdown* by James D. Barron.

RRRR-rrr-rrr-rr.

n. a "loud and raspy" snore, as in the novel *A Crazy, Mixed-Up Spanglish Day* by Marisa Montes; see also RRRRR-rrrr.

rrrr-rrr-rrrr.

n. a schoolchild's imitation of a growling dog, as described in *Captain Underpants and the Invasion of the Incredibly Naughty Cafeteria Ladies from Outer Space* by Dav Pilkey.

RRRR-rrrr.

n. the call of a hawk flying overhead, as described in *High Tide in Tucson: Essays from Now or Never* by Barbara Kingsolver.

rrrr-rrrrr.

n. the sound of a fishing reel, as described in *Wisdom of the Guides: Rocky Mountain Trout Guides Talk Fly Fishing* by Paul Arnold.

rrrrlllll.

n. the sound of an automobile spring rolling on the ground, as in the graphic novel *Uzumaki 2* by Junji Ito.

RRRRR.

1. *n.* a lawnmower.

<*Outside she pushes the RRRRR-Thing over the grass fiercely and it eats the grass for her.* —Patricia Finney, *I, Jack.*>

2. *n.* a subdued war cry.

<*"RRRRR," I growl as I run through, not quite yelling the war cry Urien wants. I may be comfortable enough with this culture to growl through clenched teeth, but not enough to open wide and yell.* —Patrick O'Donnell, *The Knights Next Door: Everyday People Living Middle Ages Dreams.*>

3. *n.* the rumble of a "car engine roar[ing] to life" (Bonny Becker, *My Brother, the Robot*).

4. *n.* the tentative title of a "hotel-of-crooks" movie script by Alfred Hitchcock, as discussed in *Alfred Hitchcock: A Life in Darkness and Light* by Patrick McGilligan.

5. *n.* the whistling of the wind at night, like “the noise of the celebration of [one's] wedding night” (Lila Abu-Lughod, *Writing Women's Worlds: Bedouin Stories*).

RRRrr.

interj. an angry growl.

<*“RRRrr,” Kelli growled from the other table. “Let's go before someone gets really hurt,” Jonathan said.* —J. Minter, *Insiders*.>

rrrrr.

1. *interj.* a growl of resentment.

<*“Sssh! You will spoil the whole thing if you don't play along.” “Rrrrr,” said Emerson. It sounded like the amplified purr of a large cat but was, in fact, a growl.* —Elizabeth Peters, *Guardian of the Horizon*.>

2. *interj.* a menacing shout that means “I'll rip your guts out” (Howard Simon, *Forbidden Research*).

3. *interj.* an emphatic expression, as when describing a particularly “tough” person (Charles Bukowski, quoted in *Bukowski and the Beats: A Commentary on the Beat Generation* by Jean-Francois Duval).

4. *interj.* an expression of disgust; see also rrrr[4].

<*“Rrrrr ...” Maggie's nose wrinkled up in disgust. The bus smelled old to Gretchen—dry papery sweat, rotting onions, newly washed linoleum.* —Thomas Harlan, *House of Reeds*.>

5. *interj.* an expression that the temperature is uncomfortably cold, as discussed in *Drama Techniques in Language Learning: A Resource Book of Communication Activities for Language Teachers* by Alan Maley and Alan Duff; see also br, brr[1], brrr[1], brrrr[5], brrrrrr[3], brrrrrrr[3], rrr[1].

6. *interj.* an impatient grumble, as in the novel *The Sisterhood of the Traveling Pants* by Ann Brashares.

7. *n.* a catlike growl.

<*‘Rrrrr,’ said Emerson. It sounded like the amplified purr of a large cat but was, in fact, a growl.* —Elizabeth Peters, *Guardian of the Horizon*.>

8. *n.* a dog's growl, as when suspicious of a stranger.

<*“Rrrrr ...” she growled, but recalled yesterday's dinner, wagged her tail, and began sniffing.* —Anton Chekhov, “Kashtanka,” *The Essential Tales of Chekhov*.>

9. *n.* a growl of someone “a little peeved,” as discussed in *What Predicts Divorce?: The Relationship Between Marital Processes and Marital Outcomes* by John Mordechai Gottman.

10. *n.* a grumble of someone being shaken awake, as in the novel *Dream Country* by Luanne Rice; a grumpy sound accompanied by a “gimlet-eyed glare” of someone still too sleepy to begin her day, as in the novel *Keep on the Borderlands* by Ru Emerson.

11. *n.* a lion's friendly purr, as in *That's Good! That's Bad!* by Margery Cuyler.

12. *n.* a noise "superior to the human voice in energy," featured in an artform called a "poème simultan" (simultaneous poem), a "contrapuntal recitative in which three or more voices speak, sing, whistle, etc., at the same time in such a way that the elegiac, humorous, or bizarre content of the piece is brought out by these combinations" (Hugo Ball, *Flight Out of Time: A Dada Diary*).

13. *n.* a roar of aggression.

<*"Rrrrr!" The roar he began when he'd launched himself at Dur continued now.* —Denise Graham, *Eye of Fortune.*>

14. *n.* a rooster noise "like water about to boil," that means "he's looking out for his hen" (James Whorton, *Frankland: A Novel*).

15. *n.* a stomach's growl of hunger; see also rrrr[9].

<Rrrrr. *My stomach growled. Four o'clock: time for an afternoon snack.* —Bruce Hale, *Farewell, My Lunchbag: A Chet Gecko Mystery.*>

16. *n.* an iguana's cough, the equivalent of its fearsome roar, as described in *The Iguana Brothers: A Tale of Two Lizards* by Tony Johnston.

17. *n.* the "dull squeaking, straining sound" of door hinge, as described in *Scion of Cyador: The New Novel in the Saga of Recluce* by L.E. Modesitt.

18. *n.* the call of the wild; the untamed moan of someone alive with primitive energy.

<*Yes, the call of the wild ... Rrrrr ... Let me loose, set me free, give me space to breathe!* —Camille Maurine, *Meditation Secrets for Women: Discovering Your Passion, Pleasure, and Inner Peace.*>

19. *n.* the growl of a "very large dog," as described in the novel *The Mayflower Project* by Katherine A. Applegate.

20. *n.* the noise of fingernails forming a crease on cloth.

<*The pinched fingernails he ran all along his pants crease, to sharpen it, made a stuttery noise in the cloth,* rrrrr. —Bill Roorbach, *Contemporary Creative Nonfiction: The Art of Truth.*>

21. *n.* the roar of ocean waves, as described in *Writing Better Lyrics* by Pat Pattison.

22. *n.* the rumbling of the ground as an island crumbles into the sea, as described in the novel *The Mysterious Island* by Tony Abbott.

23. *n.* the sound of a dump truck engine, as described in *Anastasia Has the Answers* by Lois Lowry.

24. *n.* the sound of someone's emotions getting the better of him, as in the comic book *Electric Fear.*

25. *n.* the sound of the letter r, as discussed in *Let's Read: A Complete Month-by-Month Activities Program for Beginning Readers* by Elizabeth Crosby Stull; see also rrr[7], rrrr[17], RRRR[3], rrrrrr[10], rrrrrrr[25].

<*He rattled his* rrrrrs, *sounding like the tail of a diamondback about to strike.* —Sid Fleischman, *Disappearing Act.*>

<*Make all the "disgusting" sounds you weren't supposed to make but did. Roll your rrrrr's. Spit. Even swear a little.* —Ilene Segalove, *Snap Out of It: 101 Ways to Get Out of Your Rut & into Your Groove.*>

26. *n.* the trill of a star in the sky, singing to "followers stumbling through the night" (Kevin Crossley-Holland, *The Seeing Stone*).

27. *n.* the warning call of a mother partridge.

<*His mother's warning "rrrrr" (danger) did not always keep the others from a risky path or a doubtful food, but obedience seemed natural to him.* —Ernest Seton, *Wild Animals I Have Known.*>

28. *n.* the whirring of a pencil sharpener, as described in the novel *An Invisible Sign of My Own* by Aimee Bender.

29. *v.* to burn, as a "ribbon of fire" blazes along a river in *Impasse of the Angels: Scenes from a Moroccan Space of Memory* by Stefania Pandolfo.

30. *v.* to err.

<*I said it wasn't [pronounced] "air" it was "rrrr," to rrrrr is human, people kept saying it wrong.* —Eric Wilson, "The Axe, the Axe, the Axe," *Prize Stories 1985: O'Henry Awards.*>

RRrrr RRrrr.

n. the sound of a boat engine.

<*As each wave passes, I hear something new. RRrrr ... RRrrr ... It grows louder. An engine! I leap to my knees. Coming from the island, a couple of hundred yards away, a sharp white bow, flared out at the rail, pitches forward against a wave and then crashes down with a splash.* —Steven Callahan, *Adrift: Seventy-six Days Lost at Sea.*>

rrrrr rrrrr.

n. the blaring of a police siren, as in *Cam Jansen and the Birthday Mystery* by David A. Adler; see also RRRRRR[2], rrrrrr[17].

rrrrr rrrrr rrrrr.

n. the sound of an engine turning over.

<*Oblivious of the fishermen around him, Lupino hooked up the gasoline and pumped the rubber bulb, forcing fuel into the carburetor. Then he turned the key. Rrrrr...Rrrrr...Rrrrr. The engine turned over but wouldn't start.* —Jack Rudloe, *Potluck.*>

<*Insert the key into the ignition and turn the engine over three times (rrrrr, rrrrr, rrrrr). The compression for that cylinder will then be shown on the gauge.* —Rob Reaser, *How to Maintain and Repair Your Jeep: Covers (1945-1986) and Wrangler (1987-1995) Models.*>

rrrrr rrrrrr.

n. the sound of an automobile engine, as made by a child playing with Hot Wheels toy cars in the novel *Rails Under My Back* by Jeffery Renard Allen.

RRRRR-rrrr.

n. the train-like roar of someone snoring, as in the novel *A Crazy, Mixed-Up Spanglish Day* by Marisa Montes; see also RRRR-rrr-rrr-rr.

rrrrr-rrrr-r.

n. "a parakeet's attempt to imitate the sound of a cash register" (Patricia Highsmith, "A Bird in the Hand," *Nothing That Meets the Eye: The Uncollected Stories of Patricia Highsmith.*>

rrrrr-rrrr-rrrr.

n. the sound of running.

<*Running in the rain. / Running through the snow. / Running on the beach. / Rrrrr-rrrr-rrrr!* —Lea M. McGee, *Designing Early Literacy Programs: Strategies for At-Risk Preschool and Kindergarten Children.*>

rrrrr-rrrrr-rrrrr.

n. the "deep, slow, rasping, repetitive purr" of the Seychelles Scops-owl, as described in *Birds of the Seychelles* by Ian Bullock.

rrrrrm rrrrrm rrrrrm.

n. the sound of an automobile engine, as described in the story "Half Past Four" by Ursula K. Le Guin (*Unlocking the Air: Stories*).

RRRRRR.

1. *n.* a "masculine growl" of desire, as in the novel *War and Remembrance* by Herman Wouk.

2. *n.* the howl of a police siren; see also rrrrr rrrrr, rrrrrr[17].

<*Eighty-five becomes ninety miles per hour, as the traffic is a bit lighter here. RRRRRR. Closing my eye for a brief second I hear the sirens. Taking my eyes off the road I see them, not one, but two cars chasing me.* —Tony Callan, *Fragments of a Circle.*>

3. *n.* the sound of a manual typewriter's carriage return mechanism locking up.

<*I wrote [my second novel,* No] *on a long sheet of teletype paper. I got the idea from Jack Kerouac. It kept breaking because I had a (laughter) a manual typewriter and every time I'd go this way [hit the carriage return], the machine would go RRRRRR: it would tear and then I'd have to reinsert it.* —Clarence Major, quoted in *Conversations With Clarence Major* by Nancy Bunge.>

4. *n.* the sound of attacking bomber planes.

<*"In Panama there was a very sophisticated bombardment ... RRRRRR!! ...," he imitated the*

sound of the bombers descending, "... right on top of the barracks." —Daniel Wilkinson, *Silence on the Mountain: Stories of Terror, Betrayal, and Forgetting in Guatemala.*>

RRRrrr.

n. the sound of a city bus going by, as described in *Republic: A Novel* by J.B. Powell.

rrrrrr.

1. (also rrrrr.) *n.* a squirrel's chatter, as in the novel *Marlfox* by Brian Jacques.

2. *interj.* a growl of seething anger, as when curse words fail one.

   <*"Rrrrrr," said Emerson. "You vile, contemptible old ..." Words failed him. In fact I was sure they did not, for they seldom did, but the words he would like to have employed were too inflammatory for my ears, much less those of an innocent child. For all his bravado, Kalaan was not willing to risk the wrath of the Father of Curses.* —Elizabeth Peters, *The Falcon at the Portal: An Amelia Peabody Mystery.*>

3. *interj.* a sound to fill an awkward pause in conversation, meaning, "oops, sorry ... let's change the subject" (Cydney Rax, *My Daughter's Boyfriend: A Novel*).

4. *interj.* an expression of hunger in *Ulysses* by James Joyce.

5. *n.* a growl of mock anger, as said with squeezed fists and bared teeth in *Sonny Liston Was a Friend of Mine: Stories* by Thom Jones.

6. *n.* a grumble of frustration and impatience.

   <*"Rrrrrr!" Leaping to his feet, Nathaniel strode away from the fire. Shoving his hands through his hair, he fought for patience.* —Celeste Bradley, *To Wed a Scandalous Spy.*>

7. *n.* a meditational mantra.

   <*First just hear it slightly in your mind, as the Rrrrrr generates power and volume deep within your third-chakra region. There is great power in the Rrrrrr sound. Open yourself to it—the universe will join you in your calling on third-chakra energization.* —John Selby, *Kundalini Awakening: A Gentle Guide to Chakra Activation and Spiritual Growth.*>

8. *n.* a noise made in one's throat, as to indicate an allergy to cigarette smoke in the novel *Specimen Tank* by Buzz Callaway.

9. *n.* a rolled French r.

   <*You see, the French have a funny-shaped throat to help them to pronounce all those rolling rrrrrr's. It's handy for speaking French, but try speaking English with it!* —Thomas Neenan, *Let's Blow Thru Europe.*>

10. *n.* the "voluptuous" sound of the letter r; see also rrr[7], RRRR[3], rrrr[17], rrrrr[25], rrrrrrr[25].

    <*According to my grandmother, at the naming ceremonies, our family priest cautioned my parents against giving any of us names that began with an "R." "It doesn't match your own initials," he had said, consulting his almanac. "It will surely spell disaster on some level." But my mother, who pooh-poohed anything to do with the occult, stood her ground. She adored the idea of having*

a gorgeous, voluptuous "Rrrrrr" trip off her tongue each time she might call her girls to her. —Kavita Daswani, *The Village Bride of Beverly Hills.*>

11. *n.* the buzzing of a vibrator.

<*"So I had this vibrator." June held her hands apart to indicate a magic wand approximately the size of a Saturn moon rocket. "Rrrrrr! You could probably hear it in Belgium. When I'd use it the whole house would shake."* —Lindsy Van Gelder, *The Girls Next Door.*>

12. *n.* the deep, throaty growl of a leopard, as described in *A Girl Named Disaster* by Nancy Farmer.

13. *n.* the growling of a dog, as described by Leda Mesen in *Wishes, Lies, and Dreams: Teaching Children to Write Poetry* by Kenneth Koch.

14. *n.* the menacing snarl of a mugger.

<*I hustled down the last alley on the estate, in the shadow of gigantic hedges. "Rrrrrr!" A knife leapt out of the dark, glinting for a split second under a dim yellow light. Behind it, a horrible smile slithered over the face of a man with gappy teeth and long hair.* —Andrea Ashworth, *Once in a House on Fire.*>

15. *n.* the sound of a whirling "portal through time" quivering and wobbling (Tony Abbott, *The Magic Escapes*).

16. *n.* the vicious growl of a big dog.

<*I open my door and turn on the light and just after I flick on the switch and take a few steps, I hear "rrrrrr." And there, in the middle of my room, snarling and slobbering and growling at me, is this monster dog.* —Jayson Williams, *Loose Balls: Easy Money, Hard Fouls, Cheap Laughs, and True Love in the NBA.*>

17. *n.* the whine of a prison siren, as described in the novel *The Hot Rock* by Donald E. Westlake; a sheriff's siren, as described in *Tales of Beatnik Glory* by Ed Sanders; see also rrrrr rrrrr, RRRRRR[2].

18. *v.* to go wild, like an animal.

<*I enjoy life, and I make a game out of everything. ... I like to "Rrrrrr" and take off running around the house, chasing my sister.* —Minnie Bell, *Savannah Dogs.*>

19. *v.* to roar like a lion.

<*Beodan caressed her from behind, beneath her skirt, and said something Josserek couldn't follow either, but which made her go "Rrrrrr" like a happy lioness.* Yes, I've read, I've been told, *the man from Killimaraich remembered,* kindred here make their own slang, generation by generation till a private dialect has turned into an entire language never shared with those who are not of the blood. —Poul Anderson, *The Winter of the World.*>

20. *v.* to roll the "Russian 'R.'"

<*Courses in English—"the language of the imperialists"—were suspended for a period of time, and students "Rrrrrr-ed" their way into foreign language classes (most Chinese, including myself, find the rolling Russian "R" hard to pronounce).* —Chen Chen, *Come Watch the Sun Go Home: A Memoir of Upheaval and Revolution in China.*>

rrrrrr rrrrr.

n. the creak of a flashlight's hand pump.

<*From outside came a* rrrrrr rrrrr *sound as Autumn passed under the thatch eaves. Inseat of batteries, her flashlight had a hand pump like a flour sifter.* —Lady Borton, *After Sorrow: An American Among the Vietnamese.*>

rrrrrr rrrrr rrrr rrrr.

n. the "rolling trill" of the Golden-naped Barbet, "gradually decreasing in note," as described in *A Field Guide to the Birds of Borneo, Sumatra, Java, and Bali* by John Ramsay MacKinnon.

rrrrrr rrrrr rrrrrrrr.

n. the growling of dogs, as in *The Magic Orange Tree and Other Haitian Folktales* by Diane Wolkstein.

rrrrrr scttttt.

n. the sound of snow skis making a "sweeping turn" to avoid a rocky outcropping, as described in the novel *The Towers of the Sunset* by L.E. Modesitt Jr.; see also sccctttttcchhh.

<*Rrrrrr ... scttttt ... A mass of rocks appears out of the lighter curtain of snow ahead, and he begins a sweeping turn, the only kind he dares.* —L.E. Modesitt Jr., *The Towers of the Sunset.*>

rrrrrr-r-r-r.

n. Daffy Duck's imitation of a dog, as in *Chuck Amuck: The Life and Times of an Animated Cartoonist* by Chuck Jones.

rrrrrrmmmm.

n. the sound of pommelling on a sofa in *Ulysses* by James Joyce.

RRRRRRR.

1. *interj.* a pirate's growl, as described in *The History Teacher's Really Bad Joke Book* by Richard Di Giancomo.

2. *n.* a growl of excitement; see also rrrrrrr[5].

<"*That man is sexy. Look at those broad shoulders and those teeth! RRRRRRR ... I'll tear him up!" he says, joking around.* —Maryann Reid, *Sex and the Single Sister: Five Novellas.*>

3. *n.* a warning scream of a chickaree.

<*A golden eagle came into view, his wings motionless as he rode the air current above the river. Here was a real enemy. "RRRRRRR!" [the chickaree] warned. Every bird stopped what he was doing and sat perfectly still. Eagles see movement. Birds somehow know that if they do not move, eagles and other predators will not see them.* —Jean Craighead George, *Spring Moon.*>

4. *n.* the sound of "power metal" music by the band Metallica; see also rrrrrrr[3].

<*He put this tape on of a band going "RRRRRRR!" I thought, "What the hell is this?" Of course it was Metallica.* —Ian Christe, *Sound of the Beast: The Complete Headbanging History of Heavy Metal.*>

rrrrrrr.

1. (also rrrrr.) *n.* a loud snore.

   <*Rrrrrrr. What a racket! Sampath listened to each hostile inhalation. Even in sleep, he thought, disgusted, his family showed themselves incapable of pleasant displays of consideration. Self-indulgent as always, they worked their way noisily through their dreams, keeping Sampath, meanwhile, awake and tossing.* —Kiran Desai, *Hullabaloo in the Guava Orchard.*>

2. (also rrrrrr.) *n.* a grumble "under [one's] breath," marking the transition from a "pale green spark of surprise" to a "flicker of anger" to a "sudden and very welcome return of humor" (Diane Duane, *The Book of Night with Moon*).

3. *adj.* fast paced, like the fastest heavy metal music by Metallica; see also RRRRRRR[4].

   <*[W]hen we really open up, what's really there is "rrrrrrr."* —Jim Murphy, quoted in *So What! The Good, The Mad, and the Ugly: The Official Metallica Illustrated Chronicle* by Steffan Chirazi.>

4. *n.* a "canary-like whistled trill" of the Cameroon Indigobird, as described in *A Guide to the Birds of Western Africa* by Ron Demey; the rough, aggressive call of the Yellow-rumped Cacique, as described in *New World Blackbirds* by Alvaro Jaramillo; the "soft purring rolling" call of the Cream-bellied Fruit-dove, as described in *A Guide to the Birds of the Philippines* by Robert S. Kennedy.

5. *n.* a growl of excitement; see also RRRRRRR[2].

   <*So how to put the rrrrrrr back in your romance? In three words: variety, variety, variety.* —Jane Seddon, *Daily Sex: 365 Positions and Activities for a Year of Great Sex!*>

6. *n.* a mocking imitation, likening someone's speech to the buzz of an annoying insect.

   <*He makes the noises "Rrrrrrr" and "Aaaaaaa" to imitate Glennon, as if he'd heard his words as nothing more than the buzzing of an overwrought insect inviting a swatting.* —Philip Gourevitch, *A Cold Case.*>

7. *n.* a soft grumble.

   <*Then I started hearing some movement. I hear things moving around, and I hear a little* rrrrrrr, *you know, grumbling, and "How are you?" and "Are you okay?" I heard guys talking, and I realized I wasn't alone.* —Dennis Smith, *Report from Ground Zero: The Story of the Rescue Efforts at the World Trade Center.*>

8. *n.* a squeal over a large rat running loose, as in *Maternal Meanderings* by Diane Dean-Epps.

9. *n.* a tiger's growl, as in the novel *Axis Sally* by M. Williams Fuller.

10. *n.* an audible shudder of horror.

    <*"Ever since I saw E.T. I've had a horror of something being in my closet. Imagine standing*

there trying to decide what you're going to wear, and long skinny fingers creep out of your dresses. Rrrrrrr." She shuddered. —Betsy Byars, *The Computer Nut.*>

11. *n.* an enraged, dog-like growl, likened to villainess Cruella De Vil (Judith Gould, *The Greek Villa*).

<*Auntie Mame morph[ed] into Cruella De Vil. "Rrrrrrr! That ... that twat!" Urania spat, letting loose with everything she'd kept stifled all day. "That hideous, big-jawed, culture-starved idiot of a Bronx-born twat! Who the hell does she think she is, getting off on trying to shove her coven of ghostwriters on me?* —Judith Gould, *The Greek Villa.*>

12. *n.* God's proclamation of the end of the world.

<*GOD: Rrrrrrr. I proclaim the end of the world. Rrrrrrr.* (The whole cosmic contraption starts to come apart.) *BUREAUCRAT: Rrrrrrr. That's very fine. Rrrrrrr. But where is the relevant document in this case, duly stamped and bearing the number assigned to it up there, which should have been entered in our correspondence file?* (It turns out that there was such a document, but that it got lost, so although the end of the world really does take place in actual fact, officially it doesn't count for anything.) —Konstanty Iidefons Gaiczynski, *The Little Theatre of the Green Goose Has the Honor of Presenting "The End of the World."*>

13. *n.* in Kraho mythology, the song of aquatic water spirits called Kokridho, sounding like a bull-roarer and unpleasantly loud (Claude Lévi-Strauss, *The Raw and the Cooked: Mythologiques, Volume One*).

14. *n.* the "chitter" of a sleepy dormouse, as in *W.I.T.C.H.: The Disappearance*, by Disney Enterprises; see also rrrrrrr[7].

15. *n.* the blare of an ambulance siren, as described in *Trauma and Life Stories: International Perspectives* by Kim Lacy Rogers.

<*Rrrrrrr! Sirens were blaring. They were getting louder. An ambulance drove up and stopped near where Cam, Eric, and Aunt Molly were standing.* —David A. Adler, *Cam Jansen and the Ghostly Mystery.*>

16. *n.* the creaking of a lever on a jammed rifle, as described in *A Mile in Their Shoes: Conversations With Veterans of World War II* by Aaron Elson.>

17. *n.* the deep, ominous growl of a pit bull.

<*He was short and stocky. All shoulders, head, neck. Small eyes. Evil, laughing mouth set with a row of serious teeth. Every one of which was on display. A pit bull. An angry pit bull. "Rrrrrrr," he growled low. A string of drool spilled out of his mouth.* —K.A. Applegate, *Animorphs #42: The Journey.*>

18. *n.* the howling siren of a fire engine; see also rrrrrrr-RRRRRRR.

<*"I'm a fire engine!" shouts the child. "Rrrrrrr!" We hold ears and smile patronizingly, imprisoned in our plans for the future and our memories of the past.* W.S. Merwin, *Zen Wave: Basho's Haiku and Zen.*>

19. *n.* the hum of a model train.

<*She was conscious, too, dimly now and with a different horror, of the old, unceasing voices of*

customers at the counter calling for assistance, calling to her, and of the low, humming rrrrrr *of the little train, part of the storm that was closing in and separating her from the woman.* —Patricia Highsmith, *The Price of Salt.*>

20. *n.* the hum of an alien spacecraft taking off.

<*[The UFO] just kind of sat there for a second, and I heard the engines start to go up again, "rrrrrr." And it lifted up and slowly went off and went looking around in the trees again. ... I heard it increase in pitch. It started to go "rrrrrr," and when it was doing that, it was raising up.* —Preston Dennett, *Extraterrestrial Visitations: True Accounts of Contact.*>

21. *n.* the purr of a fishing boat's motor.

<*Then he was in the lagoon, floating lazily, staring up at the cascading sunbeams that played on him while a motor's* rrrrrr *purred in his ear.* —Gregory Benford, *Across the Sea of Suns.*>

<*Ted [Williams] was out there alone. He made a mistake bringing a tarpon in. Lost him. I see him bring the rod up, break it across his knee, and throw it on the bottom of the boat. Then I see him reach down, pick up another rod, and break that one over his knee and throw it on the bottom of the boat. Then he hits the push-pull,* rrrrrr, *and he's gone.* —Leigh Montville, *Ted Williams: The Biography of an American Hero.*>

22. *n.* the rapid rattle, "like a fast electric sewing machine," of the Sombre (or Dusky) Nightjar, as described in *Birds of Western and Central Africa* by Ber van Perlo.

23. *n.* the screech of braking tires.

<*Rrrrrr! Tires screeched in protest as the wagon locked up all fours, leaving skid marks in its wake as the Duster shot by with inches to spare.* —Danny Rolling, *The Making of a Serial Killer: The Real Story of the Gainesville Student Murders in the Killer's Own Words.*>

24. *n.* the sound of a jeep's engine.

<*George was helping John move some blocks the next morning when a jeep's growing* rrrrrr *caught their attention.* —Gregory Benford, *Artifact.*>

25. *n.* the sound of the letter r, as in the novel *Attaboy, Sam!* by Lois Lowry; see also rrr[7], RRRR[3], rrrr[17], rrrrr[25], rrrrrr[10].

<*I spy with my little eye something that begins with rrrrrr.* —Lori Goodman and Lora Myers, *Wordplay: Fun games for Building Reading and Writing Skills in Children With Learning Difficulties.*>

26. *n.* the warning growl of a pig, as described in *The Story So Far: Play Therapy Narratives* by Ann Cattanach.

27. *n.* the whine of a German motorcycle engine, as described in *They Were All Young Kids: The Story of Lieutenant Jim Flowers and the First Platoon, Company C, 712 Tank Battalion, on Hill 122* by Aaron C. Elson.

28. *v.* to operate at such a fast pace that everything is a blur.

<*[M]aybe we truly are wired and just go "rrrrrr."* —Jim Murphy quoted in *So What! The Good, The Mad, and the Ugly: The Official Metallica Illustrated Chronicle*

rrrrrrr rrrrrr.

n. the hum of a machine "like something out of science-fiction movie" that dispenses cobalt treatments (Robert Byrne, *McGoorty: A Pool Room Hustler*).

<*The first time they switched on the machine it felt like my ears were all of a sudden stopped up, there was no air, I had no feeling. I was tied down, so all I could do was lie there and listen to the Rrrrrrr, Rrrrrr, and look at the spot on the machine that the rays come out of, although they are invisible.* —Robert Byrne, *McGoorty: A Pool Room Hustler.*>

rrrrrrr-RRRRRRR.

n. the howling siren of a fire engine; see also rrrrrrr[18].

<*One time, Ted was holding out or something. They wouldn't give him what he wanted, and he made the statement that if he didn't get what he was asking for, he said he was going to be a fireman. Well, Dykes heard about that. So the first time we played the Red Sox in Chicago, Jimmy Dykes had a siren. You know, the kind that you crank. And he had a fireman's hat on. When Ted Williams walked up there to hit, Jimmy starts in with that siren:* "rrrrrrr-RRRRRRR." *And he's got his fireman's hat on. And Ted Williams backed out and looked in the dugout and he started laughing.* —David Cataneo, *I Remember Ted Williams: Anecdotes and Memories of Baseball's Splendid Splinter by the Players and People Who Knew Him.*>

rrrrrrrmmmmg.

n. the sound of a hangover, as in *Diary* by Karawynn Long.

rrrrrrrnnng.

n. the ring of a telephone.

<*When he woke up, the killer headache hadn't gone away and the phone was ringing. A fourth ring. A fifth. He still made no move to pick it up.* Rnnnnnnnnng *again.* —Morrie Ruvinsky, *Dream Keeper: Myth and Destiny in the Pacific Northwest.*>

RRRRrrrr.

n. the roar of the Cowardly Lion from *The Wizard of Oz*, as discussed in *Mary Marony: Mummy Girl* by Suzy Kline.

RRRrrrrr.

n. the cry of the Incredible Hulk, as discussed in the story "What Color is Jesus" by James McBride (anthologized in *Half and Half: Writers on Growing Up Biracial and Bicultural* by Claudine C. O'Hearn).

rrrrrrrr.

1. *interj.* an enraged outburst.

<*Anouk slammed the phone down and then stood there, her clenched fists blurring in the air. Antonio was alarmed. She looked as though she was going into a seizure. What escaped from her lips sounded very much like, "Rrrrrrrr..."* —Judith Gould, *Never Too Rich.*>

2. *interj.* an expression of apprehension, as in *My Soul Is Rested: Movement Days in the Deep South Remembered* by Howell Raines.

3. *n.* a "low, terrible noise" welling up from a terrified wild cat, "as deep as a tiger's growl" (Scott Westerfeld, *Midnighters #1: The Secret Hour*); a cat's growl, seemingly unapologetic for shedding fur on one's guitar case (Bill Crider, *A Bond with Death: A Professor Sally Good Mystery*).

4. *n.* a caterwaul.

<*"Rrrrrrr," Char said, making that God-awful catfight noise.* —Laurel Handfield, *My Diet Starts Tomorrow: A Novel.*>

5. *n.* a growl of ravenous hunger, as in the comic book *Incredible Hulk Annual #13* by Alan Kupperberg.

6. *n.* a low growl of excitement.

<*While I was quietly eating and obsessing, his head dropped back against my leg, sending a frisson clear up to my waist. Rrrrrrr. Was I tempted to get hold of that tawny, wavy hair.* —Haywood Smith, *Queen Bee of Mimosa Branch: A Novel.*>

7. *n.* the "muffled whimper" of a trembling dormouse, as in *W.I.T.C.H.: The Disappearance*, by Disney Enterprises; see also rrrrrrr[14].

8. *n.* the "short throaty" rolling call of the Black-backed Antshrike, as described in *A Guide to the Birds of Colombia* by Steven L. Hilty.

9. *n.* the "short, rather high pitched rasping ripple" call of the Ratchet-tailed Treepie, as described in *Crows and Jays* by Steve Madge.

10. *n.* the "short, rather high-pitched rasping, rippling" call of the Ratchet-tailed Treepie, as described in *Birds of Thailand* by Craig Robson.

11. *n.* the buzzer at a basketball game, as described in *I Love Being the Enemy* by Reggie Miller.

12. *n.* the creaking of a falling tree, as described in *Time Heals No Wounds: The Agony of the Real War in Vietman—the Grunt's War—Told by a Soldier Who Lived Through It* by Jack Leninger.

13. *n.* the mutterings of talking in one's sleep.

<*He's talking in his sleep in that cave of his. Saying something like rrrrrrr. Tia is saying rrrrrrr too. Be quiet, Tia. It's nothing.* —Amos Oz, *A Perfect Peace.*>

14. *n.* the noise of a chainsaw.

<*[My yellow horse] Butterscotch was a little skittish all day, 'cause he didn't like it when the saw would go off. Rrrrrrr!—it made all that noise, and it scared him half to death.* —Amarillo Slim Preston, *Amarillo Slim in a World Full of Fat People: The Memoirs of the Greatest Gambler Who Ever Lived.*>

15. *n.* the noise of a stuck automobile clutch, as described in the novel *In God We Trust: All Others Pay Cash* by Jean Shepherd.

16. *n.* the soft, grumbling call of the European Nightjar, as described in *Nightjars and Their Allies: The Caprimulgiformes* by D.T. Holyoak.

17. *n.* the sound of a "rocket man" rocketing off, as in *Will I Have a Friend?* by Miriam Cohen.

18. *n.* the sound of oncoming automobile traffic, as in the comic book *Vacuum Horror* by Aaron K.

rrrrrrrr.

1. *n.* a bear's roar, as in *The Last Lap* by Peter Golenbock.

2. *n.* a lawn mower noise, as described in *The Radio Mystery* by Gertrude Chandler Warner.

3. *n.* the "distinct croaking" of Baillon's Crake, as described in *Birds and Mammals of Ladakh* by Otto Pfister.

4. *n.* the "soft little trill" of the Fernando Po Speirops, as described in *A Guide to the Birds of Western Africa* by Ron Demey.

5. *n.* the roar of the Tyrannosaur, as described in *Thunderfeet: Alaska's Dinosaurs and Other Prehistoric Critters* by Shelley Gill.

6. *n.* the roaring of an airplane during a skydiving flight, as described by Jimi Hendrix (quoted in *Jimi Hendrix: Electric Gypsy* by Harry Shapiro).

7. *n.* the sound of a tank being revved to make a U-turn in the sand, as described in *Tanks for the Memories* by Aaron Elson.

8. *v.* one's consciousness taking a quantum leap and attaining sudden enlightment, as discussed in *Zen: The Path of Paradox* by Osho.

rrrRRRrrr rrrRRRrrr rrrRRRrrr.

n. the sound of an automobile being hotwired, as described in *Cons, Scams & Grifts* by Joe Gores.

RRRRRRRRRR.

1. *n.* the squeal of braking tires.

   <*[T]he two Marines heard the trucks' large rubber tires rolling to a permanent halt, the distinctive RRRRRRRRRR hum echoing in the shattered streets of town.* —David J. Morris, *Storm on the Horizon: Khafji—The Battle That Changed the Course of the Gulf War.*>

2. *n.* a noise "like a stick being run along a picket fence," made by ravens (Jean Craighead George, *The Fire Bug Connection*).

3. *n.* the growl of rage directed against onself, as described in *The Alarm Clock of Your Life is Ringing: Time to Wake up to Happiness and Enlightenment (2nd Edition)* by Lisa Miller.

4. *n.* the mechanical hum of a robot toy walking across the floor, as described in *Arthur and the Nerves of Steal* by Marc Brown.

5. *n.* the roar of a motorbike engine racing through snowdrifts, as described in *Harry and the Wrinklies* by Alan Temperley.

RRRRRrrrrr.

n. a grumpy, growled curse, as due to nervous tension.

<*[Y]ou always knew when Joaquin was pitching, because you'd be setting there getting dressed, and all of a sudden the door would slam, and he'd come across the room, cursing, "RRRRRrrrrr, let me alone."* —Peter Golenbock, *The Spirit of St. Louis: A History of the St. Louis Cardinals and Browns.*>

RRRrrrrrr.

n. the growl of a wild cat, as described in the novel *The Chaos Balance* by L.E. Modesitt Jr.

rrrrrrrrr.

1. *adv.* in a whirl of motion.

<*At Live Aid, Bill [Graham] was a cartoon. I could see his head and feet and his arms were* rrrrrrrrr. *Like he was "The Road Runner." ... In this continual blur. With this little head on top.* —Keith Richards, quoted in *Bill Graham Presents: My Life Inside Rock and Out* by Bill Graham.>

2. *adv.* unclearly.

<*He talks like* rrrrrrrrr, *he doesn't speak clear[ly].* —Bonnie Urciuoli, *Exposing Prejudice: Puerto Rican Experiences of Language, Race, and Class.*>

3. *n.* a cheetah's roar-like purr.

<*Once we were allowed inside the cheetah cage [at the London Zoo]. The cheetahs were quite tame. There were two of them standing there, and I scratched them behind the ears. Suddenly there was a* roar—*rrrrrrrrr*—*in their throats. I thought it was growling and jumped, but the keeper laughed and said, "They're purring, ma'am."* —May Sarton, *Endgame: A Journal of the Seventy-Ninth Year.*>

4. *n.* a growl made by a dog trainer to motivate a learning puppy.

<*Let him see you see you toss his toy and encourage him by growling, "Rrrrrrrrr," or by asking him, "Do you want to get it?"* —Bobbie Anderson, *Building Blocks for Performance.*>

5. *n.* a purr of excitement, as over "the simultaneous purchase and selling of a security in order to profit from a differential in the price" (Mark Whistler, *Trading Pairs: Capturing Profits and Hedging Risk with Statistical Arbitrage Strategies*).

<*"Rrrrrrrrr ... arbitrage." It sounds sexy, doesn't it? Be careful not to fall in love with this savvy beast, for it can cause you to lose your hair with the stress it presents!* —Mark Whistler, *Trading Pairs: Capturing Profits and Hedging Risk with Statistical Arbitrage Strategies.*>

6. *n.* an ambiguous sound made by someone paralyzed with fear, as in the novel *Theo Slugg in Low Spirits* by Simon Goswell.

7. *n.* the "crying of tiny engines" of ghost-like "tiny psycho cyclers" flying through the moonlight (Denis Johnson, *Fiskadoro*).

8. *n.* the growl of a cat, "deeper than a purr" (Lilian Jackson Braun, *The Cat Who Lived High*).

9. *n.* the growl of a hungry bear, as in *Bone: Volume One* by Jeff Smith.

10. *n.* the humming of a sewing machine, as described in *Uff Da!* by C.L.G. Martin; see also rrrr rrrr rrrr[1].

11. *n.* the rumble of a burning house collapsing, as described in *Impasse of the Angels: Scenes from a Moroccan Space of Memory* by Stefania Pandolfo.

12. *n.* the snarl of a wolf, as described in *Beauty and the Beast* by A.L. Singer (*Disney's Princess Treasury*).

13. *n.* the sound of a "little film screen" coming down from the ceiling, as described in *Love All the People: Letters, Lyrics, Routines* by Bill Hicks.

14. *n.* the sound of a helicopter engine.

<*With a ni-cad battery, the engine won't go RRRRRRRRRR, RRRRRrrrrr, rrrrrrrrrr, rrrrr, rrr, rr, r, r, -----, like it does when the battery dies trying to start a car on a cold morning. Instead, it will go RRRRRRRRRR, RRRRRRRRRR, RRRRRRRR, RRRRRRRR, RRRRRRRR, -----. Once a ni-cad has lost so much charge that it can no longer motor the starter, it won't have enough charge left to power anything else either.* —R. Randall Padfield, *Learning to Fly Helicopters*.>

15. *n.* the sound of a Lamborghini engine.

<*All the guys at nursery school talked about Lamborghinis, and when they played cars they played Lamborghinis, saying "Rrrrrrrrrr" loudly in their throats as they crawled across the floor.* —Lois Lowry, *Attaboy, Sam!*>

16. *n.* the sound of a sports car shifting gears.

<*We would zip around the corner, and he would shift it into another gear—Rrrrrrrrrr. I'm trying to pray and read my Bible while lunging back and forth as Dave plays with the automatic gears.* —Joyce Meyer, *Help Me, I'm Married!*>

rrrrrrrrrr rrrrrr.

n. a drone "like a[n automatic] dishwasher," vocalized by someone in the throes of passion, as in the novel *Gets No Love* Eric Pete.

RRRrrrrrrr RRRRRrrrrr.

(also RRRrrrrrr, RRRRRrrrrrrrrRRRRRRRRrrrrrrRRRRRRR.) *n.* the mad snarling of a frustrated dog locked in the backseat of an automobile, as described in *Leading with my Chin* by Jay Leno.

RRRRRRrrrrr.

n. a sheriff's siren, as described in *Clifford: Cookie Crazy* by Gail Herman.

RRRRrrrrrrr.

n. a war cry, as in *Dude, Did I Steal Your Job? Debugging Indian Computer Programmers* by N. Sivakumar.

rrrrrrrrrrr.

1. (also rrrrrrrrr.) *n.* the squeal of tires.

<*Jerry taught me how to drive a car. He had an old Ford coupe with a rumble seat in the back and four on the floor. We would go out driving around McAllen, come to a corner, and I would turn, but you see, it took me a long time to figure out corners. I would turn but I wouldn't turn back. Rrrrrrrrrr! Wham, into the ditch. But I was a determined learner so I kept my foot on the gas. Rrrrrrrrr. Jerry didn't have the steering wheel to hang onto, so he was bouncing around pretty good and screaming at the top of his lungs, "Turn back, turn around, turn back, turn around!"* —Jim Stowell, *Traveling Light: Monologues*.>

2. *n.* a growl made by a dog trainer to motivate a learning puppy, as discussed in *Building Blocks for Performance* by Bobbie Anderson; see rrrrrrrrrr[4].

3. *n.* a rumble like an earthquake, caused by a spaceship hovering over one's house in the novel *Maximum Warp Book Two: Forever Dark* by Dave Galanter.

4. *n.* the contented croak of a parrot.

<*I'd pet his forehead and stroke his feathers and he'd say, "Rrrrrrrrrr."* —David Rice, *Crazy Loco*.>

5. *n.* the deep-throated cooing of a pigeon.

<*I swell my chest and imitate the* roucoulement *of the pigeons. My French* rrrrrrrrrr *roll.* —Anaïs Nin, *Henry and June: From "A Journal of Love," The Unexpurgated Diary of Anais Nin (1931-1932)*.>

6. *n.* the growl of a bear, as in *Myth-O-Mania: Go for the Gold Atlanta!* by Kate McMullan.

7. *n.* the roar of a "golden-haired lion." The lion, according to a Zen Buddhist riddle, symbolizes the state of "pure and clear Dharma-body" (Zen Master Seung Sahn, *The Whole World Is a Single Flower: 365 Kong-Ans for Everyday Life*).

8. *n.* the threatening growl of a guard dog, as described in the novel *Whatever Love Means* by David Baddiel.

9. *n.* tongue-rolling, as described in the novel *Emma Who Saved My Life* by Wilton Barnhardt.

rrrrrrrrrrr rrrrrrrrr.

n. the revving of a sports car engine, as described in *Help Me, I'm Married* by Joyce Meyer.

RRRRrrrRRRR RRRRrrrRRRR.

n. the whine of a distant ambulance siren.

<*I hear the sound of the siren in the distance—RRRRrrrRRRR RRRRrrrRRRR, as plaintive*

as a train whistle. —Eugene Richards, *The Knife and Gun Club: Scenes from an Emergency Room.*>

RRRRRRRRRRRR.

n. an internal grumbling that means "Why can't I get my act together. I am screwing up" (Lisa Miller, *The Alarm Clock of Your Life is Ringing: Time to Wake up to Happiness and Enlightenment, 2nd Edition*).

RRRRrrrrrrrr.

n. a deafening, paralyzing sound from an electrical generator, "like a Tyrannosaurus sicking up a bad dinner" (David Poyer, *The Command*).

<*A hoarse, deafening ROWF, followed by a steadily decreasing RRRRrrrrrrrr. She didn't know what it was, only that sparks were flying through the gratings, and she tucked and rolled instinctively, balling herself tight under the heavy steel counter.* —David Poyer, *The Command.*>

rrrrrrrrrrr.

1. *n.* a "long, sad growly sound" made by a cat when human beings get too close, as described in the novel *Ghost Cats* by Susan Shreve.

2. *n.* the creaking of an iron crank, as described in the novel *Riddley Walker* by Russell Hoban.

3. *n.* the honk of a truck horn, as described in *Love All the People: Letters, Lyrics, Routines* by Bill Hicks.

4. *n.* the warbling purr of a cat that "sounds like a Scrabble tile [is] stuck in [its] throat" (Lilian Jackson Braun, *The Cat Who Lived High*).

RRRRRRrrrrrr RRRRRRrrrrrr.

n. the "painful sounds" of someone grinding his teeth.

<*[His teeth grinding] sounded like a poor, helpless animal caught in a trap, struggling to get free, and screaming for help in a deep seated growl. It sounded like "RRRRRRrrrrrr, RRRRRRrrrrrr..." The sounds were wild, sharp, and piercing.* —Grace Cornish, *10 Good Choices That Empower Black Women's Lives.*>

RRRRRRRRRRRRR.

n. the whine of police sirens, as described in the novel *Daughters of Courage* by Red Jordan Arobateau.

RrrrrrRRRRRRR.

n. the whoosh of a "fat race-car tire" flying out of a "virtualized" video game, as described in the novel *Spy Kids Adventures: Mall of the Universe* by Elizabeth Lenhard.

rrrrrrrrrrrr.

1. *n.* a lion's roar, as described in *Does My Child Have a Speech Problem* by Katherine L. Martin.

2. *n.* an expression of anger in the poem “Black Art” by Amiri Baraka, in which the poet “finds that the normal boundaries of poetic language no longer contain the words he needs in order to express his rage” and therefore uses “raw sounds” like *rrrrrrrrrrrr* that turn “language into the verbal guns of ‘poems that kill’” (Christopher Beach, *The Cambridge Introduction to Twentieth-Century American Poetry*).

3. *n.* the angry growl of a panda bear, as in the comic strip “PvP” by Scott R. Kurtz; see also rrt.

4. *n.* the howl of an alarm, as during a civil-defense drill in *From Beirut to Jerusalem* by Thomas L. Friedman.

5. *n.* the sound of machine-gun fire, as described in *Love All the People: Letters, Lyrics, Routines* by Bill Hicks.

RRRRRRRRRRRRR.

n. an “ear-shattering roar” of a motorcycle, as described in *High Latitude, North Atlantic* by John R. Bockstoce.

RrrrRRRrrRRRRR.

n. the sound of a propeller plane.

<*“Open the hangar door, here comes the plane,” he sang, aiming the fork at her mouth like a airplane. “RrrrRRRrrRRRRR,” he rumbled, simulating the sound of a propeller plane.* —Robert Zimmerman, *Genesis: The Story of Apollo 8: The First Manned Flight to Another World.*>

rrrrrrrrrrrrr.

1. *n.* a “mechanical whirring sound” in the Futurist poetry of Carlo Carrà, as discussed in *The Aesthetics of Visual Poetry, 1914-1928* by Willard Bohn.

2. *n.* a dog’s growl.

<*“Rrrrrrrrrrrrr!” he fooled, growling like a dog.* —Rosalind Miles, *I, Elizabeth: A Novel.*>

3. *n.* a sound made while beating someone with a stick, as in the novel *Riddley Walker* by Russell Hoban.

4. *n.* the hum of a ferry boat engine.

<*Alexander stood on the boat deck of a channel ferry, the rrrrrrrrrrrrr of the engines vibrating through him, the tricolor of the French Republic snapping at the stern, as he watched Calais receding ten miles behind and daubed his nose with a sodden handkerchief.* —Richard Miller, *Sowboy: A Factual Fanciful Fiction.*>

5. *n.* the rattle of an alarm clock, as described in *Mama Lola: A Vodou Priestess in Brooklyn, Updated and Expanded Edition* by Karen McCarthy Brown.

rrrrrrrrrrrrrr / rrrrrrrrrrr.

n. the “wonderful and chaotic” scream of sirens and horns, as sung by free jazz artist Amiri Baraka (Robert G. O’Meally, *Uptown Conversation : The New Jazz Studies*).

RRRRRRRRRRRrrrrrr.

n. the sound of an "earsplitting pulsejet": "150 decibels of deafening noise" emitted by a fighting robot called "Pauline's Running Machine" (Brad Stone, *Gearheads: The Turbulent Rise of Robotic Sports*).

<*[Mark Pauline] fired up the Running Machine right then. RRRRRRRRRRRrrrrrr! The noise sprayed off the walls of the hangar. Spectators thrust their hands to their heads. Parents grabbed their children and stampeded outside. It was the loudest noise anyone had ever heard in their lives.* —Brad Stone, *Gearheads: The Turbulent Rise of Robotic Sports*.>

RRRRRRRRRRRRrrrrrrrrrrrrrr.

n. the grumble of an old automobile engine, as described in *Ash Child: A Montana Mystery Featuring Gabriel Du Pre* by Peter Bowen.

rrrrrrrsss.

n. the honk of a nose blowing like a foghorn in *Ulysses* by James Joyce; see also rrr[6].

rrrrt-rrrrt-rrrr-rrrrt-rrrrt.

n. the "harsh scolding gruff" call of an agitated Black-headed Shrike Babbler, as described in *A Guide to the Birds of Southeast Asia* by Craig Robson.

rrrs.

n. the sound of a swiping blade, as in the comic book *Alpha Flight* by Mike Gustorvich; see also sktch.

rrrsst.

n. the hissing sound of a duck, as in *The Little Yellow Duck and His Three Smiling Friends* by Gail Novak.

rrt.

n. the happy growl of a panda bear, as in the comic strip "PvP" by Scott R. Kurtz; see also rrrrrrrrrrr[3].

rt.

n. a promontory.

<*[W]e made sure to sally forth onto a rugged rt—a promontory overlooking the Adriatic sea.* —Douglas R. Hofstadter, *Le Ton Beau De Marot: In Praise of the Music of Language*.>

rtd.

n. the title of a visual poem by Mike Cannell.

Rttwlr.

n. the title of a weblog: "these letters represent the word Rottweiler, spelled without vowels" (SearchingWithin.com).

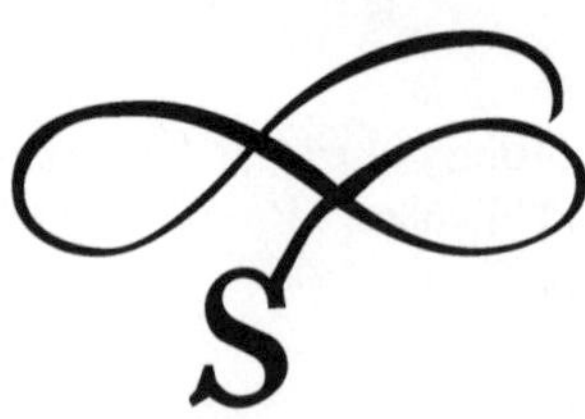

S'dzn.

n. a species of koala in the novel *The FarCall Project* by RedTurtle.

S-Dly.

n. a brave alien Luminoth who laid her body forever "before the marsh of a raining land," in the video game "Metroid Prime 2: Echoes."

S-Jrs.

n. a loyal alien Luminoth of whom it is said: "He no longer breathes, looking down at the great bridge of a holy fortress," in the video game "Metroid Prime 2: Echoes."

s-sh sh-s ch ch ch ch.

n. the sound of people moving about a room and muttering to one another.

<*I woke up again. The room around me was filled with sounds like "s-sh, sh-s, ch, ch, ch, ch..."and the noise of soft footsteps.* —Heshmat Moayyad, *Stories from Iran: A Chicago Anthology 1921-1991.*>

sccctttttcccchhh.

n. the scraping of snow skis across a rocky slope, as described in the novel *The Towers of the Sunset* by L.E. Modesitt Jr.; see also rrrrrr scttttt.

<*He totters at a scraping on the right ski but leans left and back, slowly forcing his track at an angle to the slope. Heading straight downhill would be a death sentence, even for him. Sccctttttcccchhh.* —L.E. Modesitt Jr., *The Towers of the Sunset.*>

sccssfl.

adj. successful, written in Roger Bacon's all-consonant secret code (devised in 1250), as discussed in *The Voynich Manuscript* by Gerry Kennedy.

schrrr frrr chrrr.

n. a French phrase for a repetitive sound on a telephone answering machine resembling laundry flapping on a clothesline, a needle stuck at the end of a 45 record, or the sound of a spinning washing machine, but actually the sound of street traffic and wind carried over the open line of an inadvertent cell phone call, as in "Numéro privé" by Erwan Le Goffic.

scl.

n. the title of a visual poem by Mike Cannell.

scr.

n. the scurrying of mice in the ceiling, as in the graphic novel *Uzumaki 3* by Junji Ito.

Scrnch.

n. the trademarked name of a data compression program.

scrnch.

1. *n.* the chewing sound of a “white, orange-spotted wildcat” ravenously scarfing down a pawful of cookies (Voy.com).

2. *n.* the cracking of a bone breaking or a joint dislocating.

<*Dodging by swerving to the attacker's right, he grabbed the wrist and with all his strength punched the forearm an inch below the elbow. With a sickening 'scrnch' and a painful scream the elbow was now pointing the wrong direction.* —YoungMokii, Soompi.com.>

3. *n.* the creaking of rusty bedspring coils.

<*[My computer is] directly below the bedroom upstairs. I was playing a game shortly thereafter when I heard the unmistakable *scrnch* *scrnch* *scrnch* of the box springs under their bodies. I picked up my book and went for the armchair at the bottom of the stairs until I figured they were well finished.* —WaterSpriteFlying, “'Use Your Inner Voyeur' He Says,” DearDiary.net.>

scrrrrch.

n. the screech of skidding automobile tires.

<*Scrrrrch! Kyle's car skidded to a halt in front of Ranma's new house, and the pigtailed man immediately jumped out.* —Black Dragon, “Guardian: A Ranma 1/2 Fanfiction.”>

sh.

1. *interj.* a sound meaning “be quiet!” See shhh[2].

<*Sh! ... Mr. Phipps, what is your attitude toward censorship in a public library? —The Complete Monty Python's Flying Circus.*>

<*Ell stroked her impossibly long, lush red hair; it coiled around her wrist like a living thing while another section caressed her shoulder. 'Sh,' the woman told her hair, and gave the coil braceleting her wrist a tender nuzzle with her lips. 'Not now. Wait.'* —Pat Cadigan, *Dervish is Digital.*>

2. *n.* the sound of a lost voice.

<*Her mouth was open but her voice wouldn't come. “... sh.”* —Brooks Hansen, *Perlman's Ordeal.*>

sh'.

n. a word meaning *life* in the novel *The FarCall* by RedTurtle.

sh-h-h-h-h.

n. a shushing sound, as in "Sex differences? Sh-h-h-h-h" by Robert Samuelson, *Washington Post.*

sh-hhhh.

v. hush, as spoken in a whisper.

<*Helmina whispered, "Sh-hhhh. Don't go in the dining room. Papa has had some bad news.* —Doris Stensland, *Ole's Promise.*>

sh-sh.

n. the hiss of a "spotty snake," as in *Just So Stories* by Ruyard Kipling.

sh-sh-sh.

n. the sound of maracas or other shakable percussion instruments, as described in *Complete Idiot's Guide to Playing Drums* by Michael Miller; see also ch-ch-ch[7].

shf.

1. *n.* a stifled sob, as at a funeral, in the graphic novel *Uzumaki 2* by Junji Ito.

2. *n.* the sound of a shirt being pulled up, as in the graphic novel *Uzumaki 3* by Junji Ito.

shff.

1. (also shfff, sshfff, sshffff.) *n.* the sound of shoveling dirt, as in the graphic novel *Uzumaki 2* by Junji Ito.

2. *n.* a short spelling of *sheriff.*

<*The final conclusion of the meeting was to let the Shff go on.* —Dorothy Kubik, *A Free Soil—A Free People: The Anti-Rent War in Delaware County, New York.*>

shfff.

n. the sound of clothing pulled over one's head, as in the graphic novel *ShadowFall* by Kaichi Satake.

Shh.

n. a hush sound; see also shhhht[2], ssss[6], ssssss-sssssshhh.

<*The ground was sandy, and there was a gentle hissing. It was a fairy-whisper; or perhaps Divine Nature saying Shh, calling all the things of the world to silence while he slept.* —Stan McDaniel, *The Letterseeker.*>

shh shh shh.

n. the call of the Grey-Hooded Parrotbill, as described in *A Field Guide to the Birds of China* by John MacKinnon.

shh-h-h-hhh.

n. a sound meaning "be quiet!"; see also shhh[2].

<*Have you ever seen someone tell someone else to be quiet by putting their finger over their lips and saying shh-h-h-hhh?* —Cindy Crenshaw, "Emergent Literacy.">

shh-hhh.

n. a hissing shush, as in the novel *Youth in Revolt* by C.D. Payne.

shhfffff.

n. the sound of a window sliding open, as in the graphic novel *Uzumaki 2* by Junji Ito.

shhh.

1. *n.* a sound vibration worthy of exploration, as discussed in *Whole Body Meditations: Igniting Your Natural Instinct to Heal* by Lorin Roche.

2. *n.* the most common spelling for the sound meaning "be quiet!"

<*Nor found Manek at last on the stairs outside the door to Auntie Guest's rooms. "Shhh," he said as they came near, and Nor tapped him anyway, saying, "You're out." "Shhh," he said again, more urgently.* —Gregory Maquire, *Wicked: The Life and Times of the Wicked Witch of the West.*>

shhh-hhh.

n. a whispered shush, as to caution someone to be careful in *Bones of the Master: A Journey to Secret Mongolia* by George Crane.

shhhff.

n. the sound of pulling bedclothes over oneself, as in the graphic novel *ShadowFall* by Kaichi Satake.

SHHHH-hhhh.

n. a cautioning hiss, as in *Children in the Worshipping Community* by David Ng and Virginia Thomas.

shhhh-hhhh.

n. a dying breath.

<*"Just go to dying," Tsung Tsai said and closed his eyes and let one breath softly out. "Shhhh-hhhh," he sighed and breathed no more.* —George Crane, *Bones of the Master: A Journey to Secret Mongolia.*>

shhhhht.

n. the hiss of a carbonated beverage can being opened; see also psss[2], sssss[8].

<*He opened the refrigerator, pulled out a beer. Shhhhht, it sighed when he popped the top.* —Janet Fitch, *White Oleander: A Novel.*>

shhhht.

1. *n.* a shooing sound; see also shht.

<*She'll shoo the men from their cameras. 'Shhhht... I'll take it,' she'll say.* —Evelina Galang, *Her Wild American Self: Short Stories.*>

2. *n.* a shushing sound; see also Shh, ssss[6], ssssss-sssssssshhh.

<*'Shhhht!' Sunderland put his forefinger to his lip.* —John J. Gobbell, *The Last Lieutenant.*>

shhhlck.

n. the sound of someone's cheek getting gashed by a sword, as in the graphic novel *Falcon Twin* by Brenden Mecleary.

shhhlllkk.

(also shhllllllkk, ssshlkkt.) *n.* the sound of someone being impaled by a sword, as in the graphic novel *Falcon Twin* by Brenden Mecleary.

shhhrrrtt.

n. a word of the Bocce language from *Star Wars*, as transcribed in the comic strip "PvP" by Scott R. Kurtz.

shhht.

1. *n.* a warning hiss.

<*'Shhht,' Tessa warned them.* —Evelina Galang, *Her Wild American Self: Short Stories.*>

2. *n.* shit; see also shzzt[1].

<*'Oh shhht,' he mouthed. 'I was just going to change the disc.'* —Victor McGlothin, *Autumn Leaves: A Novel.*>

3. *n.* the alarm cry of a kangaroo.

<*Linda had surprised a gray kangaroo there that morning; it had made its characteristic 'shhht' sound of alarm and thudded hastily away.* —Gabrielle Walker, *Snowball Earth: The Story of the Great Global Catastrophe That Spawned Life as We Know It.*>

shhp.

1. *n.* the sound of a human snail slithering on the floor, as in the graphic novel *Uzumaki 2* by Junji Ito.

2. *n.* the sound of a window sliding open, as in the graphic novel *Uzumaki 2* by Junji Ito.

3. *n.* the sound of an anesthetic being administered, as in the graphic novel *ShadowFall* by Kaichi Satake.

shht.

n. a shooing sound; see also shhhht[1].

<*"I told you I don't want that dog in here. Shht!" She shooed him away from the puddle of soup on the floor beside Jordie's chair.* —Kathleen Eagle, *This Time Forever.*>

shhwfff.

n. the sound of a brassiere being whisked out from beneath one's clothing, as in the comic book *Mystic #39* by Aaron Lopresti and Matt Ryan.

shksp-p-p-p.

n. a sound made by a six-month-old baby, as described in the novel *Edwin Mullhouse* by Steven Millhauser.

shlgg.

n. a noncommittal mutter, as in the story "Potch" by Leo Rosten (anthologized in *A Passion for Books: A Book Lover's Treasury of Stories, Essays, Humor, Love and Lists on Collecting, Reading, Borrowing, Lending, Caring for, and Appreciating Books* by Harold Rabinowitz).

shllkrr.

n. a copper-red metal in Stan McDaniel's novel *The Letterseeker.*

<*The hair of Gretta Hunterchief, friend Threescar, is as red as beaten shllkrr in the firelight.* —Stan McDaniel, *The Letterseeker.*>

shlp.

n. the gruesome sound of intestines falling out of a rotten corpse, as in the graphic novel *Uzumaki 2* by Junji Ito.

shlt.

n. the sound of a needle-like tongue spearing someone's neck, as in the graphic novel *Uzumaki 2* by Junji Ito.

shmpf.

n. the sound of a defibrillator, as in the graphic novel *ShadowFall* by Kaichi Satake.

Shzzt.

n. the name of an elfin thief in the role-playing game "Greyhawk Campaign."

shzzt.

1. *n.* shit; see also shhht[2].

<*Teenage drama shzzt.* —MyOtaku.com.>

<*You can't take shzzt like this personally.* —LoveShack.org.>

<*That stinks a pile-o-shzzt.* —S10forum.com.>

2. *n.* the sound of an electronic discharge.

Shzzt'Trk.

n. a character in "The Knight Clash" by Marco Dinaro.

shzzz.

n. a snarling artillery round, as in *No One Smiled on Leyte* by Deane Marks.

shzzzzzzztt.

n. the sound of a needle scraping the edge of a record.

<*For some reason I put the needle on the empty space [and] all I heard was "SHZZZZZZZTT!"* —DirtyChimp182, "The Right Stuff Forum.">

skkrt.

n. the sound of a razor blade scraping whiskers, as in the comic book *Schizo #2* by Ivan Brunetti.

sklch.

n. the sound of a talking vacuum cleaner's electrical cord crushing the skull of a murderer whose head it has tied up, as in the comic book *Vacuum Horror* by Aaron K.

sklklkl.

n. the sound of a talking vacuum cleaner from outer space sucking the brain out of a girl so that she can enjoy eternal life as a vacuum cleaner, in the comic book *Vacuum Horror* by Aaron K.

skng.

n. an impatient mutter, as in the story "Potch" by Leo Rosten (anthologized in *A Passion for Books: A Book Lover's Treasury of Stories, Essays, Humor, Love and Lists on Collecting, Reading, Borrowing, Lending, Caring for, and Appreciating Books* by Harold Rabinowitz).

Skrp.

n. the name of a rat.

<*Skrp's people are bright enough, but they seem to have a bit of a blind spot when it comes to labels on bottles.* —Terry Pratchett, *Guards! Guards!*>

skrrk.

n. the sound of a throat being cut or a voice being forcibly silenced through psychic power.

<*Think of all the people in America who stick their dogs outside first thing in the morning. They almost invariably bark and wake up the neighbors. So there's this wave of irritation traveling across the country, picking up momentum with every people who's awakened. By the time it gets to Oregon, half the people in the country are pissed. Somewhere along the way it reaches critical mass, and one person who really wants some peace and quiet focuses that power—probably without even knowing he's doing it—and skrrk.' She drew her finger across her throat.* —Jerry Oltion, *Abandon In Place.*>

skrrkkkll.

n. the sound of a weapon being levitated through telekinetic powers, as in the comic book *X-Men Adventures #11* by John Herbert.

skrrr.

n. the sound of an automobile changing gear, as in *Building a Very Large Sandcastle* by Morten Nisker.

skrrrk-skrrrrk-kk-kk-kk-kk-kk.

n. the high pitched, fast call of the Northern Brownbill bird, as described in *Birds of Kenya and Northern Tanzania* by Dale A. Zimmerman.

skrrrrnnnch.

n. the sound of a train car being lifted out of the way by an angry person's bare hands, as in the comic book *Gen13 #0* by Jim Lee, Alex Garner and Wendy Fouts.

skrrt.

n. the buzzing sound of radio static.

<_*SKRRT*enant Gordon? We've got a little situation brewing down here._ —Jason Corley, _Gotham Day_.>

skrsh.

n. the crunch of a foot stomping on giant mollusk eggs, as in the graphic novel *Uzumaki 2* by Junji Ito.

Skszp.

n. the name of lyricist Stephen Trask's character in the film "Hedwig and the Angry Inch."

sktch.

1. *n.* a scratching sensation as one's mind races with irritating memories.

   <*Sktch. Sktch. Audie felt the sensation of sandpaper rubbing against the inside of his skull.* —Whitehorse, "Soul Worms," EastOfTheWeb.com.>

2. *n.* the sound of a swiping blade, as in the comic book *Alpha Flight* by Mike Gustorvich; see also rrrs.

3. *n.* the sound of opening an envelope, as in the graphic novel *ShadowFall* by Kaichi Satake.

sljb.

n. the title of a visual poem by Mike Cannell.

sll.

(also slllp.) *n.* the sound of a person slithering across the floor like a snail, as in the graphic novel *Uzumaki 2* by Junji Ito.

slll-p.

n. the sound of a slurp from a soda can, as in the graphic novel *The Makeshift Miracle* by Jim Zubkavich.

slmp.

v. slumping, collapsing to the ground, as in the graphic novel *Uzumaki 3* by Junji Ito.

slrp.

(also sllp, slllp.) *v.* to slurp a beverage, as from a coffee cup or soda can, as in the comic strip "PvP" by Scott R. Kurtz.

smmrr.

n. an inarticulate mutter from someone whose mouth is held shut, as in the comic strip "PvP" by Scott R. Kurtz.

smrr.

n. an ocean wave, as in Stan McDaniel's novel *The Letterseeker*.

smsk.

n. the smack of a kiss, as in the comic strip "PvP" by Scott R. Kurtz.

sndng.

v. sending, written in Roger Bacon's all-consonant secret code (devised in 1250), as discussed in *The Voynich Manuscript* by Gerry Kennedy.

snff.

n. a sniffing sound.

<*It is not war—it is a chastizement. Snff!* —Rudyard Kipling, *Kim*.>

snfft.

(also snff, snnfff, snnnnfff.) *n.* a sniffle accompanying tears, as in the graphic novel *ShadowFall* by Kaichi Satake.

snkt.

n. the sound of a switchblade, as in the comic book *Vacuum Horror* by Aaron K.

snnfff.

1. *n.* a deep inhalation of a pleasant scent.

<*For an intoxicating berry scent, try [the] Votivos Red Currant candle. Snnfff... It's sensational!* —Janice Hoffmann, "Five Simple Tips on Using Your Senses.">

2. *n.* a sniffle, as from crying.

<*Suddenly tears sprang into her eyes, and her throat sounded tight. "And... snnfff..."* —Suzy Pizzuti, *Say Uncle*.>

snnkk.

n. the whoosh of a door sliding shut, as in the graphic novel *ShadowFall* by Kaichi Satake.

snnnffff.

v. to sniff deeply, as in the comic strip "PvP" by Scott R. Kurtz.

snnrrk.

(also snnrrrk.) *n.* a snore, as in the comic strip "PvP" by Scott R. Kurtz; see also snnrzzz, znrrk.

snnrzzz.

(also snrzzzzz.) *n.* a snore, as in the comic strip "PvP" by Scott R. Kurtz; see also snnrrk, znrrk.

snrff.

n. a sniffing sound from a "floppy-eared dog" in the kitchen, as in *It Came From Beneath the Sink!* by R.L. Stine.

snrrrl.

n. the snarl of someone having been bitten by the Wolfman, as transcribed in the comic strip "PvP" by Scott R. Kurtz; see also hrrrk, nngh[7].

Sphnx.

1. *n.* an alternate spelling of the Egyptian Sphinx, presumably lending it an air of mystery and antiquity.

2. *n.* the name of a character in the Yu-Gi-Oh! card game.

3. *n.* the name of a pop music band from the Seventies.

<*As students at St. Bede's Grammar School in Bradford, United Kingdom, Terry Uttley, the only founding member left in the new 'Smokie' group, teamed up with his musical friends, Chris Norman and Alan Silson, to form a group named 'The Yen,' which was later changed to 'The Sphnx.'* —Joel Savage, Blogcritics.com>

splp.

n. the sound of a bare foot walking through mud, as in the graphic novel *Uzumaki 2* by Junji Ito.

splsh.

n. the beat of a boat's oars upon furious ocean waves; see also plsh, pltt.

<*Splsh! Splt! Elgo stood beside Reynor, both on the same oar, corded muscles standing out in bold relief as they hove the blade to a furious beat, working synchronistically.* —Dennis L. McKiernan, *Dragondoom.*>

splt.

n. a splashing sound, as in *Dragondoom* by Dennis L. McKiernan; see splsh.

sppt.

n. the sound of someone struggling not to drown in a vat of fresh cream, as in the graphic novella *Hearts and Minds* by Scott McCloud; see also hgkh, blpb.

spptt.

n. the sound of expectorating while brushing one's teeth, as in the comic book *Schizo #2* by Ivan Brunetti.

sprtl.

n. a sound indicating that one's "personal holo-projector" has a bent antenna, as in the comic strip "PvP" by Scott R. Kurtz.

Sqwrt.

n. the name of a character in "Sqwrt's Tale" by Bem Ajani Jones-Bey, about a boy facing the hardship of having a name with no vowels.

srrrr.

n. the short, unmusical trill of the Common Tody-Flycatcher bird, as described in *A Guide to the Birds of Panama* by Robert S. Ridgely.

sshhhllk.

n. the sound of a slashing knife, as in the graphic novel *Falcon Twin* by Brenden Mecleary.

sshhlllrrr.

n. the sound of "serious respiratory distress," as in the graphic novel *ShadowFall* by Kaichi Satake; see also hhrrkkrk.

sshhrrkssh.

n. the sound of flesh ripped apart by a sword, as in the graphic novel *Falcon Twin* by Brenden Mecleary.

sshhssh.

n. the woosh of a lunging attack, as in the comic story "Rogue's Curse" by Wendy Pini.

sss.

1. *n.* a hissing sound of disapproval.

<*What was that 'sss ... sshssh' business?* —David L. Lindsey, *A Cold Mind.*>

2. *n.* the hiss of a bathtub filled with acid, as discussed in the play *Awake and Sing* by Clifford Odets.

3. *n.* the sound of the letter s; see also ssss[11].

<S says "sss"—(the sss sound in this case is heard at the end of the letter name). —"Alphabet Letter Memorizing Trick," ReadingKey.com.>

4. *n.* the sound of white noise, as described in "What to Listen For in Cymbals" by Bill Cahn.

SSS SSS.

v. to rustle fabric.

<Ms Nelson's dress goes SSS, SSS to the door and I hear her turn the lock above the knob. —J.B. Powell, *Republic: A Novel.*>

sssft.

n. the angry snarl of a duck whose treasure and flying carpet have been stolen, as in *Walt Disney's Comics in Color, Volume 7* by Carl Barks.

ssshhhhh.

n. an overwhelmed exhalation.

<If he had been able to hear, he would have heard, in the nearly perfect silence, the sound of Tom Cullen's imagination at work—the lip-vibrating brrrrrr *as he drove the cars onto the Fisher-Price tarmac ... the* ssshhhhhhh *as the lift inside went up and down.* —Stephen King, *The Stand: Expanded Edition.*>

ssshhhhhhh.

n. the sound of a garage lift.

<Sullivan's mouth opened, but all the things there were to say overwhelmed him, and he just exhaled a descending "Ssshhhhh." —Tim Powers, *Expiration Date.*>

ssshp.

n. the sound of paint rollers on a wall.

<I could hear their sticky little rollers moving over that wall, ssshp, ssshp, ssshp. —Nicholson Baker, *Vox.*>

ssslllrr.

n. the slurping sound of a whirlpool swallowing a raft, as in the graphic novel *Uzumaki 3* by Junji Ito.

Ssss.

n. a "Sand wedge" golf club, as discussed in *In the Loop: A Crash Course in the Golf Culture* by John Renslow.

ssss.

1. *n.* an attention-grabbing sound; a variation of psst, as in *Timeline* by Michael Crichton; see also fsst[2], psss[1], ssstt.

2. *n.* the wet hiss of a leaking garden hose.

<*And when the Cloudy laughs, it's a garden hose sound—ssss. A little bit leaking out at a time.* —Liz Curtis Higgs, *Help! I'm Laughing and I Can't Get Up: Fall-down Funny Stories To Fill Your Heart And Lift Your Spirit.*>

3. *interj.* an exhalation of sensual pleasure.

<*"Ssss, do that again, baby," she begged.* —Michael Baisden, *The Maintenance Man: A Novel.*>

4. *interj.* the startling hiss of an imprisoned Dread Gnome, as in *The Shadowlands* by Emily Rodda.

5. *n.* a "deep but soft" sound "like the echo of the ocean inside a seashell" (Donna Farki, *Yoga Mind, Body & Spirit: A Return to Wholeness).*

6. *n.* a shushing sound; see also Shh, shhhht[2], ssssss-sssssssshhh.

<*"Ssss!" She held a hand up, shushing me, her eyes focusing in the way people do when someone picks up the phone on the other end.* —Sue Grafton, *C is for Corpse.*>

7. *n.* the hiss of a non-spotted snake, as in *Just So Stories* by Ruyard Kipling.

8. *n.* the sound of "a sudden fiery splash of lava burst[ing] from the volcano floor" in *Journey to the Volcano Palace* by Tony Abbott.

9. *n.* the sound of a breath.

<*Her mother breathes, "Ssss, be strong."* —Gus Lee, *Chasing Hepburn: A Memoir of Shanghai, Hollywood, and a Chinese Family's Fight for Freedom.*>

10. *n.* the sound of a sword blade being sheathed.

<*The combined slippery sound, the high-pitched metallic ssss of polished steel against steel, again made Savage's skin prickle.* —David Morrell, *The Fifth Profession.*>

11. *n.* the sound of the letter s, as described in *The Voice That Means Business: How to Speak With Authority, Confidence and Credibility Anytime, Anywhere* by Linda Shields; see also sss[3].

12. *n.* the sound of the letter s, as described in the novel *Just Call Me Stupid* by Tom Birdseye.

13. *pron.* "what's," as in the colloquialism "Ssss up?" as discussed in *Customers Are People: The Human Touch* by John McKean.

Ssss Ssss Ssss.

n. the sound of a train.

<*"Ssss Ssss Ssss," she called, making the sound of a train.* —Geoff Ryman, *The Child Garden: A Low Comedy.*>

ssss ssss ssss.

n. the light sizzling sound of snowflakes hitting a body of water.

<*[L]ow white clouds, flakes of snow swirling ahead and disappearing into the sea with a faint ssss, ssss, ssss.* —Kim Stanley Robinson, *The Wild Shore: Three Californias*.>

ssss ssss ssss ssss.

n. "the idiosyncratic urgings of cowpokes" (Lawrence Scanlan, *Wild About Horses: Our Timeless Passion for the Horse*).

ssss tsss.

n. a subtle sound betraying a person's presence on the other end of an otherwise silent telephone line, as in *Independence Day* by Richard Ford.

sssss.

1. *interj.* a hiss of frustration.

<*"Sssss!" he hissed in frustration, swinging his head from side to side.* —Sara Douglass, *Enchanter*.>

2. *n.* a "droning silence" like a long-drawn s-sound (Heshmat Moayyad, *Stories from Iran: A Chicago Anthology 1921-1991*).

3. *n.* a philosophical conception of the "space" between tension and compression.

<*Sssss is the between, the excluded middle, of tension and compression. Even the form, S, is a marker of this. Flaccidity, flow, or snake movement of alternating tension and compression.* —R. Shields, *Anti-Methods: Expressive Forms of Researching Culture*.>

4. *n.* a prefatory whisper.

<*"Sssss!" A whisper prefaced all his remarks. "I think—yes, by Heaven, I'll make a* saucier *of you!"* —Idwal Jones, *High Bonnet: A Novel of Epicurean Adventures*.>

5. *n.* a sound betraying pent-up hostility or rage.

<*You know that sssss sound he's always makin'? You know what that is? That's cigarettes burning the backs of his legs when he don't do his chores. Anybody wonder where his rage comes from?* —Chris Crutcher, *Ironman*.>

<*My brother pops his knuckles, his throat moving, a puff of hostile sssss sounds coming out.* —Joy Nicholson, *The Tribes of Palos Verdes: A Novel*.>

6. *n.* a splash of water.

<*He tossed the water across the air. Sssss! The water struck something in midair and spilled down it.* —Tony Abbott, *Journey to the Volcano Palace*.>

7. *n.* a tinkling sound heard at a urinal.

<*And then someone comes in and takes a leak: bang of door and zip of zipper and the stream in the urinal, a faint sssss at first, then silence as it tapers down.* —Vince Passaro, *Violence, Nudity, Adult Content: A Novel*.>

8. *n.* the hiss of a carbonated beverage can being opened; see also psss[2], shhhhht, sssss[8].

<*Moore pulled open the top of a Bud. The sssss preceded the tiny bubbles that leapt at him.* —Ken Morris, *The Deadly Trade: A Novel.*>

9. *n.* the low hiss of the Wyvern.

<*For every low Wyvernian sssss, Julie heard a hosanna or a shout of joy.* —James Morrow, *Only Begotten Daughter.*>

10. *n.* the sound of a cigarette extinguished in water.

<*The hot end of her cigarette made a sssss sound as she dipped it into the water of her tub.* —Merry McInerney-Whiteford, *If Wishes Were Horses: A Novel.*>

11. *n.* the sound of an arrow piercing one's chest, as in *The Hummingbird King: A Guatemalan Legend* by Argentina Palacios.

12. *n.* the tangible shock of ice-cold water on bare feet, like a zap of electricity.

<*Back in the bathroom, she dumped the bucket of freezer snow on top of the puddle that had been the ice cubes. Then she ran cold water, filled the bathtub calf-deep, and stepped into it. Sssss ... The shock of cold feet zapped straight through Issy's body to her brain.* —Nalo Hopkinson, *Skin Folk.*>

sssss sssss sssss.

n. the sound of someone "crazily imitating" a hissing radiator, as in *Not About Nightingales* by Tennessee Williams.

Sssss-ssss-ssss-ssss.

n. a stopped-up laugh.

<*[T]hen going into a stopped-up laugh, Sssss-ssss-ssss-ssss- until somebody would try to break up his sequence by asking him how was the tennis playing going these days.* —Tom Wolfe, *The Electric Kool-Aid Acid Test.*>

sssss**hhhh.**

n. the sound of air whooshing past a skydiver's ears, as described by Jimi Hendrix (quoted in *Jimi Hendrix: Electric Gypsy* by Harry Shapiro).

ssssss.

1. *n.* the hissing of a snake.

<*They all squirm and go ssssss but I know they don't mean anything by it.* —David Maine, *The Preservationist.*>

2. *n.* the sound of steam in a Chinese laundry, as described in *The Woman Warrior: Memoirs of a Girlhood Among Ghosts* by Maxine Hong Kingston.

ssssss-sssssssshhh.

n. a shushing sound; see also Shh, ssss[6], shhhht[2].

<*I put my index finger up to my lips, whispered 'Ssssss-sssssssshhh,' and slipped behind the wheel of the Miata.* —Linda Fairstein, *Cold Hit.*>

Sssssss.

n. the title of a film from 1973.

<*I learned about evil from [Dad's] metal FBI car radio. The sound of evil goes like this: sssssss. This is what I listen to when Dad drives me to St. Bede on his way to work. ... Ssssss. Evil flies in like a dart. It hides in the static infiltrating the car. Ssssss.* —Maura Conlon-McIvor, *FBI Girl: How I Learned to Crack My Father's Code.*>

sssssss sssss sssssss.

n. the whispers of a town gossip.

<*Mr. Crackle said crossly, "Sssssss, sssss, sssssss. The two little town gossips."* —Betty MacDonald, *Hello, Mrs. Piggle-Wiggle.*>

sssssssss.

1. *n.* the hissing of a pipe, described by Leda Mesen in *Wishes, Lies, and Dreams: Teaching Children to Write Poetry* by Kenneth Koch.

2. *n.* the hissing of air through teeth.

<*From Jeanne, from other towel-surrounded heads along the beach I hear nothing but the occasional intake—Sssssssss—a stoic hissing through the teeth, a long exhale.* —Donald W. George, *Japan: True Stories of Life on the Road.*>

3. *n.* the sound of a fine mist emerging from a can that contains a genie, as in *The Unknown Witches of Oz: Locasta and the Three Adepts* by Dave Hardenbrook.

sssssssss ssss sssss.

n. the hiss of watchgeese, as in *Scion of Cyador* by L. E. Modesitt.

sssssssss-ttt.

n. the sound of airbrakes on a bus.

<*As he approached Houston, the bus always got more loaded with people and express, and the highway became crowded with cars and trucks and other hazards. And then suddenly, like rolling off the edge of a table, it was over. Sssssssss-ttt went the brakes and off went the people, the express and all of that tension.* —Jim Lehrer, *White Widow.*>

sssssssssshhhh.

n. the hiss of the "iron fist" energy strike, imbued "with all the deadliness of the mystical dragon['s] ... molten heart" (Sal Buscema, *Incredible Hulk #300*).

ssssst.

(also sssst sssst, sssssssst, ssssssssst, ssssssssssssssssst, ssssssssssssssssssssst.) *n.* the sound of a telescope racing "to catch up with the Earth's rotation," as in *Shoemaker by Levy: The Man Who Made an Impact* by David H. Levy.

sssst.

1. *n.* the hissing sound of a duck, as in *The Little Yellow Duck and His Three Smiling Friends* by Gail Novak.

2. *n.* the sound of squirting water in a Chinese laundry, as described in *The Woman Warrior: Memoirs of a Girlhood Among Ghosts* by Maxine Hong Kingston.

ssst.

n. the sound of an android or robot malfunctioning, as in *The Metallic Touch*; see vzzkt.

ssstt.

n. an attention-grabbing sound; a variation of psst, as *The Letterseeker* by Stan McDaniel; see also fsst[2], psss[1], pssst[3], psst[2], ssss[1].

<*Ssstt! ... Don! Look!* —Robert Saar, *Trout Days and Onion Nights.*>

sszzzl.

n. the sizzle of "discharges of highly-concentrated flames at [a] temperature deemed sufficient to incinerate even [a] female mutant's apparently heat-resistant flesh" (Rich Buckler, *Marvel Super-Heroes 6*).

stg.

n. the title of a visual poem by Mike Cannell.

stp.

n. the sound of a quiet step, as in the graphic novels *Uzumaki 2* and *Uzumaki 3* by Junji Ito.

strr.

n. a verbalized pause.

<*Strr ... So, okay. I'll bring over da boxes.* —Leo Rosten, "Potch," anthologized in *A Passion for Books: A Book Lover's Treasury of Stories, Essays, Humor, Love and Lists on Collecting, Reading, Borrowing, Lending, Caring for, and Appreciating Books* by Harold Rabinowitz.>

swwsssshhh.

n. an electronic swoosh.

<*To fill things out, XBXRX have also included a limited assortment of electronic bweeEEows and swwsssshhhs here and there.*>

t'chk t'chk.

interj. a sympathetic cluck in response to sobering news.

<*"Struck down," said the Rector, "struck down by this wretched scourge of influenza. Quite helpless. Delirious. They have sent for Dr. Baines." "T'chk, t'chk," said Mrs. Venables.* —Dorothy L. Sayers, *The Nine Tailors*.>

t't't't't.

n. the stuttering trill of the Killdeer bird during courtship, alarm, and aggressive encounters, as described in *Stokes Guide to Bird Behavior, Volume 2* by Donald Stokes.

t-krrrk.

n. the dry, rhythmic call of the inconspicuous Yellow-Eared Toucanet bird, as described in *A Guide to the Birds of Panama* by Robert S. Ridgely.

t-t-t-rrrrrrrr.

n. the rolling, speeding-up call of the Blue-eared Barbet, as described in *Toucans, Barbets and Honeyguides: Ramphastidae, Capitonidae and Indicatoridae* by Lester L. Short.

t-t-t-t-t.

n. a stutter.

<*He trembles and cannot speak, only stutter, in what may be the shortest line ever written in blank verse: 'T-t-t-t-t ...'* —Thomas Pynchon, *The Crying of Lot 49*.>

t-t-t-t-t-t-t.

n. the soft, rapid, excited call of the Ruby-Throated Hummingbird, as described by Tomm Lorenzin in "Birdsong Mnemonics."

t-t-trrr.

n. the loud call of the Pale-Eyed Pygmy-Tyrant bird, as described in *A Guide to the Birds of Panama* by Robert S. Ridgely; see also trrrrr[2].

tch.

1. *interj.* a sound indicating a sudden realization.

<*Door looked down at her scroll some more and then looked around the hall, more carefully. She made a face. "Tch," she explained, and took off back down the stairs, the way they had come.* —Neil Gaiman, *Neverwhere*.>

2. *interj.* a sound of disbelief.

<*A chorus of* tuts *and* tsks *and* tchs *ran around the table as Mrs. Higgler and Mrs. Dunwiddy and Mrs. Bustamonte and Miss Noles clicked their tongues and shook their heads.* —Neil Gaiman, *Anansi Boys.*>

3. *interj.* a sound of disgust.

<*She went off with a young man ... on a horse. Tch. I ask you.* —Neil Gaiman, *Smoke and Mirrors.*>

tchhhhhhh.

n. the thump of a heartbeat.

<*His heart was beating so hard beneath his sternum, he could hear it when he opened his mouth... tchhhhhhh tchhhhhhh tchhhhhhh tchhhhhhh.* —Tom Wolfe, *A Man in Full.*>

tchk.

1. *interj.* a sound made by Rikki Tikki Tavi, a character from *The Jungle Book* by Rudyard Kipling.

2. *n.* the sound of a stone shifting, as when nudged by a foot.

<*The sound of dripping water had faded away again; there was nothing now to be heard but their own breaths, and the faint sound of their paw-pads on the dry, rough stone—sometimes a* tchk *as one of them kicked or shifted a bit of stone, and the sound fell flat and loud into the surrounding stillness.* —Diane Duane, *The Book of Night with Moon.*>

tchp.

n. the short, sharp call of the Buff-Bellied Hummingbird, as described in *Hummingbirds: A Wildlife Handbook* by Kim Long.

tchrrrrk tchrrrrk.

n. the "harsh grating" call of the Brown Bush Warbler, as described in *A Guide to the Birds of Southeast Asia* by Craig Robson.

tck.

1. *interj.* a sound of displeasure or annoyance.

<*Then the first man came back, this time careless enough to kick over the small cake of black ink as he passed. "Tck!" the seaman exclaimed in annoyance.* —Diana Gabaldon, *Voyager.*>

2. *n.* a clucking command to a horse.

<*"Tck." He clucked to our horse and urged it up alongside the leader's, engaging the burly shadow in quiet Gaelic conversation.* —Diana Gabaldon, *Outlander.*>

tfh htf.

n. the title of a visual poem by Mike Cannell.

tftktstt.

n. in the Tashlhiyt dialect of Berber, this means "you sprained it."

tgggghhhh.

n. time, as spoken by someone whose mouth is sealed with fear over a massive snake "with yellow, swirling slits for eyes and huge fangs" (Robert Asprin, *Myth-Ion Improbable*).

th t.

n. the title of a visual poem by Mike Cannell.

thd.

n. a thud, as in the graphic novel *Uzumaki 2* by Junji Ito.

Thfft.

n. the sound of a cork slowly pulled from a champagne bottle so as to maintain the bubbles; see also pffft[7].

<*Exactly on cue, a quiet Thfft emitted, as the cork came free.* —Rex Pickett, *Sideways: A Novel.*>

thfyhtf.

n. the title of a visual poem by Mike Cannell.

thgg.

n. the sound of one hand grasping another, as in the graphic novel *Uzumaki 3* by Junji Ito.

thgh.

conj. though, written in Roger Bacon's all-consonant secret code (devised in 1250), as discussed in *The Voynich Manuscript* by Gerry Kennedy.

thmp.

n. a thumping or banging sound.

<*'Why---' thmp / 'are you being' / thmp thmp bng-bmp / 'so fucking nice to me?' / he asked. / thmp thmp*. —Terra Elan McVoy, "Dragonfly.">

thnk.

n. the clang of balls in a skee ball machine, as in the graphic novel *Sordid City Blues* by Charles Schneeflock Snow.

thnn.

n. an incoherent word (presumably "thank") spoken through a parched throat, just upon waking.

<*He was startled, had let his head fall, sleepily, and he snapped awake, stood, saw the young man*

holding the door for him, and he tried to say something, his mouth dry and thick. "Thnn uuu," he said, and cleared his throat, stepped through the door. —Jeffrey M. Shaara, *Gods and Generals.*>

thrkkklll.

n. the crackle of a roiling "timestorm" as it changes the present and removes from existence all that one knows, bit by bit, as in the comic book *X-Men Adventures #8* by John Herbert.

thrp.

n. the sound of one's boot tripping over the ledge of a roof, as in the graphic novel *ShadowFall* by Kaichi Satake.

Thrrl.

n. a given name for males.

<*Hrrl my ancestor was not red-bearded. This Thrrl can be neither his ghost nor his kin. He takes a brave name wrongly.* —Stan McDaniel, *The Letterseeker.*>

Thrrp.

n. a god, Charioteer of the Sun.

<*"And rightly so," said the high priest of Thrrp, the Charioteer of the Sun.* —Terry Pratchett, *Pyramids.*>

thrrp.

1. *n.* a noncommittal mutter, as in the story "Potch" by Leo Rosten (anthologized in *A Passion for Books: A Book Lover's Treasury of Stories, Essays, Humor, Love and Lists on Collecting, Reading, Borrowing, Lending, Caring for, and Appreciating Books* by Harold Rabinowitz).

2. *n.* the moment one catches a fish on a hook.

<*In the meadow sometimes I would forget and let my shadow cross the quiet brook; and then I would approach from the east and drop my fly around the bend, and let it float gently, to tease the watching brown, until thrrp ... I had him. What joy!* —Mary McClure Goulding, *Changing Lives Through Redecision Therapy.*>

ths.

pro. this, written in Roger Bacon's all-consonant secret code (devised in 1250), as discussed in *The Voynich Manuscript* by Gerry Kennedy.

tk-rrrrrrrrrrrr.

n. the "low-pitched guttural repercussion[s]" of the Rufous Nightjar, as described in *Nightjars and Their Allies: The Caprimulgiformes* by D.T. Holyoak.

tk-tk-tk-tk-tk-tk-tk.

n. a repeated clicking sound.

<*"Tk-tk-tk-tk-tk-tk-tk," a rapid-fire clicking noise echoed from deep within Hunter's throat, and leftover blood dripped from his beak as he slowly advanced upon the final victim of the hour.* —Black Dragon, "Guardian: A Ranma 1/2 Fanfiction.">

tkk.

n. the sound of cutting embroidery thread with one's teeth.

<*She bit the thread of the embroidery she was doing with her little sharp teeth, tkk!* —Donn Byrne, *The Wind Bloweth.*>

tkkststt.

n. in the Tashlhiyt dialect of Berber, this means "you took it off."

tkt.

n. the click of a door opening, as in the comic book *Alpha Flight* by Mike Gustorvich.

tmp.

1. *n.* the patter of running feet, as in the graphic novels *Uzumaki 2* and *Uzumaki 3* by Junji Ito.

2. *n.* the sound of feet running down a staircase, as in the graphic novel *ShadowFall* by Kaichi Satake.

tnk tnk tnk.

n. the sound of typing on a keyboard.

<**click* *wrrrr* *tnk tnk tnk*. i'm a crazy man at the keyboard. sure a typewriter would make me seem cooler, but i write all my stories in emails, and then send them to myself, at a different email address.* —Paul Jarvis, "Pseudofamous.">

Tnn.

n. a primeval sea dragon who was defeated by the god Baal.

<*In the Canaanite Baal and Anat poems from Ugarit in Syria, Anat and Baal both speak of having crushed Sea, destroyed Flood, bound the sea dragon (tnn), and crushed the sea serpent (ltn).* —Fuller Theological Seminary.>

tnng.

n. the sound of a ricocheting projectile, as in the comic book *Steampunk #1* by Chris Bachalo and Richard Friend.

Tnnnsh.

n. the name of a warrior bat in the novel *Wink-Eye Creek* by Doug Hiser.

<*[The doe's] right front hoof smashed into Tnnnsh, crushing his skull and he dropped to the ground to be trampled.* —Doug Hiser, *Wink-Eye Creek.*>

tprw.

n. the sound of a horn (cited by Jeff Miller, "A Collection of Word Oddities and Trivia").

tptptp.

n. the sound of feet running quickly, as in the graphic novel *Uzumaki 2* by Junji Ito.

trksph.

n. a muffled expression by someone whose mouth is sealed by duct tape, as in the novel *Heart Seizure* by Bill Fitzhugh.

trr-trr-trr.

n. the short rattling call of the Rusty-Throated Parrotbill bird, as described in *A Field Guide to the Birds of China* by John MacKinnon.

trrk trrk trrk trrrrk.

n. the "monotonous, repeated" call of the Orange-fronted Barbet, as described in *A Field Guide to the Birds of Borneo, Sumatra, Java, and Bali* by John Ramsay MacKinnon.

trrp.

n. the soft croaking call of the elusive Slate-Headed Tody-Flycatcher bird, as described in *A Guide to the Birds of Panama* by Robert S. Ridgely.

trrp-trrrrrrrrr.

n. the loud, piercing call of the Woodland Kingfisher, as described in *Birds of Southern Africa* by Ian Sinclair.

trrr.

n. the alarm call of the Sedge Warbler, as described in *A Guide to the Birds of Western Africa* by Ron Demey.

trrr trrr trrr.

n. the grating call of the Dwarf Cuckoo, as described in *A Guide to the Birds of Columbia* by Steven L. Hilty.

trrrr.

n. a low grating call of the Sooty Thrush, as described in *Thrushes* by Peter Clement.

trrrr trrrr trrrr.

n. the "sibilant low" call of the Yellow-eyed Babbler, as described in *A Guide to the Birds of Southeast Asia* by Craig Robson.

trrrr-r-r.

n. the "creaking, rasping" song of Baillon's Crake bird, as described in *The Handbook of Bird Identification for Europe and the Western Palearctic* by Mark Beaman.

trrrr-trrr-trrr.

n. the high-pitched squeak of the Fire-Tailed Myzornis bird, as described in *A Field Guide to the Birds of China* by John MacKinnon.

trrrrr.

1. *n.* the "hard, rolling" call of an agitated Clamorous Reed Warbler, as described in *A Guide to the Birds of Southeast Asia* by Craig Robson.

2. *n.* the fast, clicking call of the African (Bluebilled) Firefinch, "like a fishing reel as the line is played out," as described in *Birds of Southern Africa* by Ian Sinclair; the "long dry trills" of the Pale-Eyed Pygmy-Tyrant, as described in *A Guide to the Birds of Columbia* by Steven L. Hilty; the "dry rattling" of the Kittlitz's Plover, as described in *A Guide to the Birds of Western Africa* by Ron Demey; see also t-t-trrr.

trrrrrr.

n. the "thin wooden rattle" of the Spotted Antpitta bird, as described in *A Guide to the Birds of Columbia* by Steven L. Hilty.

trrrrrrrr.

n. the call of the Chestnut-Crested Cotinga bird in Peru and Bolivia, as described in *A Guide to the Birds of Columbia* by Steven L. Hilty; the "long harsh rattling" trill of the Tchagra species of shrike, as described in *Shrikes and Bush-Shrikes* by Tony Harris.

trrrrrrrrrr-RRRRRRRRRRRRR.

n. the "far-carrying trill" of the Trilling Cisticola, "lasting several seconds and increasing in volume," as described in *Birds of Kenya and Northern Tanzania* by Dale A. Zimmerman.

trrrrrrt trrrrrt.

n. the "harsh squeaky" call of the Grey-faced Tit Babbler, as described in *A Guide to the Birds of Southeast Asia* by Craig Robson.

trrrrt.

n. the rattling call of the Little Pied Flycatcher, as described in *A Guide to the Birds of Southeast Asia* by Craig Robson.

trrt-trrt.

n. the call of Levaillant's Cisticola bird, as described in *Birds of Kenya and Northern Tanzania* by Dale A. Zimmerman.

trrt-trrt-trrt.

n. the scolding call of the Hill Blue Flycatcher, as described in *A Guide to the Birds of Southeast Asia* by Craig Robson.

trrt-trrt-trrt-trrt.

n. the harsh cry of the Crimson-Breasted Shrike bird, as described in *Birds of Southern Africa* by Ian Sinclair; the arresting call of the furtive Squirrel Cuckoo bird, as described in *A Guide to the Birds of Panama* by Robert S. Ridgely.

Trst.

1. *n.* a gulf in Italy; a populated place in the Friuli-Venezia Giu region of Italy.

2. *n.* a harbor city in Slovenia.

<*I went to give a lecture in the beautiful ancient harbor city of Trst (as it is known to the many Slovenians who live in it or right across the border).* —Douglas R. Hofstadter, *Le Ton Beau De Marot: In Praise of the Music of Language.*>

ts.

n. an "imperial" shush.

<*"Ts." All is silent. Harry is at his imperial best. He wears a raspberry beret and Peugeot sunglasses, all prepared for his debut at Cannes. "Ts. Ts ts ts, now then, does everybody know what to do?"* —Buzz Callaway, *Specimen Tank.*>

ts-ts.

n. an expression of irritability.

<*He went through the pages irritably, going ts-ts occasionally* —Anthony Burgess, *Earthly Powers.*>

tschschsch.

n. the German sound of leaking gas, as in "Hemmerling Painting 52" by Rolf Hemmerling.

tsk.

1. *interj.* a sound indicating annoyance or impatience.

<*The Houston Chronicle wrote a tsk-tsking editorial deciding the city's top bookkeeper suffered from a "judgment deficit."* —Eric Gerber, *On City Life.*>

2. *n.* the high-pitched alarm sound of excited Chirping Sparrows, as described in *Know Your Bird Sounds, Volume 1: Yard, Garden, and City Birds* by Lang Elliott.

tsktsk.

1. (also tsk-tsk.) *v.* to make disapproving noises.

<*Everyone then began tsk-tsk-tsking at Irwin's plight and marveling at Everett's heroism, tsk-tsk, marvel-marvel, over and over.* —David James Duncan, *The Brothers K.*>

2. *n.* "tsktsk" noises of disapproval.

<*I got eight tsktsks.* —Richard Marcinko, *Task Force Blue.*>

3. *v.* to say "tsk-tsk."

<*You must be prepared for scathing looks, stern "tsktsk"s, and even outright denunciations from passers-by whose mission in life is to mind other people's business.* —Elizabeth Wetzel, *A Is For Aggravation.*>

tsssk.

n. a disapproving hiss.

<*'Tsssk, tsssk,' a chilling voice laughed.* —Katrionah Rosalette, *Fading Echoes*.>

tsssp.

n. the soft call of the rather silent Little Weaver bird, as described in *A Guide to the Birds of Western Africa* by Ron Demey.

tsssssshhhhhhhh.

n. the hiss of a bus' doors closing, as in the poem "dead bus" by James Hörner.

tst.

1. *interj.* a command for a horse to move.

   <*Tst! Yah! Get on with you!* —Charles Dickens, *A Tale of Two Cities*.>

2. *interj.* a warning cry.

   <*"Tst! Joe!" cried the coachman in a warning voice, looking down from his box.* —Charles Dickens, *A Tale of Two Cities*.>

3. *n.* a dismissive utterance.

   <*"Tst! That's just a story, a thousand years old. Only stupid people still think Changmian is a bad-luck place to live."* —Amy Tan, *The Hundred Secret Senses*.>

4. *n.* a hissing sound meaning "be quiet!"

5. *n.* the sound of a head being chopped off.

   <*"Tst! Chopped head off over one hundred year ago. Now look fine, no problem."* —Amy Tan, *The Hundred Secret Senses*.>

6. *n.* the weak call of the Rufous-Winged Tanager bird, as described in *A Guide to the Birds of Columbia* by Steven L. Hilty; the sharp voice of the Red-Flanked Lorikeet in flight, as described in *A Photographic Guide to the Birds of Indonesia* by Morten Strange.

tst tst.

1. *n.* an expression of concern, compassion, or regret.

   <*"Misery! Tst! Tst!" She looked at me. "This too sad."* —Amy Tan, *The Hundred Secret Senses*.>

2. *n.* an expression of surprise or disbelief.

   <*[O]ne almost hears the "tst" "tst" as he observes the quantites of onion sauce consumed by Philip Larkin and his girlfriend, or the poor quality of claret served at one of the numerous literary luncheons he attends.* —Richard Harney, "The Right Set: Anthony Powell Journals 1982-1986.">

Ttt.

n. the name of a character in the novel *The Martian Chronicles* by Ray Bradbury.

<*Do you think it fair of Mr. Ttt to be so ill-mannered?* —Ray Bradbury, *The Martian Chronicles*.>

ttt.

1. *n.* the sound of a dripping water tap, as described in "More Than Words" by the New Zealand Ministry of Education.

2. *n.* the sound of a peculiar exhalation.

<*He shakes his head and exhales with a "ttt" sound, a strange mannerism his father used to have.* —Denise Minor, "Day of the Dead," *The Noe Valley Voice*.>

3. *n.* the sound of the letter t, as described by kindergarten teacher Diane Smith; see also tttt[2].

tttt.

1. *n.* the "rattling sound" of the Plate-billed Mountain-toucan, "likely made by the tongue against the ramphotheca," as described in *Toucans, Barbets and Honeyguides: Ramphastidae, Capitonidae and Indicatoridae* by Lester L. Short; see also dddd[2], kkkk[3].

2. *n.* the sound of the letter t, as described in *The Voice That Means Business: How to Speak With Authority, Confidence and Credibility Anytime, Anywhere* by Linda Shields; see also ttt[3].

<*Where's the* tttt *sound in* ghost? —Peggy Kaye, *Games for Learning: Ten Minutes a Day to Help Your Child Do Well in School, from Kindergarten to Third Grade*.>

ttttt.

n. "a sharp, soft tapping sound," as described in *Tongue Tie—From Confusion to Clarity: A Guide to the Diagnosis and Treatment of Ankyloglossia* by Carmen Fernando.

ttttttttt.

n. the "fast, almost froglike trill" of the Andean Tapaculo bird, as described in *A Guide to the Birds of Columbia* by Steven L. Hilty.

twch.

n. the sound of bodies twitching and writhing, as in the graphic novel *Uzumaki 3* by Junji Ito.

tz-tz-tz-tz-tz-tz.

n. the high-pitched alarm call of the Black-Faced Warbler bird, as described in *A Field Guide to the Birds of China* by John MacKinnon.

tz-tz-tz-tz-zz-zz-zz.

n. the buzzing song of the Lesser Whitethroat bird, as described in *A Field Guide to the Birds of China* by John MacKinnon.

tzgr.
n. in the Tashlhiyt dialect of Berber, this means "she crossed."

Tzng.
n. a Chinese family name.

tzng.
n. the sound of an unfamiliar word, as from a foreign language.

<*For me, the text isn't important in the* Wayfarer*; it's just the music. You know, it's "Tzng, tzng, tzng . . ."; it doesn't mean anything to me. It's childhood memories. I could sing "La, la, la," and it would have the same effect for me.* —Matthias Goerne, quoted by Jason Serinus in "Interview: The Art of Baritone Matthias Goerne," *Secrets of Home Theater & High Fidelity*.>

Tzrg.
n. the name of the warrior goblin chief of the Stonedeep Tribe; see also Glnk.

<*It looked like Glnk was going to stand up to the hobgoblin, which was something Tzrg—the Stonedeep Tribe's legitimate chief—couldn't do.* —T. H. Lain, *The Savage Caves*.>

tzrrr.
n. the grasshopper-like call of the Grass (Sedge) Wren, as described in *A Guide to the Birds of Panama* by Robert S. Ridgely.

tzzt.
n. the sharp, metallic clang of clashing swords, as in *My First Dungeon Experience* by Katherine.

tzzz.
n. the "sharp buzzing" call of the Crested Flycatcher-Shrike, as described in *Shrikes and Bush-Shrikes* by Tony Harris.

tzzzzt.
n. the sound of automobile windshield wipers.

<*Wipers, they go up: TZZZZT, they go down, they go up: TZZZZT, they go down.* —Edward Burkhart, *A Tale of Two Cities*.>

tzzzzzt.
n. the buzzy call of the diminutive Black-Capped Pygmy-Tyrant bird, as described in *A Guide to the Birds of Panama* by Robert S. Ridgely.

tzzzzzzz.
n. the whoosh of an arrow flying through the air, as in the comic "Terinu" by Peta Hewitt.

v kmm thr rffoo nn.

n. a mumbled line of dialogue (presumably meaning "I'm here to rescue you") by the character "Kenny" from the animated television series *South Park* (Matt Graham, "South Park: Angband comes to South Park").

vmmm.

1. *n.* the hum of a submarine's central control system.

   <*Book flicked some switches and suddenly—vmmm—a small collection of green lights burst to life all around Schofield.* —Matthew Reilly, *Scarecrow*.>

2. *n.* the sound of a machine gun's mechanism, as in the comic book *Dirty Pair: Run From The Future #4* by Adam Warren.

vmmmm.

1. *n.* the hum of a superhero's "hover power," as in the comic strip "PvP" by Scott R. Kurtz.

2. *n.* the sound of an automobile accelerating, as in the comic book *Vacuum Horror* by Aaron K.

vppp.

n. the sound of communications signal going out, as in the graphic novel *ShadowFall* by Kaichi Satake.

vrmm.

n. the purr of an accelerating motor.

<*[J]ust see you two on a motorcycle, vrmm, vrmm—can you picture it? You are there: vrmm, vrmm.* —Edmund White, *A Boys Own Story*.>

vrrp.

n. the sound of exploding ammunition.

<*The crackling of the flames and the "vrrp" and "fft" of the exploding ammunition seemed to fill the troops with inordinate glee.* —Johannes Steinhoff, *Messerschmitts Over Sicily: Diary of a Luftwaffe Fighter Commander*.>

vrrrm.

1. *n.* the sound of a machine gun's mechanism, as in the comic book *Dirty Pair: Run From The Future #4* by Adam Warren.

2. *n.* the sound of a physical transformation; the manifestation of a super power, as in the comic book *Gen13 #1* by J. Scott Campbell and Alex Garner.

vrrrrmm.

n. the hum of an automobile engine, as in the graphic novel *Uzumaki 3* by Junji Ito.

vrrrt.

n. the sound of a wig coming off, as in "The One Thousand Swinging Nights (and Another Night on the Side...)" by Sam Inabinet.

vrrrt-vrrrt.

n. the sound of corduroy fabrics rubbing together.

<*Husky thighs in corduroy pants should not go 'vrrrt-vrrrt.'* —Chad A. Nester.>

vrrrttttttt.

n. the sound of automatic weapons fire, as in the graphic novel *ShadowFall* by Kaichi Satake.

vrrt.

1. *n.* the crash of a metal chair being hurled against the partition of an office cubicle, as in "What You've Always Wanted to Say" by Jim Esch.

2. *n.* the sound of a robot's working mechanisms.

<*Vrrt! Vrrt! Hello! I am a robot.* —M. Zole, "Death to the Extremist.">

vshh.

n. the sound of a switchblade flying through the air, as in the comic book *Vacuum Horror* by Aaron K.

vssh.

(also wshh.) *n.* the sound of a vacuum cleaner sucking air, as in the comic book *Vacuum Horror* by Aaron K.

vv.

n. the sound of the letter v, as in the novel *Doona* by Anne McCaffrey; see also vvv, vvvv.

vvrrrr.

n. the swooshing of double-blade swords, as in the graphic novel *The Eternity Axis* by Kelley Cain.

vvrrrrr.

n. the "husky" call of the Eurasian Collared Dove, as described in *A Guide to the Birds of Southeast Asia* by Craig Robson.

Vvv.

n. the name of a character with glowing yellow eyes in the novel *The Martian Chronicles* by Ray Bradbury.

vvv.

n. the sound of the letter v, as described by first grade teacher Meg Smith; see also vv, vvvv.

vvv-vvv.

n. a typical sound made by a baby attempting to talk, as discussed in *Wonder Weeks: How to Turn Your Baby's 8 Great Fussy Phases into Magical Leaps Forward* by Hetty Vanderijt.

vvvv.

n. the sound of the letter v, as described in *The Voice That Means Business: How to Speak With Authority, Confidence and Credibility Anytime, Anywhere* by Linda Shields; see also vv, vvv.

vwhnnnn.

n. the throbbing hum of a ball of energy, as in the graphic novel *Falcon Twin* by Brenden Mecleary.

vwwwhnnnnnn.

n. the whine of an emergency alarm, as in the graphic novel *Falcon Twin* by Brenden Mecleary.

vzt.

1. *n.* the crisp sound of a sharp blade slicing through the air, as in comic books.

2. *n.* the sound of a tranquilizer gun dispatching a werewolf, as in "Alternate Universe Survivors #7" by J. Leigh Nelson.

vzzkt.

n. the sound of an android or robot malfunctioning.

<*I barely have the strength to *vzzkt* stay a-*crackle* alive.* —The Metallic Touch.>

vzzmmm.

n. the hiss and hum of a super-weapon, as in the comic book *World's Finest #3* by Dave Taylor.

vzzzz.

n. the sound of an electric food-mixer.

<*Advertising which attempts to seduce gives no information and tells a story without it being obvious which product is being advertised. Consider a cinema/television advert. While massaging a client, a masseuse asks another lady whether 'it Voooh? - Vzzzz? - Rmmm?'; she illustrates what she means by energetically slapping, clapping and kneading the back of her client. We cannot help wondering what she is talking about. The answer is provided in the last shot showing*

an electric food-mixer which makes the sounds, 'Voooh - Vzzzz- Rmmm'. The film leaves a twenty-second gap which the viewer will perhaps try to fill by an analogy which comes not from the advertiser but from the receiver. —Pierre Sorlin, *The Mass Media.*>

W'T'N.

n. the equivalent of JHVH-1; a true prophet who "shall give succor and sustenance," as taught by Rev. Ivan Stang in *The Book of the SubGenius: Being the Divine Wisdom, Guidance, and Prophecy of J. R. 'Bob' Dobbs, High Epopt of the Church of the SubGenius, Here Inscribed for the Salvation of Future Generations and in the Hope that Slack May Someday Reign on this Earth.*

w-w-w-w-w.

n. the crying of a baby, as described in *Wishes, Lies, and Dreams: Teaching Children to Write Poetry* by Kenneth Koch.

wght.

v. wait, as spoken with a mouth filled with toothpaste, as in *My Monastery is a Minivan: 35 Stories from a Real Life* by Denise Roy.

wh.

1. *n.* a questioning sound, as in *Life, the Universe and Everything* by Douglas Adams.

2. *pron.* what, as in the graphic novel *Uzumaki 2* by Junji Ito.

whd.

pro. what, as spoken with a mouth filled with toothpaste, as in *My Monastery is a Minivan: 35 Stories from a Real Life* by Denise Roy.

whdd.

n. the wet thud of someone's face hitting the ground with twelve Gs of force, as in the comic book *Dirty Pair: Run From The Future #3* by Adam Warren.

whf.

n. the sound of a rolled magazine whooshing toward a mosquito, as in the graphic novel *Uzumaki 2* by Junji Ito.

whff.

n. the sound of an arm swooshing through the air, as in the graphic novel *Uzumaki 3* by Junji Ito.

whhfff.

interj. a moan of protest, as by someone with a traumatized, bloody nose in the novel *The Long Dark Tea-Time of the Soul* by Douglas Adams.

whhhh.

n. the breezy sound of blowing air through one's lips, as in the story "Blowbob" in "More-Fisted TALES of 'BOB.'"

whhhhhhhh—h.

n. the naturally musical sound of leaves rattling (considered to be whispering spirits), as described in *Visions of Sound: Musical Instruments of First Nation Communities in Northeastern America* by Beverley Diamond.

whhhhsssttt.

n. the sound of a burning sulfurous mist/haze, as described in *The Chaos Balance* by L. E. Modesitt Jr.

whhhhsttt.

n. the sound of a white-red fireball flaring across the morning sky, as described in *The Chaos Balance* by L. E. Modesitt Jr.

whhhrrr.

n. an expression indicating that one has a headache after experiencing "matter transference."

<*'Whhhrrr...' said Arthur Dent.* —Douglas Adams, *The Hitchhiker's Guide to the Galaxy.*>

whhp.

1. *n.* the whoosh of a basset hound's wagging tail, as in the comic strip "PvP" by Scott R. Kurtz.

2. *n.* the whoosh of a punched fist, as in the comic book *Legend of the Dark Knight #1* by Gene Ha.

whhp-wwhhp.

n. the sound of "episiotomy snips" during childbirth, as described in *She's Having a Baby and I'm Having a Breakdown* by James D. Barron.

whhppp.

(also whhhppp, whhp.) *interj.* a loud, deep cry.

<*In the lull between gusts, she could hear Aldoff's bellow, as he stood at the base of the hillside. Whhppp! Whhppp! Whhppp!* —L.E. Modesitt Jr., *In Endless Twilight.*>

whhsstt.

(also whhssttt, whhsttt, whsstt, whhhsttt, whsssttt.) *n.* the sound of a rocket flaring overhead.

<*Whhssttt... whhsttt! Two more rockets flared off the hillcrest.* —L. E. Modesitt Jr., *The Order of War.*>

whmmpf.

n. the thud of a thrown pillow, as in the graphic novel *ShadowFall* by Kaichi Satake.

whmp.

n. the thud of a blow to the head, as in the graphic novel *ShadowFall* by Kaichi Satake.

whnngg.

n. the sound of a falling body impacting a balcony railing, as in the graphic novel *ShadowFall* by Kaichi Satake; see also krnch.

whp.

n. the sound of a talking vacuum cleaner's electrical cord flying through the air as it ties up a murderer, in the comic book *Vacuum Horror* by Aaron K.

whrr.

1. *n.* an emphatic spoken by a rat.

<*Gleet gave Alex an appraising look, and nodded. "Whrr, you should fit through all right."* —Eve Forward, *Animist.*>

2. *n.* the howl of a police siren, as discussed in *More Boys' Toys of the Fifties and Sixties* by Thomas W. Holland.

3. *n.* the whirring made by a revolving object or motor.

whrr whrr.

n. what one car says to another, as discussed in *Blood and Guts in High School* by Kathy Acker.

whrr-whrr-whrr.

n. the chirping of a bird

<*Joan had a canary, whose cage sat next to Donnie's favorite chair in the living room. The bird would sing and whistle happily: "Whrr-whrr-whrr, whrr-whrrr."* —Eddie B. Allen, *Low Road: The Life and Legacy of Donald Goines.*>

whrrmbbb.

n. the sound of an emotional embrace, as in the graphic novel *ShadowFall* by Kaichi Satake.

whrrr.

1. (also whhrrr.) *n.* throbbing pain, with such quick pulses that the pain becomes a tangible hum.

<*[H]is unseen hunter refused to let him turn, driving him with the shadowy presence, with the silent whrrr of pain.* —L.E. Modesitt Jr., *The Forever Hero.*>

2. (also whrrrr). *n.* the sound of an automobile engine reluctant to start.

<*There amidst the broken glass, Jesse raised up and immediately tried to restart the Regal. Whrrr... whrrrr... Finally it came to like with a popping protest. The once-regal Buick limped off smoking with nineteen holes drilled into it.* —Danny Rolling, *The Making of a Serial Killer: The Real Story of the Gainesville Student Murders in the Killer's Own Words*.>

3. *n.* a whirring sound.

<*"Whrrr!" whirred the runners.* —Anton Chekhov, "A Joke," *Early Short Stories, 1833-1888*.>

4. *n.* the alarm call of the Black-Faced Laughingthrush, as described in *A Photographic Guide to the Birds of India and the Indian Subcontinent, Including Pakistan, Nepal, Bhutan, Bangladesh, Sri Lanka, and the Maldives* by Bikram Grewal.

5. *n.* the imagined mechanical buzzing of active eardrums.

<*Listen carefully and you can hear the sound of our listening. Whrrr, whrrr.* —Jim Lehrer, *Blue Hearts*.>

6. *n.* the sound of "spinning spears," as described in the novel *Into the Land of the Last* by Tony Abbott.

7. *n.* the sound of a cargo bay door opening, as described in *Big Silver Space Shuttle* by Ken Wilson-Max.

8. *n.* the sound of a flaming arrow, as described in *Into the Fire* by Dennis KcKiernan.

9. *n.* the sound of a grouse fleeing its territory; see also ppptr-rrrrrrr.

<*I turn to walk back to the dog, and* whrrr!, *a grouse tears up through the undercover and is gone.* —Dennis Walrod, *Grouse Hunter's Guide: Solid Facts, Insights, and Observations on How to Hunt the Ruffed Grouse*.>

10. *n.* the sound of a gun turret locking on target, as in the graphic novella *Hearts and Minds* by Scott McCloud.

11. *n.* the sound of an operating photocopy machine.

<*A pressed button, a* whrrr, *the procedure repeated, and into the tray slid two copies.* —Michael Doris, *The Crown of Columbus*.>

12. *n.* the whir of falling debris.

<*In the morning heat fragile ice towers and rotten rocks were breaking loose, filling Big Al Gully with the echoing whrrr and boom of falling debris.* —Stephen Venables, *Everest: Alone at the Summit*.>

13. *n.* the whirring of a broken clothes dryer, as described in *Words and Wisdom of the Appliance Doctor* by Joseph Gagnon.

whrrrr-whrrr.

n. the sound of a helicopter.

<*[W]hrrrr-whrrr makes me dizzy.* —George Crane, *Bones of the Master: A Journey to Secret Mongolia.*>

whrrrrr.

n. the whirring motor of "two huge electric beaters" (Mary-Kate and Ashley Olsen, *In Action #3: Fubble Bubble Trouble*).

whshh.

n. the whoosh of "rent flesh," as by a cook "cutting up a bullock" (Zhuang Zhou, *Zhuangzi*, quoted in *Classical Chinese Literature* by John Minford.

whssh.

n. the whoosh of cards flying through the air, as in the comic book *Dirty Pair: Start the Violence* by Adam Warren.

whst.

n. the sound of a dueling vacuum cleaner's electrical cord flying through the air as it ties up an automobile, in the comic book *Vacuum Horror* by Aaron K.

whzzkt.

(also whzzzkt.) *n.* the sound of a slashing knife, as in the graphic novel *Falcon Twin* by Brenden Mecleary.

wk.

n. the aggressive screech of an Ewok, as described in *The Star Wars Trilogy* novelization by George Lucas.

wrrhl.

n. a noncommittal answer, as spoken with congested sinuses.

<*"I can't* believe *the Japanese are going to start hunting [whales] again." "Wrrhl."* —Christopher Buckley, *Thank You for Smoking.*>

wrrr.

1. *n.* an incoherent mutter by Keith Richards of the band The Rolling Stones, decipherable only by Mick Jagger, as discussed in *Rebel Heart: An American Rock 'n' Roll Journey* by Bebe Buell.

2. *v.* were, as spoken by someone "slurring his words out of pure exhaustion," as in the novel *Doona* by Anne McCaffrey.

wrrr-rrrr-wrrr.

v. to spin.

<*"Last night I cannot sleeping. My mind go wrrr-rrrr-wrrr." He pursed his lips to make a motor noise and twirled a finger in front of his nose like a propeller.* —George Crane, *Bones of the Master: A Journey to Secret Mongolia.*>

wrrrr.

n. the sound of typing on a keyboard.

<**click* *wrrrr* *tnk tnk tnk*. i'm a crazy man at the keyboard. sure a typewriter would make me seem cooler, but i write all my stories in emails, and then send them to myself, at a different email address.* —Paul Jarvis, "Pseudofamous.">

wrtng.

n. writing, written in Roger Bacon's all-consonant secret code (devised in 1250), as discussed in *The Voynich Manuscript* by Gerry Kennedy.

wsst.

n. the sound of a talking vacuum cleaner's electrical cord flying through the air in search of an outlet, as in the comic book *Vacuum Horror* by Aaron K.

wv.

n. the title of a visual poem by Mike Cannell.

Www.

n. the name of a character with glowing yellow eyes in the novel *The Martian Chronicles* by Ray Bradbury.

www.

n. the sound of the letter w.

WWWWW.

n. a marking on a Maui map indicating Haleakala Crater Road (Highway 378), "one of the fastest-ascending roads in the world. This grand corniche has at least 33 switchbacks; passes through numerous climate zones; goes under, in, and out of clouds; takes you past rare silversword plants and endangered Hawaiian geese sailing through the clear, thin air; and offers a view that extends for more than 100 miles" (Jeanette Foster, *Frommer's Maui 2005 with Molokai and Lanai*).

wwwww.

n. an upside-down spelling of *mmmmm.*

<*"Mmmmm" said the Bear. Which, it occurred to him, was essentially Wwwww inverted.* —Rafi Zabor, *The Bear Comes Home.*>

wwwwwft.

n. a German word for the sound of an automobile's broken passenger door window dropping down (Timm Schuch, "Meine Begleiter.")

wzzk.

n. the whoosh of a "widow's bite blast" attack, as in the comic book *Amazing Adventures #8* by Bill Everett.

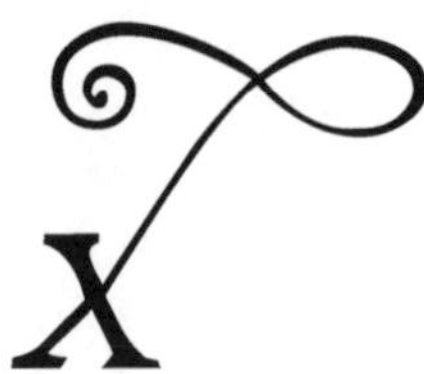

XBXRX.

n. the name of a garage-punk rock band based in Oakland, California.

<*To fill things out, XBXRX have also included a limited assortment of electronic bweeEEows and swwsssshhhs here and there.* —Spencer Owen, Pitchfork Media.>

Xt!.

n. "a language spoken by a race of insectoid aliens. This language has no vowels and all the 'consonants' are click-like sounds" (Adam Walker, "Languages of the Commonwealth").

Xxx.

n. the name of a character in the novel *The Martian Chronicles* by Ray Bradbury.

<*Mr. Xxx peered seriously into his file. He went "Tsk" and shut the file solemnly.* —Ray Bradbury, *The Martian Chronicles*.>

xxx.

adj. of an adult nature; erotic; hardcore (such as a film with graphic sexual content).

<*Of course, it would be much easier to forget He Who Shall Remain Nameless and move on if I stopped having XXX-rated dreams about him.* —Megan McCafferty, *Second Helpings: A Novel*.>

xxxx.

adj. a potent brew of ale.

<*At least it provided the world with some new Australian images that don't involve kangaroos,* Crocodile Dundee, *or lugubrious halfwits drinking Castlemaine XXXX at dusty outback pubs.* —Bill Bryson, *In a Sunburned Country*.>

XXXXX.

1. *n.* a person of unknown identity.

<*Now she knew who XXXXX was.* —William Boyd, *Brazzaville Beach*.>

2. *n.* lots of kisses, as written at the end of a letter; see also XXXXXX.

<*Clarissa takes the flowers into the kitchen, where Sally has left a note ("Lunch w. Oliver—did I forget to tell U?—back by 3 latest, XXXXX").* —Michael Cunningham, *The Hours: A Novel*.>

XXXXXX.

n. lots of kisses, as written at the bottom of a letter, usually alongside OOOOOO (hugs), as discussed in *Brief Encounters* by Emily Coleman; see also XXXXX[2].

xxxxxxxxxx.

n. a soft sound of encouragement used by a trainer to let an animal know that "he is headed for success" (Kayce Cover, "Bridges," SynAlia.com).

xxxxxxxxxxxxxxxxxxxxxxxxxxxxxxxxx.

n. an inaudible statement that sounds similar to "truth and information are not the same thing" but is actually something else.

<*XXXXXXXXXXXXXXXXXXXXXXXXXXXXX! he said.* What? *I yelled over the wind. It was starting to carry him away.* I said, XXXXXXXXXXXXXXXXXXXXXXX XXXXXX! *he yelled back.* Truth and information are not the same thing! *he shouted, and he shot up into the sky instantaneously, shrinking to a tiny black dot that hung briefly in the air and then winked out. I stood staring up at the spot where he had been. That wasn't what he'd been trying to tell me, that truth and information weren't the same thing. He'd been saying something else but I just hadn't been able to get it. XXXXXXXXXXXXXXXXXXXXXXXXX XXXX. I focused my concentration; there was a sizzling sound. It had been pressed into the sand in front of me in green glass symbols: XXXXXXXXXXXXXXXXXXXXXXXXXXXXX. Okay, now I'd retain it and work on a translation later. Probably take me the rest of my life, I thought.* —Pat Cadigan, *Mindplayers*.>

z—nds.

n. a self-censored spelling of the mild oath "zounds," a contraction of "God's wounds."

<*Talking one day of Chinese waggons, which were made so light as to sail over mountains: 'Z—nds,' said Peter, 'where's the wonder of that?'* —Jonathan Swift, *A Tale of a Tub.*>

z-z.

(also z-z-z.) *n.* the sound of a parrot sleeping, as in the comic book *Donald Duck and the Pirates* by Walt Disney.

z-z-z.

n. the buzzing of bees.

<*I knew from past experience that the oxen were afraid of the buzzing sound of bees. So we made the z-z-z sound and the oxen raised their tails somewhat and went faster. We were satisfied with the speed and stopped the buzzing, however the buzzing was resumed, not by us, but by a real bee. The oxen raised their tails very high and went into a gallop. We knew right away that we could get into serious trouble, because there was no way to stop oxen on the run.* —Nahum Meir Halpern, *From Slavery to Freedom.*>

zblrt-tbpttpt.

n. a magic spell to conjure blurred vision (Balanced Alternative Technologies Multi-User Dimension, Bat.org).

zhr-r-r-rrrrrrrrrrr.

n. the "purring or snoring" call of the Yellow-spotted Barbet, as described in *Birds of Kenya and Northern Tanzania* by Dale A. Zimmerman.

zhzh.

n. the rhythmic hum of a hovercraft, as described by K. V. Krishnan in "Are you from Palghat?"

zmmmmmm.

n. the sound of a vortex created by the lashing arms of the hounds of hell, as in the comic book *Divine Right #1* by Jim Lee and Scott Williams.

znrrk.

(also znnrk.) *n.* a snore, as in the comic strip "PvP" by Scott R. Kurtz; see also snnrrk, snnrzzz.

zrp.

n. the sound of an android or robot malfunctioning, as in *The Metallic Touch*; see vzzkt.

zrrr.

n. a savage growl of revenge.

<*Ruthless, lifelong revenge. Zrrr.* —William H. Gass, *Omensetter's Luck: A Novel.*>

ztt ztt.

n. the sound of gas grenades shooting forth, as in the comic book *Amazing Adventures #8* by Bill Everett.

zxtt.

n. the title of a visual poem by Mike Cannell.

ZXZX.

n. the title of an invention by Crispin Jones designed to play the early athletic events simulation video game "Track & Field."

<*ZXZX offers a way of thinking about the cheating devices available to digital games players. It also poses the question—what does it mean to cheat or deceive a computer?* —Mr-Jones.org.>

zz-zz-zz.

n. the buzzing ("possibly begging") call of the Black-headed Batis, as described in *Shrikes and Bush-Shrikes* by Tony Harris.

zzhzzh.

interj. a slurred exclamation, as in *A: A Novel* by Andy Warhol.

zzrrr.

n. the "descending grating" call of the Crested Flycatcher-Shrike, as described in *Shrikes and Bush-Shrikes* by Tony Harris.

zzsssh.

n. the sound of a destructive "nova effect" explosion, caused by defective cyborg robots created to explore the stars (Jack Kirby, *2001: A Space Odyssey #8*).

Zzt.

n. a computer adventure game developed by Epic, using text-mode graphics and spanning over one thousand different worlds.

Zzz.

n. the name of a character with glowing yellow eyes in the novel *The Martian Chronicles* by Ray Bradbury.

zzz.

1. (also Zs.) *n.* the sound of a person snoring; sleep.

<*Cut to shot of old man asleep in chair with head slumped forward on his chest. He has two [semaphore] flags which he waves. Subtitle: 'ZZZ... ZZZ...' —The Complete Monty Python's Flying Circus.*>

2. *n.* a sound heard by fishermen, as when a fish pulls hard on a lure.

<*Take 'zzz,' for example. There are several familiar occasions when fishermen hear this sound. The first is in a fishing camp at night. The sound is coming from the next bunk over and lasts for hours—sometimes right until dawn. Many fishermen are so enamored by this sound that they will stay up long hours just listening to it even though it means being dead tired the next day. On rarer (and more pleasant) occasions, this sound can also be heard from your reel as a huge fish grabs your lure and heads for deeper water, peeling off line as it goes. Just this past May while fishing the Big Horn in Montana I heard this sound several times. Much to the dismay of the friend who was guiding me, however, the 'zzz' sound was usually followed by another sound often described as 'snap.'* —"The Sounds of Fishing," *Addison Independent.*>

3. *n.* a Swahili word for the sound of a flying bee; see also z-z-z.

4. *n.* a typical sound made by a baby attempting to talk, as discussed in *Wonder Weeks: How to Turn Your Baby's 8 Great Fussy Phases into Magical Leaps Forward* by Hetty Vanderijt.

5. *n.* the buzz of a vibrating tattooing needle; see also zzzz[2].

<*The needle vibrated and as it hit McKenzie's flesh, it made a zzz sound. A shock went down McKenzie's spine, a shock that he later said "scared the hell out of me."* —Stacey Longval, "Senior Gets Fifth Tattoo," *Crimson Review.*>

6. *n.* the buzzing of a neon sign.

<*Driving by, it flashed from the corner of our eye—a neon sign, something with a "zzz" sound.* —"Best African Art and Jewelry," *Baltimore City Paper.*>

7. *n.* the high-pitched buzz of a computer networking router (DSLreports.com).

8. *n.* the hiss of audio distortion, as described by Dennis Hartwick in "Me, Myself, My System," *SoundStage! Magazine.*

9. *n.* the howling of a strong wind.

<*According to the next day's news, the winds reached 75 mph on the ground, and we were on a mountain. Around 1 AM there was a ZZZ sound, and the bottom of the door flap was open. Wind swelled up the tent like a box kite.* —Douglas J. Shaw, "Doug and Laurel Go West.">

10. *n.* the scamper of a mouse, described by Zaida Rivera in *Wishes, Lies, and Dreams: Teaching Children to Write Poetry* by Kenneth Koch.

11. *n.* the sound of a force field generator.

<*I haul myself over to the field generator, very glad that it is a standard Starfleet design, uncomplicated and unburdened by various modifications. It hums loudly, generating a rather*

annoying "zzz" sound, but it makes no fuss as I pry open the front and start examining the circuitry inside. —Seema, "Lines in the Sand: The Darkest Hour, part VII.">

12. *n.* the sound of a lens withdrawing into the body of a camera (PBase.com).

13. *n.* the sound of the letters x and z (ReadingKey.com); see also zzzz[3].

14. *n.* the title of a recording by Leif Elggren and Thomas Liljenberg of over an hour of sleeping and snoring sounds.

zzz-zzz-zzz.

n. the buzzing of a mosquito.

<*Styles of Beyond's [album] Megadef begins with a buzz. Not a metaphorical this-shit-is-hot buzz, but the needling, invasive sound of a mosquito tickling your ear. The zzz-zzz-zzz, panned in stereo no less, is first a novelty, then a nuisance, and eventually yanks you to the brink of frenzy. Before the pestering drone carries you over the edge, though, Styles of Beyond unleash the pent-up pressure like a sonic geyser. The experience is unnerving. It's also enthralling.* —Oliver Wang, *LA Weekly.*>

zzzkk.

n. the sound of mechanical warriors suffering electrical malfunctions, as in the comic book *Dirty Pair: Start the Violence* by Adam Warren.

zzzkt.

n. a crackle of electricity, as in the graphic novel *Falcon Twin* by Brenden Mecleary; see also kzzkt.

zzznrk.

n. the snort of someone talking in his sleep, as in the comic strip "PvP" by Scott R. Kurtz.

zzzp.

n. the sound a zipper makes, as in the graphic novel *ShadowFall* by Kaichi Satake; see also zzzz[1].

zzzrt krzkk bzzz pzzzt.

n. "horrid noises" pouring from a re-wired drum machine; "a bizarre series of crackles and static, like an overloaded transformer" (Paul Di Filippo, *Neutrino Drag*).

zzzrt-zzzzrt-zzzrt-zzzrt.

n. the "loud, repetitive" call of the Black-Chested Prinia bird, as described in *Birds of Southern Africa* by Ian Sinclair.

zzzsssh.

n. the hiss of air blasts from jet-boots, as in the comic book *Mister Miracle #17* by Jack Kirby.

zzztt.

n. the crackling of an electronic field, as in the comic book *Electric Fear*.

zzzz.

1. *n.* the sound a zipper makes; see also zzzp.

<*Zzzz, he says the zipper goes.* —William H. Gass, *The Tunnel.*>

2. *n.* the sound of a tattooing gun; see also zzz[5].

<*His boxed head cannot hear the high zzzz's of the biker's tattooing gun.* —Jack Fritscher, *Stand By Your Man.*>

3. *n.* the sound of the letter z, as described in *The Voice That Means Business: How to Speak With Authority, Confidence and Credibility Anytime, Anywhere* by Linda Shields; see also zzz[13].

zzzzp.

v. to move with a sudden hissing sound.

<*Knowledge—Zzzzzp! Money—Zzzzzzp!—Power! That's the cycle democracy is built on!* —Tennessee Williams, *The Glass Menagerie.*>

zzzzzhch.

n. the sound of electrical interference, as in "Evolutions" by Travis Hogbin.

zzzzzz zzzzzz.

n. the "monotonously repeated song, even through the heat of the day, a high insectlike buzz" of the Yellow-Browed Sparrow, as described in *A Guide to the Birds of Columbia* by Steven L. Hilty.

zzzzzzz kkkkkkk szzzzz.

n. the crackle of a lightning bolt.

<*He raised his elbow blades into position and slashed the wire. Zzzzzzz. Kkkkkkk. Zzzzzz. A blue flash! A visible charge of controlled lightning arced from the wires to [him]. He shook and trembled in the grisly grips of electrocution.* —K.A. Applegate, *Animorphs #33: The Illusion.*>

zzzzzzzz/jjjjj.

n. an "enlivening" sound explored in "Continuum" therapy.

<*Ten minutes of exploring with the sound* zzzzzzzz/jjjjj *stimulated a series of sensations that increased the acuity of both my vision and hearing. As a result, I felt more alive. This aliveness altered my sense of self as deeply as did interpretation and insight.* —Don Hanlon Johnson, *The Body in Psychotherapy: Inquiries in Somatic Psychology.*>

All-Vowel Words

a i-eee ai-eeee.

interj. a ritualistic cry in a Black Hawk tribal dance.

<*He looked to Sparrow Hawk like a dandy as his braves all began a dance screaming sharply, "A i-eee Ai-eeee!"* —Meridel Le Sueur, *Sparrow Hawk.*>

a'u.

n. the Hawaiian name for all marlin species of fish.

<*Striped Marlin (A'u) [is] great for poke [that is, served raw, cut in bite-size chunks and marinated the Hawaiian way].* —Sophia Schweitzer, "What's that Fish on my Plate?" (CoffeeTimes.com)>

a-a-a.

n. a hesitation in speaking.

<*"Young man, do you have your ticket?" asked the conductor. "A-a-a, I'm sorry, I ate it by mistake," said the little boy.* —The Southern California Scenic Railway Association, "A Conductor Joke.">

a-a-a-a-a-a-oooooo.

n. the sobbing moan of the lovelorn, as in the ska song "All My Tears (Come Rolling)."

<*A-a-a-a-a-a-oooooo, I love you / All my tears come rolling, all my tears come rolling over you, you, you.* —Alton Ellis, "All My Tears (Come Rolling).">

a-oooo a-oooo.

n. the howling of a wolf.

<*[Don't leave Ely, Minnesota without j]oining a nighttime wolf howl with the International Wolf Center.... Stand at the edge of the forest and let 'er rip: A-oooo, A-oooo. Sometimes, the wolves even answer back.* —Diane Bair and Pamela Wright, "Ely, Minnesota," Away.com.>

a-ooooo a-ooooo.

n. the howling of a dog, as in *The Case of the Haunted Scarecrow* by James Preller.

a-oooooo.

1. *n.* a "long, low howl" emanating from a spooky old house, as in *The Case of the Haunted Scarecrow* by James Preller.

2. *n.* the chilling cry of coyotes breaking the silence of a campout, as in *The Case of the Marshmallow Monster* by James Preller.

Aa.

1. *n.* a "wild and romantic" river in Engelberg, Switzerland (Switzerland Tourism).

2. *n.* a canal in the heart of Denmark.

<*The Aa runs through the southern end of the downtown and winds it way due south toward Midtfyn.* —Tom Galvin, "Odense: A Trip to the Birthplace of Hans Christian Andersen.">

3. *n.* a river in Latvia.

<*The crusaders donned their weapons, put the trappings on their horses, and with their infantry, the Livonians, and their whole company crossed the Aa river, went on through the night, and approached the pagans.* — William L. Urban, *The Baltic Crusade.*>

4. *n.* a river in the Antwerpen region of Belgium.

<*Coastal Flanders covers the area from the North Sea to the Lys river and is bordered by the Aa river to the West.* —"The Traditions of Flanders," Brasserie-St-Sylvestre.com.>

5. *n.* a river in the Brabant region of the Netherlands.

<*The Boundary Aa River (in German Grenz Aa) has been for years a minor source of irritation [between the Netherlands and Germany].* —The Geographer, Office of Research in Economics and Science, Bureau of Intelligence and Research, "International Boundary Study No. 31: Germany-Netherlands Boundary.">

6. *n.* a river in the Nord-Pas-de-Calais region of France.

<*The town of Saint-Omer stands on [a] hillside on the edge of the river Aa marshes.* —"Saint Bertin's Abbey, St. Omer," TheOtherside.co.uk.>

7. *n.* a stream in the Nordrhein-Westfale region of Germany.

<*The bubbling Aa River ran alongside now and then with its waters tumbling crystal clear over pebbles. If Mutti had let me splash in there, that would have made my day.* —Dorothea von Schwanenfluegel Lawson, *Laughter Wasn't Rationed: A Personal Journey Through Germany's World Wars and Postwar Years.*>

8. *n.* a traditional Norwegian fishing village (also spelled Å); a small town in the Nordland and Troms regions of Norway.

<*British policeman Paul Perry plans to ride his bicycle from "A" to "B," he said Tuesday, adding that this jaunt will carry him from Norway to Nebraska. Perry's journey, expected to kick off Friday, would take him from the fishing village of Aa, some 1,500 kilometres north of the capital, Oslo. From Aa, he plans to ride 10,000 kilometres through Norway, Sweden, Denmark, Germany, the Netherlands, Belgium and to France, before taking a ferry to Britain and riding across the country to take a ship to New York. He'll then cycle north into Canada, making his way to Ottawa before pedalling to Toronto and then to Windsor before dipping back into the United States at Detroit. If he's successful, Perry said he'll end his trip in Bee, Nebraska.* —Associated Press, "Cop to Bike From 'Aa to Bee'.">

9. *n.* a variety of orchid.

<*[T]he incredible tiny altiplano bog orchid* Aa nervosa *was in full bloom in April this year [in Atacama, Chile].* —Alto Andino Nature Tours, BirdingAltoAndino.com.>

10. *n.* a village in Estonia.

<*A total of 15 Iraqi refugees who are awaiting adjudication of their status remain in a holding center in the town of Aa, near the city of Kohtla Jarve in northeastern Estonia.* —Bureau of Democracy, Human Rights, and Labor, U.S. Department of State, "Human Rights Practices for 1998 Report.">

11. *n.* an intermittent stream in Ethiopia.

12. *n.* an island in the Vava'u region of Tonga.

aa.

n. volcanic lava with a rough surface.

<*I was afire, dry afire, all the inside of me like a burnt cinder, like aa lava, like the harpooner's tongue dry and gritty with sand.* —Jack London, *Island Tales.*>

aa-ooo-aa-ooo-aaaa-ooooo.

n. a coyote's baying at the moon; a primitive howl in honor of the dead.

<*[T]he upturned faces near the stage, awash with the splashover of swirling colors from the light show, seem to glow with enthusiasm and delight, and each time the band takes up a different song there arises from out there in the dark a wild chorus of the hall, whooping and howling and yipping like coyotes baying at the moon, aa-ooo-aa-ooo-aaaa-ooooo, a savage, animal, tribal thing one knows instinctively they do only for the dead, in honor of the dead.* —Ed McClanahan, *My Vita, If You Will: The Uncollected Ed McClanahan.*>

AAA.

n. the ringing of an alarm clock.

<*AAA! AAA! AAA! AAA! AAA! My alarm clock screamed at me to get up.* —Bobby Bradley, "The Young Writer's Club: StoryBook No. 1203.">

Aaa.

1. *n.* a shorthand notation used by musician Gustav Mahler in his manuscripts "to identify [thematic] elements that he would repeat or rework later in the compositional process" (James L. Zychowicz, *Mahler's Fourth Symphony*).

2. *n.* the name of a character in the novel *The Martian Chronicles* by Ray Bradbury.

<*Half an hour later, Mr. Aaa, seated in his library sipping a bit of electric fire from a metal cup, heard the voices outside in the stone causeway.* —Ray Bradbury, *The Martian Chronicles.*>

aaa.

1. *interj.* a cry of pain; see also aaaa[8], aiee[1], aiieee[2].

<*"Aaa!" Gabrielle winced in pain and grabbed her arm, as blood squeezed out between her fingers.* —Tim Wellman, "Killing Time.">

2. *interj.* a mumble of "vowels without consonants" (John Altman, *The Watchmen*).

3. *n.* the sound of the letter a, "like a screaming person" described in the Ponca City Public Schools curriculum; see also aaaa[12].

aaa-eee.

n. a baby's first mutterings, as discussed in *Let the Baby Drive: Navigating the Road of New Motherhood* by Lu Hanessian.

aaa-eeeee.

n. a scream of intense pain.

<"*Aaa-eeeee!" The scream was terrible. "You're killing me! You're pulling me apart!"* —James Jones, *The Thin Red Line.*>

aaa-ooooo.

n. the signature howl of radio DJ Wolfman Jack.

<*I wantcha ta reach over the radio, darlin', right now, and grab my knobs. Aaa-ooooo!* —Wolfman Jack, *Have Mercy*, qtd. by Ben Fong-Torres, *The Hits Just Keep on Coming: The History of Top 40 Radio.*>

aaaa.

1. *interj.* a cry of disbelief.

<*"Aaaa! You're taller than me! My granddaughter is taller than me!" She looks up at me, her forehead grazing my chin.* —Laura Moriarty, *The Center of Everything: A Novel.*>

2. *interj.* a cry of panic.

<"*Aaaa!" BeeBee shrieked. "My arms are gone."* —Gail Carson Levine, *The Wish.*>

3. *interj.* a dying cry when it is "too late for words, whether sane or no," as when a madman is buried beneath "a landslide he had unwittingly begun" (Bill Everett, *Amazing Adventures #8*).

4. *interj.* a mortal cry, as when one is impaled by an arrow in the comic book *Savage Sword of Conan #18* by John Buscema.

5. *interj.* an expression of discomfort or fear.

<*Something rustled near Christopher's feet. Aaaa! A rat as big as a cat scampered across his boot.* —Gail Carson Levine, *The Princess Tales, Volume 1.*>

6. *interj.* an expression of frustration.

<*"Aaaa!" I shook the dirt out of my hair, flapped it out of my ears.* —Richard Bach, *Illusions.*>

7. *interj.* an expression of satisfaction.

<*He reached over for the [liquor] bottle, unscrewed the cap, took the longest pull he could stand.* Aaaa, goddamn. Won't take long like that. —Kaye Gibbons, *A Virtuous Woman.*>

8. *interj.* an extended cry of pain; see also aaa[1], aiee[1], aiieee[2].

<*I took out the ice-pick from the raincoat, gripped it in my hand and, with my eyes closed, dealt him a terrible blow on the head. Trotsky gave a cry that I shall never forget. It was a long 'aaaa,' endlessly long, and I think it still echoes in my brain.* —Dmitri Volkogonov, *Trotsky: The Eternal Revolutionary.*>

9. *interj.* the sound of a realization; a-ha!

<*Aaaa, knew you was scared.* —Henry Roth, *Call It Sleep: A Novel.*>

10. *n.* a baby's babble. Babies between eight and twelve months "tend to chain their vowel sounds: aaaa, aa, aaaa" (Tara Losquadro Liddle, *Why Motor Skills Matter: Improving Your Child's Physical Development to Enhance Learning and Self-Esteem).*

<*"You're forty minutes old," the father says, "and crying already?" "Aaaa," says the baby.* —Annie Dillard, *For the Time Being.*>

<*[E]verybody's first words in this world are, "Please save me! Aaaa, please save me!"* —Seung Sahn, *The Compass of Zen.*>

11. *n.* the sound of French words shouted by thousands of troops, as in *War and Peace* by Leo Tolstoy.

12. *n.* the sound of someone singing the letter *a*; see also aaa[3].

<*Behind her she hears a woman beginning to sing classical vocals, a single vowel,* aaaa, *raised and lowered, broken into syllables, pulled out in a single, shivering note.* —Chitra Divakaruni, *Queen of Dreams: A Novel.*>

aaaa-ya.

interj. a sound of disgust.

<*Aaaa-ya! How can you use such sickening language?* —David Henry Hwang, *M. Butterfly.*>

AAAAA.

interj. the desolate cry of uniform buildings which are constructed side by side in a monotonous fashion, out of harmony with their surroundings.

<*If buildings are the letters of the alphabet they are not used to make coherent words but to utter the desolate cries of AAAAA! Or OOOOOO!* —Gordon Cullen, qtd. in *Architectures: Modernish and After* by Andrew Ballantyne.>

aaaaa.

1. *n.* a sound of pain, as in the comic book "DV8 #4" by Humberto Ramos and Sal Regla, and as in the graphic novel *Uzumaki 2* by Junji Ito.

2. *n.* the sound of a baby crying, as described in the novel *Edwin Mullhouse* by Steven Millhauser.

aaaaaaa.

n. a mocking imitation, likening someone's speech to the buzz of an annoying insect.

<*He makes the noises "Rrrrrrr" and "Aaaaaaa" to imitate Glennon, as if he'd heard his words as nothing more than the buzzing of an overwrought insect inviting a swatting.* —Philip Gourevitch, *A Cold Case.*>

aaaaaaaoooooooo.

n. the "long-drawn-out howl" of someone both drunk and homesick, as in *Psalm at Journey's End: A Novel* by Erik Fosnes Hansen; see also aooooooo.

aaaaaeeeee.

n. the sound of a six-month-old baby singing, as described in the novel *Edwin Mullhouse* by Steven Millhauser.

aaaaoooooooooo.

interj. a cry of sweet victory, as in *The Sandman: Preludes and Nocturnes* by Neil Gaiman.

aaiee.

interj. a cry of sheer terror, as when one is chased by the living dead in the graphic novel *Uzumaki 2* by Junji Ito.

aaiiii-eeee.

interj. a shriek of surprise; see also aiieee[4].

<*"Aaiiii-eeee!" She didn't even bother to muffle her voice this time.* —Shari Macdonald, *A Match Made in Heaven.*>

Aauaua.

n. a river in Brazil, as discussed in "A Collection of Word Oddities and Trivia" by Jeff Miller.

Ae.

n. an island in the Marshall Islands.

ae.

n. one (Scottish), as in the traditional Scottish folk song "Ae fond Kiss."

Aea.

n. a capital in the Tarabulus region of Libya.

<*[Some minstrels say that the Argonauts'] visit to Libya took place before the voyage to Aea began, when Jason went in the Argo to consult the Delphic Oracle and was driven off his course by a sudden storm.* —Robert Graves, *The Greek Myths, Volume 2.*>

Aeaea.

(also Aiaie.) *n.* the legendary Tyrrhenian Sea home of Circe.

<*Never would they have landed if they had known what lay before them. They had come to Aeaea, the realm of Circe, a most beautiful and most dangerous witch. Every man who approached her she turned into a beast.* —Edith Hamilton, *Mythology: Timeless Takes of Gods and Heroes*.>

Aeai.

n. a stream in the Solomon Islands.

aeai.

n. a rogue artificial intelligence program, tens of thousands of times more intelligent than a human, in the novel *River of Gods* by Ian McDonald.

aeee aeee.

interj. an emphatic yes.

<*Petey broke into a huge smile and nodded his head. "Aeee, aeee," he squealed.* —Ben Mikaelsen, *Petey*.>

aeei.

interj. a scream of pain, as from a burn.

<*"Aeei!" One brief scream is the only sound that may leave Lorn's quarters. He takes a deep breath, and moves to the two bodies, each sprawled with most of its skull burned away.* —L. E. Modesitt, *Scion of Cyador*.>

aeioi.

adj. containing the vowels *a*, *e*, *i*, *o*, and *u*, such as the word "sequoia" (Razilcc Mary Purdue, AndréJoyce Fan Club).

Ai.

1. *n.* a Banda island of eastern Indonesia, famous for growing spices.

<*On Ai Island, one of the 6 Banda Islands where we spent a majority of our time, there was no electricity, no cars, no motorcycles, no restaurants, no western signs, including Coca-Cola signs... it was great!! But there also weren't any feminine products or sunscreen, which we badly needed. Sunscreen was the main reason why we wouldn't have been able to stay on that beautiful island one day longer even if our visas weren't about to expire!* —Sonya Stewart, "Prosperity Burger.">

2. *n.* a former fortified royal city of the Canaanites, now a ruin in West Bank.

<*Wail, O Heshbon, for Ai is laid waste!* —Jeremiah 49:3, *Old Testament* (NRSV).>

3. *n.* a populated place in Nigeria.

4. *n.* a populated place in Russia; a river in the South Ural mountains of Russia, the subject of artist David Burlyuk's 1917 painting "Ai River."

5. *n.* a populated place in the Chiang Mai region of Thailand.

6. *n.* a populated place in the P'yongan-namdo region of North Korea.

7. *n.* a populated place in the Shimane region of Japan.

8. *n.* a populated place in the Solomon Islands.

9. *n.* a scenic river (literally "Love River" in Chinese) flowing through the heart of Kaohsiung City in southern Taiwan and location of the romantic Kaohsiung Lantern Festival.

<*A sudden rise in temperature yesterday in Kaohsiung City could be responsible for the deaths of 20,000 tonnes of fish in the Ai River.* —Chiu Yu-Tzu, "Tonnes of Fish Die on Ai River," *Taipei Times*.>

10. *n.* a stream in the Efate region of Vanuatu (formerly New Hebrides).

11. *n.* a village and island in Indonesia, with high cliffs popular for diving and reefs featuring "great quantities of soft coral in red, beige, purple, and orange hues" (SongLine Cruises of Indonesia).

12. *n.* an island in the Marshall Islands.

ai.

1. *interj.* a grunt of sexual frustration.

<*'Ai!' Thierknut grunted, and sat upon the edge of his cot trembling with man-heat.* —Stan McDaniel, *The Letterseeker*.>

2. *n.* a small salmon-like fish of Japan, indigo blue in color.

<*There is one type of sumi [ink] … that is referred to as ai-zumi because it has a bluish quality to it.* —Bob Brudd, "The Language of Koi," *Water Gardening Magazine*.>

3. *n.* a species of South America sloth.

<*While the Unau sloth has two toes on the front feet, the Ai sloth has three.* —Geetika Anand, "Inverted Life.">

Ai Ai.

(also AIAI.) *n.* a woeful cry; "alas! alas!"; in Greek mythology, Apollo's inscription of sorrow on the hyacinth flower that sprang from the blood of the dying prince Hyacinthus.

<*A grief-stricken Apollo raised a purple flower from [Hyacinthus'] blood, on which the letters Ai, Ai were traced. This was so that his cry of woe would have existence on earth forever. As our native variety of hyacinth had no trace of these mystic letters, our earlier botanists called it* Hyacinthus nonscriptus, *or "not written on."* —WorkingForWildlife.org.>

ai ai ai.

interj. a howling sound.

<*Ai! Ai! Ai!* There's *a Homeric yawp; but what's the use of howling? who will hear and what will change?* —William H. Gass, *The Tunnel.*>

ai ai aiaiaiai aiai.

n. a joyous cry of the Yanomama Indian shaman of South America.

<*[H]is voice sounded clear, vibrant with joy, as he shouted, "Ai ai aiaiaiai, aiai!"* —Florinda Donner, *Shabono: A Visit to a Remote and Magical World in the South American Rain Forest.*>

Ai Aoua.

n. a spring in the Al Biqa region of Lebanon.

ai eee.

n. a yelp which begins a chant of the Pulap people of Oceania. This "beautiful chant is a greeting of respect to Sagur, the legendary chief of Pulap," who "resides in bamboo floating at sea" (Stephen D. Thomas, *The Last Navigator*).

ai-eee.

interj. a cry of happiness.

<"*Ai-eee!" she cried. "I am happy. Thank you."* —Anna L. Waldo, *Sacajawea.*>

ai-yaaa.

interj. a cry of impatience at oneself.

<*Ai-yaaa! I'm so clumsy! So awkward and stupid.* —Gus Lee, *Chasing Hepburn: A Memoir of Shanghai, Hollywood, and a Chinese Family's Fight for Freedom.*>

ai-yai-ai.

n. the Russian expression for "tsk-tsk," as discussed in *Hear! Here!* by Michele Slung.

ai-yeee ai-yeee.

n. the squeal of a piglet, as in *The Best of Girls to the Rescue* by Bruce Lansky.

Aia.

1. *n.* a Babylonian goddess, spouse of Utu/Shamash, as discussed in *Divine Encounters: A Guide to Visions, Angels, and Other Emissaries* by Zecharia Sitchin.

2. *n.* a pass in Ethiopia; a village in Ethiopia.

3. *n.* the mythical "end of the earth," home of the legendary Golden Fleece in the *Argonautica.*

   <*Aeetes was originally lord of Aia, a mythical land on the Ocean stream at the eastern edge of the world.* —Donald J. Mastronarde, *Euripides: Medea.*>

4. *n.* the mythological setting of Cecilia Dart-Thornton's Bitterbynde series of epic fantasy novels.

<*Nothing lay beyond the Ringstorm—it was a barrier around the rim of Aia to stop ships from falling over the edge into nothingness.* —Cecilia Dart-Thornton, *The Ill-Made Mute.*>

aia.

1. *adv.* the Hawaiian word for "there."

2. *n.* an Indian or South African nursemaid or governess; see Aiya[1].

Aiai.

1. *n.* a populated place in the Maputo region of Mozambique.

2. *n.* son of the fishing god Ku'ula, as discussed in *Hawaii: The Big Island Trailblazer: Where to Hike, Snorkel, Surf, Bike, & Drive* by Jerry Sprout.

Aiaie.

1. (also Aeaea.) *n.* a mythological island discussed in *The Odyssey* by Homer.

   <*Apollonios gives the name of Aiaie to the residence of Circe in order to distinguish it from the original Aia.* —Metrum.org, "The Voyage of the Argo.">

2. *n.* a populated place in Ethiopia.

Aiao.

n. a populated place in the Porto region of Portugal.

Aie.

1. *n.* a populated place in Italy.

2. *n.* a stream in Indonesia.

3. *n.* an abandoned populated place in the Shan State region of Myanmar (formerly Burma).

aie.

(also aiee.) *interj.* an expression of grief or despair.

<*Aiee, I'm late to meet some people for dinner.* —David Moore.>

Aiea.

n. a city in Hawaii.

<*On the road to Aiea it showered twice, and twice the rain clouds came streaming across the volcanic Koolau Mountains.* —Harry Mazer, *A Boy at War: A Novel of Pearl Harbor.*>

aiee.

1. *interj.* a cry of pain; see also aaa[1], aaaa[8], aiieee[2].

<*She fell on the steps and began to moan "Aiee! Aieee!" Even these cries of pain seemed florid.* —John Cheever, *The Stories of John Cheever.*>

2. *interj.* a cry of panic.

<*It's swimsuit season. Aiee!* —Jennifer Crawford, "A Cat by Any Other Name," Jenipurr.com.>

3. *interj.* a cry of self-frustration.

<*Aiee! I am an idiot!* —Layla Lawlor, TalkAboutComics.com.>

4. *interj.* a squeal of excitement.

<*You gonna love it like a pig loves corn! Aiee!* —Joseph R. Thompson, *University of Southern Maine Free Press*, reporting on a Cajun food festival.>

aieee.

1. *interj.* a call for help; see also aiieee[1].

<*But the police stopped because they could hear my frozen feet screaming.* Aieee! Help me! *They could hear this. "You hear screaming?" They looked over and saw this snow girl shaking like a washing machine gone* berserk. *And my feet were screaming.* Aieee!. —Francisco Goldman, *The Long Night of White Chickens.*>

2. *interj.* a cry of feigned fear.

<*"Aieee!" he cried in mock terror and tried to run.* —Bernard Doove and Boyce Garald Kline Jr., "The Admiral and the Chakat 5.">

3. *interj.* a ghastly, unrestrained howling.

<*Then suddenly the Sabbath decorum was shattered. A wailing arose in a corner of the room. "Aieee! Get away from me!" It was a ghastly howling, altogether unrestrained.* —Walter Wangerin Jr., *The Book of God.*>

4. *interj.* a joyous cry.

<*[S]he reached to cup the head of the infant so that she might guide its passage into the world. "Aieee, yes! It is very good!" she exclaimed again as the baby surged out of the mother on a hot tide of blood and fluid.* —William Sarabande, *The Sacred Stones: A Novel of the First Americans.*>

5. *interj.* a rebel yell.

<*Loud rebel yells pierced the air as Woody and Sonny urged them on, celebrating each swallow with a high-pitched "Aieee! Aieee! Aieee!"* —Carl Franz, *The People's Guide to Mexico.*>

6. *interj.* a scream meant to frighten.

<*Morning Star screamed, "Aieee!" The deer didn't pause to look, merely bolted into the trees and vanished, smoke on the wind.* —Bob Arter, "Apache Shorts," *Gator Springs Gazette.*>

7. *interj.* a scream of hysterics, as in "Another Genie's Life" by Eddie Glover.

8. *interj.* a shout of pain and anguish.

<*Which god's bloodlust made this happen? / Mothers screaming / Young girls screaming / Families mourning / Aieee! Yelling! / Aieee! Shouting! / As house after house / Joined the shrill chorus, / And handed on the torch of pain.* —Euripides, *Phoenician Women*, translated by Andrew Wilson.>

9. *interj.* a warning of attack, as in karate.

<*Aieee! Slam! Smash!* —Carol M. Shifflett, "'Real' Aikido.">

10. *interj.* an expression of yearning.

<*When the geese returned they would continue their journey. My heart leaped when I heard this. They might travel to the land of the Shoshoni! Aieee! If only I could journey with them.* —Peter Roop, *Sacagawea: Girl of the Shining Mountains.*>

11. *interj.* boo!

<*"Aieee!" said the first ghost, jumping out from behind a tree.* —Gloria Dominic, *Brave Bear and the Ghosts: A Sioux Legend.*>

12. *n.* a microcosm of the world of poetry.

<*Craft was just a dry Englishman, brought up on the flat breast of Political Economics, incapable of understanding the world of poetry that an* aieee *could contain!* —Eca De Queiros, *The Maias.*>

13. *n.* an expression of frustration.

<*Aieee, all this bureaucratic garbage!* —Paul Preuss, *Arthur C. Clarke's Venus Prime 5.*>

14. *n.* an involuntary mutter signifying a sudden realization or remembrance.

<*He watched her walk away, and suddenly remembered the woman under the street lamp, the last time he'd come to the bar. "Aieee," said Jules softly, not realizing he'd spoken.* —Jamie Harrison, *The Edge of the Crazies.*>

15. *n.* the last gasp of a dying person; see also eeee.

<*He held the smoking pistol still aimed at Tenorio, but a second shot was not needed. Tenorio's face twisted with the pain of death. "Aieee..." He moaned and tumbled into the dust.* —Rudolfo Anaya, *Bless Me, Ultima.*>

AIEEEE.

(also AIEEEEEEEEEEEE.) *n.* the orchestral wail of "the horror of the moment," as upon a terrible realization.

<*She reached the back of the church and saw the pile of bulletins. She wondered if her name was printed inside. She excitedly grabbed a handful and opened one up to take a peek. AIEEEE. A thousand violins shrieked chords of horror in the crisp air. The cellos played a pedal-point of doom and a lonely bassoon tootled its mournful wail in the distance. AIEEEEEEEEEEEE. Louder and louder the noise grew, as the horror of the moment made itself painfully aware. A paper cut. An enormous, king-sized (3 kings-sized) paper cut right across her fingertip. And not*

just any finger. Her right index finger. The most important organ-playing finger of them all. —Green Tuna, "The Tale of the Bloody Keys," GreenTuna.Blogspot.com.>

aieeee.

1. *interj.* a cry of excitement, as in the story "Déjà Blue" by Shawn Raventhorn.

2. *interj.* a cry of pain.

   <*The knight's body convulsed.* "Aieeee!" —Christopher Stasheff, *The Oathbound Wizard.*>

3. *interj.* a cry of shock, as by feeling something ice-cold, in the story "Orange" by Joseph Palmer.

4. *interj.* a sound standing for all the words that can't be said at once.

   <*Eddie jumped into Hank's arm, flung himself against Hank's chest, chattering madly, and feeling that he had a long and desperate story to tell. "Aieeee!" Eddie was even inventing new words.* —Patricia Highsmith, *The Selected Stories of Patricia Highsmith.*>

5. *interj.* a yell of frustration, as in "Tail of the Fox" by Bruce Cox.

6. *interj.* an expression of amazement.

   <*I remember once saying to a man I was infatuated with, who wanted to have a huge family, that I would love to have ten children with him! Aieeee! What love—or lust—can make us say!* —Pepper Schwartz, *Everything You Know About Love and Sex is Wrong: Twenty-Five Relationship Myths Redefined to Achieve Happiness and Fulfillment in Your Intimate Life.*>

7. *interj.* the sound of the exertion of intense willpower.

   <*Aieeee! I physically restrained him from taking another step.* —Melissa de la Cruz, *Cat's Meow: A Novel.*>

8. *n.* the squeal of a brown bat, as described by Francisco Azinsan in "Stopping to Ask for Directions."

aieeeee.

1. (also aieee.) *n.* a wail of despair, as upon hearing news of a loved one's death.

   <*She is not prepared for Verlie's reaction. A wail—"Aieeeee"—that goes on and on, from Verlie's wide mouth, and her wide, wild eyes. "Aieee—"* —Alice Adams, *The Stories of Alice Adams.*>

   <*"Aieeeee," wailed Dwarf, eyes wide at once with despair and hopelessness.* —Niel Hancock, *Faragon Fairingay: The Circle of Light, Book 2.*>

2. (also aieeee.) *interj.* a cry for help.

   <*"Aieeeee, aieeee, aieeee!" cried the wolf. "Help me, oh help me!" he cried, "and I shall reward you justly." For this is the way of wolves in tales of this kind.* —C.P. Estes, "The Wolf's Eyelash.">

3. *interj.* a cry of frustration, as when at the end of one's wits.

<*Marauding deer nibbling your roses, chomping your baby tomatoes, stomping your feeble attempts at deer fencing, aieeeee!* —Jacqueline Girdner, "A Glimpse into the Mysteries of the Next Millennium.">

4. *interj.* a cry of nervous excitement, as on the night of one's first musical gig (Rob O'Connell).

5. *interj.* a warning call, as in *Keep the River on Your Right* by Tobias Schneelbaum.

6. *interj.* a whimper of pain.

<*"Aieeeee," she whimpers as the [sea's] salt water meets the gunshot wound and the split across her nose.* —Matt Lawrence, *Dying to Get Here: A Story of Coming to America.*>

7. *interj.* an attacker's yell.

<*[Spelling Bee] Moderator: Aieeee. / Boy: Could you use it in a sentence, please? / Moderator: "The native screamed 'Aieeeee' as he lunged with his knife." / Boy: Aieeeee! A-I-E-E-E-E-E-E. Aieeee! / (buzzer sounds) / (back to Dennis in the studio) / Dennis Miller: Come on, the kid choked. It's "I" before "E," and there's five E's in "Aieeeee."* —Saturday Night Live, "Weekend Update With Dennis Miller," transcribed by SNLtranscripts.jt.org.>

8. *interj.* an enraged groan.

<*"Aieeeee!" Tenorio groaned with rage and hate, but there was nothing he dared to do.* —Rudolfo Anaya, *Bless Me, Ultima.*>

Aii.

n. a well in Djibouti.

aii-eee.

interj. a shout of approval, as described in *From Sea to Shining Sea* by James Alexander Thom.

aiieee.

1. *interj.* a call for help; see also aieee[1].

<*"Aiieee!" cried my host. "Aiieee! Aiieee!" I cocked my head to listen to the echoes. "Aiieee!"* —Ian Watson, *Yaleen.*>

2. *interj.* a cry of pain; see also aaa[1], aaaa[8], aiee[1].

<*As he goes out into the hall, a hand reached up and grabs his ear. He lets out a sharp "Aiieee" as the door closes behind him.* —John Berendt, *Midnight in the Garden of Good and Evil.*>

3. *interj.* a cry of panic, as at the sight of blood; see also aiiii-eeee.

<*Serafina points at the wrist and cries out: "Aiieee!"* —Tennessee Williams, *The Rose Tattoo.*>

4. *interj.* a shriek of surprise; see also aaiiii-eeee.

<*"I'll take my chances with the dogs!" Sunbright screamed. "What dogs?" Candlemas asked, then, "Aiieee!"* —Clayton Emery, *Dangerous Games.*>

aiii.

interj. a shriek of pain.

<*There was a flare of flame. "Aiii! I burn!" the thing cried.* —Piers Anthony, *Wielding a Red Sword.*>

aiiii-eeee.

interj. a cry of panic, as at the sight of blood; see also aiieee[3].

<*She cut her wrist, my daughter, she cut her wrist! Aiiii-eeee!* —Tennessee Williams, *The Rose Tattoo.*>

aiiiiiii-eeeee.

interj. an ecstatic cry of victory.

<*"Aiiiiiii-eeeee!" he cried like a fiend when he found the object of his search.* —Rudolfo Anaya, *Bless Me, Ultima.*>

Aio.

1. *n.* a populated place in Ethiopia.

2. *n.* an abandoned populated place in the Solomon Islands.

Aioi.

1. *n.* a t-shaped bridge in Hiroshima, Japan. The word "describes two trunks growing from the same root" (Jiro Takei, *Sakuteiki: Visions of the Japanese Garden*).

<*And there was Aioi Bridge. It slid right under the crosshairs, a tiny T right in a gap of clouds.* —Kim Stanley Robinson, "The Lucky Strike," *The Best Alternate History Stories of the 20th Century.*>

2. *n.* a village in the Hokkaido and Hyogo regions of Japan.

<*If you followed the bank [of the Nozeri brook] for about three-quarters of a mile downstream, you came to the village of Aioi. There is a statue of Kannon, the goddess of mercy, in this village.* —Natsume Soseki, *Botchan.*>

Aioio.

n. an island in French Polynesia.

Aioua.

n. a populated place in the Shepherd region of Vanuatu (formerly New Hebrides).

Aiouea.

n. a genus of plants of the laurel family. Botanist Susanne Renner identified nineteen neotropical species of Aiouea for the book *Lauraceae, Part I (Aniba and Aiouea)*.

Aiu.

n. a plain in Ethiopia.

Aiua.

1. *n.* a populated place in the Ceara region of Brazil.

2. *n.* a populated place in the Sandaun region of Papua New Guinea.

aiua.

1. *n.* a pre-existent soul; the thread-like spirit-essence binding all life in the universe, as discussed in *Ender's Game* and related novels by Orson Scott Card.

   <*I continue to exist because the aiua whose irresistible will called me into existence continues to imagine me. Continues to need me, to control me, to be my will.* —Orson Scott Card, *Children of the Mind.*>

2. *n.* a word from "some imaginary language ... of circus people familiar with all manner of swindling," encouraging the wheel of fortune to turn, as in *The Sand Child* by Tahar Ben Jelloun.

Aiy.

n. a populated place in the Al Karak region of Jordan.

aiy—eeee.

n. a soft, pitiful cry, "like a long sigh from the deepest darkest nightmare," as described in the story "At Fortune's Way" by Li Yongping.

Aiya.

1. (also aia.) *n.* an Indian governess.

   <*When I was a young boy, our family lived in India and I heard from our Aiya (a mother's helper" who become like an aunt) many stories like these.* —Michael Gurian, *The Wonder of Girls: Understanding the Hidden Nature of Our Daughters.*>

2. *n.* a Crimean cape, home to "a large-scale botanic reserve" of evergreen trees (Crimea Ministry of Tourism).

3. *n.* a stream in Nigeria.

aiya.

1. *interj.* a Chinese chiding expression.

   <*I sensed the ghost of my grandmother in the room. "Aiya! What a stupid girl," I could hear her saying. "This is what happens when you let them become Americans." I imagined other wispy-edged relatives, more frowning and head shaking.* —Amy Tan, "Family Ghosts Hoard

Secrets that Bewitch the Living," *Writers on Writing, Volume II: More Collected Essays from The New York Times.*>

2. *interj.* a Chinese exclamation meaning "Aha!" as discussed in *The Eternal Storyteller: Oral Literature in Modern China* by Vibeke Børdahl.

3. *interj.* a Chinese exclamation meaning "drat!"

   <*"Aiya!" said Farmer Wang in the front seat, slapping his forehead. "We didn't bring our* shen fen zheng*!"My heart sank. It was too late to turn back to fetch their government-issued identification cards.* —Jan Wong, *Red China Blues: My Long March From Mao to Now.*>

4. *interj.* a Chinese exclamation of joy.

   <*Aiya! You got five out of six in Lotto!* —San Diego Chinese Women's Association.>

5. *interj.* a Chinese exclamation of profound astonishment.

   <*Aiya! She switch majors from Business to Art History!* —San Diego Chinese Women's Association.>

6. *interj.* a Chinese exclamation of surprise.

   <*"Aiya!" [Yu Zuomin] is said to have exclaimed. "It's over! It's over! I never thought it would happen so quickly!"* —Bruce Gilley, *Modern Rebels: The Rise and Fall of China's Richest Village.*>

7. *interj.* a Chinese expression meaning "are you kidding?" or "don't be silly."

   <*Pei swallowed, tears pushing against her eyes. "You don't have to stay here anymore, you could return to Hong Kong with me. …" Moi laughed. "Aiya, what would I do there? My home is here. It always has been."* —Gail Tsukiyama, *The Language of Threads: A Novel.*>

8. *interj.* a Chinese expression of awe.

   <*"Aiya!" Golden Dog exclaimed, "there really are two suns in the world!"* —Pingwa Jia, *Turbulence: A Novel.*>

9. *interj.* a Chinese expression of disappointment or regret.

   <*"Aiya," he sighed, "my foolish boy. He has stopped drawing and seems to have become interested in sports. What will we do with him?"* —Mark Salzman, *Iron and Silk.*>

10. *interj.* a Chinese expression of disapproval.

    <*Report Card: Five A, one B? Always a B in Math. Aiya.* —San Diego Chinese Women's Association.>

11. *interj.* a Chinese expression of disbelief.

    <*Aiya! You're not going to paint the floor without sweeping and mopping first, are you?* —John Dalton, *Heaven Lake.*>

12. *interj.* a Chinese expression of distaste.

<*You expect me to drink that herbal medicine concoction of yours? Aiya!* —San Diego Chinese Women's Association.>

13. *interj.* a Chinese expression of doubt.

<*Do I have to wear that lemon yellow/lime green sweater my mother made? I wonder if she would notice if I "accidentally" donated it to Goodwill? Aiya.* —San Diego Chinese Women's Association.>

14. *interj.* a Chinese expression of irritation.

<*Clean your room. Aiya! Why you live like a pig?* —San Diego Chinese Women's Association.>

15. *interj.* a Chinese expression of outrage.

<*Never clean your rice cooker with that steel scouring pad! Aiya!* —San Diego Chinese Women's Association.>

16. *interj.* a Chinese expression of shock.

<*What? Ketchup on Yang Chow Fried Rice ... Aiya!* —San Diego Chinese Women's Association.>

17. *interj.* a Chinese lamentation.

<*Aiya ... why me ... ungrateful child ... Aiya.* —San Diego Chinese Women's Association.>

18. *interj.* a Chinese shriek of pain.

<*"Aiya! My chest, my heart!" His father clutched at his robe. "She's a demon. She's trying to kill me.* —May-Lee Chai, *The Girl from Purple Mountain: Love, Honor, War, and One Family's Journey from China to America.*>

19. *interj.* a flirtatious greeting, as in the novel *Schism: Part One of Triad* by Catherine Asaro.

20. *interj.* a Malaysian expression meaning "oh my!"

21. *interj.* a Nepali word for "ouch."

<*"Ouch!" he said, and it struck her that he didn't say "aiya" like a Nepali would.* —Samrat Upadhyay, "This World," *Stories in the Stepmother Tongue.*>

22. *interj.* an exclamation that one is dying, as discussed in *The Anthropology of Buddhism and Hinduism: Weberian Themes* by David N. Gellner; a Chinese utterance of resignation.

<*Ch'en Ts'ung ... was so worn out that he suddenly shrieked in the middle of the night, "Aiya, I am finished!" ... his face had turned very pale and his pulse had stopped beating.* —Nankai University "August 18" Red Guards describing their winter 1966-67 experiences in researching the Case of the Sixty-One Renegades, quoted by Pamela Lubell, *The Chinese Communist Party During the Cultural Revolution: The Case of the Sixty-One Renegades.*>

23. *interj.* an expression of rage fueled by grief.

<*Who was left? Only one of his wives was still breathing. Three of his children. An image of his infant son rose up—as cold as a pebble.* Aiya. *He made the heartbreak into rage.* —Jeff Long, *The Descent.*>

Aiyai.

n. a populated place in Greece.

aiyai aiyai.

n. a chant in the song "Boom Boom Fire" by D. Essex.

Aiyaiya.

1. *n.* a populated place in Ghana.

2. *n.* the weary song of the buffalo, traveling under cover of the fog of his own breath as wolves nip at his heels, from the Nez Perces chant "Medicine-Song of the Buffalo" transcribed by Edward S. Curtis ("The North American Indian," Set #254, Vol. 8).

Aiyau.

1. *n.* a pool in the A'ali an Nil region of Sudan.

2. *n.* a populated place in the Madang region of Papua New Guinea.

Aiye.

1. *n.* a populated place in Nigeria.

2. *n.* the title of a 2004 film directed by A. Venkatesh, named after a shout of frustration.

<*Says director Venkatesh, "My hero is a calm and a patient guy involved in family life. But then one day he's harassed to such an extent that he turns back and shouts at his tormentor 'Aiye...!' The consequences of this action turn his life upside down."* — Malini Mannath, "Aiye," ChennaiOnline.com.>

1 . aooooo. *n.* the howl of a coyote, as transcribed by dance workshop teacher Laura Kennedy in her tribute to "Dancing Coyote," her shamanic spirit guide and muse.

<*Aooooo! Dancing Coyote reminds us to step out of our comfort zones—to take risks, allow silliness to be and surrender to our crazy wisdom. He invites us to embrace the fullness of our beings and follow our hearts' desires despite our fears.* —Laura Kennedy, "The Legend of Dancing Coyote.">

Aiyo.

n. a stream in Sudan.

Aiyo Aiyo.

1. *n.* the name of a music album by the artist Betty Spaghetty.

2. *n.* the name of a music album by the artist Rimi Natsukawa.

Ao.

1. *n.* a populated place in the Hyogo, Ishikawa, Mie, Nagasaki, and Toyama regions of Japan.

2. *n.* a populated place in the Sor-Trondelag region of Norway.

3. *n.* a stream in Central African Republic.

4. *n.* a stream in Zaire.

5. *n.* a village in the New Guinea Jungle, discussed in *Where the Spirits Dwell: An Odyssey in the New Guinea Jungle* by Tobias Schneebaum.

6. *n.* a well in the Kanem region of Chad.

ao.

n. a Maori and Polynesian name for the personification of light and the upper world of the living.

Ao Yai.

n. a bay in the Chanthaburi and Trat regions of Thailand.

<*Many of the islanders live in the small village behind the long pier that juts out from the middle of Ao Yai, just north of the shallow khlong.* —Paul Gray, *The Rough Guide to Thailand's Beaches & Islands.*>

Aoa.

1. *n.* a stream in Central African Republic.

2. *n.* a stream in the Solomon Islands.

Aoai.

n. one of five ministers of Chozzar, a spiritual dragon (equated to Poseidon) revered by the Naasseni (a Gnostic school of the Ophites), as discussed in *Encyclopedic Theosophical Glossary*.

aooooooo.

n. a forceful howl "like a fearful caged wild animal," of someone both drunk and homesick, as in *Psalm at Journey's End: A Novel* by Erik Fosnes Hansen; see also aaaaaaaoooooooo.

Aou.

1. *n.* a locality in the Ambrym region of Vanuatu (formerly New Hebrides).

2. *n.* a plain in the Eastern region of Zambia.

3. *n.* a populated place in the Miyagi region of Japan.

4. *n.* a ridge in New Caledonia.

5. *n.* a stream in the Beyla region of Guinea.

6. *n.* a stream in Togo.

7. *n.* an ancient Celtic god, as discussed in *Irish Druids and Old Irish Religions* by James Bonwick.

8. *n.* an electronic dance song by the artist Mitsumoto, on the album "Sounds of Feedback Vol. 1."

9. *n.* one of five ministers of Chozzar, a spiritual dragon (equated to Poseidon) revered by the Naasseni (a Gnostic school of the Ophites), as discussed in *Encyclopedic Theosophical Glossary*.

Aoua.

1. *n.* a cry of determination.

<*Aoua! let not that old devil start to rise.* —Frank O'Hara, "Chanty," *Poems Retrieved.*>

2. *n.* a lake in Morocco, near Marrakech.

3. *n.* a populated place in Cameroon.

4. *n.* a populated place in French Polynesia.

5. *n.* a populated place in Mali.

6. *n.* a populated place in the Woleu-Ntem region of Gabon.

7. *n.* a stream in Central African Republic.

8. *n.* a woman's given name, as in some African nations.

9. *n.* the title of a song by Maurice Ravel, based upon a poem by Evariste-Désiré de Forges, Vicomte de Parny at the time of the French Revolution.

<*Ravel selected three of Parny's 12 "Madagascar" verses as song texts. He completed one, "Aoua!", in time for a performance in Paris during the summer. The song provoked a hostile audience demonstration. As the text indicates, the poem was a bitter warning about the destructive white invaders of Madagascar, and audience members objected to such an anti-colonial message at a time when French soldiers were fighting in Morocco.* —Will Hertz, "Maurice Ravel: Chansons madécasses (Madagascan Songs).">

Aoue.

1. *n.* a populated place in New Caledonia.

2. *n.* a well in the Borkou-Ennedi-Tibe region of Chad.

Aoueoua.

n. a hill in Mauritania.

Aoueoue.

n. an intermittent stream in Togo.

Aoui.

n. a hill in New Caledonia; a stream in New Caledonia.

Aouoye.

n. a populated place in Mali.

Aouya.

1. *n.* a populated place in Central African Republic.

2. *n.* a river in Saint Andrew, Dominica.

Aoya.

n. a city in the Tottori region of Japan.

<*[W]hen architects in the small seaside town of Aoya in Tottori Prefecture, Japan started clearing land for the construction of a new overpass back in 1998, they couldn't have known they would stumble upon one of the most amazingly preserved archaeological sites the world has ever seen. And even more incredible than all the other artifacts, was the discovery of preserved human DNA from not one, but three human skulls, all about 1800 to 2000 years old. This find has placed Aoya on the map, and given Japan the distinction of being one of only six places in the world to have made such a discovery.* —Matt Goerzen, "The Tottori Skulls: Bridging the Great Divide," *The Foreigner: Japan.*>

Au.

1. *n.* a mission in the West New Britain region of Papua New Guinea; a populated place in the Morobe, New Ireland and West New Britain regions of Papua New Guinea.

2. *n.* a populated place in Czech Republic.

3. *n.* a populated place in Switzerland.

4. *n.* a populated place in the Jubbada Hoose region of Somalia.

5. *n.* a populated place in the Laane-Virumaa region of Estonia.

6. *n.* a populated place in the Niederosterreich, Oberosterreich, Salzburg, Steiermark, Tirol, and Vorarlberg regions of Austria.

7. *n.* a populated place in the Rajasthan region of India; a stream in India.

8. *n.* a populated place in the Solomon Islands.

Au Yeao.

n. an intermittent stream in the Siemreab-Otdar Mea region of Cambodia.

auaua.

1. (also auauua.) *n.* the sound of crying, as in "Lady's Man" by T. George Cronum.

2. *n.* an incomprehensible utterance of pain, from the ubiquitous German joke about a man mistakenly diagnosed with hemorrhoids who tells the proctologist, "get someone with longer fingers—I have a sore throat!"

Auaue.

n. a populated place in French Polynesia.

Auay.

n. a populated place in the Huancavelica region of Peru.

Aue.

1. *n.* a populated place in the Niederosterreich, Steiermark and Tirol regions of Austria.

2. *n.* the name of an angel, as discussed in *John Dee's Five Books of Mystery: Original Sourcebook of Enochian Magic.*

aue.

1. *interj.* a cry of terror or anguish.

<*"Aue, the moths, the moths," she cries out, and her voice is harsh with terror.* —Keri Hulme, *The Bone People.*>

2. *n.* Polynesian expression of sorrow, surprise.

Aui.

n. a stream in the Ida-Virumaa region of Estonia.

Auia.

1. *n.* a stream in the Cabo Delgado region of Mozambique.

2. *n.* a waterhole in the Jubbada Hoose region of Somalia.

Auio.

n. a populated place in the Cuanza Sul region of Angola.

Auu.

n. a hill in Uganda.

Auy.

n. a well in Western Sahara.

Auya.

n. a populated place in the Sandaun region of Papua New Guinea.

Ay.

1. (also Ai.) *n.* an island and village in Indonesia, near Great Banda Island, famous since the 15th century for its nutmeg plantations.

<*Rozengain had little nutmeg and was therefore of no interest to Captain Colthurst, whilst Ai had an extremely treacherous shoreline which deterred all but the most foolhardy of mariners. Nevertheless, it was "the paradice of all the rest [for] there is not a tree on that iland but the nutmeg."* —Giles Milton, *Nathaniel's Nutmeg: Or, The True and Incredible Adventures of the Spice Trader Who Changed The Course Of History.*>

2. *n.* a populated place in Kazakhstan; a stream in Kazakhstan.

ay.

1. *adv.* ever, always.

2. *adv.* indeed, verily.

<*Ay, you shall be together even in the silent memory of God.* —Kahlil Gibran, *The Prophet.*>

3. *adv.* so.

<*"Ay, ye little runt, ye think ye can face me even up an' live to talk about it?" bellowed the giant.* —R. A. Salvatore, *The Icewind Dale Trilogy.*>

4. *adv.* yes; see also aye[1].

<*[I]t was a moment before he grasped the force of her remark. "Ay," he replied, shaking his head.* —Patrick O'Brian, *The Truelove.*>

5. *interj.* eh?

<*Vacation, ay?* —F. Paul Wilson, *Crisscross.*>

6. *interj.* hey.

<*"Ay, Dougal!" shouted a tattered hostler, running up to grab the halter of the lead horse.* —Diana Gabaldon, *Outlander.*>

ay ay.

n. a cry of fright, as upon seeing an apparition, as in *A Cry of Stone* by Michael O'Brien.

ay ya.

n. a Zulu warrior chant, as discussed in *Don't Let's Go to the Dogs Tonight: An African Childhood* by Alexandra Fuller.

Ay'i.

n. a well in Djibouti.

ay-ay-aya.

interj. the yell of a runner in training.

<*Broe yells "AY-AY-AYA!" and takes off over one hurdle, then another, set up willy-nilly on the track.* —Chris Lear, *Sub 4:00: Alan Webb and the Quest for the Fastest Mile.*>

ay-yeee.

interj. a howl of victory, as in the story "The Wonderful Ice-Cream Suit" by Ray Bradbury (*A Medicine for Melancholy and Other Stories).*

Aya.

1. *n.* a populated place in Central African Republic; a stream in Central African Republic.

2. *n.* a populated place in Mali.

3. *n.* a populated place in the Guera region of Chad.

4. *n.* a populated place in the Miyazaki region of Japan.

5. *n.* a river basin in southeast Nigeria, home to hydroprojects battling water scarcity (*Global Journal of Pure and Applied Sciences).*

6. *n.* a stream in Cameroon.

7. *n.* a stream in the Tartumaa region of Estonia.

8. *n.* a stream in the Woleu-Ntem region of Gabon.

9. *n.* a town and scenic river in Japan, north of Mount Karakuni, which boasts the nation's "largest evergreen [oak] forest, in which the Aya River springs are located. The 142m Teruha Suspension Bridge spans the Aya River Gorge where the water from the spring flows" (*Kyushu Newsletter).*

Ayay.

n. a populated place in the Ayacucho region of Peru.

Ayaya.

1. *n.* a "shaman-haunted, fjord-like" bay near Lake Baikal, Siberia, "where reindeer have been reintroduced" (Richmond Simon, *Lonely Planet: Russia & Belarus*).

2. *n.* a populated place in the Estuaire region of Gabon.

ayayau.

(also ayau.) *interj.* an exclamation of pain, as from being hit in the head with a rock in the Peruvian folktale "The Condemned Lover" (Richard M. Dorson, *Folktales Told Around the World).*

Aye.

1. *n.* a populated place in Equatorial Guinea.

2. *n.* a populated place in the Luxembourg region of Belgium.

3. *n.* a stream in Central African Republic.

4. *n.* an intermittent stream in Togo; a populated place in the Tsevie region of Togo.

aye.

1. *adv.* yes; see also ay[4].

<*"Aye?" "Aye!" Violet cried. "Aye!" Klaus shouted. "Aye!" Sunny shrieked. "Hooray!" Phil yelled. Captain Widdershins peered down in annoyance at Phil, whom he would have preferred said "Aye!" along with everyone else.*" —Lemony Snicket, *The Grim Grotto.*>

2. *n.* an affirmative vote or voter.

<*On behalf of the majority of the proxies assigned to management I vote 'aye' and the ayes have it.* —Saul Alinsky, *Rules For Radicals.*>

aye-aye.

n. a nocturnal lemur of Madagascar which probes for insects with a long-nailed finger, as discussed in *The Aye-Aye and I: A Rescue Journey to Save One of the World's Most Intriguing Creatures from Extinction* by Gerald Durrell.

Ayee.

n. a populated place in Cameroon.

ayee yaee yaee.

interj. a Zulu expression of a delight and amazement (Gisele Turner, "Zulu Blues").

Ayeye.

n. a hill in Uganda.

Ayi.

n. a stream in Uganda.

Ayia.

n. a mountain in the Limassol region of Cyprus; a populated place in the Nicosia and Paphos regions of Cyprus; a ruin in the Famagusta region of Cyprus.

Ayii.

n. a forest in Uganda.

Ayo.

1. *n.* a hill in the Guera region of Chad.

2. *n.* a populated place in the Arequipa and Huancavelica regions of Peru.

3. *n.* a populated place in Zaire.

Ayo Ayo.

1. *interj.* a call of greeting.

<*Reaching the lobby, Tone screamed out, "Ayo! Ayo!" to a hungry pack of drug addicts standing around.* —Antoine Thomas, *No Regrets*.>

2. *n.* a populated place in the La Paz and Potosi regions of Bolivia.

<*[Ayo Ayo] is a historical site by excellence, cradle of the revolutionary Indians such as Tupaj Katari, seat of colonial temples and witness of historical events of the nation.* —*BoliviaContact.com*.>

Ayou.
n. a populated place in Benin.

Ayu.
n. a populated place in the Karan State region of Myanmar (formerly Burma), as discussed in "The Many Faces of Ayu" (*Time Asia*).

ayu.
1. *n.* a river fish similar to trout.

<*[The Sagami River] is also known as the "ayu river" because of its abundance of ayu (sweetfish).* —Keihin Office of River.>

2. *n.* the Burmese word for "fool."

<*[A] soccer match is one of the few occasions when ordinary Burmese can give vent to their anger and frustrations. Marshall attends a soccer match in Rangoon where the audience, in unison, shouts "ayu, ayu, ayu, ayu," or "fool, fool, fool, fool," at a portly colonel who is there to present a trophy to the winning team. When Marshall asks a fellow spectator how they dare to do this, the reply is simple: There are too many people taking part in this open ridicule. Gatherings of more than five people are technically illegal in Burma, but at a soccer match disgruntled civilians can sit together and scream abuse until they are hoarse. And unless the authorities want to arrest 5,000 rowdy fans, there is little they can do to stop the ridicule.* —Bertil Linter, "Book Review: *The Trouser People* by Andrew Marshall," *Far Eastern Economic Review*.>

Ayuy.
n. a populated place in the Morona-Santiago region of Ecuador.

Ayy Aay Ay Ay.
n. the name of a mariachi album by El Mariachi Arriba Juarez.

Ayyu.
n. a stream in Kyrgyzstan.

E Yu.

n. an island in the Zhejiang region of China.

E'ya Yo' yoyo'.

n. a chant from a Lakota Indian Ghost Dance asserting "a claim to the land and its resources" (S. E. Wilmer, *Theatre, Society and the Nation: Staging American Identities*).

E-u.

n. a populated place in the Shan State region of Myanmar (formerly Burma).

Ea.

1. *n.* a Basque town in Spain.

<*My father ... was born in Ea, Spain in 1926.* —Jess M. Nachiondo.>

2. *n.* a capital in the Tarabulus region of Libya.

3. *n.* Babylonian God of wisdom, the sea, and patron of the healing arts.

<*In Babylonia the great god Ea was reputed to be the inventor of magic, and his son Marduk, the chief deity of Babylon, inherited the art from his father.* —Sir James George Frazer, *The Golden Bough: A Study in Magic and Religion.*>

ea.

n. river, stream, or drainage channel.

Ea Ea.

n. a locality in French Polynesia.

Ea Yao.

n. a stream in Vietnam.

Eaea.

n. a populated place in the West New Britain region of Papua New Guinea.

Eao.

n. a populated place in the Rio Grande do Sul region of Brazil.

Eau.

n. an island in the Yap region of Micronesia.

eau.

n. watery perfume, from the French word for "water."

<*I smelled a little eau de something over the smells of baby powder and warm milk.* —Nelson DeMille, *Night Fall.*>

Ee.

1. *n.* a canalized stream in the Friesland region of the Netherlands; a populated place in the Friesland region of the Netherlands.

2. *n.* a stream in the Solomon Islands.

ee.

1. *n.* eye (Scottish).

2. *n.* one of the magic words comprising the name of Skeezer Queen Coo-ee-oh, in the novel *Glinda of Oz* by L. Frank Baum.

<*"Well, Coo-ee-oh used just three magic words, one to make the bridge work, and one to make the submarines go out of their holes, and one to raise and lower the island. Three words. And Coo-ee-oh's name is made up of just three words. One is 'Coo,' and one is 'ee,' and one is 'oh.' ... If 'Coo' sends out the boats, it is probable that 'ee' works the bridge," suggested Ozma.* —L. Frank Baum, *Glinda of Oz*

3. *n.* the letter e.

<*Has anybody here seen Kelly? Key ee double ell wy.* —James Joyce, *Ulysses.*>

e-e-e-e.

n. an "ejaculation of wordless awe" in "Social Control in an African Society" by the Boston University African Studies Center (1963).

ee ee ee.

n. the jabbing sound of the hornbell.

<*A six-foot skinny Negro woman was rolling her bones at the man's hornbell, and he just jabbed it at her, "Ee! ee! ee!"* —Jack Kerouac, *On the Road.*>

ee-ee-ee.

n. the short, high call of the Northern Flicker woodpecker, as described in *A Guide to the Birds of the West Indies* by Herbert Raffaele.

ee-uuu.

interj. a sound of disgust.

<*"Looked like snot to me." "Ee-uuu." Will giggled. "It did to me, too, but you said I wasn't allowed to say gross stuff when we're eating."* —Judi McCoy, *Wanted: One Perfect Man.*>

eeaa.

n. a cry of sheer terror, as when one is chased by the living dead in the graphic novel *Uzumaki 2* by Junji Ito.

eee.

1. *interj.* a cry of shock.

<*Tiphany carried Tooter over to Vanessa and pressed his cold, wet body against the back of her neck. "Eee!" Vanessa screamed, nearly dropping her camera.* —Cecily von Ziegesar, *Gossip Girl #6: You're the One That I Want.*>

2. *interj.* a joyful exclamation of the Toraja people of highland Sulawesi, Indonesia.

<*"Eee, grandchild," she exclaimed, embracing me almost jubilantly and offering up her share of meat.* —Toby Alice Volkman, *Feasts of Honor: Ritual and Change in the Toraja Highlands.*>

3. *interj.* a shriek of glee.

<*"Eee!" Nieh said, a high-pitched sound of glee.* —Harry Turtledove, *Colonization: Aftershocks.*>

4. *interj.* a shriek of surprise; see also eeeeee[10].

<*Eee, Mr. Herriot, I didn't expect to see you. I thought you were in the army.* —James Herriot, *All Creatures Wise and Wonderful.*>

5. *interj.* a sigh.

<*Eee, this guy.* —Hank Stuever, *Off Ramp: Adventures and Heartache in the American Elsewhere.*>

6. *interj.* oh; see also eeee[15], eeeee[9].

<*"Eee, you cheeky monkey" was what my mother said to me all the time when I was a kid.* —Mike Etherington, *The Very Best of the British.*>

7. *n.* a shriek like electronic feedback, powerful enough to cut through the traffic noise on Broadway: "A strange, nasty sound, high-pitched, insistent" (David Denby, *Great Books).*

8. *n.* radiowaves from a spiral galaxy, as in the graphic novel *Uzumaki 3* by Junji Ito.

9. *n.* the distant echo of a syllable being called out.

<*Presently the voice moved farther away and we could hear only the plaintive echoing. "Eee?" "Eee?" of the repeated second syllable of each of our names, like a distant calling bird.* —Sue Miller, *The Distinguished Guest.*>

10. *n.* the sharp sound of the rock rabbit (pika).

<*A sharp "eee" sound in a rockfield near or above treeline is the prime clue to the presence of pikas.* —James Halfpenny, *Field Guide to Mammal Tracking in North America.*>

11. *n.* the sound of the letter e, as described in the Ponca City Public Schools curriculum; see also EEEE.

12. *n.* the trilling end of the Red-Eyed Chirper's song, as described in *Stokes Birdfeeder Book: The Complete Guide to Attracting, Identifying, and Understanding Your Feeder Birds* by Donald Stokes.

eee eee eee eee ooo.

n. an expression that one's love has been in vain, from the song "Love in Vain" by Robert Johnson.

eee eee ooo aaa aaaa.

n. the chatter of a monkey, mimed by a character in the script *(Domestic) Animal Instinct* by Gregory P. Dorr and Alan Ryman.

eee eeee eeeee.

interj. a chilling, threatening cry, as of an attacker.

<*"EEE! EEEE! EEEEE!" The sound sent chills through his body. He looked up and saw a Fen standing over him. The Fen held a stick—it could have been a spear—high over his head.* —Walter Dean Myers, *Shadow of the Red Moon.*>

eee-eee.

n. the shriek of a monkey, as described in *Tigers at Twilight* by Mary Pope Osborne.

eee-eee-eee.

1. *n.* the flight call of the Cut-Throat Finch, as described in *Birds of Southern Africa* by Ian Sinclair.

2. *n.* the sound of someone manically blowing a wooden recorder, as described in *Not Even Wrong: Adventures in Autism* by Paul Collins; see also eeee eeee eeee.

eee-EEEE-eee-ooo.

n. the eerie, supersonic whine of sonar.

<*For the first time, Dan heard the keel sonar. It came right up through the steel fabric of the hull, an eerie high note, like whale songs he'd heard on a National Geographic special. It went from tone to tone, eee-EEEE-eee-ooo, trailing off in a supersonic whine that sent a shiver up his back. He imagined it burrowing down from the storm-lashed surface, twisted by currents and inversions, reverberating down, down, down into two thousand fathoms of inky sea.* —David Poyer, *The Circle.*>

eee-ooo eee-ooo.

n. the sound of a police siren, as in the manga "20th Century Boys Volume 7."

eee-ooo eee-ooo eee-ooo.

n. a child's musical babble.

<*"Eee-ooo, eee-ooo, eee-ooo," Robertito bellowed as he scooted across the room, his right*

hand flapping energetically beside his head. … Francisca chased merrily after her son, finally duplicating his pace and maintaining a parallel movement, "Eee-ooo, eee-ooo, eee-ooo," she sang, submerging her echo into a musical context. He increased his speed. Francisca escalated her own steps. Against the harmony of cooing and strange babble, they passed before my eyes like dancers inaugurating a new ballet. —Barry Neil Kaufman, *A Miracle to Believe In.*>

eee-ooo-eee.

n. the singing of a genie, as described in *Flight of the Genie* by Tony Abbott.

eee-ooo-ii.

n. the outburst of the peacock, which Flannery O'Connor describes as sounding "like a cheer for an invisible parade" (*Mystery and Manners: Occasional Prose).*

<*[The peacock] appears to receive through his feet some shock from the center of the earth, which travels upward through him and is released: Eee-oo-ii! Eee-ooo-ii!* —Flannery O'Connor, *Mystery and Manners: Occasional Prose.*>

EEE-ya-ya-ya.

n. a chant to the primeval god Cthulhu, as in *Tales of the Cthulhu Mythos* by H. P. Lovecraft.

EEEE.

n. the sound of the letter e, as discussed in *Tantra of Sound: How to Enhance Intimacy With Sound.*

eeee.

1. (also eeeee.) *interj.* the screeching of fighting rats, as in *R-T, Margaret, and the Rats of Nimh* by Jane Leslie Conly.

2. *interj.* a cry of pain upon stepping on hot coals, as in *The Great Tejon Club Jubilee: Stories* by Gerald W. Haslam.

3. *interj.* a cry of passion.

   <*Eeee, I have never*, ever *been done like this.* —Corson Hirschfield, *Too High.*>

4. *interj.* a cry of surprise.

   <*Suddenly she grasped it and raised it by its ferocious tail, at which point it gave a very human gasp, a surprised* eeee! —Louise Erdich, *The Last Report on the Miracles at Little No Horse: A Novel.*>

5. *interj.* a scream of shock, as in response to a rude remark.

   <*"Eeee, send him to the Vice, Miss, he's talking dirty about the restroom," Slapsie Annie screamed.* —Danny Santiago, *Famous All Over Town.*>

6. *interj.* a shriek brought on by a staggeringly foul odor, as in *The Annotated Chronicles* by Margaret Weis.

7. *interj.* a shriek of alarm, as when someone is "freaking out."

<*"Eeee!" Woe Betide screamed, freaking out.* —Piers Anthony, *Currant Events: Xanth #28.*>

8. *interj.* a shriek of excitement.

<*[L]ifting arms high in the air with an excited "eeee" sound.* —Ian McCurrach, *Special Talents, Special Needs: Drama for People With Learning Disabilities.*>

9. *interj.* a shriek of terror.

<*"Eeee!" she wails, levitating into the air.* —Francess Lantz, *Luna Bay #5: Hawaii Five-Go!*>

<The old man's eyes flew wide with terror. *"Eeee—" he shrilled, then clapped both hands across his mouth to stifle his own screams.* —Dennis L. McKlernan, *The Dragonstone.*>

10. *interj.* a squeal of inspiration.

<*Just then Angelica's eyes lit up as she squealed, "EEEE, mommy has a good idea."* —Libby Keatinge, *Beverly Hills Tutor.*>

11. *interj.* a sympathetic exclamation.

<*"I was so terrified all alone in the creepy dark full of cobwebs that I tried to flee—" "Eeee!" crowed Roberta.* —Beverly Cleary, *Ramona's World.*>

12. *interj.* ah, as in "eeee God" (synonymous with "egad"); see also eeeee[8].

<*Will I ever do anything that important in my life? Or, eeee God, have I peaked?* —Iris Krasnow, *Surrendering to Motherhood: Losing Your Mind, Finding Your Soul.*>

13. *interj.* an expression of astonishment.

<*Eeee, I've never seen the good Father so angry. Never. Astonishing!* —James Clavell, *Shogun.*>

14. *interj.* an inquisitive crooning; eh?

<*Grace pinched and patted his arm and crooned. "Eeee, Son-ny, is that you? You look so different."* —Kathleen Eagle, *This Time Forever.*>

15. *interj.* oh; an expression of longing; see also eee[6].

<*"Eeee, to be so rich," Shorin whispered to Ori when they had first found out.* —James Clavell, *Gai-Jin.*>

16. *interj.* the shriek of a giant brown bug twice the size of a football, as in *The Mysterious Island* by Tony Abbott.

17. *interj.* the sound of a visceral reaction; a reaction to something disturbing, frightening, or sickening.

<*What makes someone behind you cry "Oh!" or "Eeee!" What makes you wince?* —David Ball, *Theater Tips and Strategies for Jury Trials*.>

18. *interj*. yikes; an exclamation of mild surprise or fear.

<*Eeee, Skully knocking on the morning room window.* —J. P. Donleavy, *The Ginger Man*.>

19. *n*. a horse's scream, as described in *The Chaos Balance* by L. E. Modesitt Jr.; see also eiiiiii.

20. *n*. a sound meaning "hurry along" in Papua New Guinea.

<*Grandmothers recall wandering toddlers from doorways and windows, "Eeee! Gaingeen, Gaingeen! [referring to the bogey spirit who threatens children].* —William A. Corsaro, *The Sociology of Childhood*.>

21. *n*. an apology.

<*"Eeee, dearies, I'm sorry," said Gramma from under her skirt. "I'm a miserable sinner."* —B. J. Chute, *Greenwillow*.>

22. *n*. an eagle's cry.

<*Occasionally the high-pitched "eeee" of an eagle can be heard overhead, and at night there are the thumps of armadillos under the floors of the shabby little cabins, and from the creek and swamp the raucous squawk of limpkins.* —Bailey White, *Sleeping at the Starlight Motel: And Other Adventures on the Way Back Home*.>

23. *n*. an Eskimo affirmation; yes.

<"Eeee, eeee. *Yes, yes," answered the others.* —James Houston, *White Dawn: An Eskimo Sage*.>

24. *n*. an expression of disbelief.

<*"Eeee... can... can the land change so much, in this million years?* —Thomas Harlan, *House of Reeds*.>

25. *n*. the aggressive screech of an Ewok, as described in *The Star Wars Trilogy* novelization by George Lucas.

26. *n*. the calling of the letter e.

<*The cheerleaders were in their glory. They screamed up at the bleachers: "GIMME AN E!" The bleachers screamed back: "EEEE!"* —Jerry Spinelli, *Stargirl*.>

<*"So I says, Ernie," screeching out the last eeee in Ernie, "Get off my back."* —Lynn Breedlove, *Godspeed: A Novel*.>

27. *n*. the cheering chorus of an audience, as during a heroic recitation by a Tanzanian storyteller, as discussed in *Africa (World Encyclopedia of Contemporary Theatre, Volume 3)* by Don Rubin; see also yeeee.

28. *n*. the last gasp of a dying person; see also aieee[15].

<*"Eeee..." The marine aiming the launcher fell forward, burning.* —L. E. Modesitt Jr., *The Order of War.*>

29. *n.* the mating call of the Wood Thrush during courtship chases, as described in *Stokes Guide to Bird Behavior, Volume 2* by Donald Stokes.

30. *n.* the musical call of a goat, as described in *Life in a Jewish Orphanage* by Ahuva Goldenthal.

31. *n.* the sound of howling wind.

<*A wee little wind piped eeee.* —James Joyce, *Ulysses.*>

32. *n.* the squeak of a mouse, as described by Zaida Rivera in *Wishes, Lies, and Dreams: Teaching Children to Write Poetry* by Kenneth Koch.

33. *v.* to shake or vibrate crazily, as in the physical comedy of The Three Stooges.

<*To me it looked like Al's jeans went* eeee, *like the Stooges—his pants legs are vibrating, his legs are shaking so hard.* —Connie Fletcher, *What Cops Know.*>

Eeee e E E.

n. a herder's call.

<*First there appeared a lone rider over the hill and then the others came. (As if calling to herders) Eeee e E E!* —Dennis Tedlock, *The Dialogic Emergence of Culture.*>

eeee eeee.

n. the "high, thin whistle call" of the Cedar Waxwing bird, as described in *Stokes Guide to Bird Behavior, Volume 1*, by Donald Stokes.

eeee eeee eeee.

n. the bad sound of someone blowing a recorder poorly; see also eee-eee-eee[2].

<*I blow the recorder. I make a sound. EEEE! EEEE! EEEE! A bad sound comes, like angry birds.* —Karen Hesse, *The Music of Dolphins.*>

eeee yaaa.

interj. a Tarzan-like cry of masculine power.

<*"Eeee yaaa!" Troy fell down on one of the easy chairs and beat his chest.* —Gentry Lee, *Cradle.*>

eeee-aaaay.

interj. a lament; a sorrowful cry.

<*EEEE-AAAAY! EEEE-AAAAY! Oh Weep for Mara whose people are no more.* —David Eddings, *The Rivan Codex: Ancient Texts of the Belgariad and the Malloreon.*>

eeee-ee.

interj. a snarl of rage.

< *Then she sucked in her breath through her teeth at the sight of von Rossbach. "Eeee-ee," she said.* —S. M. Stirling, *T2: Rising Storm.*>

eeee-eee-eeee.

n. the sound of chalk screeching on a blackboard or another writing implement scraping across a surface.

<*Ellen made the slightest eeee-eee-eeee noise as the dry lipstick screeched down the mirror.* —Kristen Kemp, *I Will Survive.*>

eeee-eeee-eeee-EEEE-eeee-eeee.

n. the discordant trill of a crude falsetto, as during vocal exercises.

<*She, too, glanced carelessly over her shoulder, smiling and Eeee-eeee-eeee-EEEE-eeee-eeee-ing without interruption.* —Carole Nelson Douglas, *Another Scandal in Bohemia: A Novel of Suspense Featuring Sherlock Holmes and Irene Adler.*>

eeee-uuu.

interj. something stinks!

<*"Eeee-uuu." I pinched my nostrils. "What, I smell?"* —David Payne, *Gravesend Light: A Novel.*>

eeee-yaaa.

interj. an attack cry, as described in *Lilly Robbins, M.D.* by Nancy N. Rue.

eeeee.

1. *interj.* a cry of disbelief.

<*Eeeee! Solly proposed! I keep pinching myself to be sure this is real.* —Daniel Evan Weiss, *Swine's Wedding.*>

2. *interj.* a cry of fear, as in the comic book *Do You Dare Enter the House of Mystery.*

3. *interj.* a fearful expression, as in response to a supernatural tale.

<*Her children, obviously familiar with the legend, made fearful sounds ("eeeee!") but encouraging smiles as she began it.* —Catherine A Lutz. *Unnatural Emotions: Everyday Sentiments on a Micronesian Atoll and Their Challenge to Western Theory.*>

4. *interj.* a scream of rage.

<*In an instant, you feel a rage inside. You shout EEEEE! as you unsheath your sword and swing your shield before you.* —William J. Knaus, *Take Charge Now! Powerful Techniques for Breaking the Blame Habit.*>

5. *interj.* a shriek of embarrassment.

<*[Someone steps on my strapless dress] and boing, my boobs pop out, eeeee! Well my date grabbed me so no one would see and gave me his jacket and I ran to the bathroom. He was so sweet about it but I was really, really embarrassed.* —Richard G. Calo, *The First & Original Book of Prom.*>

6. *interj.* a shriek of pain.

<*Eeeee! The pain. I cannot help it! The pain. My limbs are in agony!* —Dave Freer, *Rats, Bats, & Vats.*>

7. *interj.* a solemn exclamation; oh.

<*Eeeee, I'm a dead man.* —L. A. Marzulli, *The Unholy Deception.*>

8. *interj.* ah, as in "eeeee God" (synonymous with "egad"); see also eeee[12].

<*I thought, "Eeeee, God!" But that's what they was lookin' for. They wanted to make the biggest hillbilly in Bakersfield into somethin' he wasn't!* —Richard Kienzle, *Southwest Shuffle: Pioneers of Honky Tonk, Western Swing, and Country Jazz.*>

9. *interj.* oh; the sound of a belated realization.

<*Eeeee, I didn't recognize them.* —Michael Herzfeld, *The Poetics of Manhood.*>

10. *n.* a last word.

<*[Mallie's] got her list with everyone's answers on it, everyone who might have heard it [Starr's last word]. Even Kathy from Jewell's with all the makeup. I saw Kathy's answer in there, written down in Mallie's faithful script: Eeeee.* —Alison McGhee, *Rainlight.*>

11. *n.* a terrible wail of grief, as over a dead child.

<*Three whole bright-blustery days in March she screamed, till, finely sifted, her plaint reduced itself to eeeee.* Gunter Grass, *The Flounder.*>

12. *n.* sensual pleasure: "no eeeee's of pleasure but their own" (Toni Morrison, *Love*).

<*[He] set his teeth very softly in the tender flesh at the side of my neck. "Eeeee," I said, and shivered uncontrollably.* —Diana Gabaldon, *Drums of Autumn.*>

13. *n.* the creaking of an old wooden canal boat, as described in *The Magic Escapes* by Tony Abbott.

14. *n.* the cry of the tenor horn.

<*[E]verything came out of the horn, no more phrases, just cries, cries ... "EEEEE!"* —Jack Kerouac, *On the Road.*>

15. *n.* the final cry of the cicada, beseeching the tide to come in but saying "nothing about the spirit land, nothing about what is going to happen to you after you die," from an Australian Aboriginal myth discussed in *Ancestral Connections: Art and an Aboriginal System of Knowledge* by Howard Morphy.

<*Garanyirrnyirr [cicada] is a very strange animal. He yells out "eeeee," and then dies. Very hard, he takes his own life. He sings out for the salt water to come in, and then he dies, for the tide*

to come in, and when it comes in he dies. —Howard Morphy, *Art and an Aboriginal System of Knowledge.*>

16. *n.* the screech of someone who had the air knocked out of his lungs.

<*The ball got through the corner of the screen and caught him in the ribs. You could hear him go, "EEEEE!" It was like all his breath left him.* —Pete Diprimio, *Hoosier Hitmen: Indiana University Baseball.*>

17. *n.* the sound of a far-off train.

<*theres that train far away pianissimo eeeee* —James Joyce, *Ulysses.*>

18. *n.* the sound of an instant camera regurgitating a photograph.

<*Andy [Warhol] would come with his Polaroid and sit there at the table. Everybody was carrying on and he'd say nothing, but periodically he goes brrr with the machine and then this long thing comes out eeeee. I always thought it was just like sticking his tongue out at the company. Puking on them in a way.* —Victor Bockris, *Warhol: The Biography.*>

19. *n.* the thin sound of a cornet, communicating knowledge "before alphabetic, literate language," as described by Toni Morrison in *Song of Solomon.*

20. *n.* the thin, wavering call of the Great Thrush in flight, as described in *Thrushes* by Peter Clement.

eeeee ee e.

n. the incoherent mutterings of a dental patient whose mouth has been coated with a tincture of opium.

<*Matthew tried to say: where am I? Instead he said, Eeeee ee e?* —Edwin Shrake, *The Borderland: A Novel of Texas.*>

eeeee uuuuu.

interj. yuck, as in the variation of the "Pease Porridge" nursery rhyme told in *All About Pockets: Storytime Activities for Early Childhood* by Christine Petrell Kallevig.

eeeee-eee.

n. a high, awful squeak: "A sound comes out of his mouth like a nail being crowbarred out of a plank of green pine; Eeeee-eee" (Ken Kesey, *One Flew Over the Cuckoo's Nest*).

EEEEE-eeeee.

n. the war cry of a cannibal tribe.

<Great cries of EEEEE-eeeee!! hit the air and ears as we ran into a fire-lit hut. —Tobias Schneelbaum, *Keep the River on Your Right.*>

eeeee-ooooo-eeeee.

n. an eerie melody, reminiscent of the spooky theme to the "Twilight Zone" television series.

<*"Eeeee-ooooo-eeeee, we're in Crestone," he joked, his voice climbing and descending the scale in an eerie* Twilight Zone *tone, a reference to what many Coloradoans thought of this town of New Age and Eastern-religion devotees.* —William Celis, *Battle Rock: The Struggle Over a One-Room School in America's Vanishing West.*>

eeeee-yo.

n. a sound of physical exertion, as during self defense.

<*If a big dog comes at you... then grab both of its front legs, pull them out sideways—eeeee-yo!—and snap its back.* —Nicola Barker, *Behindlings: A Novel.*>

eeeeee.

1. (also eeee.) *interj.* the cheering cry of animals in the Ashanti folktale "Anansi Proves He Is the Oldest," retold in *A Treasury of African Folklore, Second Edition*, by Harold Courlander.

2. (also eeee.) *n.* the muffled vowel sound of an inaudible statement.

<*The officer was saying something. All Lang could make out was the vowel sound, the "eeee" that would have been a shriek if it hadn't been spoken in such a soft voice. "What?" "Eeeeee." A hand reached toward the ignition.* —Mary Gardner, *Boat People: A Novel.*>

3. (also eeeee.) *n.* the sound of a baby singing.

<*The sounds become wetter and drop to a gurgle or gargle, rise suddenly to another grinning eeeeee which changes in pitch: eeeeeeEEEEEEeeeeeeEEEEEEE.* —Steven Millhauser, *Edwin Mullhouse.*>

4. *interj.* a comic book fanboy's squeal of excitement at meeting a mythological creature, as in the comic strip "PvP" by Scott R. Kurtz.

5. *interj.* a cry of shock, as upon discovering the living heart of a baby in the refrigerator in *The Original Last Wish Baby* by William Seebring.

6. *interj.* a high-pitched cry of surprise, as when one is struck by cold air.

<*A fairly stoic child, he wiggled and squirmed, but didn't screech, instead making high-pitched "Eeeeee" noises.* —Diana Gabaldon, *The Outlandish Companion.*>

7. *interj.* a scream as someone falls.

<*"Eeeeee!" Chena screamed, putting a good six E's into it. She dropped out from under him like a rock.* —Piers Anthony, *Yon Ill Wind: A Xanth Novel.*>

8. *interj.* a scream to shoo away spiders and other "filthy crawly things," as in *The Angel's Command: A Tale From the Castaways of the Flying Dutchman* by Brian Jacques.

9. *interj.* a shriek of gratitude, disbelief, and happiness.

<*"Eeeeee!" shrieked Bindi into the microphone. ... "This is such an honor! I can't believe it! I'm so happy! Thank you all!"* —Susan G. Sizemore, *Heaven and Hell.*>

10. *interj.* a shriek of surprise, as when someone unexpectedly bursts into the room; see also eee[4].

<"*Can't you stop this damned thing, Mr. Johnson? I mean it's only a formality. They simply... Eeeeee!" With a crash and a splintering of rotten wood, we burst through the barricade.* —Patrick Dennis, *Around the World With Auntie Mame.*>

11. *interj.* a wail of anguish, as in *A Cry of Stone* by Michael O'Brien.

12. *interj.* an energetic confirmation; "and how!"

<*"People really used to make people cleanse broken taboos?" Rasoa responded, "Eeeeee! Once when a man came from Niarovana, he tried to drag his canoe across town rather than rowing around. Taboo! We made him get a bull and cleanse the transgression, but now no one does that anymore."* —Jennifer Cole, *Forget Colonialism? Sacrifice and the Art of Memory in Madagascar.*>

13. *interj.* giddyup (a command for a horse to move).

<*Then El Mehdi shouted, "Eeeeee!" to his horses, and the carriage began to creak as it started down the road.* —Paul Bowles, "The Successor," *The Stories of Paul Bowles.*>

14. *interj.* the cry of a torture victim, as in a Japanese comic book.

<*"I'm teaching myself Japanese," Wags said. He showed Nat what he was reading: a comic book. Two Japanese men were about to torture a Japanese woman. The only word on the page was Eeeeee!* —Peter Abrahams, *Crying Wolf.*>

15. *interj.* the Italian expression for "whee!" as discussed in *Hear! Here!* by Michele Slung.

16. *interj.* the primal wail of a banshee.

<*You'd wailed like you thought the Banshee might wail and Rachel had crawled under your parents' bed, set herself perfectly in the centre so that reaching under from either side you missed her entirely. EEEEEE you screamed, jumping up and down on the mattress until she skittered out and made for the living room where your brother was watching the Stanley Cup playoffs. EEEEEE.* —Aislinn Hunter, *What's Left of Us.*>

17. *n.* a gleeful chuckle.

<*"Eeeeee, perhaps you'd better not," Haru, a short, wizened fisherman, chortled.* —James Clavell, *Shogun.*>

18. *n.* a man's romantic wooing, "like some dirty kind of animal," as described in *Barrios and Borderlands: Cultures of Latinos and Latinas in the United States* by Denis Lynn Daly Heyck; see also ooooo.

19. *n.* the scream of a slain ghoul.

<*So I drew a picture of a beautiful lady with long hair driving a sword right into the eye of a ghoul with blood and jelly squirting out and the ghoul shouting, screaming, "EEEEEE!" in big red letters.* —Brian Doyle, *Boy O'Boy.*>

20. *n.* the shriek of suffering and dying horses, as described in *The Chaos Balance* by L. E. Modesitt Jr.

21. *n.* what the famous figure in Munch's painting "The Scream," "the official spokesperson of angst," says to Elvis Presley in a humor piece entitled "All Shook Up" by Bobbie Ann Mason, quoted in *More Mirth of a Nation: The Best Contemporary Humor* by Michael J. Rosen.

Eeeeee eeeeee / Eeeeee eeeeee / Eeeeeeeeee / Eeee eeee eeee eeee.

n. a stanza from the song "Going Away Blues" by Lottie Kimbrough, as transcribed in *The Blues Line: Blues Lyrics from Leadbelly to Muddy Waters* by Eric Sackheim.

Eeeeee Eeeeee Eeeeee.

n. a transcription of the stringed instrumentation theme from the score to the film *Psycho.*

<*[Danny Elfman] had an idea about sampling the shower scene from Psycho and slowing down the "Eeeeee! Eeeeee! Eeeeee!" strings and making a rhythm out of it.* —David Morgan, *Knowing the Score: Film Composers Talk About the Art, Craft, Blood, Sweat, and Tears of Writing for Cinema.*>

eeeeee eeeeeeee.

n. the sound of a singer attempting a higher octave.

<*I don't know if I can get up that high. Eeeeee... Eeeeeeee... I can still do it, I haven't lost my voice yet.* —Sue Graham Mingus, *Tonight At Noon: A Love Story.*>

eeeeee-yeeee.

interj. the exultant scream of a Confederate infantryman.

<*The sudden drumming of hooves brushed me off the dusty pike and petrified me into rigidity as a troop dressed in gray and dirty tan galloped by screaming "Eeeeee-yeeee" exultantly.* —Ward Moore, "Bring the Jubilee," *The Best Alternate History Stories of the 20th Century.*>

EEEEeee.

interj. "shut up!" as in *Baby Catcher: Chronicles of a Modern Midwife* by Peggy Vincent.

eeeeeee.

1. *interj.* a "collective scream" of terror in response to "a peril beyond comprehension," as in *Once Upon a Winter's Night* by Dennis L. McKiernan.

2. *interj.* a cry of disinclination to get out of bed, ostensibly due to fear of sunlight.

<*Gavin screamed. "EEEEEEE! Daylight!"* —Alice Borchardt, *The Silver Wolf.*>

3. *interj.* a cry of panic that the world is ending due to global warming.

<*The greenhouse effect is running out of control. Is it warm in here or is it... EEEEEEE!!! THE END OF THE WORLD!!!* —P. J. O'Rourke, *Age and Guile Beat Youth, Innocence, and a Bad Haircut.*>

4. *interj.* a squeal at having one's hiding place discovered, as in *The Prophecy* by K. A. Applegate.

5. *interj.* the desperate shriek of a person on fire.

<*[W]ith each tortured breath he sucked flames into his lungs. "Eeeeeee!" the human torch shrieked.* —David Sherman, *Starfist: Steel Gauntlet.*>

6. *n.* an animal howl indicative of an emotional breakdown.

<*You turned and ran toward a wall, turned again and rushed to the opposite wall, wailing and wailing a high, horrible note: Eeeeeee!* —Walter Wangerin Jr., *Mourning Into Dancing.*>

7. *n.* the call of the Cedar Waxwing bird, "a high sibilant eeeeeee, slightly tremulous" (Steven L. Hilty, *A Guide to the Birds of Columbia*).

8. *n.* the scream of a police car siren.

<*EEEEEEE! A squad car tore suddenly down the street, sirens screaming, red, white, and blue lights flashing on the top in an alternating pattern.* —Lisa Scottoline, *Legal Tender.*>

9. *n.* the sound of teeth gnashing in frustration and anger.

<*"Eeeeeee," my mother gnashes her teeth. Her hands do a slow-motion dance of frustration.* —Lisa Lerner, *Just Like Beauty: A Novel.*>

eeeeeee eeeee.

n. the squealing sound of a barnyard sow, as in *Loose Balls: Easy Money, Hard Fouls, Cheap Laughs, and True Love in the NBA* by Jayson Williams.

eeeeeee eeeeeee eeeeeee.

interj. a scream of grief, as from a mother mourning a dead baby.

<*"Don't seem like it's breathing no more," he explained. EEEEEEE. EEEEEEE. EEEEEEE, the mother screamed.* —Denis Johnson, *Already Dead: A California Gothic.*>

eeeeeee-yiee.

interj. an answering call of the elusive and violent Yanomami Indians who dwell in the rain forest between Orinoco and the Amazon, as described in *In Trouble Again: A Journey Between Orinoco and the Amazon* by Redmond O'Hanlon.

<*"Eeeeeee-yiee!" came an answering cry from outside the shabono.* — Redmond O'Hanlon, *In Trouble Again: A Journey Between Orinoco and the Amazon.*>

eeeeeeee.

n. a piercing cry.

<*A cry pierced the hall—Eeeeeeee! a glass door slammed, the clatter of heels and then—Who was that!* —William Gaddis, *A Frolic of His Own.*>

eeeeeeee eeeeeeeee.

n. the sound of a rocket-powered elevator ascending, as in the comic book "Hyperco" by Aaron K.

eeeeeeeee.

n. the flute-like musical sound of trees rubbing together, as described in *Visions of Sound: Musical Instruments of First Nation Communities in Northeastern America* by Beverley Diamond.

eeeeeeeee eeeeee.

interj. a mad scream of fear.

<*"Eeeeeeee! Eeeeee!" Mary Elliot was screaming, and then she was sobbing, "God have mercy!"* —James Alexander Thom, *From Sea to Shining Sea.*>

eeeeeeeeeeee.

1. *n.* a "magnificent piercing" cry of a baby, rising out of a "rich yowl," as described in the novel *Edwin Mullhouse* by Steven Millhauser.

2. *n.* the howl of a cascading "man-made storm of released energy," as in the comic book *Amazing Adventures #10* by Mike Sekowsky.

3. *n.* the siren of a fire engine, as described by Melissa Blitz in *Wishes, Lies, and Dreams: Teaching Children to Write Poetry* by Kenneth Koch.

eeeeeeEEEEEEeeeeeeEEEEEEE.

n. the sound of a baby singing, as described in the novel *Edwin Mullhouse* by Steven Millhauser; see eeeeee[3].

eeeeeeeeeeeeeeeeeeeeeeeeeeeeeeeeeee.

n. the brain's reaction to what Tom Wolfe calls an "all-embracing look of total acid [LSD] understanding."

<*[F]inishing off in a sailing tremulo laugh as if she has just read your brain and it is the weirdest of the weird shit ever, your brain eeeeeeeeeeeeeeeeeeeeeeeeeeeeeeeeeee.* —Tom Wolfe, *The Electric Kool-Aid Acid Test.*>

eeeeeeeyayayayay eeeee.

n. a lyric (ostensibly from "Johnny B. Goode") sung by The Sex Pistols' Johnny Rotten to the tune of "Through My Eyes," as discussed in *Exploding: The Highs, Hits, Hype, Heroes, and Hustlers of the Warner Music Group* by Stan Cornyn.

eeeeoooo.

interj. a cry of pain caused by terrible spiral warts, as in the graphic novel *Uzumaki 3* by Junji Ito.

eeeiii-eeeeee.

n. the screech of the Golden Eagle.

<*Just then Juan Salvador heard the screech of a great Golden Eagle, "EEEIII-EEEEEE!" as he went leaping, bouncing across the beautiful, open desert toward the salt flat.* —Victor Villasenor, *Thirteen Senses: A Memoir.*>

eeeooo.

interj. an expression of disgust, as in response to a worm.

<*“That’s for worms.” “Eeeooo,” Raun grimaced, “you gonna put them on the hook?”* —Walt Kaufmann, “Raun.”>

Eeu.

n. a bay in French Polynesia.

eeuuu.

n. an expression of revulsion, as used by journalist Jay Boyar in his Orlando Sentinel review of the 2004 film “White Chicks.”

eeyaaa.

interj. an exclamation of discomfort.

Ei.

1. *n.* a populated place in the Hyogo region of Japan.

2. *n.* a stream in Russia.

ei.

interj. an exclamation of bewilderment, as in *The Tunnel* by William H. Gass.

Eia.

1. *n.* a populated place in the Morobe region of Papua New Guinea.

2. *n.* a populated place in the Rogaland region of Norway.

Eiao.

n. an island in the Marquesas archipelago.

<*He felt his divine powers leaving him with the sunrise and with his last breath he murmured, “This is Eiao!”* —The Marquesan creation legend, as told by Hilary Rogers, *Lonely Planet Tahiti & French Polynesia.*>

Eiau.

1. *n.* a populated place in the Central region of Papua New Guinea.

2. *n.* an island in French Polynesia.

Eie.

n. a farm in the More og Romsdal region of Norway.

eiiiiiii.

n. the neigh of a horse; see also eeee[19].

<*The knight rode on the horse's back and shouted: "Ooooooo!" and the horse neighed "Eiiiiii!"* —Yoram Kaniuk, *Adam Resurrected*.>

Eiy.

1. *n.* a hill in Western Sahara.

2. *n.* a populated place in the Zanjan region of Iran.

Eiyo.

n. a populated place in the Kyongsang-bukto region of South Korea.

Eo.

n. a populated place in New Caledonia.

Eooa.

n. an island in the Tongatapu region of Tonga, discussed in *A Voyage to the Pacific Ocean, Undertaken by the Command of His Majesty, for Making Discoveries in the Northern Hemisphere, in the Resolution and Discovery, in the Years 1776, 1777, 1778, 1779 and 1780* by Captain James Cook.

Eou.

n. an intermittent stream in the Santo/Malo region of Vanuatu (formerly New Hebrides).

Eoua.

1. *n.* a Pacific island formed of coral rock, discussed in *The Structure and Distribution of Coral Reefs* by Charles Darwin.

2. *n.* a populated place in Mali.

Eoya.

n. a populated place in the Andaman and Nicoba region of India.

Eu.

1. *n.* a populated place in the Haute-Normandie region of France.

2. *n.* an island in the Yap region of Micronesia.

euoi.

interj. an expression of Bacchic frenzy, derived from a secondary name of the wine god.

<*[T]hey shouted the song of Bacchos sounding tongue with tongue, crushing the fruit with many a skip of the foot, crying "Euoi!"* —Carl Kerenyl, *Dionysos*.>

euouae.

n. a term from Gregorian music formed from the vowels of "seculorum Amen," which ends the Latin hymn "Gloria Patri," as discussed in *The Forms and Orders of Western*

Liturgy from the Tenth to the Eighteenth Century: A Historical Introduction and Guide for Students and Musicians by John Harper.

Ey.

n. a farm in the Rangarvallasysla region of Iceland.

Eya.

n. a populated place in the Irrawaddy region of Burma.

<*I then discussed with the lama the route to Zhongdian via Eya, and soon afterwards Lao Li came to me, once more pale and trembling. "Sir," he said, "don't go through Eya. A few days ago it was raided by sixty bandits from Gong-ling. They stole a hundred pack animals and killed some people."* —Heinrich Handel-Mazzetti, *A Botanical Pioneer in South West China: Experiences and Impressions of an Austrian Botanist During the First World War.*>

Eye.

1. *n.* a populated place in Nigeria.

2. *n.* a populated place in United Kingdom.

3. *n.* a stream in Zaire.

eye.

n. the organ of sight.

Eyee.

n. a populated place in Cameroon.

Eyo.

1. *n.* a populated place in Cameroon; a stream in Cameroon.

2. *n.* a stream in Central African Republic.

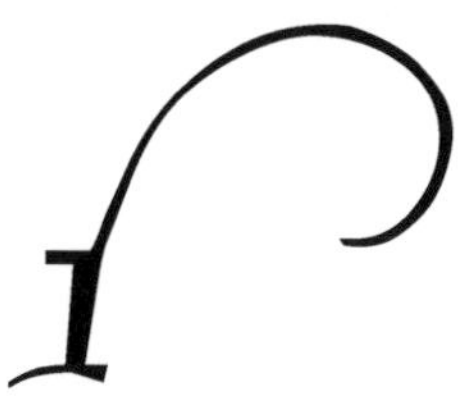

I aya oa a.

n. an incoherent expression one makes while yawning.

<*"I aya oa a," she said in yawnspeak, a language—not unlike Hawaiian—for its paucity of consonants.* —Christopher Moore, *Fluke: Or, I Know Why the Winged Whale Sings.*>

I Yi Yi Yi Yi.

n. a song from the Carmen Miranda musical *That Night in Rio.*

I'o.

(also Iao, Io). *n.* a Hawaiian name for the "Great Spirit" or divine field, as discussed in *Spirit Medicine: Healing in the Sacred Realms* by Hank Wesselman.

I-iyo.

n. a populated place in the Nueva Vizcaya region of the Philippines.

I-u.

n. a populated place in the Western region of Papua New Guinea.

i-yi-yi-yi.

n. an exclamation of wonderment, as in the Madonna song "I Want You."

Ia.

1. *n.* a stream in Ethiopia.
2. *n.* a stream in Ghana.
3. *n.* an intermittent stream in the Santo/Malo region of Vanuatu (formerly New Hebrides).
4. *n.* the Sumerian river god of wisdom, as discussed by Fred Hamori in "Mesopotamian and Finn-Ugor God Names Compared to Sumerian."

Ia Oue.

n. a stream in Vietnam.

Ia-Oue.

n. a Greek spelling of the god Jehovah (Peter Kirk); see Iaou[2].

Iaa.

n. a populated place in the Niassa region of Mozambique.

Iai.

1. *n.* a populated place in the Cuanza Sul region of Angola; a stream in the Cuanza Sul region of Angola.

2. *n.* a stream in Malawi.

3. *n.* an island in New Caledonia.

iai.

n. the art of sword-drawing in Japanese martial arts.

<*Iai was developed long after peace had been established. On the battlefield, iai was hardly necessary [as warriors were fully clad in armor].* —Kenji Tomiki, "The Nature of Modern Martial Arts.">

Iaia.

1. *n.* a stream in Benin.

2. *n.* a stream in the Zaire region of Angola.

3. *n.* an intermittent stream in Ethiopia.

4. *n.* an intermittent stream in the Zambezia region of Mozambique.

5. *n.* the name of a space fantasy warrior princess paper doll character

<*Iaia can defend her world against the greatest odds.* —Brenda Sneathen Mattox, fancyephemera.com.>

6. *n.* the title of an album of Brazilian music by Mônica Salmaso.

Iaie.

1. *n.* a stream in the Huambo region of Angola.

2. *n.* the title of a music album by Spanish chanteuse Lidia Pujol.

Iaio.

1. *n.* a populated place in Ethiopia.

2. *n.* the name of a character in Pier Paolo Pasolini's 1961 film *Accattone.*

<*One of the most heartbreaking, and heartfelt, scenes finds Accattone with Iaio, the young son he had abandoned along with his estranged wife.* —Jim Clark, "Accattone: Pasolini's 1st of 25 Films.">

iaio.

n. a variety of beetle with aggressive larvae found in the rice patties of the Erbo Delta (Barcelona Field Studies Centre SL, "Ebro Delta: Flora and Fauna").

Iao.

1. (also I'o, Io). *n.* a Hawaiian name for the "Great Spirit" or divine field, as discussed in *Spirit Medicine: Healing in the Sacred Realms* by Hank Wesselman

2. *n.* a demiurge in the gnostic system of primordial powers, as discussed in *A Dictionary of Angels: Including the Fallen Angels* by Gustav Davidson.

3. *n.* a valley and state park on the Hawaiian island of Maui, as discussed in *Lonely Planet: Hawaii* by Glanda Bendure.

4. *n.* the god Jehovah, "the ineffable name of God, Yahweh" (Martin W. Meyer, *The Ancient Mysteries: A Sourcebook of Sacred Texts of the Mystery Religions of the Ancient Mediterranean World*); see also Iaue, Iaou[2], Ya.

<*[Iao is] the form usually taken by Jehovah's name in magical texts of the Hellenistic age.* —Arthur B. Cook, "The Solar Wheel in Greece.">

<*The Hebrew name of God, IAO, fascinated sorcerers by its vowels, always crucial in ancient magic.* —Dr. Daniel Botkin, "Linguistic Superstition And The Sacred Name Only Movement.">

iao.

n. small fish used as bait.

< *I thought that iao—that's the nehu-looking animal—was extinct already. But about October, when I made some sampling, it was fantastic—big ones out there again.* —George Uyemura, *Environment-Hawaii.org.*>

Iaou.

1. *n.* an intermittent stream in Benin.

2. *n.* the God of the Jews; "the greatest of all the gods, the supreme divinity," according to the oracle of Apollo at Claros (Elijah Benamozegh, *Israel and Humanity*); see also Iaue, Iao[4], Ieue[2], Ya.

iaou.

1. *n.* a cat noise, less melodious than the French spelling *miaou.*

2. *n.* a French word for the sound of a bird's call, as in the Arthur Rimbaud poem "Brussels."

Iau.

n. a populated place in the Northern region of Papua New Guinea.

Iaue.

n. the god Jehovah; see also Iao[4], Iaou[2], Ya.

<*I believe that most who use Yahueh, or Yahuweh, use it instead of IAUE because many who first come into contact with IAUE at first glance find it difficult to pronounce. We are not used to seeing a word made up of all vowels, and Yahueh seems easier to pronounce.* —Bill Burton, "The Key to the Key of Knowledge.">

Iaya.

n. a stream in the Southern region of Zambia.

Ie.

1. *n.* a populated place in the Okinawa region of Japan.

2. *n.* a stream in the Bretagne region of France.

ie.

(also ieie.) *n.* Pacific Islands screw pine whose fiber is used for weaving.

iee-iee-iee-iuu.

n. the "quickly repeated, rather mournful, high-pitched, bouncing, descending" song of the Spectacled Barwing, as described in *A Guide to the Birds of Southeast Asia* by Craig Robson.

Iei.

n. a populated place in Ethiopia.

Ieie.

n. a populated place in the Nampula region of Mozambique.

Ieiya.

n. an island in Japan.

Ieue.

1. *n.* a stream in Central African Republic.

2. *n.* the "Great Spirit," discussed in the 1882 book *Oahspe: A New Bible in the Words of Jehovih and His Angel Ambassadors*; the god Yahweh; see Iaou[2].

Ii.

1. *n.* a populated place in Finland just north of Oulu.

2. *n.* a populated place in the Okinawa and Yamaguchi regions of Japan.

3. *n.* a slope in Palau.

Iii.

1. *n.* a populated place in the Yamaguchi region of Japan.

2. *n.* the name of a character with glowing yellow eyes in the novel *The Martian Chronicles* by Ray Bradbury.

<*Mr. Iii answered his door. He was on his way to a lecture, but he had a minute, if they would hurry.* —Ray Bradbury, *The Marian Chronicles.*>

iii.

n. the sound of the letter i, as described in *Reading Made Easy: A Guide to Teach Your Child to Read* by Valerie Bendt.

iiiyy.

n. a battle cry, as in the comic book *The Savage Sword of Conan.*

Iio.

n. a populated place in the Oulu region of Finland.

Iiya.

n. a populated place in the Shizuoka region of Japan.

Io.

1. (also I'o, Iao). *n.* the great spirit "voice of all worlds singing," as in *Singer from the Sea* by Sheri S. Tepper.

2. *interj.* in Ezra Pound's poem "Cantos," "The cry of 'Io' is 'Hail!'" (George Kearnes, *Ezra Pound: The Cantos*).

3. *n.* a moon of Jupiter.

   <*In 1979, the Voyager spacecraft flew through the Jovian system, and one of the most exciting discoveries made by the Voyager spacecraft was the presence of active erupting volcanoes on Io.* —NASA.>

4. *n.* a populated place in South Korea.

5. *n.* a stream in Cameroon.

6. *n.* a woman's given name.

   <*They were warming again to enmity, perhaps because Io's blue dress filled the corners of their eyes, and Io's small, rounded and pleasing voice was saying something gay and unintelligible to a group of colliers just within earshot.* —Ellis Peters, *Fallen Into the Pit.*>

7. *n.* in Classical mythology, another name for Dionysus.

8. *n.* in Classical mythology, the daughter of Inachus.

   <*Inachus, a river-god and legendary king of Argos, was the father both of the Goddess Io, who became Isis when she reached Egypt, and of the hero Phoroneus, founder of the Pelasgian race, who has already been identified with the God Bran, alias Cronos.* —Robert Graves, *The White Goddess.*>

9. *n.* the blind, elderly chief of the gods in *The Last Hero: A Discworld Fable* by Terry Pratchett.

10. *n.* the universal void, as discussed in *Spiritwalker: Messages from the Future* by Hank Wesselman.

io.

1. *interj.* a shout of triumphant joy, as in the traditional Thanksgiving song "Singing, the Reapers Homeward Come."

   <*Singing, the reapers homeward come, Io! Io! / Merrily singing the harvest home, Io! Io! / Along the field, along the road, / Where autumn is scattering leaves abroad, / Homeward cometh the ripe last load, Io! Io!* —Author unknown, "Singing, the Reapers Homeward Come.">

2. *n.* a North American yellow moth.

   <*The io moth / Has mam-moth eyes / That are not real— / They're a disguise / To ward off birds / And other creatures, / Like garter snakes / And science teachers.* —Douglas Florian, "The Io Moth," *Insectiopedia.*>

Ioa.

1. *n.* a populated place in the Harjumaa region of Estonia.

2. *n.* a volcanic crater valley in the north of Maui, home to frigate birds and other rare sea birds.

ioa.

n. the frigate bird of Hawaii.

Ioaa.

n. a capital in the Ioannina region of Greece.

Ioi.

n. a populated place in the Central region of Papua New Guinea.

Ioii.

n. a stream in the Nzerekore region of Guinea.

Ioiya.

n. a populated place in Nigeria.

Iou.

n. a populated place in the Milne Bay and Western regions of Papua New Guinea.

Ioui.

n. a ridge in New Caledonia.

Ioye.

n. a populated place in the Raplamaa region of Estonia.

Iu-ai-iu.

n. a populated place in the Northern region of Papua New Guinea.

Iua.

n. a stream in the Cabo Delgado region of Mozambique.

Iue.

n. a rock in the Cuanza Sul region of Angola.

Iuo.

n. a stream in the Huambo region of Angola.

iuu-iuu iuu-iuu iuu-iuu iuu-iuu.

n. the melancholy whistled territorial call of the Stork-billed Kingfisher, as described in *A Guide to the Birds of Southeast Asia* by Craig Robson.

Iya.

1. *n.* a mountain in Indonesia.

2. *n.* a populated place in the Azarbayjan-e Bakht region of Iran.

3. *n.* a populated place in the Eastern Highlands region of Papua New Guinea.

4. *n.* a secluded, historic mountain valley in the Shikoku region of Japan.

   <*[I]n the upstream area of the River Yoshino, high and steep mountains present spectacular views of Iya Valley.* —"Tokushima Prefecture," jtb.co.jp.>

5. *n.* an "evil spirit giant" whose foul breath brought sickness to the Lakota Indians (Lydia Whirlwind Soldier, "Lakota Studies").

Iyai.

n. a populated place in the Yomou region of Guinea.

iyaiya-yaya.

n. a chant in an ancient Inuit spirit song, "expressing the influence of the unique and difficult environment on the peoples' soul" (Alvin M. Josephy, *500 Nations: An Illustrated History of North American Indians*).

Iye.

1. *n.* a populated place in the Harjumaa and Hiiumaa regions of Estonia.

2. *n.* a stream in Indonesia.

Iyeee.

n. a woman's name.

<*As was my custom through those years, I would explore far and wide, and on my return, would share my adventures and discoveries with Aunt Iyeee. And in turn, she would tell me one of her magical tales of our frontier family, of "The Blood" as she called it, and of "The Days." You see, Aunt Iyeee always held firm that our blood had mixed with Comanche blood along the way.*

—Anthony Raddio, "Because the Past Only Happened Once," BrandXIndian.com.>

iyeee.

1. *interj.* a cry of pain.

   <*I have a mad headache today. Iyeee.* —Snowboard.com.>

2. *interj.* a Samurai yell, as in the novel *Bait* by Mark Weatherbe.

3. *interj.* a scream of panic.

   <*"Iyeee!!!" I sputtered, as I lost my footing and slid down the bank toward the creek.* —Gary John Rush, *Emergency Toilet Paper: An Outdoorsman's Bathroom Guide.*>

Iyei.

n. a populated place in Indonesia.

Iyeye.

n. a hill in Uganda.

iyeye.

n. "people" in the language of the Catawba Indian nation.

Iyi.

n. a forest in Uganda.

Iyo.

n. a populated place in Benin.

iyoooo.

(also iyoo ooo.) *n.* a chant from the Igbo Folk Epic from Sub-Saharan Africa, as discussed in *Traditional Storytelling Today: An International Sourcebook* by Margaret Read MacDonald.

Iyuyu.

n. a stream in Tanzania.

Iyye.

n. a populated section in the Saaremaa region of Estonia.

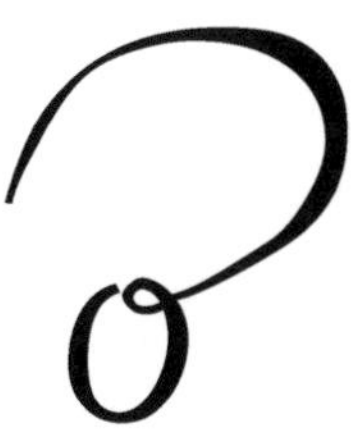

O Ya.

n. a stream in the Nzerekore region of Guinea.

O Yeao.

n. a stream in the Kracheh region of Cambodia.

O Yeo.

n. an intermittent stream in the Siemreab-Otdar Mea region of Cambodia.

O'e.

n. a stream in the Solomon Islands.

O'io.

n. a populated place in the Solomon Islands.

o—o—o—o.

interj. a moan (as from cold-weariness), spoken with chattering teeth.

<*Pikel's typical moan of "Oooo," came out more as "O—o—o—o," as his teeth chattered through the sound.* —R. A. Salvatore, *The Fallen Fortress*.>

O-aa.

n. the daughter of a king living at the earth's core in the fantasy world of Pellucidar (Edgar Rice Burroughs, *Savage Pellucidar*).

o-eee.

interj. the Swedish expression for "whee!" as discussed in *Hear! Here!* by Michele Slung.

o-o.

interj. the Italian expression for "yoo-hoo," as discussed in *Hear! Here!* by Michele Slung.

O-ooa.

n. an island in the Ha'apai region of Tonga.

O-yu.

n. a stream in Russia.

Oa.

1. *n.* a cape in the Pohnpei region of Micronesia; a populated locality in the Pohnpei region of Micronesia.

2. *n.* a populated place in Mali.

3. *n.* a populated place in the Solomon Islands.

4. *n.* a stream in the Macenta region of Guinea.

5. *n.* the name of "the lost world at the geographic center of the Milky Way where the Guardians of the Universe made their home and headquarters for eight billion years. If the light of the original Oa's nameless star were much brighter, it would still be visible to astronomers on Earth who looked back over forty million years of time to see it" (Elliot S! Maggin, *Kingdom Come*).

Oae.

n. a populated place in French Polynesia.

Oaia.

n. a populated place in Romania.

Oao.

n. an island in the Yap region of Micronesia.

Oau.

1. *n.* a hill in New Zealand.

2. *n.* a populated place in the Solomon Islands.

Oayo.

n. a populated place in the Eastern region of Zambia.

Oe.

1. *n.* a Japanese family name. <*Kenzaburo Oe was the 1994 Nobel Laureate in Literature.*>

2. *n.* a populated place in Finland.

3. *n.* a populated place in the Liege region of Belgium.

4. *n.* an area in Japan; a populated place in the Hokkaido, Nagasaki, Shiga, Shimane, and Wakayama regions of Japan; a populated area in the Aichi region of Japan.

oe.

1. *n.* a grandchild (Scottish).

2. *n.* a violent whirlwind off the Faroe islands (a group of Danish islands in the North Atlantic between Iceland and the Shetland Islands), as discussed in *The American Practical Navigator* by Nathaniel Bowditch.

Oea.

n. a capital in the Tarabulus region of Libya.

Oeaei.

n. the wife of the Egyptian god Ra-amen, as discussed in *An Archaic Dictionary, From the Egyptian, Assyrian, and Etruscan Monuments and Papyri* by William R. Cooper (cited by Jeff Miller, "A Collection of Word Oddities and Trivia").

Oeo.

n. a populated place in New Zealand.

Oey.

1. *n.* a populated place in Switzerland.

2. *n.* a populated place in the Lorraine region of France.

Oi.

1. *n.* a bay in French Polynesia.

2. *n.* a farm in the Hedmark region of Norway.

3. *n.* a populated place in Indonesia.

4. *n.* a populated place in the Aichi, Gifu, Hiroshima, Okayama, Saitama, and Shimane regions of Japan.

5. *n.* a populated place in the Chiang Rai region of Thailand.

6. *n.* a populated place in the Kyongsang-bukto region of South Korea.

oi.

interj. used to attract attention.

<*Oi, haven't I seen you somewhere before? —The Complete Monty Python's Flying Circus.*>

Oia.

1. *n.* a populated place in Italy.

2. *n.* a populated place in the Aveiro region of Portugal.

3. *n.* a populated place in the Kikladhes region of Greece.

Oia-Oia.

n. an intermittent stream in the Manica region of Mozambique.

oiaio.

adv. the Hawaiian word for "truly."

Oie.

n. a farm in the Sor-Trondelag region of Norway; a populated place in the More og Romsdal and Vest-Agder regions of Norway.

Oio.

1. *n.* a populated place in New Zealand.

2. *n.* a populated place in the Solomon Islands.

Oiu.

n. a populated place in the Viljandimaa region of Estonia.

Oiye.

n. an area in Japan.

Oo.

1. *n.* a populated place in the Midi-Pyrenees region of France.

2. *n.* an extinct honey-eating bird of Hawaii whose feathers were used in ceremonial robes.

<*The Oo trophy is now so rare that the Bishop Museum in Honolulu keeps a solitary taxidermy specimen in a dark safe. If you happen to be in England, you may see a cape once worn by Hawaiian kings made of 20,000 bright yellow Oo thigh feathers at the Pitt-Rivers Museum at the University of Oxford.* —Marcie Carroll, *The Unofficial Guide to Maui.*>

3. *n.* an island in the Marshall Islands.

oo.

1. *n.* an exclamation, as in James Joyce's *Ulysses*.

2. *pron.* you.

<*Oo never heard such a sad little song.* —Lewis Carroll, *Sylvie and Bruno.*>

oo-aaaaa.

n. the "deep, wailing, drawn-out" cry of the Satyr Tragopan, as described in *Birds of Nepal* by Richard Grimmett.

oo-EEE-ooo.

n. a swelling in a musical performance.

<*The quartet swelled oo-EEE-ooo between the verses.* —Mark Childress, *Tender.*>

Ooa.

1. *n.* a reef in French Polynesia.

2. *n.* an island in the Marshall Islands.

ooaa.

n. a bird of the Meliphagidae family, found on the island of Kauai.

Ooi.

n. a populated place in the Gelderland region of the Netherlands.

ooo.

1. *adv.* yes.

<*Ooo, you're right.* —Edward Lee, *Succubi.*>

2. *interj.* a moan of sympathy.

<*He rolled on the ground, back curved fetal-like, eyes wide. Every man in the general vicinity gave a collective, sympathetic "Ooo."* —Harlan Coben, *Deal Breaker.*>

3. *interj.* an appreciative cooing.

<*Clouds wafted by, and the cosmos was inchoate. "Ooo, lovely!" Luna breathed, hugging Zane from behind.* —Piers Anthony, *On a Pale Horse.*>

4. *interj.* an exclamation marking a realization; see also ooooo[12], oooooo[15].

<*Ooo, if I were wearing boots, I'd be shaking in them.* —Sherriyn Kenyon, *Night Pleasures.*>

5. *interj.* an exclamation of shock, as upon being drenched with water.

<*"Ooo!" Lucidia cried. "Why did you do that?"* —Piers Anthony, *Cube Route.*>

6. *interj.* an expression of a strong feeling; see also ooo-eee[4], oooo[18].

<*Ooo, this guy is tough.* —Ross W. Greene, *The Explosive Child: A New Approach for Understanding and Parenting Easily Frustrated, Chronically Inflexible Children.*>

7. *interj.* an expression of anticipation, longing, or relish as from hunger.

<*She watched as they drove past the Café du Monde. "Ooo, I bet a beignet would be good for dessert."* —Sherriyn Kenyon, *Fantasy Lover.*>

8. *interj.* an expression of enthusiasm.

<*"Ooo, I'd like that, too!"* —Lynn Grabhorn, *Excuse Me, Your Life is Waiting: The Astonishing Power of Feelings.*>

9. *interj.* an expression of pain, as in James Joyce's *Ulysses*; see also oooo[3], ooooo[4], oooooo[3], ooooooo[11].

10. *interj.* oh.

<*Ooo, definitely something her hero would have done.* —Kinley MacGregor, *A Pirate of Her Own.*>

11. *n.* the hooting of an owl, as described in “More Than Words” by the New Zealand Ministry of Education.

12. *n.* an indecipherable syllable of a distant voice carried by the wind.

<“...ooo!” A distant voice like a feeble wave has curled up to die on our shore. The phrase, the word, was lost on the way and the result is an undecipherable message. Yet it strikes me like a blow. —Antoine de Saint-Exupery, *Wind, Sand and Stars*.>

13. *n.* the sound of the letter o, “like an owl makes” as described in Ponca City Public Schools curriculum.

ooo eee.

1. *n.* a wooing call.

<*Ooo eee, ooo eee baby / Won’t you let me take you on a sea cruise?* —Glenn Frey, “Sea Cruise.”>

2. *n.* part of a love spell chanted in the song “Witch Doctor” by David Seville.

ooo eee eee.

n. the cries of a pregnant mother in labor.

<*“Listen, I’ve got to deliver the baby breech. Lay back and breathe. You hear me?” “Ooo...eee... eee,” she screamed, the people on the tv screaming with her.* —Janice Daugharty, *Dark of the Moon*.>

ooo ooo ooo.

1. *n.* the call of the gibbon, as in the Goodies’ song “The Funky Gibbon.”

2. *n.* the song of the “white winged dove,” as in the Stevie Nicks song “Edge of Seventeen.”

ooo ooo ooo ooo ooo ooo ooo.

n. the song of the siren Lorelei of the Rocks, as recounted in the Chance Gardener song “Lorelei.”

ooo ooo oooo.

n. a belly laugh, as in *Bridges Out of Poverty: Strategies for Professionals and Communities* by Philip DeVol.

ooo oooo oooo.

interj. a sob of shock.

<*Minnie sat surveying me malevolently through a knot hole and plaintively crying “Ooo... Oooo... Oooo,” as if shocked to the core by my perfidy.* —Gerald Durrell, *A Zoo in My Luggage*.>

ooo-eee.

1. *interj.* an exclamation of wonder, as in *The Brave* by Robert Lipsyte; see also oooo-eee, oooo-eeee, ooooo-eeeee.

   <*She gobbled her buttered popcorn and stared at the screen, where a stripper was biting off a snake's head. "Ooo-eee," somebody said in the darkness.* —Roger Ebert, *I Hated, Hated, Hated This Movie.*>

2. *interj.* an expression of feeling dizzy or overwhelmed.

   <*Niels, old friend, I'm suddenly so dizzy... Ooo-eee! That pain in the back of my head just went off the scale! I feel like I can't hold on.* —Robert Hutchinson, *The Old Man of the Mountain.*>

3. *interj.* an expression of praise; a compliment.

   <*Ooo-eee, bright girl!* —Dana Cameron, *A Fugitive Truth: An Emma Fielding Mystery.*>

4. *interj.* an expression of strong feeling; see also ooo[6], oooo[18].

   <*Ooo-eee, I'm here to tell you, boy, it was one sorry hereafter.* —Reginald McKnight, *African American Wisdom.*>

5. *interj.* an expression of wide-eyed wonder.

   <*And now look at us? Ooo-eee! Taking rocket ships to work.* —William Jack Sibley, *Any Kind of Luck.*>

6. *n.* a pig's squeal.

   <*Ooo-eee! Ooo-eee! cried the pigs.* —George Ella Lyon, *Come a Tide.*>

7. *n.* a wooing call.

   <*Ooo-eee, ooo-eee my baby.* —Annie McLoone, "Ooo-Eee.">

ooo-eee-ooo.

n. an eerie, cosmic melody.

<*"To Match the Sun" is arguably the best song on the [Jane's Addiction] album [*Strays*], starting out with an eerie science fiction "ooo-eee-ooo" and transitioning into a sort of uplifting hard rock power ballad.* —Nicole Saidi, "Jane's Addiction Strays From Path to Greatness.">

ooo-eee-ooo-eee-ooo.

1. *n.* the spooky feeling of déjà vu.

   <*I suppose the kind of ooo-eee-ooo-eee-ooo factor that we get when we encounter the old deja vu is there in me.* —Kenneth Branagh, interviewed by Tom Hibbert, "What Makes Kenny Run," *Empire Magazine.*>

2. *n.* the theme from the film "The Good, the Bad, and the Ugly," as transcribed on amcgltd.com.

ooo-eee-ooo-eee-ooo-eee-ooo.

n. the first seven notes from the theme to the game show "Jeopardy," as transcribed on EchoJournal.org.

ooo-oo-oo.

n. the sound of the letter O.

<*We'll open a little hole at the end of the round egg to show how the O-noise runs out all thin, ooo-oo-oo.* —Rudyard Kipling, *Just So Stories.*>

Ooo-ooo ooo-oooo OOOOO.

interj. a monkey-like shriek.

<*Suddenly, Mr. Krupp sprang off his desk and began swinging from the fluorescent light fixtures. "Ooo-ooo ooo-oooo OOOOO!" he shrieked, leaping from one side of the room to the other.* —Dav Pilkey, *The Adventures of Captain Underpants: An Epic Novel.*>

ooo-ooo-ooo-ooo-ooo.

n. the mournful, repetitive call of the White-Faced Storm-Petrel bird, uttered in breeding colonies, as described in *The Handbook of Bird Identification for Europe and the Western Palearctic* by Mark Beaman.

ooo-ooo-ooo-ooo-ooo-eee.

interj. an expression of carrying a heavy load, as in the Grand Funk Railroad song "Responsibility" and the Chicago song "Wishing You Were Here."

ooo-oooo-ooooo.

n. a dog's full-bodied howl, as in response to a baby's piercing cry; see also ooooo[25].

<*"Ooo-oooo-ooooo!" Paws outstretched, Moondoggie lowered his head, dug in his heels and refused to budge. Ooo-oooo-ooooo!* —Suzy Pissuti, *Say Uncle.*>

OoOo.

1. *interj.* the moan of a ghost.

<*She yanked, and the ghost lurched forward. "OoOo!" it complained.* —Piers Anthony, *Xone of Contention: A Xanth Novel.*>

2. *n.* mental turmoil; the pounding of a headache.

<*"OoOo!! OoOo!!" There's something struggling in my head, trying to punch my eyeballs out from the inside.* —Tim Krabbe, *The Rider.*>

oooo.

1. *interj.* a cry of excitement.

<*The mail! The mail is here! Oooo!* —Harlan Coben, *Tell No One.*>

2. *interj.* a cry of mock horror.

<*“Oooo!” Wilhelm St. Guillaume shrilled in mock horror as he teased a handful of Anouk’s gleaming soft raven hair with extravagant flourishes.* —Judith Gould, *Never Too Rich.*>

3. *interj.* a cry of pain; see also ooo[9], ooooo[4], oooooo[3], ooooooo[11].

<*Creslin shrugs. “Oooo...” His shoulder indicates that the gesture was unwise.* —L. E. Modesitt Jr., *The Towers of the Sunset.*>

4. *interj.* a gentle chastisement.

<*Her laughter tickled in his ear. “Oooo... can this be jealousy I hear in my lord’s voice? For his own son?”* —Marsha Canham, *The Last Arrow.*>

5. *interj.* a goblin’s cry of outrage, as in *Man From Mundania* by Piers Anthony.

6. *interj.* a romantic utterance; oh.

<*So, she’s in her hive and all these male bees are just buzzing around saying, “Oooo baby, I feel lucky tonight.”* —Ellen Degeneres, *My Point... And I Do Have One.*>

7. *interj.* a sarcastic response.

<*“Oooo,” she said in a less than impressed voice.* —Sherrilyn Kenyon, *Dance With the Devil.*>

8. *interj.* a sensual moan, as during lovemaking.

<*Oooo. Make it last, baby.* —Stacy Reed, “Night Talk,” *Herotica 4: A New Collection of Erotic Writing By Women.*>

9. *interj.* a shriek of gaiety, as when Amanda accidentally “baptizes” herself with lemonade in *The Glass Menagerie* by Tennessee Williams.

10. *interj.* a sound of disapproval.

<*“Oooo,” Sister Mary Ursula said as though Wulfgar had said the one thing she dreaded more than hearing that scrying was about to take place.* —Vivian Vande Velde, *Heir Apparent.*>

11. *interj.* a sound of disgust.

<*Oooo, Momma, he stinks.* —Katherine Paterson, *Bridge to Terabithia.*>

12. *interj.* a squeal of delight.

<*“Oooo, wonderful!”* she exclaimed, delighted. “This is just perfect!” —Piers Anthony, *Xanth 14: Question Quest.*>

13. *interj.* a wail of tearful unhappiness.

<*“Oooo!” the face wailed, and the tears flowed so copiously that they started to pool on the floor.* —Piers Anthony, *Cube Route.*>

14. *interj.* an affirmation.

<*Did it ever occur to you that you don’t know what the hell you’re talking about?” “Oooo!” He*

smiled. "That occurs to me just about all the time." —Mary McGarry Morris, *A Dangerous Woman.*>

15. *interj.* an appreciative exclamation, as in response to a drink of fine ale.

<*Buffett drank down three good swallows. "Oooo," he said slowly. "Jubilation."* —Jeffery Deaver, *Bloody River Blues.*>

16. *interj.* an ecstatic squeal.

<*Her two schoolfriends were ecstatic. "Oooo! Are you going to? Are you really going to?"* —Alan Booth, *The Roads to Sata: A 2000-Mile Walk Through Japan.*>

17. *interj.* an expression anticipating a bad conclusion; an acknowledgment that aggression has been instigated.

<*So Jack's holding out on you big-time! Oooo, not good, Jack.* —Sarah Andrews, *Killer Dust.*>

18. *interj.* an expression of a strong feeling; see also ooo[6], ooo-eee[4].

<*Oooo, it's the most romantic story, really.* —Julia London, *Wicked Angel.*>

19. *interj.* an expression of a sudden revelation or remembrance.

<*While she was drawing the vats and the connecting hoses, she suddenly cringed and exclaimed, "Oooo! I just remembered. I put my hands in that water."* —Dolores Cannon, *The Custodians: Beyond Abduction.*>

20. *interj.* an expression of embarrassment.

<*"And then you ring for the nurse to take it [the bedpan] away." "You mean she sees it? Oooo, how embarrassing."* —Danny Santiago, *Famous All Over Town.*>

21. *interj.* an expression of sadness.

<*"Oooo," said Rose, furrowing her brow and tilting her head, as if the news was very sad.* —Scott Spencer, *Endless Love.*>

22. *interj.* an expression of shame.

<*"Oooo," Pikel moaned, ashamed of his perceived laziness.* —R. A. Salvatore, *Night Masks.*>

23. *interj.* an expression of shock.

<*"Oooo, what you said!" the pebble exclaimed. "Wash out your mouth with soapstone!"* —Piers Anthony, *Centaur Aisle.*>

24. *interj.* oh.

<*Oooo I'm so glad.* —Toni Morrison, *Love.*>

25. *n.* a chilling cry of mourning; see also oooo oooo[1].

<*"Oooo," she wailed and the back of his neck went cold.* —Peter Straub, *Ghost Story*.>

26. *n.* a melancholy moan.

<*The other dwarf, his older brother, shrugged and gave a plaintive, "Oooo" sound.* —R. A. Salvatore, *The Thousand Orcs*.>

27. *n.* a sound of relief.

<*He was reading the Wall Street Journal so the coast was clear. Oooo.* —Harlan Coben, *Drop Shot*.>

28. *n.* a vocalist's crooning.

<*We've been doing this for so long, we know what "oooo's" go where.* —Lynn Grabhorn, *Excuse Me, Your Life is Waiting: The Astonishing Power of Feelings*.>

29. *n.* an ultra-fine grade of steel wool.

<*Slight surface scratches may be buffed with dry oooo steel wool.* —Cheryl Mendelson, *Home Comforts: The Art and Science of Keeping House*.>

30. *n.* the scarcely audible call of the Chatham Island Pigeon, as described in *The Complete Guide to Antarctic Wildlife: Birds and Marine Mammals of the Antarctic Continent and the Southern Ocean* by Hadoram Shirlhai.

31. *n.* the scream of the Swamp Gaboon, as in *The Last of the Really Great Whangdoodles* by Julie Andrews Edwards.

oooo eee.

n. the haunting call of the snowy owl.

<*Over and over / at dinner she calls, oooo ... eee.* —Frances Mayes, "Sestina For the Owl," *The Discovery of Poetry: A Field Guide to Reading and Writing Poems*.>

oooo eeeee.

n. the wailing winds of a typhoon.

<*He stood in the pilothouse, safe from the flying spray, his elbow hooked around the captain's chair, and grinned into the teeth of the typhoon, which wailed louder than ever, "OOOO! EEEEE!"* —Herman Wouk, *The Caine Mutiny: A Novel*.>

oooo ooee eeee.

n. an expression of dread upon finding oneself stranded in a strange place at night, as in the song "Cross Road Blues" by Robert Johnson, as transcribed in *Trouble in Mind* by Leon F. Litwack.

oooo ooee eeeee.

n. an expression of "the very pain of existence and the anguish of alienation from which music sets us free," in the lyrics to "I Just Can't Be Satisfied" by

Muddy Waters, transcribed by Paul Gordon in *Tragedy After Nietzsche: Rapturous Superabundance*.

oooo oooo.

1. *n.* a grievous moan, as in *Paul* by Walter Wangerin Jr.; see also oooo[25].

2. *n.* a negative response.

<*He scowled, shaking his head no. "Oooo, oooo," he growled.* —Ben Mikaelsen, *Petey.*>

Oooo Ooooo Oooooooo.

n. Tarzan's yell, as described in "Marketplace" by Bhavna S. Doegar.

oooo-ee.

n. a short, forlorn whistle of a train, as in the blues song "Blues in the Night" by Harold Arlen; see oooo-ee-a-oooo-ee.

oooo-ee-a-oooo-ee.

n. the forlorn whistle of a train, reminiscent of a blues song melody.

<*Now the rain's a fallin', hear the train a callin', oooo-ee / Hear the lonesome whistle blowin' 'cross the trestle, oooo-ee / Oooo-ee-a-oooo-ee, ol' clickety-clack / Comes echoing back the blues in the night.* —Harold Arlen, "Blues in the Night.">

oooo-eee.

interj. an exclamation of wonder; see also ooo-eee[1], oooo-eeee, ooooo-eeeee.

<*She looked really interested then and wanted to know which of the guys in line was mine, and when I pointed to Michael she went, "Oooo-eee, he's a looker," which filled me with internal pride but also made me feel like smacking her.* —Meg Cabot, *Project Princess.*>

oooo-eeee.

interj. an exclamation of wonder; see also ooo-eee[1], oooo-eee, ooooo-eeeee.

<*"Oooo-eeee, I tell you," he suddenly burst out, and if he had been alone he would have left it there, but with Junior he had to finish it. "That was something else."* —Clark Blaise, *Pittsburgh Stories.*>

oooo-eeee-oooo.

interj. the ominous utterance of the Mud Monster from the deep.

<*"Oooo-eeee-oooo. You'll never escape the Mud Monster from the deep." John Steiner, his hands dripping with watered-down clay, chased Fiona around the room.* —Ann M. Martin, *Claudia and the New Girl.*>

oooo-eeeee.

n. the yelp of a wolf, as described in *Stray Sheep* by Tatsutoshi Nomura.

OOOoo.

interj. an expression of excitement, as when the lights go out in the school auditorium in *Arthur's Thanksgiving* by Marc Brown.

ooooo.

1. *adv.* truly; indeed.

<*Ooooo, I was the happiest soul going down that highway.* —Steve Cheseborough, *Blues Traveling: The Holy Sites of Delta Blues.*>

2. *interj.* a cooing over something cute, like a nest of darling calico kittens in *Hard Ball* by Will Weaver; see also ooooooo[23].

3. *interj.* a coy, romantic murmur.

<*She looked right back, but with romance in her beady black eyes, and murmured coyly, "Oooooo!"* —George Selden, *Harry Cat's Pet Puppy.*>

4. *interj.* a cry of pain; see also ooo[9], oooo[3], oooooo[3], ooooooo[11].

<*Ooooo, I am bursting apart at the seams.* —John Ross, *Murdered by Capitalism: A Memoir of 150 Years of Life and Death on the American Left.*>

5. *interj.* a lusty expression of approval, as of a person's looks.

<*Sweeping her spaghetti-length lashes up and down Rick's body, Vivien cooed, "Ooooo,* nice." —LaVyrle Spencer, *A Heart Speaks.*>

6. *interj.* a moan of sensual pleasure.

<*I rewarded Mary with a massage. "Ooooo. That feels wonderful. Some more there. Yes."* —Eric Brende, *Better Off: Flipping the Switch on Technology.*>

7. *interj.* a sarcastic expression.

<*Ooooo, brave words from the land of the walking dead.* —Stephen Hunter, *Point of Impact.*>

8. *interj.* a sound affirming the contrary.

<"*Oh,* you *aren't fat," the stylish lady said. "Ooooo I am too," Mrs. Turpin said.* —Flannery O'Connor, "Revelation," *Flannery O'Connor: Collected Works.*>

9. *interj.* a sound indicating a rush of excitement, as by sports fans in *Shoot for the Hoop* by Matt Christopher.

<When Dawn showed up, Mark felt a rush of excitement, saying to himself, "Ooooo. There she is!" —Savitri L. Bess, *The Path of the Mother: With the Divine Guidance of the Holy Mother, Ammachi.*>

10. *interj.* a squeal of awed delight, as in *And Eternity* by Piers Anthony.

<*Jenny clapped her hands, letting out an "ooooo" of delight.* —Susan Carroll, *Winterbourne.*>

11. *interj.* a thrilled exclamation.

<*"Ooooo!" Knut and Silhouette cried together, putting five O's into it. It was hard to tell who was more thrilled.* —Piers Anthony, *Cube Route.*>

12. *interj.* an exclamation marking a realization; see also ooo[4], oooooo[15].

<*So do you get that implication? Matt: Ooooo!* —Peter Ralston, *Ancient Wisdom New Spirit: Investigations into the Nature of "Being."*>

13. *interj.* an exclamation of wide-eyed wonder, as at a majestic landscape; see also oooooo[2].

<*The color of the mountains, Michael! Ooooo, look at the color of the mountains!* —Ward Just, *A Soldier of the Revolution.*>

14. *interj.* an expression of a shiver of righteous indignation.

<*Mummie shivered. "Ooooo, it makes my blood run cold."* —Michael Lee West, *Crazy Ladies: A Novel.*>

15. *interj.* an expression of marvel.

<*"Look, Master Frito," said Spam, pointing up the road. "Elfs, lots of 'em. Ooooo, I must be dreaming. I wish the old Fatlip could see me now."* —Harvard Lampoon Staff, *Bored of the Rings: A Parody of J.R.R. Tolkien's The Lord of the Rings.*>

16. *interj.* an expression of mock fright, as in *A World of Thieves: A Novel* by James Carlos Blake.

<*"Ooooo. Sounds so scary. Look at me! I'm tremblin' all over."* —Charles R. Swindoll, *Moses: A Man of Selfless Dedication.*>

17. *interj.* an expression of shock, as from a cold temperature.

<*Ooooo... it was so cold out here!* —James D. Doss, *The Night Visitor: A Shaman Mystery.*>

18. *interj.* an indication that one is unimpressed.

<*"Ooooo," she said, her back still turned and sounding unimpressed.* —Elizabeth Haydon, *Prophecy: Child of Earth.*>

19. *interj.* an involuntary exclamation, as from a blow to the body.

<*"Ooooo!" The involuntary exclamation was forced from him, expelled by the force of the slingstone that had hit his side as he had twisted inside the dark passage.* —L. E. Modesitt Jr., *The Forever Hero.*>

20. *interj.* the growl of a simmering rage.

<*I look away from her, furious. Ooooo, that little Miss Cuchifrita! Wait till we land—I'm gonna get her back good in Hollywood!* —Deborah Gregory, *Cheetah Girls Supa-Dupa Sparkle.*>

21. *n.* a chant from the Igbo Folk Epic from Sub-Saharan Africa, as discussed in *Traditional Storytelling Today: An International Sourcebook* by Margaret Read MacDonald.

22. *n.* a chiding remark, as to someone exhibiting a lack of patience.

<*Ooooo, testy.* —Terry Osborne, *Sightlines: The View of a Valley Through the Voice of Depression.*>

23. *n.* a man's romantic wooing, "like some dirty kind of animal," as described in *Barrios and Borderlands: Cultures of Latinos and Latinas in the United States* by Denis Lynn Daly Heyck; see also eeeeee[18].

24. *n.* a moaning sound preceding tears.

<*I wanted to cry, but all that came out was an "ooooo" sound. I "ooooo"-ed for days.* —Deborah Howe, *Bunnicula: A Rabbit-Tale of Mystery.*>

25. *n.* the sound of "a dog baying at the moon" (Shelby Foote, qtd. in *Shelby Foote: A Writer's Life* by C. Stuart Chapman); see also ooo-oooo-ooooo.

26. *n.* the spooky moan of the Grim Reaper; see also oooooo oooooo.

<*It was staring me in the face—"Ooooo"—the Man of Death ... had come spooking after me to moan at my mother's doormat.* —Jack Kerouac, *Doctor Sax: Faust Part Three.*>

27. *n.* the toot of a tugboat whistle.

<*[T]he sky was clear and bright with stars and moon and a light breeze was blowing and you could hear the tugs in the harbor chugging and the deep ooooo from their whistles floated across the bay and rolled down 2nd avenue.* —Hubert Selby, *Last Exit to Brooklyn.*>

ooooo oooooooooo.

n. a loud moaning like that of a tortured spirit.

<*Soon a soft moaning sound floated on the wind. "Ooooo ... oooooooooo."* —Mary-Kate & Ashley Olsen, *Two of a Kind #29: Love-Set-Match.*>

OOooo-ee.

interj. a "long high-pitched, thrilling scream" of a surfer reacting to a powerful ocean swell, as in *Bully: Does Anyone Deserve to Die* by Jim Schultze.

ooooo-eeeee.

interj. an exclamation of wonder; see also ooo-eee[1], oooo-eee, oooo-eeee.

<*"Ooooo-eeeee!" yelled Pè Gerard.* —Frances Temple, *Tonight, the Sea.*>

ooooo-oo.

n. the toot of a train's whistle.

<*[H]e was making a chugging noise in his throat like some kind of engine, and as he turned the corner he let out a piercing "Ooooo-oo" (it was a train whistle, he told her afterwards) so he did not hear her call.* —Mary Norton, *The Borrowers.*>

ooooo-ooooo.

n. a chant sung by warriors in a bonding ceremony to prepare for battle.

<[W]e swayed back and forth, heads leaning to one side. "Ooooo-ooooo," we whispered in a low growl. "Ooooo-ooooo," the sound came out from deep inside, sending a shiver along the line of arms. —Tobias Schneebaum, *Keep the River on Your Right.*>

ooooo-oooooo.

n. a long whisper of astonishment.

<*[A] flash of flame appeared between my hands and shrieks of astonishment went up and long whispers of Ooooo-oooooo and two fingers reached out and closed themselves on the fire and a shout of pain gave it reality, and they backed away an instant but returned and I lit another. Ooooo-oooooo, they whispered.* —Tobias Schneebaum, *Keep the River on Your Right.*>

ooooo-oooooooo-ooooooo.

n. a headhunter chief's tender whisper to a sacred syrinx aruanus shell, as in *Where the Spirits Dwell: An Odyssey in the New Guinea Jungle* by Tobias Schneelbaum.

oooooo.

n. lots of hugs, as written at the bottom of a letter, usually alongside XXXXXX (kisses), as discussed in *Brief Encounters* by Emily Coleman.

OOOooo.

interj. a moan of sensual pleasure, as in *Hand I Fan With* by Tina McElroy Ansa.

OOoooo.

n. the rush felt by a junkie who has just shot up.

<*OOoooo then the delicious itches began instantaneously all over—not just my nose, but in my chin, cheeks, eyes, head, body—rush after rush of leaden breath pressure annihilating the solar plexus.* —Jan Kerouac, *Baby Driver.*>

OoOoOo.

interj. a moan of seasickness, as in *Vale of the Vole* by Piers Anthony.

oooooo.

1. *interj.* a coo of appreciation, as over receiving a glass of orange juice in bed in *New York Dead* by Stuart Woods.

2. *interj.* a coyote-like cry of wide-eyed wonder, as at a majestic landscape; see also ooooo[13].

   <*Like Valley of Fire, [Red Rock Canyon is] a surreal and lovely landscape of outer-space-like rock formations, perfect for hiking or even just driving through while emitting cries of "oooooo!!!"* —Mary Herczog, *Las Vegas for Dummies, Second Edition.*>

3. *interj.* a cry of pain; see also ooo[9], oooo[3], ooooo[4], ooooooo[11].

<*Look at my head, it's all bloody and cut and—oooooo, it hurts!* —Victor Villasenor, *Thirteen Senses: A Memoir.*>

4. *interj.* a cry of whimsy, of being swept up in a fantasy.

<*He grinned when she began to waltz around the room. "Oooooo, and I feel like a princess," she sang.* —Mary Kay Remick, *Searching for Blanche: A Novel.*>

5. *interj.* a long moan meant to sound spooky.

<*"You're not scaring me," said the girl. "Oooooo," moaned Rose. "Oooooo," echoed Lila.* —Joan Holub, *Tatiana Comes to America: An Ellis Island Story.*>

6. *interj.* a moan of pity, sympathy.

<*She... heaves a big, delicious sigh of emotional support and, trying to raise my morale says, "Oooooo, Huck, you poor boy!"* —Timothy Leary, *Surfing the Conscious Nets: A Graphic Novel.*>

7. *interj.* a nervous reaction at the possibility of the supernatural.

<*"Well, I know how this sounds," I said, "but I do think there is some kind of... I don't know... spirit or something living in the flat." A little laugh escaped him, and then he made a scary face and an oooooo sound, antics that were clearly nervous reactions, not intended to ridicule.* —Dennis McFarland, *A Face at the Window.*>

8. *interj.* a noise made on talk shows "in an effort to spur the confrontation on," as in the play *...Do Not Collect $200* by J. Wiltz (*Ten Minute Plays From Oxford*, edited by Neil White).

9. *interj.* a sound meaning "how sexy," as in *Document Zippo* by L. A. Ruocco.

10. *interj.* a sound of self-deprecation.

<*Oooooo / I know / how weak / I am.* —Fr. Jon Bruder, *My Search for Life's Meaning—I Found My God... In My Heart...*>

11. *interj.* a star-struck exclamation, as at receiving a phone call from Frank Sinatra in *Paul McCartney: Many Years From Now* by Barry Miles.

12. *interj.* a teasing, taunting call of children, as in *Drinking Coffee Elsewhere* by ZZ Packer.

13. *interj.* a wincing moan meaning "that isn't good," as in *Grave Peril* by Jim Butcher.

14. *interj.* an embarrassed reply, as to an intimate secret from a confidant, in *The Great Pint-Pulling Olympiad: A Mostly Irish Farce* by Roger Boylan.

15. *interj.* an exclamation marking a realization; see also ooo[4], ooooo[12].

<*Oooooo, I've got an idea.* —Ellen Degeneres, *My Point... and I Do Have One.*>

16. *interj.* an exclamation of being overwhelmed.

<*"Oooooo," said Charles. "I really must be going. This is all very delicious, but it's not something for my tender ears."* —Earl Emerson, *Portland Laughter.*>

17. *interj.* an exclamation of praise.

<*Oooooo! You're getting good.* —Bobbi McCutcheon, *Father Mars, Mother Earth.*>

18. *interj.* an exclamation of titillation.

<*Listening in on someone else's intimacies, [Oscar] Wilde implies, wouldn't have you going "Oooooo!" but "Ugh."* —Regina Berreca, *Too Much of a Good Thing is Wonderful.*>

19. *interj.* an exclamation of wonder or surprise, as from a crowd.

<*There was an "Oooooo!" from the crowd. People jumped back in surprise.* —Anne Rivers Siddons, *Nora, Nora: A Novel.*>

20. *interj.* an expression of "feigned awe," as in *Robin Cousins* by Martha Lowder Kimball.

21. *interj.* an expression of a sudden revelation.

<*Oooooo, now that's a plus I hadn't considered.* —Timothy Wade Huntley, *Earthgame.*>

22. *interj.* an expression of awe, as when marveling over the abilities of a gifted individual.

<*When I told people I was writing a book on self-esteem they looked at me with awe and said, "Oooooo!" and sighed deeply like I possessed some cherished gift.* —Lindsey Hall, *Self-Esteem Tools for Recovery.*>

23. *interj.* the desolate cry of uniform buildings which are constructed side by side in a monotonous fashion, out of harmony with their surroundings.

<*If buildings are the letters of the alphabet they are not used to make coherent words but to utter the desolate cries of AAAAA! Or OOOOOO!* —Gordon Cullen, qtd. in *Architectures: Modernish and After* by Andrew Ballantyne.>

24. *interj.* the moan of a bellyache from "stinkin' meatballs" in the play *Not About Nightingales* by Tennessee Williams.

25. *interj.* the mocking voice of a higher power speaking through a channel, as in response to a howling for help.

<*One of the gods spoke back through Bellarose: "Oooooo! Bubble bubble, toil and nothin' but trouble!"* —Vance Cornell, *Indian Summer: The Return of the Myth of the Running Man.*>

26. *interj.* the sound of a feigned swooning.

<*Mrs. Valentine Biggs put fingertips to brow and said, "Oooooo," seeming about to swoon in the manner of Scarlett O'Hara.* —Jon Hassler, *Simon's Night.*>

<*Oooooo! Mercy me, I do believe I'll faint!* —Vicki Grove, *The Starplace.*>

27. *n.* a sound of "fawning admiration," as in *Suitably Modern: Making Middle-Class Culture in a New Consumer Society* by Mark Liechty.

oooooo ooooo.

interj. a wail of wanton depravity.

<*The aide was the first to break the silence in the banquet room. "Oooooo, ooooo," he wailed, "hit me, beat me, make me write bad checks!"* —Christine Wiltz, *The Last Madam: A Life in the New Orleans Underworld.*>

oooooo oooooo.

n. the howl of "Death with the head of a dog," as in the poem "Fin Wè Mò" by Danielle Legros Georges (*Maroon*); see also ooooo[26].

oooooo-eeeeee-oooooo-eeeeee-oooooo.

n. the wavering tones of a piercing, unearthly howl, like the combined shrieks of a departed multitude.

<*All of a sudden a noise pierced the air—a howl, a singing screech that started low and got ever higher and louder. No living creature was behind that sound. It reached a peak of height and loudness, and wavered there between two tones, rising and falling, oooooo-eeeeee-oooooo-eeeeee-oooooo, on and on and on, like the scream of the ghosts of every dead person ever buried in Orange County, or the final shrieks of all those killed by the bombs.* —Kim Stanley Robinson, *The Wild Shore: Three Californias.*>

OOOoooo.

interj. a moan of appreciation, as for a delicious drink.

<*I'd go in there in the wintertime, take a cup, and get a cup full of that ice-cold kraut juice. OOOoooo, it was good. Lot better than this canned kraut that you buy today.* —Joseph Earl Dabney, *Smokehouse Ham, Spoon Bread & Scuppernong Wine: The Folklore and Art of Southern Appalachian Cooking.*>

ooooooo.

1. *interj.* a collective reaction of approval, as from an audience discussed in *Hello Darling, Are You Working?* by Rupert Everett.

   <*A deep "Ooooooo" went through the crowd. They approved.* —Anna L. Waldo, *Sacajawea.*>

2. *interj.* a croon of gentle teasing.

   <*"Ooooooo," she crooned, "looks like you've got an admirer."* —Emma Kallok, *Diary of Chickabiddy Baby.*>

3. *interj.* a cry of consternation.

   <*Ooooooo, doggone that show-off bird. He fooled me again.* —Judith Martin, *Dandelion*, from the anthology *Plays Children Love: Volume II.*>

4. *interj.* a cry of desperation and humiliation, as in *Warriors Don't Cry: A Searing Memoir of the Battle to Integrate Little Rock's Central High* by Melba Pattillo Beals.

5. *interj.* a cry of dismay.

<*He remembered ... [h]ow the lariat, always kept on the front seat of the car coiled neatly, had opened across his father's chest as if to spell out one last cry of dismay: ooooooo.* —Gretel Ehrlich, *Heart Mountain.*>

6. *interj.* a cry of euphoria, as in *Winnie-The-Pooh* when Piglet flies into the air while inside Kanga's pocket (A. A. Milne, *The Complete Takes & Poems of Winnie-The-Pooh.*>

7. *interj.* a ghostly moan.

   <*They didn't seem, well, ghostly. No going "Ooooooo" or trying to scare anyone.* —Diane Duane, *A Wizard Abroad: The Fourth Book in the Young Wizards Series.*>

8. *interj.* a gleeful exclamation, as upon witnessing the splendor of a rich person's house.

   <*"Ooooooo, Mama, can you believe this?" Freda asked, as she glided through one room after another. "Just don't touch nothing, girl, this shit ain't fake."* —Terry McMillan, *Mama.*>

9. *interj.* a moan of agony, anguish; the realization that something is "horribly, painfully wrong," as in *Dark Sapphire* by Lisa Jackson.

10. *interj.* a moan of indecision, as in *The Book of Sorrows* by Walter Wangerin Jr.

11. *interj.* a moan of pain, as from being shaken by one's hair in *Finnegan's Week* by Joseph Wambaugh; see also ooo[9], oooo[3], ooooo[4], oooooo[3].

12. *interj.* a shuddering reaction to being sprayed with water, as in *What's Eating Gilbert Grape* by Peter Hedges.

13. *interj.* a warrior's cry.

    <*When the heat makes the bamboo explode, the warriors stamp their feet, cry Ooooooo, and move to the battlefield in single file, prancing and singing along the way.* —Marvin Harris, *Cows, Pigs, Wars, and Witches: The Riddles of Culture.*>

14. *interj.* an expression of marvel.

    <*Ooooooo, Nicky, that's a strange one.* —Stephen Hunter, *Point of Impact.*>

15. *interj.* the Russian expression for "whee!" as discussed in *Hear! Here!* by Michele Slung.

16. *interj.* the sound of vomiting; an expression of disappointment, as by a crowd reacting to a bad golf swing.

    <*I did a stroke and hit my toe and knocked the ball straight the opposite way. Everybody went, "Ooooooo." It sounded like a big upchuck.* —Charlie Jones, *Be The Ball: Golf Instruction Book For the Mind.*>

17. *n.* a beseeching expression.

    <*Come on, talk... ooooooo just tell us!* —Marvin Sutton, *Santa & Marvin.*>

18. *n.* a command to a horse.

<*The knight rode on the horse's back and shouted: "Ooooooo!" and the horse neighed "Eiiiiii!"* —Yoram Kaniuk, *Adam Resurrected.*>

19. *n.* a gentle chastisement.

<*"Ooooooo," Rhonda teased. "Big Stud gets cranks when he don't get enough sleep."* —Sharolett Koenig, *Plight of the Children.*>

20. *n.* a groan of anger, as "issued out of... trembling lips, between gnashing, gritted teeth," in *Night Masks* by R. A. Salvatore.

21. *n.* a profound and drawn-out sigh, as in *The Fallen Fortress* by R. A. Salvatore.

22. *n.* an imitation of the song of the humpback whale: a tremulous, bass groan, "ululating, elegaic, and otherworldly" (Brenda Peterson, *Build Me an Ark: A Life With Animals.*)

23. *n.* cute; see also ooooo[2].

<*She has milky brown skin and huge brown eyes, the kind artistic people draw when they are doodling puppies and other small animals and they want to make you say, "Ooooooo. For CUTE."* —Jane Kurtz, *Memories of Sun: Stories of Africa and America.*>

24. *n.* the whistling sound of the wind.

<*[T]his was the only one that had the wind whistling around it, making an Oooooo sound.* —Lyn Buchanan, *The Seventh Sense: The Secrets of Remote Viewing as Told by a "Psychic Spy" for the U.S. Military.*>

25. *n.* the wolfish howl of a mental patient.

<*Passing the mental hospital located in the town, they stopped to stare at the building, whereupon, in the quiet hush of twilight, they could hear the patients' wolfish screams echoing from inside. "Oooooo," one patient wailed. The voices stayed with Sylvia.* —Paul Alexander, *Rough Magic: A Biography of Sylvia Plath.*>

ooooooo-eee.

interj. a child's squeal during a game of tag, as in *Untangling My Chopsticks: A Culinary Sojourn in Kyoto* by Victoria Abbott Riccardi.

oooOOOooo.

interj. a howling sound of excitement.

<*I danced anxiously about on the sidelines saying 'oooOOOooo' as they struggled to deal with the creature.* —Katherine, *My First Dungeon Experience.*>

ooooooooo EEEEEEEEEEE eeeeeeeeeeeee.

(also Ooo EEEEEEE, ooooo EEEEEE.) *n.* the pained wailing of the elements.

<*It was a deep, sorrowful whine coming from nowhere and everywhere, a noise above the crashing of the waves and the creaking of the ship and the roar of the black-smoking stacks, "Ooooooooo EEEEEEEEEEE eeeeeeeeeeeee," a universal noise as though the sea and the air were in pain, "Ooo EEEEEEE, ooooo EEEEEE—"* —Herman Wouk, *The Caine Mutiny: A Novel.*>

oooooooooo-ooooo.

n. the endless spew of cruel language in Hell.

<*For eternity we'll sit across that big campfire of Hell and he'll say cruel things to me and it will be his torture and mine. Oooooooo-ooooo...*" —Edward Lewis Wallant, *The Tenants of Moonbloom.*>

oooooooooo oooooooooooo ooooooooooooooooo.

interj. a whoop of "maximum derision," as in the novel *A Man in Full* by Tom Wolfe.

oooooooooooo.

n. the "lamenting note" of a "long-drawn-out howl" of someone both drunk and homesick, as in *Psalm at Journey's End: A Novel* by Erik Fosnes Hansen; see also ooooooooouuuuuu.

ooooooooouuuuuu.

n. the pained bellow of someone both drunk and homesick, as in *Psalm at Journey's End: A Novel* by Erik Fosnes Hansen; see also oooooooooooo.

Ooua.

n. a populated place in Mali.

Oouay.

n. a populated place in the Gueckedou region of Guinea.

Ooy.

n. a populated place in the Gelderland region of the Netherlands.

Ooya.

1. *n.* a populated place in Burkina Faso.

2. *n.* a stream in Central African Republic.

Ou.

1. *n.* a populated place in South Korea.

2. *n.* a populated place in the Solomon Islands.

3. *n.* an intermittent stream in the Cape Province region of South Africa.

ou.

n. an expression of concession.

Oua.

1. *n.* a mountain in the Guera region of Chad; a populated place in the Moyen-Chari region of Chad; a stream in Chad.

2. *n.* a populated place in Burkina Faso.

3. *n.* a populated place in Central African Republic; a stream in Central African Republic.

4. *n.* a populated place in Mali.

5. *n.* a populated place in the Woleu-Ntem region of Gabon; a stream in the Woleu-Ntem region of Gabon.

6. *n.* a populated place in the Zambezia region of Mozambique.

7. *n.* a stream in Cameroon.

8. *n.* a stream in the Beyla, Macenta and Nzerekore regions of Guinea.

Oua Ia.
n. a stream in New Caledonia.

Oua Oua.
1. *n.* a hill in Mauritania.

2. *n.* a populated place in the Saint-Louis region of Senegal.

3. *n.* a stream in Ghana.

4. *n.* a stream in Togo.

oua oua.
n. a baby's chatter in *The Cherry Orchard* by Anton Chekhov.

oua oua oua.
n. a muttered "good day," as in "A Family" by Guy de Maupassant.

Oua Ouiou.
n. a stream in New Caledonia.

Oua Ya.
n. a stream in the Nzerekore region of Guinea.

Oua-Oue.
n. a populated place in New Caledonia.

Ouai.
1. *n.* a locality in New Caledonia; a mountain in New Caledonia.

2. *n.* a populated place in the Fria region of Guinea.

3. *n.* a well in Algeria.

Ouaie.
n. a rock in the Batha region of Chad.

Ouao.
n. a populated place in Benin.

Ouaou.
n. a stream in the Kissidougou region of Guinea.

Ouaoua.
1. *n.* a populated place in the Guera region of Chad.
2. *n.* a stream in Central African Republic.
3. *n.* a stream in the Mali region of Guinea.

Ouaouiye.
n. a populated place in the Al Hasakah and Ar Raqqah regions of Syria.

Ouaya.
1. *n.* a populated place in Mali.
2. *n.* a populated place in the Biltine and Lac regions of Chad.

Ouaye.
n. a populated place in the Mayo-Kebbi region of Chad.

Ouayo.
n. a ridge in New Caledonia.

Ouayou.
n. a populated place in Burkina Faso.

Oue.
1. *n.* a hill in New Zealand; a populated place in New Zealand.
2. *n.* a populated place in Burkina Faso.
3. *n.* a populated place in Cameroon.
4. *n.* a populated place in New Caledonia.
5. *n.* a populated place in the Gueckedou region of Guinea; a stream in the Kissidougou region of Guinea.
6. *n.* a stream in Central African Republic.

Oue Oue.

1. *n.* a stream in Djibouti.

2. *n.* a stream in the Macenta region of Guinea.

Oue Ya.

n. a stream in the Nzerekore and Yomou regions of Guinea.

Oue‘a.

n. a populated place in the Djibouti region of Djibouti.

Oue-Oue.

n. a well in the Borkou-Ennedi-Tibe region of Chad.

Ouei.

n. a peak in New Caledonia.

Oueoi.

n. an ancient Tuscan city in Etruria, as discussed in “A Collection of Word Oddities and Trivia” by Jeff Miller.

Oueou.

n. a ridge in New Caledonia.

Ouey.

n. a hill in the Guera region of Chad.

Oueya.

1. *n.* a populated place in Cameroon.

2. *n.* a populated place in the Nzerekore and Yomou regions of Guinea; a stream in the Beyla region of Guinea.

Oueya Oue.

n. a stream in New Caledonia.

Oueye.

n. a populated place in the Gueckedou region of Guinea.

Oui.

1. *n.* a populated place in Benin.

2. *n.* a populated place in Burkina Faso.

3. *n.* a populated place in the Nimba region of Liberia.

4. *n.* a stream in Central African Republic.

5. *n.* an island in New Caledonia.

Ouia.

1. *n.* a populated place in French Polynesia.

2. *n.* a populated place in Mali.

3. *n.* an island in the Ha apai region of Tonga.

Ouio.

n. a stream in New Caledonia.

Ouiya.

n. a populated place in Central African Republic.

Ouiye.

n. a populated place in the Diffa region of Niger.

Ouo.

1. *n.* a Gnostic Naasseni sect: a school of the Ophites "which regarded the spiritual dragon or serpent as the redeeming power" (*Encyclopedic Theosophical Glossary*).

2. *n.* a populated place in Burkina Faso.

3. *n.* a populated place in Mali.

4. *n.* a populated place in New Caledonia.

5. *n.* a stream in Benin.

6. *n.* a stream in Cameroon.

7. *n.* a stream in the Nzerekore region of Guinea.

8. *n.* one of five ministers of Chozzar, a spiritual dragon (equated to Poseidon) revered by the Naasseni (a Gnostic school of the Ophites) (*Encyclopedic Theosophical Glossary*).

Ouo-Ouo.

n. a populated place in the Malakula region of Vanuatu (formerly New Hebrides).

Ouoae.

n. one of five ministers of Chozzar, a spiritual dragon (equated to Poseidon) revered by the Naasseni (a Gnostic school of the Ophites), as discussed in *Encyclopedic Theosophical Glossary*.

Ouou.

1. *n.* a populated place in the Pangasinan region of the Philippines.

2. *n.* a stream in Central African Republic.

Ouoya.

n. a stream in the Gueckedou region of Guinea.

ouu.

1. *interj.* a scolding word; "shame on you."

<*[He] came up and shook his finger scoldingly and said, "Ouu, Bobby— ... you got in trouble. You better be good."* —Jerry Spinelli, *The Library Card.*>

2. *interj.* oh.

<*Ouu, thank you, God bless you, you're so nice.* —K. C. Constantine, *Saving Room for Dessert: A Rocksburg Novel.*>

3. *interj.* the deep grunt of football players primed for action.

<*Us footballers all jumped up and pumped our fists and went, "Ouu! Ouu!" The coach grinned and pumped us one back and we went wild.* —Jerry Spinelli, *Crash.*>

4. *n.* a mumble of a dying person, as in *The Sandman: Preludes and Nocturnes* by Neil Gaiman.

ouuu.

1. *adv.* truly.

<*I hear the palmetta bug saying something. Yeah, saying, "Ouuu, it's nice here. I don't believe this woman washes herself, yeah."* —Elmore Leonard, *Rum Punch.*>

2. *interj.* a grunt of physical exertion, as when kicking someone in *Maniac Magee* by Jerry Spinelli.

3. *interj.* an expression of disgust or revulsion, as at a snakeskin jacket in *Battle of Angels* by Tennessee Williams.

4. *n.* a cry of pain upon stepping on hot coals, as in *The Great Tejon Club Jubilee: Stories* by Gerald W. Haslam.

ouuu-ee.

(also ouuuee.) *interj.* an expression of strong emotion; indeed.

<*Fats [Domino] incanted: "Ouuu-ee baby, ouuuee! Baby don't you let your dog bite me!"* —Gerald W. Haslam, *Coming of Age in California: Personal Essays.*>

Ouya.

1. *n.* a populated place in Central African Republic.

2. *n.* a populated place in Mali.

Ouya Ouya.

n. a distributary in the Forecariah region of Guinea.

Ouyaoua.

n. a ridge in New Caledonia.

Ouyaye.

n. a populated place in Burkina Faso.

Ouye.

1. *n.* a populated place in Central African Republic.

2. *n.* a populated place in Mali.

3. *n.* a populated place in the Niamey region of Niger.

4. *n.* an intermittent stream in the Logone Oriental region of Chad.

5. *n.* an intermittent stream in the Macenta region of Guinea.

Ouyeye.

n. a populated place in the Nzerekore region of Guinea.

Ouyou.

n. a populated place in Togo.

Oy.

n. a populated place in the Bohol region of the Philippines.

oy.

1. *interj.* a cry of caution.

   <*"Oy! Watch out!" yells someone behind me—and to my horror I realize I've stepped off the pavement in front of a cyclist.* —Sophie Kinsella, *Shopaholic Takes Manhattan.*>

2. *interj.* a shout for help, so as to establish one's location.

   <*"Help! Oy! Oy!" Mr. Bunter groped towards the voice, feeling cautiously before him with his walking-stick.* —Dorothy L. Sayers, *Clouds of Witness.*>

3. *interj.* a Yiddish expression of vexation, exasperation; "what now?".

   <*"What's 'oy'?" He smiled. "God, you're goyische. It's Jewish for 'Jesus Fucking Christ, that was mortifying.'"* —Ann Packer, *The Diver From Clausen's Pier: A Novel.*>

4. *interj.* an expression of annoyance, frustration, or dismay, as at relatives who repeat the same stories over and over in *The Bitch in the House: 26 Women Tell the Truth About Sex, Solitude, Work, Motherhood, and Marriage* by Cathi Hanauer.

5. *interj.* an expression of disbelief.

   <*It used to be, if we gals wanted to look like a model, all we had to do was be born with extraordinary genes, grow to five-foot ten, subsist on lettuce, and maybe develop a coke habit. Now, it seems, we've also got to have our looks "enhanced" by an underpaid production assistant*

with a fifty-thousand-gigabyte hard drive. As my grandmother used to say: Oy. —Susan Jane Gilman, *Kiss My Tiara: How to Rule the World as a SmartMouth Goddess.*>

6. *interj.* an expression of grief.

<*Mama cried, Oy, no, it can't be.* —David Grossman, *See Under: Love.*>

7. *interj.* an expression of pain.

<*When Jack's boot impacted on his shin he opened his eyes and shouted, "Oy!"* —Neal Stephenson, *The Confusion.*>

8. *interj.* an expression of regret.

<*Oy, such a waste of good money and paper.* —F. Paul Wilson, *Crisscross: A Repairman Jack Novel.*>

9. *interj.* an expression of validation.

<*"Oy," June says. "I knew that somewhere in this country there had to be a woman who still uses the term 'little girls' room.'"* —Richard Russo, *Straight Man: A Novel.*>

10. *interj.* hey.

<*He looked a bit startled at first, like he was thinking, "Oy what are you looking at, mate?"* —Louise Rennison, *Away Laughing on a Fast Camel: Even More Confessions of Georgia Nicolson.*>

11. *interj.* oops.

<*I'm sure they pad their orders for those last-minute, oy-I-forgot-to-order-a-turkey shoppers.* —Diane Morgan, *The Thanksgiving Table: Recipes and Ideas to Create Your Own Holiday Tradition.*>

oy oy oy.

interj. the shouts of baseball fans in the bleachers, as in "Cohen at the Bat," a parody of "Casey at the Bat," discussed in *Ellis Island to Ebbets Field: Sports and the American Jewish Experience* by Peter Levine.

oy-oy-oy.

interj. a cry of panic.

<*"Oy-oy-oy," cried Yossel's mother, "my little son is possessed by a dybbuk."* —Yaacov Peterseil, *Jewish Sci-Fi Stories for Kids.*>

Oya.

1. *n.* a goddess of violent storms, fertility, and the river Niger, as discussed in *Oya: In Praise of an African Goddess* by Judith Gleason.

2. *n.* a populated place in Indonesia.

3. *n.* a populated place in the Galicia region of Spain.

4. *n.* a populated place in the Sarawak region of Malaysia.

5. *n.* a populated place in Togo.

6. *n.* a section of a populated place in the Jarvamaa region of Estonia.

7. *n.* a stream in Central African Republic.

8. *n.* a stream in Uganda.

Oya-oy.
n. a populated place in the Iloilo region of the Philippines.

Oyao.
n. a populated place in Zaire.

Oye.
1. *n.* a populated place in Central African Republic.

2. *n.* a populated place in the Bourgogne and Nord-Pas-de-Calais regions of France; a stream in the Nord-Pas-de-Calais region of France.

3. *n.* a populated place in Zaire.

4. *n.* a stream in Guinea.

Oyeao.
n. a marsh in New Caledonia.

Oyeu.
n. a populated place in the Rhone-Alpes region of France.

Oyeyu.
n. a populated place in Uganda.

Oyii.
n. a hill in Uganda.

Oyo.
1. *n.* a hill in the Ash Sharqiyah region of Sudan; a populated place in the Ash Sharqiyah region of Sudan; a well in the Darfur region of Sudan.

2. *n.* a populated place in the Guera region of Chad; a well in the Borkou-Ennedi-Tibe region of Chad.

3. *n.* a populated place in the Kalinga-Apayao region of the Philippines.

4. *n.* a populated place in the Siguiri region of Guinea.

5. *n.* a stream in Zaire.

Oyou.

n. a populated place in the Haut-Ogooue region of Gabon.

Oyu.

1. *n.* a populated place in the Viljandimaa region of Estonia.

2. *n.* a populated place in Uganda.

Oyuyo.

1. *n.* a family name.

2. *n.* a populated place in the Puno region of Peru.

U'u.

n. squirrelfish of Hawaii.

u'u'u'u'u'u.

n. the "monotonous" call of the Rufous-tailed Tailorbird, as described in *A Guide to the Birds of Southeast Asia*

u-u.

interj. the Portuguese expression for "yoo-hoo," as discussed in *Hear! Here!* by Michele Slung.

Ua.

1. *n.* a populated place in the Milne Bay region of Papua New Guinea.

2. *n.* a stream in the Akershus region of Norway.

Uaa.

n. a populated place in Ethiopia.

Uae.

n. a populated place in Guinea-Bissau.

uaea.

n. a Samoan word meaning "wire," as discussed in *Tuvaluan: A Polynesian Language of the Central Pacific* by Niko Besnier.

Uai.

1. *n.* a populated place in the Eastern Highlands region of Papua New Guinea.

2. *n.* a stream in the Eastern region of Kenya.

Uaia.

n. a populated place in the Tete region of Mozambique.

Uaio.

n. a stream in Ethiopia.

Uaiu.

n. a mountain in Ethiopia; a populated place in Ethiopia.

Uaiua.

n. a populated place in the Nampula region of Mozambique.

Uaiya.

n. a populated place in the Al Istiwa'iyah region of Sudan.

Uao.

n. a populated place in the Lanao del Sur region of the Philippines.

Uau.

1. *n.* a populated place in Ethiopia; a stream in Ethiopia.

2. *n.* a populated place in the Uige region of Angola; a stream in the Namibe and Uige regions of Angola.

UaUa.

n. a name for the creator god meaning "One and Only," "One Without Second," "One Alone" (Ernest P. Moyer, *The Legacy of Adam and Eve*).

Uaua.

1. *n.* a family name, especially in Hawaii.

2. *n.* a populated place in the Bahia region of Brazil.

3. *n.* a populated place in the Batangas region of the Philippines.

4. *n.* a populated place in the Zambezia region of Mozambique.

5. *n.* a stream in Ghana.

6. *n.* a tribe of early settlers in the Nubia region of north-east Africa; a name for lower Nubia.

<*The first inhabitants of the region beyond Egypt appear to have been the Uaua, whose name occurs in an inscription on a tomb at Memphis of the VIth Dynasty, and again constantly in subsequent inscriptions down to the time of the Ptolemies, as the chief negro race to the south of Syene. —Encyclopedia Britannica, 11th Edition.*>

Uayu.

n. a mountain in Ethiopia.

Ue.

1. *n.* a stream in New Caledonia.

2. *n.* a stream in the Bengo region of Angola.

Uea.

n. an island in New Caledonia.

Ueia.

n. a hill in the Cuanza Sul region of Angola; a stream in the Cuanza Sul region of Angola.

Ueiua.

n. a populated place in the Zambezia region of Mozambique.

Ueu.

n. a stream in the Uige region of Angola.

Ueua.

n. a stream in the Uige region of Angola.

Ueye.

n. a populated place in the Koundara region of Guinea.

Uia.

1. *n.* a bay in French Polynesia.
2. *n.* a populated place in New Zealand.
3. *n.* a populated place in the Cuanza Sul and Cunene regions of Angola; a stream in the Cuanza Sul region of Angola.
4. *n.* a populated place in the Ifugao region of the Philippines.
5. *n.* a populated place in the Viljandimaa region of Estonia.
6. *n.* an island in the Ha apai region of Tonga.

Uie.

n. an intermittent stream in Ethiopia; a stream in Ethiopia.

Uioa.

n. a populated place in the Cabinda region of Angola.

Uiuia.

1. *n.* a populated place in Mozambique.
2. *n.* a stream in the Huambo region of Angola.

Uiya.

n. a populated place in the Viljandimaa region of Estonia.

Uo.

1. *n.* a Japanese given name.

   <*Uo was a broad-shouldered, rocklike man with vast hands and a broken nose, and he wore a pained expression.* —James Clavell, *Shogun.*>

2. *n.* a populated place in Ethiopia.

3. *n.* a stream in Cameroon.

Uoiauai.

n. a native language in Brazil, as discussed in "A Collection of Word Oddities and Trivia" by Jeff Miller.

uooo.

1. *n.* a chant from the Igbo Folk Epic from Sub-Saharan Africa, as discussed in *Traditional Storytelling Today: An International Sourcebook* by Margaret Read MacDonald.

2. *pro.* you, as pronounced in a garbled fashion by a dental patient in *Stories From a Life in Progress* by Lou Ann Thomas.

Uu.

1. *n.* a stream in the Eastern region of Kenya.

2. *n.* a stream in the Solomon Islands.

Uue.

n. a populated place in the Northern region of Papua New Guinea.

uuoooo.

n. mesmerization induced by looking at a spiral, as in the graphic novel *Uzumaki 2* by Junji Ito.

Uuu.

n. the name of a character with glowing yellow eyes in the novel *The Martian Chronicles* by Ray Bradbury.

<*Mr. Uuu clapped the captain's shoulder. "It's so good to see another man from Earth. I am from Earth also."* —Ray Bradbury, *The Marian Chronicles.*>

uuu.

1. *n.* an incoherent word (presumably *you*) spoken through a parched throat, just upon waking.

   <*He was startled, had let his head fall, sleepily, and he snapped awake, stood, saw the young man holding the door for him, and he tried to say something, his mouth dry and thick. "Thnn uuu," he said, and cleared his throat, stepped through the door.* —Jeffrey M. Shaara, *Gods and Generals.*>

2. *n.* the sound of the letter u, as described in *Reading Made Easy: A Guide to Teach Your Child to Read* by Valerie Bendt; see also UUUU.

UUUU.

n. the sound of the letter u; "the vowel sound of the first chakra" (Jonathan Goldman, *Tantra of Sound: How to Enhance Intimacy With Sound*); see also uuu[2].

<*This UUUU sound is made in the back of the throat.* —Jonathan Goldman, *Tantra of Sound: How to Enhance Intimacy With Sound.*>

Uya.

n. a stream in Kazakhstan.

Uyae.

n. an atoll in the Marshall Islands.

Uyaoy.

n. a populated place in the La Union region of the Philippines.

uyaoy.

(also uyauy.) *n.* a Filipino folk dance: "an Ifugao wedding festival dance, which makes use of gongs and is usually performed by the affluent wealthy people. Those who have performed this dance are entitled to the use of gongs at their death" (GlobalPinoy.com).

Uye.

1. *n.* a populated place in Ethiopia.

2. *n.* a stream in Zaire.

Uyea.

n. an island of the Shetland Islands in Scotland, home to a colony of Puffin birds and breeding ground for grey seals; a stretch of water between Uyea Isle and the Shetland mainland's northern coastline.

<*Uyea is joined to the Mainland by a lovely sandy ayre. The rocks here are Lewissian gneiss, some of the most ancient [nearly three billion years old] in the world. On the long walk in, the track passes the Beorgs of Uyea where the felsite used to make "Shetland Knives" is found.* —Orkney & Shetland Touring Company.>

Uyo.

n. a populated place in Nigeria.

Uyoyo.

n. a populated place in the North-Western region of Zambia.

Uyua.

n. a populated place in the Casanare region of Colombia.

Uyuyi.

n. a hill in Tanzania; a populated place in Tanzania.

Uyuyo.

n. a populated place in the Puno region of Peru.

y-i-e-e-e.

n. the war cry of a Native American, as in the comic book *Donald Duck in Indian Country* by Walt Disney.

y-i-i-i-i.

n. the war cry of a Native American, as in the comic book *Donald Duck in Indian Country* by Walt Disney.

Ya.

1. *n.* a farm in the Jonkoping region of Sweden.

2. *n.* a populated place in Burkina Faso.

3. *n.* a populated place in Liberia.

4. *n.* a populated place in Zaire; a stream in Zaire.

5. *n.* a short form of the name of God, YHWH; see also Iao[4], Iaou[2], Iaue.

   <*At Elat Chayyim, God is referred to in prayers simply as "Ya," intriguingly close to the Rastafarian Ja.* —Robert Eisenberg, *Boychicks in the Hood: Travels in the Hasidic Underground.*>

6. *n.* a stream in Central African Republic.

7. *n.* a stream in the Faranah region of Guinea.

8. *n.* a stream in the Hedmark region of Norway.

9. *n.* a wadi in the Al Istiwa'iyah region of Sudan.

10. *n.* an intermittent stream in Benin.

11. *n.* an intermittent stream in Cameroon; a stream in Cameroon.

ya.

1. *interj.* a yell of triumph, as in *The Long Night of White Chickens* by Francisco Goldman.

2. *pron.* you (informal). <*Hey, ya big dope.*>

3. *pron.* your (informal). <*Ya father's big moustache.*>

Ya Ya.

n. a man's nickname.

<*[T]he area was full of booby traps, and Ya Ya was moving very carefully, each step in a deliberate, catlike motion.* —Ed Kugler, *Dead Center: A Marine Sniper's Two-Year Odyssey in the Vietnam War.*>

ya-ya.

v. to talk or discuss.

<*Whenever all us girls are together, she says, "Gumbo Ya-Ya!" This means "everybody talking at the same time," which is what we sure do.* —Rebecca Wells, *Divine Secrets of the Ya-Ya Sisterhood: A Novel.*>

Ya-yu.

n. a populated place in Taiwan.

Yaa.

1. *n.* a populated place in the Gulf region of Papua New Guinea.

2. *n.* a populated place in the Oaxaca region of Mexico.

3. *n.* a stream in Russia.

4. *n.* a stream in Sudan.

yaa.

interj. the Arabic expression for "yoo-hoo," as discussed in *Hear! Here!* by Michele Slung.

yaaa.

1. *interj.* "a yelp of disgust, as if surprised by a spider in the bath" (David Mitchell, *Number9Dream*).

2. *interj.* a sound to accompany a dramatic gesture in the play *Mount Tempai and Tumult in the Palace*, as discussed in *Traditional Japanese Theater* by Karen Brazell.

3. *interj.* an exclamation of happiness; see also yay[1].

   <*"Yes, you can use it." "Yaaa!" screamed the boy.* —Ray Bradbury, "Dark They Were, and Golden-Eyed," *A Medicine for Melancholy and Other Stories.*>

4. *interj.* the shout of a martial arts practitioner, as discussed in *Art of Shaolin Kung Fu: The Secrets of Kung Fu for Self Defense, Health and Enlightenment* by Wong Kiew Kit.

5. *n.* a variation of "yeah."

   <*"Yaaa," the voice said, "now you have to be a preacher, wise guy."* —Flannery O'Connor, "An Afternoon in the Woods," *Flannery O'Connor: Collected Works.*>

6. *v.* shoo!

<*Get out of here. Get out. Yaaa!* —Julie Andrews Edwards, *The Last of the Really Great Whangdoodles.*>

yaaa yaaa ya-ya-ya-ya yaaa yaaa.

n. the chorus of Nelson Riddle's "Lolita Ya Ya" song.

<*He hears the music—Nelson Riddle's "Lolita Ya Ya" theme, with its high-pitched chorus of mechanically speeded-up wordless vocalizers, Chipmunk music for the spiritually adrift—Yaaa yaaa, ya-ya-ya-ya yaaa yaaa.* —Geoffrey O'Brien, *Sonata for Jukebox: Pop Music, Memory, and the Imagined Life.*>

yaaaa.

1. *inter.* a scream of pain, as in *Mobile Guerrilla Force: With the Special Forces in War Zone D* by James C. Donahue.

2. *inter.* a vocalization upon waking up from a nightmare, as in *East Along the Equator: A Journey Up the Congo and Into Zaire* by Helen Winternitz.

3. *interj.* a meaningless expression that has a cathartic effect on the person who yells it.

<*Wildly excited, Tas threw back his head. He opened his mouth and cried a loud "Yaaaa" that had absolutely no meaning but just felt good.* —Margaret Weis, *Dragons of a Vanished Moon.*>

4. *interj.* a scream of aggression, as during a fight with a wild dog in *The Long Night of White Chickens* by Francisco Goldman.

5. *interj.* a shriek of alarm.

<*Before I can grab it, my "lunch" is in my lap! "Yaaaa!!!!" I scream. There goes my new cheetah blouse!* —Deborah Gregory, *Cheetah Girls Supa-Dupa Sparkle.*>

6. *interj.* giddyup (a command for a horse to move); see also yeeeee[2].

<*"Yaaaa!" Henry shouted, spurring the stallion to follow.* —Wendy Loggia, *Ever After: A Cinderella Story.*>

yaaaaaa yeeee yaaa yaaaaa yeee yaaaa.

n. the "cacophonous chorus of high-pitched, shrill voices, joining in a long ululation" during a Russian Orthodox worship service, as described in *Highlanders: A Journey to the Caucasus in Quest of Memory* by Yo'av Karny.

Yaaya.

n. a stream in Russia.

Yae.

1. *n.* a populated place in Nigeria.

2. *n.* a populated place in the Hiroshima region of Japan.

3. *n.* a populated place in the Oaxaca region of Mexico.

Yai.

1. *n.* a mountain in the Nakhon Sawan and Phetchaburi regions of Thailand.
2. *n.* a populated place in the Hainan region of China.
3. *n.* a populated place in the Lara region of Venezuela.
4. *n.* a populated place in the Yomou region of Guinea.

Yaia.

1. *n.* a well in the Obock region of Djibouti.
2. *n.* an intermittent stream in Ethiopia.

Yaio.

n. a populated place in Burkina Faso.

Yaiyo.

n. a populated place in Ethiopia.

Yao.

1. *n.* a city in the Osaka region of Japan.
2. *n.* a mythical emperor of China.
3. *n.* a populated place in Central African Republic.
4. *n.* a populated place in the Batha region of Chad.
5. *n.* a populated place in the Nan region of Thailand.
6. *n.* a stream in the Ogooue-Lolo region of Gabon.

Yaou.

1. *n.* a hill in French Guiana.
2. *n.* a stream in Central African Republic.

Yaoue.

1. *n.* a hill in New Caledonia; a stream in New Caledonia.
2. *n.* a stream in Central African Republic.
3. *n.* a stream in the Ogooue-Maritime region of Gabon.

Yaoya.

n. a locality in Nicaragua.

Yaoyaoa.

n. a populated place in the Batha region of Chad.

Yaoyo.

n. a stream in Central African Republic.

Yau.

1. *n.* a hill in Nigeria; a populated place in Nigeria.

2. *n.* a populated place in Uzbekistan.

3. *n.* a stream in Ghana.

Yaua.

1. *n.* a populated place in the Samar region of the Philippines.

2. *n.* an area in the Eastern region of Kenya; a hill in the Eastern region of Kenya.

Yaui.

n. a populated place in the Quezon region of the Philippines.

yaui.

v. Mongolian for "let's go."

<*Finally, she put her hands to the side of her head in the sleeping position and meekly said "yaui," which means, "let's go" in Mongolian. She was propositioning me! Somewhat shocked at the offer, in broad daylight no less, I abruptly replied "no yaui," not realising that I had mixed up English and Mongolian.* —Stan Jung, "Lost in Ulaanbaatar.">

Yauya.

1. *n.* a stream in Nicaragua.

2. *n.* a village in the Andes mountains of northern Peru.

<*In July 1974, I set off on a journey to Yauya, a village high in the Peruvian Andes. In archaeological circles, this small town is well known because of Julio Tello's 1919 discovery there of a large stela from the Chavín culture (900-200 B.C.), Peru's earliest civilization.* —Richard L. Burger, "Letter from Peru: Andean Odyssey," *Archaeology*.>

YauYau.

1. *n.* a populated place in the East New Britain region of Papua New Guinea.

2. *n.* a village in Suriname (formerly Dutch Guyana), near the Feroelasie Rapids of the Suriname River.

<*Our destination was a village of approximately 1,000 called YauYau on a splendid bend in the Suriname River, just below the Feroelasie Rapids, said to be the most dangerous on the river.* —Danny Thorn, "A Visit to Suriname.">

Yauye.

n. a populated place in the Eastern Highlands region of Papua New Guinea.

Yay.

n. a populated place in the Lara region of Venezuela.

yay.

1. *interj.* an exclamation of happiness; see also yaaa[3].

<*No more dinosaurs! Yay!* —Michael Crichton, *Jurassic Park.*>

2. *n.* an affirmative vote; see also yea[2].

<*It was he who described being a Permian football player as like being a gladiator, like walking into the Roman Coliseum with all those thousands in the stands yelling yay or nay, all wishing they could be you down there on that field.* —H. H. Bissinger, *Friday Night Lights: A Town, A Team, and A Dream.*>

YaYa.

n. a woman's nickname.

<*I made a friend named Yanis. (Sometimes I call her YaYa.)* —Richard Steckel and Michele Steckel, *The Milestones Project: Celebrating Childhood Around the World.*>

Yaya.

1. *n.* a hill in Ghana; a stream in Ghana.

2. *n.* a lake in the Louga region of Senegal.

3. *n.* a man's given name, as a West African shaman discussed in *Conscious Dreaming: A Spiritual Path for Everyday Life* by Robert Moss.

<*It was you who had Yaya whipped.* —George R. R. Martin, *A Storm of Swords.*>

4. *n.* a populated locality in the Matanzas region of Cuba.

5. *n.* a populated place in Burkina Faso.

6. *n.* a populated place in Ethiopia.

7. *n.* a populated place in French Guiana.

8. *n.* a populated place in Nigeria.

9. *n.* a populated place in Sri Lanka; a section of estate in Sri Lanka.

10. *n.* a populated place in the Canakkale region of Turkey.

11. *n.* a populated place in the Grand'-Anse region of Haiti.

12. *n.* a populated place in the Lima region of Peru.

13. *n.* a populated place in the Tahoua region of Niger.

14. *n.* a populated place in Zaire.

15. *n.* a river in Russia.

16. *n.* a river in the Amazon rain forest, as discussed in *One River* by Wade Davis.

17. *n.* a stream in Central African Republic.

18. *n.* a waterhole in the Coast region of Kenya.

19. *n.* a well in the Obock region of Djibouti.

20. *n.* a woman's given name, as in *Dreams of Trespass: Tales of a Harem Girlhood* by Fatima Mernissi.

21. *n.* an intermittent stream in Togo.

22. *n.* an open town market in Ethiopia, as discussed in *Rules of the Wild: A Novel of Africa* by Francesca Marciano.

23. *n.* elder mother of the Towa tribe, as discussed in *Voice of the Eagle* by Linda Lay Shuler.

24. *n.* grandmother, in Greek, as discussed in *Travelers' Tales Greece: True Stories* by Larry Habegger.

<*To them all she was "Yaya," the Greek for grandmother.* —Hugo Vickers, *Alice: Princess Andrew of Greece.*>

25. *n.* the first woman on earth, as in the creation story of the Tainos peoples of Puerto Rico, discussed *Stories From Puerto Rico* by Robert L. Muckley.

26. *n.* the name of the Turkish infantrymen of the early Ottoman forces (1324-59), as discussed in *The Janissaries* by David Nicolle.

yaya.

1. *adj.* a derogatory expression meaning "out to lunch."

2. *n.* a sacred dance of the Apache Indians, as discussed in *Latin American Folktales: Stories from Hispanic and Indian Traditions* by John Bierhorst.

3. *n.* a slang term for a British "upper-class twit," as discussed in *Lonely Planet: Britain* by David Else.

4. *n.* a type of tree in Cuba.

<*Then, in new shoes, with heavy loads, we climb the very steep hillside, through the delicate leaves of the yaya tree.* —Jose Marti, *Jose Marti: Selected Writings.*>

5. *n.* pent-up energy, stress.

<*See, it's not that we're looking for a war. We just want to get our yayas out on each other, scream and yell and jump and pound on each other.* —Lynn Breedlove, *Godspeed: A Novel.*>

<*Dog lovers ... often unleash their pups to let them get their yayas out—despite laws against going off leash.* —Ann Oldenburg, *Dog Lover's Companion to Washington D.C. & Baltimore: The Inside Scoop on Where to Take Your Dog.*>

6. *n.* the Incan word for father, as discussed in *The Incas* by Terence N. Daltroy.

7. *n.* the Pueblo Indians' word for mother, as discussed in *A Native American Encyclopedia: History, Culture, and Peoples* by Barry M. Pritzker.

Yaye.

1. *n.* a populated place in Nigeria.

2. *n.* a populated place in the Diourbel region of Senegal.

3. *n.* a stream in Zaire.

4. *n.* an intermittent stream in Benin.

Yayi.

n. a populated place in Zaire.

Yayie.

n. a populated place in the Bong region of Liberia.

Yayo.

1. *n.* a populated place in Burkina Faso.

2. *n.* a populated place in Ethiopia.

3. *n.* a populated place in the Chuquisaca region of Bolivia.

4. *n.* a populated place in the Lima region of Peru.

5. *n.* a stream in Central African Republic.

6. *n.* a stream in Ghana.

7. *n.* an area in the Borkou-Ennedi-Tibe region of Chad; a well in the Borkou-Ennedi-Tibe region of Chad.

8. *n.* an intermittent stream in Benin.

Yayoi.

n. a period in Japanese history from 300 B.C. to 300 A.D.

<*The Aoya-Kamijichi ruins are known in archaeological circles as "an underground museum of the Yayoi Period" following the discovery of various artifacts, including hunting tools [and preserved brain tissue], at the location.* —"Yayoi Brain Tissue Preserved in Ruins," *The Japan Times.*>

Yayou.

1. *n.* a populated place in Ethiopia.

2. *n.* a populated place in the Nord region of Haiti.

Yayu.

1. *n.* a huge carnivorous beast in Chinese mythology, ordered to be slain by the mythical Emperor Yao.

2. *n.* a malevolent creature from Chinese mythology, a maneater appearing "as a god with a snake's body and a human face" who makes the sounds of a baby (Richard E. Strassberg, *A Chinese Bestiary: Strange Creatures from the Guideways Through Mountains and Seas).*

3. *n.* a populated place in Ethiopia.

4. *n.* a Zen Buddhist poet, as discussed in *Zen Art for Meditation* by Horioka Holmes.

5. *n.* the Hindu god of air and wind (variant spelling of "Vayu").

yayu.

1. *n.* a fictional grub.

   <*It should have been as easy to draw the secret from his mouth as it is to pull the yayu grub from its hole in the ouil tree.* —Phyllis Gotlieb, *Flesh and Gold.*>

2. *n.* an outdoor Korean mask dance "from the region east of the Naktong River" (Peter H. Lee, *A History of Korean Literature).*

Ye.

1. *n.* a populated place in Benin.

2. *n.* a populated place in Burkina Faso.

3. *n.* a populated place in Indonesia.

4. *n.* a populated place in the Canarias region of Spain.

5. *n.* a populated place in the Mon State region of Myanmar (formerly Burma).

6. *n.* a stream in Cameroon.

7. *n.* a stream in the Beyla and Nzerekore regions of Guinea.

8. *n.* an intermittent stream in Central African Republic; a stream in Central African Republic.

ye.

pron. the plural form of "thou"; see also yeeeeee[2]. <*O ye of little faith.*>

Ye Ya.

n. a stream in the Yomou region of Guinea.

Ye-e.

n. a populated place in the Karan State, Mandalay, Pegu, Rakhine State, Sagaing, and Shan State regions of Myanmar (formerly Burma).

ye-e-e.

interj. the Arabic expression for "phooey!' as discussed in *Hear! Here!* by Michele Slung.

Ye-u.

n. a populated place in the Mandalay, Sagaing and Shan State regions of Myanmar (formerly Burma).

ye-ye-ye.

n. the howls of a dozen wild boars, as described in *Children of the Plains* by Paul B. Thompson; see also yeee yeee.

Ye-ye-ye-ye-ye-ye-ye-ye-ya-ya-ya.

n. a lyric from the song "The Communicator" by Madness.

Ye-yo.

n. a populated place in the Kayah State region of Myanmar (formerly Burma).

Yea.

n. a populated place in the Victoria region of Australia.

yea.

1. *adv.* an affirmation or assent. <*Yea, I want ice cream.*>

2. *n.* an affirmative vote; see also yay[2]. <*I vote yea to the bill.*>

Yee.

1. *n.* a Chinese family name.

2. *n.* a populated place in Indonesia.

yee yeee.

interj. an ecstatic expression of a religious frenzy.

<*Yee! Yeee! I kidnapped the future and ransomed it for the past.* —Rev. Ivan Stang, *The Book of the SubGenius: Being the Divine Wisdom, Guidance, and Prophecy of J.R. 'Bob' Dobbs, High Epopt of the Church of the SubGenius, Here Inscribed for the Salvation of Future Generations and in the Hope that Slack May Someday Reign on this Earth.*>

yee-aay-ee.

interj. an exultant shout, as by a hunter.

<*Then above the confused sounds Stuart Tarleton's voice rose, in an exultant shout, "Yee-aay-ee!" as if he were on the hunting field.* Margaret Mitchell, *Gone With the Wind.*>

yeee.

1. *interj.* a cry of terror.

<*Suddenly the happiness on their faces turned to terror. "Yeee! Look! Look!" one cried.* —Stephen D. Sullivan, *The Phoenix.*>

2. *interj.* a squeal of pain.

<*The voice from the bathroom made him jump. "Yeee!" he answered, as he caught the glans of his penis in the zipper.* —Michael Fredrickson, *A Cinderella Affidavit.*>

3. *n.* the singing sounds of a mountain hollow when a fierce wind passes through; see also yuuu.

<*[When filled with wind, the mountain forest hollows] roar like waves, whistle like arrows, screech, gasp, cry, wail, moan, and howl, those in the lead calling out yeee!, those behind calling out yuuu!* —Zhuangzi, *Zhuangzi: Basic Writings.*>

yeee yeee.

n. the howl of a wounded wild boar, as described in *Children of the Plains* by Paul B. Thompson; see also ye-ye-ye.

yeee-yeee.

n. the begging call of the young Merlin bird, as described in *A Field Guide to the Birds of China* by John MacKinnon.

yeeee.

1. *interj.* a scream for help, as upon being tied to an explosive device in the graphic novel *Great Teacher Onizuka #12* by Tohru Fujisawa.

2. *interj.* a throaty gasp of shock, as upon stumbling upon a hanged man in the graphic novel *Great Teacher Onizuka #12* by Tohru Fujisawa.

3. *interj.* a vocalized shudder, as in response to a bad rhyme in *Flyboy Action Figure Comes with Gasmask* by Jim Munroe.

4. *interj.* an exclamation of sincerity; truly.

<*A mean hog's real meal, all right. That's no lie, let me tell you. Mean. Yeeee.* —William H. Gass, *Omensetter's Luck: A Novel.*>

5. *interj.* an expression of mirth; see also yeeeee[3].

<*"Yeeee ... doggie! Do ya see what I see?" The man's windburned face was split in a wide grin.* —Dorothy Garlock, *Restless Wind.*>

6. *n.* the cheering chorus of an audience, as during a heroic recitation by a Tanzanian storyteller, as discussed in *Africa (World Encyclopedia of Contemporary Theatre, Volume 3)* by Don Rubin; see also eeee[27].

yeeeee.

1. *interj.* a squeal of delight, as in *Goddesses #3: Muses on the Move* by Clea Hantman.

2. *interj.* a whistled equivalent to "giddyup" (a command for a horse to move); see also yaaaa[6].

<*“Yeeeee!” the man whistled shrilly, urging his mount into full gallop and waving at Cybele to follow suit.* —Roger J. Didio, *Atlantis: A Take of the Earth.*>

3. *interj.* an expression of mirth; see also yeeee[5].

<*“Yeeeee doggies,” he cackled, “that’s by-God funny.”* —Ralph Compton, *The Killing Season.*>

yeeeee-yiiiii.

interj. a banshee-like whoop of rage and fury, “cursing every foul demon of fate” (Irving Warner, *Wagner, Descending: The Wrath of the Salmon Queen).*

yeeeeee.

1. (also yeeeeeeee). *interj.* a comical cry of shock.

<*It was a hell of a funny sound, like a siren with a slippy chain that can’t quite get started. “Yeeeeee!” he said. “Yeeeeee!” It sounded funny as hell, and he looked funny as hell.* —Jim Thompson, *The Killer Inside Me.*>

2. *pron.* the plural form of “thou”; see also ye.

<*Much of everything seems to be a matter of racketeering, frauds, fakes, catchdollar tricks, falsehood and the like. Yeeeeee Gods!* —James C. Whorton, *Inner Hygiene: Constipation and the Pursuit of Health in Modern Society.*>

yeeeeeee.

1. *interj.* a screamed scolding by an Aikido master, as in *Remembering O-Sensei: Living and Training with Morihei Ueshiba, Founder of Aikido* by Susan Perry.

2. *interj.* an ear-splitting cry of agony, as discussed in *For the Love of Mike: More of the Best of Mike Royko* by Mike Royko.

yeeeeeeee yeeeeee.

interj. a bone-chilling wail, as in *The Illusion* by K. A. Applegate.

Yeeu.

n. a stream in Cameroon.

Yeeyo.

n. a waterhole in the Jubbada Hoose region of Somalia.

Yei.

1. *n.* a populated place in the Al Istiwa’iyah region of Sudan.

2. *n.* a populated place in the Logone Oriental region of Chad.

Yeo.

1. *n.* a populated place in the Thies region of Senegal.

2. *n.* a populated place in the Victoria region of Australia.

Yeo Yeo.

n. a railroad station in the New South Wales region of Australia.

Yeou.

n. a populated place in Burkina Faso.

Yeoua.

1. *n.* a populated place in Central African Republic.

2. *n.* a stream in Nigeria.

Yeu.

n. an abandoned populated place in the Quang Nam-Da Nang region of Vietnam.

Yeua.

n. a stream in Ethiopia.

Yeui.

n. a populated place in the Hwanghae-namdo region of North Korea, meaning "courtesy."

Yey.

1. *n.* a populated place in the Al Istiwa'iyah region of Sudan.

2. *n.* a stream in the Djibouti region of Djibouti.

Yeya.

1. *n.* a mine in the Santiago de Cuba region of Cuba.

2. *n.* a populated place in the Shan State region of Myanmar (formerly Burma).

Yeye.

1. *n.* a populated place in Nigeria.

2. *n.* a populated place in the Haut-Ogooue region of Gabon.

3. *n.* a populated place in Zaire; a stream in Zaire.

Yeyi.

n. a populated place in the Shan State region of Myanmar (formerly Burma).

Yeyo.

n. a populated place in the Magwe and Sagaing regions of Myanmar (formerly Burma).

Yi.

1. *n.* a stream in Cameroon.

2. *n.* a stream in Central African Republic.

3. *n.* a stream in Uruguay.

4. *n.* in China, the hero deity who saved the earth from destructuve drought when all 10 suns appeared in the sky simultaneously. <*Yi shot down nine of the ten suns with his magic bow.*>

Yia.

n. a stream in Zaire.

yiiiii.

1. *n.* a cheer of appreciation.

   <*Everyone was waving and milling about and cheering. "Yiiii, eeeee! Hooooklaaaa!"* —Anna L. Waldo, *Sacajawea.*>

2. *n.* a sound of surprise or of being startled, as in the comic book *Kull the Destroyer.*

Yiye.

n. a stream in the Eastern region of Sierra Leone.

Yiyoyo.

n. a stream in Cameroon.

Yiyu.

n. a populated place in the Arunachal Pradesh region of India.

Yo.

1. *n.* a populated place in Burkina Faso.

2. *n.* a populated place in Nigeria.

3. *n.* a populated place in the Kagoshima region of Japan.

4. *n.* a populated place in the Sandaun region of Papua New Guinea.

5. *n.* a populated place in Togo.

6. *n.* a stream in Cameroon.

7. *n.* a stream in Central African Republic.

8. *n.* a stream in the Nzerekore region of Guinea.

9. *n.* a stream in the Woleu-Ntem region of Gabon.

10. *n.* an island in the Marshall Islands.

yo.

n. the number eleven, as said by a craps player who doesn't like to say the actual number for superstitious reasons.

<*He likes to put a little zip in his dialogue, so when he tosses his chip to the stickman he'll yell: "Gimme me the yo." ... [A] couple of other cats like the sound of the word and they begin a steady stream of chips being sailed to the center of the table, while the sound[s] of yo-yo-yo-yo-yo-yo fill the air.* —John Patrick, *So You Wanna Be a Gambler: Advanced Craps.*>

Yo-Yo.

n. a bayou (officially known as the Old Sabine River) in the Toledo Bend Lake reservoir of Louisiana.

yo-yo.

(also yoyo.) *n.* a toy which spins on a string.

<*The yoyo spun and twirled, looped, double looped! It would do anything she wanted it to do!* —Teri Perl, *Women and Numbers: Lives of Women Mathematicians Plus Discovery Activities.*>

Yoa.

1. *n.* a lake in the Borkou-Ennedi-Tibe region of Chad.

2. *n.* a populated place in Cameroon; a stream in Cameroon.

3. *n.* a populated place in the Yomou region of Guinea.

Yoay.

n. a populated place in the Santa Cruz region of Bolivia.

Yoe.

1. *n.* a farm in the New South Wales region of Australia.

2. *n.* a stream in Cameroon.

3. *n.* a stream in the Quang Nam-Da Nang region of Vietnam.

Yoi.

1. *n.* a populated place in Burkina Faso.

2. *n.* a well in the Kurdufan region of Sudan.

Yoo.

1. *n.* a hill in the Gueckedou region of Guinea.

2. *n.* a mountain in the Western region of Fiji.

3. *n.* a stream in Cameroon.

4. *n.* a well in the Agadez region of Niger.

Yooua.

n. a ruin in the Nzerekore region of Guinea.

You.

1. *n.* a populated place in Burkina Faso.
2. *n.* a populated place in the Chimbu region of Papua New Guinea.
3. *n.* a populated place in the Kanem region of Chad.
4. *n.* a populated place in the Quang Nam-Da Nang region of Vietnam.
5. *n.* a stream in Guinea.
6. *n.* an intermittent stream in Togo.

you.

pro. a person being addressed.

Youa.

n. a populated place in the Nzerekore region of Guinea.

Youa Ya.

n. a stream in the Yomou region of Guinea.

Youa Youa.

n. a populated place in the Chari-Baguirmi region of Chad.

Youe.

1. *n.* a populated place in the Mayo-Kebbi region of Chad.
2. *n.* a stream in Central African Republic.
3. *n.* an intermittent stream in Benin; a populated place in Benin.

Youi.

1. *n.* a populated place in Cameroon.
2. *n.* a populated place in the Yomou region of Guinea.
3. *n.* a well in the Agadez region of Niger.

Youoye.

n. a populated place in Nigeria.

Youyouo.

n. a stream in Cameroon.

Yoya.

1. *n.* a populated place in the Darfur region of Sudan.

2. *n.* a populated place in the Eastern Highlands region of Papua New Guinea.

3. *n.* a populated place in the Eastern region of Sierra Leone.

Yoye.

1. *n.* a populated place in the Thies region of Senegal.

2. *n.* a stream in Central African Republic.

Yoyi.

n. a mountain in the Southern region of Sierra Leone.

Yoyie.

n. a populated place in the Bong region of Liberia.

YoYo.

1. *n.* "a missile-defense radar deployed around Moscow," as discussed in *I Always Wanted to Fly: America's Cold War Airmen* by Wolfgang W. E. Samuel.

2. *n.* a nickname.

<*Exactly how Bernie Schiffran came to be called YoYo wasn't clear. It may have been for the "Yo!" with which he greeted people, as if he were Rocky Balboa, or for the way he moved, as if being unspooled and gathered up on a string.* —Alexander Wolff, *Big Game, Small World: A Basketball Adventure.*>

Yoyo.

1. *n.* a populated place in Burkina Faso.

2. *n.* a populated place in the Darfur region of Sudan.

3. *n.* a populated place in the Nyanga region of Gabon.

4. *n.* a populated place in Uganda.

5. *n.* a port town in Nigeria.

6. *n.* a river and crescent-shaped forest reserve in Ghana, north of the town of Enchi.

7. *n.* a stream in Cameroon.

8. *n.* a stream in Central African Republic.

9. *n.* the name of a chimp born in the Ngamba Island Chimpanzee Sanctuary near Entebbe, Uganda.

yoyo.

1. *adj.* loco, out of one's mind.

   <"*The poor chap might be slightly yoyo, but I've been reading about it. He's one of these idiot servants.*" "*Savants,*" *said the Dean patiently.* —Terry Pratchett, *Hogfather.*>

2. *n.* a "crash diet" involving an up-and-down cycle of gaining and losing weight, in which one rotates between feast and famine, named after the yo-yo toy.

   <*By my mid-forties, I had become increasingly aware that yoyo dieting was unhealthy and compounded the problem, making it easier to gain and harder to lose weight.* —Carolynn Hillman, *Love Your Looks: How to Stop Criticizing and Start Appreciating Your Appearance.*>

3. *n.* a dolt; a clueless person.

   <*I've had it up to my eyebrows with the yoyos them dopes in Anchorage send me; most of you couldn't find your ass with two hands and a flashlight.* —Daba Stabenow, *Midnight Come Again.*>

   <*[T]he word 'human' will take on a whole new meaning, and most yoyos will never be the wiser.* —Rev. Ivan Stang, *The Book of the SubGenius: Being the Divine Wisdom, Guidance, and Prophecy of J.R. 'Bob' Dobbs, High Epopt of the Church of the SubGenius, Here Inscribed for the Salvation of Future Generations and in the Hope that Slack May Someday Reign on this Earth.*>

4. *n.* a high-speed aircraft maneuver named after the yo-yo toy, "used when overtaking a slower aircraft in a hard turn" (Daniel P. Raymer, *Aircraft Design: A Conceptual Approach*).

   <*In the high speed yoyo discussed earlier, the aircraft quickly pitches up, then rolls and turns at approximately corner speed for a few seconds, then rolls to almost inverted flight, pitches up (down) again, and then rolls out and dives.* —Daniel P. Raymer, *Aircraft Design: A Conceptual Approach.*>

5. *n.* a sharp gardening implement.

   <*Then there was the garden and yard equipment—hoes, rakes, shovels, ax handles, mowing machines, yoyo blades, caneknives.* —Ernest J. Gaines, *A Lesson Before Dying: A Novel.*>

6. *n.* a Tunisian fritter "made with egg dough that is leavened with baking powder instead of yeast and is perfumed with vanilla and orange zest" (Joyce Esersky Goldstein, *Saffron Shores: Jewish Cooking of the Southern Mediterranean*).

7. *v.* to go up and down, as the yo-yo toy.

   <*Do not let security audit logs yoyo in size.* —Jay Ramachandran, *Designing Security Architecture Solutions.*>

8. *v.* to swing back and forth, as the yo-yo toy.

   <*You yoyo between friends, lovers, parents, relatives, student squats, public libraries, park benches, jail.* —Stella Hyde, *Darkside Zodiac.*>

Yoyoi.

n. a well in the Darfur region of Sudan.

Yoyou.

n. a populated place in Burkina Faso.

Yu.

1. *n.* a brook crossing Chengguan town, China.
2. *n.* a legendary Chinese master who drained the land and made the mountains.
3. *n.* a populated place in Burkina Faso.
4. *n.* a populated place in the Hyogo, Toyama and Yamaguchi regions of Japan.
5. *n.* a populated place in Zaire.

yu.

interj. the Chinese expression for "whoops!" as discussed in *Hear! Here!* by Michele Slung.

Yu'ao.

n. the name of a bridge in Macao spanning the Jialing River.

Yu-ao.

n. a rock in Taiwan.

Yua.

n. a populated place in Nigeria.

Yuao.

n. a village in Taiwan.

> <*Between the villages of Tulan and Yuao is an attraction which causes endless wonder and amusement to tour parties. This is an irrigation channel where, due to an optical illusion, the water appears to run uphill.* —Simon Reeve, "Taiwan's Rocky Coast.">

Yue.

n. a populated place in the Mayo-Kebbi region of Chad.

Yui.

n. a populated place in the Fukushima, Kagoshima and Shizuoka regions of Japan.

Yuo.

1. *n.* a populated place in the East Sepik region of Papua New Guinea.
2. *n.* a populated place in Zaire.

Yuu.

n. a populated place in the Yamaguchi region of Japan.

Yuu-Yuu.

n. the name given to a rare crested ibis born on Sado Island, Japan, in 1999.

yuuu.

n. the singing sounds of a mountain hollow when a fierce wind passes through; see also yeee[3].

<*[When filled with wind, the mountain forest hollows] roar like waves, whistle like arrows, screech, gasp, cry, wail, moan, and howl, those in the lead calling out yeee!, those behind calling out yuuu!* —Zhuangzi, *Zhuangzi: Basic Writings.*>

yuuuu.

interj. a cry of disgust.

<*Yuuuu! You go to that horseshit place?* —Gus Lee, *Chasing Hepburn: A Memoir of Shanghai, Hollywood, and a Chinese Family's Fight for Freedom.*>

Yuya.

1. *n.* a lake garden in Nanjing, China, near the Sun Yat-sen Mausoleum.
2. *n.* a locality in the Tarapaca region of Chile.
3. *n.* a man's given name, especially in Japan.
4. *n.* a populated place in the Eastern region of Sierra Leone.

Yuyi.

1. *n.* a populated place in the Oaxaca region of Mexico.
2. *n.* a woman's given name, especially in Spanish-speaking nations.

Yuyo.

1. *n.* a populated place in the Ayacucho and Huancavelica regions of Peru.
2. *n.* a populated place in the El Beni and La Paz regions of Bolivia.

yuyo.

n. a tangy seaweed used in traditional Peruvian recipes, as discussed in *Bon Appétit.*

Yuyu.

1. *n.* a populated place in Ethiopia.
2. *n.* a populated place in Zaire; a stream in Zaire.

yyyyyyyyyyyy.

n. a “rapturous French” sound made by a baby, as described in the novel *Edwin Mullhouse* by Steven Millhauser.

Printed in Great Britain
by Amazon.co.uk, Ltd.,
Marston Gate.